Articulations of Difference

ARTICULATIONS OF DIFFERENCE

Gender Studies and Writing in French

EDITED BY DOMINIQUE D. FISHER
AND LAWRENCE R. SCHEHR

STANFORD UNIVERSITY PRESS
Stanford, California
1997

Stanford University Press
Stanford, California

Printed in the United States of America

CIP data are at the end of the book

We dedicate this book
to the memory of George H. Bauer,
scholar, teacher, and friend

CONTENTS

CONTRIBUTORS

MARTINE ANTLE is associate professor of French at the University of North Carolina at Chapel Hill. She is the author of *Théâtre et poésie surréalistes*, articles on Marguerite Duras, surrealism, and the contemporary novel, and has edited a collection of essays entitled *The Object in France Today.*

JOHN R. BARBERET is assistant professor of French and comparative literature at Case Western Reserve University. He has written articles on Marxism, Balzac, and Sade and is preparing a book on the diffusion and reception of books from Balzac to Baudelaire, entitled *Habent sua fata libelli.*

GEORGE H. BAUER was, at the time of his death, professor of French at the University of Southern California. He was the author of *Sartre and the Artist*, as well as of numerous articles on Barthes, Sartre, Duras, and Duchamp.

DAVID F. BELL is professor of French at Duke University. He has published several books, including *Models of Power* and *Circumstances: Chance in the Literary Text.* He is currently working on the notion of probability in the nineteenth century and on its importance in narrative of that era.

LAURENCE ENJOLRAS is associate professor of French at the College of the Holy Cross. She is the author of *Femmes écrites: bilan de deux décennies.*

DOMINIQUE D. FISHER is associate professor of French at the University of North Carolina at Chapel Hill. She has published *Staging of Language and Language(s) of the Stage*, as well as articles on Gautier, Baudelaire, Mallarmé, and Foucault, among others. She is presently working on a book on Algerian literature.

ROBERT HARVEY is associate professor of French at the State University of New York at Stony Brook. He is the author of *Search for a Father* and is the co-editor and co-translator of *Toward the Postmodern* by Jean-François Lyotard. He is currently writing a book on the functions of laughter in literature and the visual arts.

MELANIE HAWTHORNE is associate professor of French at Texas A&M University. She is currently working on a book about Rachilde and has published a translation of Rachilde's *The Juggler*. She is also the co-editor, with Richard J. Golsan, of a book of essays on gender and the right in France.

GARETT R. HEYSEL finished his dissertation at The Ohio State University. It is entitled "Viewing Things Differently: Specularized Desire and the Avant-Garde Body." He is teaching at Connecticut College.

ALPHONSO LINGIS is professor of philosophy at Pennsylvania State University. Among his numerous books are *Libido: the French Existential Theories*, *The Community of Those Who Have Nothing in Common*, *Deathbound Subjectivities*, *Excesses*, and *Foreign Bodies*.

CHARLES D. MINAHEN is associate professor of French at The Ohio State University. He is the author of *Vortex/t: The Poetics of Turbulence*, editor of *Figuring Things: Char, Ponge, and Poetry in the Twentieth Century*, and co-editor of *Situating Sartre in Twentieth-Century Thought and Culture*.

LAURENCE M. PORTER is professor of French and comparative literature, and member of the core faculty of the African Studies Center, at Michigan State University. He also served as Andrew W. Mellon Distinguished Visiting Professor at the University of Pittsburgh. He has published eight books and ninety articles and book chapters on topics ranging from deconstruction to desire to feminism to popular culture, and on authors from Shakespeare to Flaubert, Freud, Goethe, Dostoevsky, and García Márquez.

VERNON A. ROSARIO is a resident in psychiatry at the University of California, Los Angeles, Neuropsychiatric Institute. He is co-editor with Paula Bennett of *Solitary Pleasures: The Historical, Literary, and Artistic Discourses of Autoeroticism* and the editor of *Science and Homosexualities*. He is a co-author of *Gay and Lesbian Life in the United States*, which will be published by Oxford University Press in 1999.

MIREILLE ROSELLO has worked on surrealist black humor, on Michel Tournier, on oppositional tactics in Caribbean literature, and on the figure of the infiltrator (*Infiltrating Culture*). She is currently completing a study on the reappropriation of ethnic stereotypes.

LAWRENCE R. SCHEHR is professor of French at the University of South Alabama. His books include *The Shock of Men*, *Alcibiades at the Door*, *Rendering French Realism*, and *Parts of an Andrology*.

NIGEL E. SMITH is assistant professor of French at West Georgia College. He has published articles on Balzac, Gautier, and Latouche, and is presently working on a study of Romantic representations of androgyny.

Articulations of Difference

Introduction

DOMINIQUE D. FISHER AND LAWRENCE R. SCHEHR

Articulations of Difference is a collection of essays dealing with the representations, theories, and problematics of homosexuality in writing in French in the nineteenth and twentieth centuries. It is far from encyclopedic; indeed we could not hope to bring closure to a subject that, for various reasons that we will discuss below, can never comfortably fit into one set of neatly defined parameters. Instead, we have encouraged multiple approaches to a variety of material in order to provide readers with a plural reading of what we shall, for the moment, call homosexuality over the past two centuries in the French-speaking world. The book focuses on literature but includes other self-conscious writing such as medical discourse and lexicography because these are all privileged sites within Western ideology, though they are not the only such sites. Indeed, one could imagine a collection of studies dealing with the manifestations of the subject in popular culture as well, and a recent collection on the historical context for homosexuality has just been published by Jeffrey Merrick and Bryant Ragan, Jr. By focusing predominantly on the literary, the authors of the essays in our book examine how self-conscious, written language is a privileged means to understanding how homosexuality is a component in the representation of ideology, desire, and structures in the nineteenth century, and how, in the twentieth century, homosexuality emerges in its own right as a subject for representation and study.

Let us start with literature, then, by making a list: Balzac, Flaubert, Baudelaire, Verlaine, Rimbaud, Proust, Gide, Colette, Cocteau, Sartre, de Beauvoir, Genet. A canonic list to be sure, the list of a canon that reflects a great deal of the standard nineteenth- and twentieth-century canon in French literature. It is also an incomplete list of authors who have engaged the question of homosexuality in their literary writings, in their correspondence, or in their daily lives. It is a subject that has for these two hundred years been seen as suitable to literary endeavor. Of course, there have been changes in the representation of the homosexual and homosexuality over these two centuries. To a great extent, in the early nineteenth century the homosexual was lumped together with the romantic figure of the androgyne. But this was not the only possibility: a reading of Balzac's *Pierrette*, for example, shows a monstrous mass of intertwined figures of sexuality, including implications of incest, sadomasochism, and lesbianism, which remain, to a greater or lesser extent, undifferentiated in that novel. And in *The Apparitional Lesbian*, Terry Castle has shown how the figure of what we would now call the lesbian was associated with ghosts and phantoms. These figures only begin to be seen clearly as the homosexual subject takes an independent form in the late nineteenth century. This independence was formed through the construction of homosexuality as a pathology; an apology for the individual subject arose as well, replacing the image of the homosexual as a Romantic figure, or homosexual sex as an isolated act.

This remains the case despite the condemnation of Baudelaire for obscene poetry, the marginalization of Verlaine's and Rimbaud's pornographic poetry, and the incarceration of Jean Genet. This remains the case despite the original private printing of Gide's landmark *Corydon*, which was an apologia for the naturalness of Greek love. And for every supposed transformation of Proust's chauffeur Agostinelli into the fictional Albertine, with whom the narrator of the *Recherche* has a love affair, it remains nonetheless true that the powerful creation of Charlus and the revelation of the sexual preferences of numerous characters in Proust's novel are two of the most important motors for the production of textuality in his massive opus.

At a first level, then, and only in a preliminary fashion, one might sketch an unproblematic historical line through French literature of the past two centuries and see numerous occurrences of homosexuality in writing. One could immediately make an explicit comparison to another frame of reference, Anglo-American literature over the same time period. For Balzac's Vautrin, who as the Abbé Herrera in *Splendeurs et misères des courtisanes* unabashedly serves as the homosexual protector of Lucien de Rubempré, substitute Dickens's Fagin, who secretly ogles Oliver Twist while the latter sleeps. For the personal or private lives of Proust and Gide, substitute the outrageous person of Oscar Wilde, prancing about, "posing as a Son-domite," as the Marquess of Queensbury illiterately wrote. For their explicit writings, substitute the oblique, the precious, and the cryptic phrases of *The Importance of Being Earnest.* For the blithe matter-of-fact approach to lesbian loves in the work of Colette, substitute the shock of *The Well of Loneliness* that courageously brought lesbianism into the open, but not without a rhetoric of the pathological. The French-speaking world has public and private spheres, public and private discourses, founded in a world of difference. The English-speaking world has the overarching metaphor of the closet, associated as it is with the prison. The English-speaking world has repression and explosion: one must break down the closet door, one must break out of the closet.[1] Whereas in the Anglo-American world it is perfectly acceptable to characterize homosexuality in a universal fashion as "transgression," as do Jonathan Dollimore and Diana Fuss, in the French-speaking world it may be nothing more than a private nonquestion.

Perceiving the closet as the grounding metaphor for homosexual writing—whatever that may be or mean—has had a wide-ranging effect. Specifically, tearing down the closet in an active, revolutionary sense marked the period of gay liberation of the late 1960's in the United States. Suddenly, one proclaimed one's homosexuality, or better yet, one refused the psychologizing label of "homosexuality" and one proclaimed one's gayness. It was an era of explosive discourse, revolutionary action: gay people came out of the closet, declared themselves proud to be what or who they were, recognized themselves as gay, established gay identities. In one of many borrowings from the French, gay liberation took a farce and turned *La Cage aux Folles* into a Broadway musical that blared the ideological exaggeration of identity into a war-cry and came up with what amounts to a gay anthem: "I Am What I Am." In the United States, being gay was a process of coming out of the closet, finding one's peers, and assembling the parts of one's identity.

The movement of gay liberation that followed May 1968 in France was both more radical and far less optimistic than the liberation theology expounded by the purveyors of a gay identity.[2] Specifically, we are referring to

1. In French, *être dans le placard* means to be in prison, but it does not directly connote homosexuality. The American expression has now been somewhat adopted, however, with reference to the closeted homosexual.

2. Frédéric Martel's *Le Rose et le noir* provides a substantial post-1968 history of homosexuals in France. His *Matériaux* is an important source for bibliographic and cultural information (also in *Le Rose et le noir*).

the work of Guy Hocquenghem, who was its most eloquent militant for men, and the work of Monique Wittig, who in works like *Les Guerrillères* asked profound radical questions about the inclusiveness or the apartness of the lesbian and of lesbians. In French thought, the problem of establishing an identity was beset with a whole radical critique of the subject him-, her-, or itself, as well as a generalized critique of phallocentrism and heterocentrism. Hocquenghem, for one, endlessly criticized the complete heterosexualization of space and the policing of bodies as part of a heterosexual machine endlessly seeking to reproduce itself. For Hocquenghem, the other was never fully banished, despite the confirmation of the self in some complacent statement of self-identity. For the other was both the heterosexual and the Maghrebin man, Hocquenghem's example of the other who fit no category in a bivalent opposition. Wittig challenged language to be nonheterosexual, nonphallocentric, and language came up short. In her book *The Straight Mind*, Wittig views the categories of "man" and "woman" as political categories—in other words, as temporal, historical constructs, and not as some eternal framework. Indeed, in "La Pensée straight," Wittig shows that this "sexual" difference functions to mask conflicts of interests at every level, including the ideological one. Thus, for her, lesbians are not "women" because the word "woman" only has meaning as a construct within ideological and economic systems organized by, or according to, heterosexuality. In their writing both Wittig and Hocquenghem hearkened back to the gay surrealist René Crevel, for whom memory itself was heterosexual and therefore suspect. Finally, both for Hocquenghem and for Wittig as for Sartre before them, we are all other, all a series of differences from the essentialist position of a subject sure of its identity. We are all alienated and nomadic subjects, structured by those differences.

How does all this translate into academic discourse? Let us first start with the French tradition, because there is a landmark work that defines a privileged moment in the academic discipline. In 1979 George Stambolian and Elaine Marks edited an extraordinary collection of essays, *Homosexualities and French Literature*. Quite simply, the book brought the subject into the open as an intellectual endeavor. Certainly, French literature and culture had not been as secretive, hypocritical, or repressive as their Anglo-American counterparts. But the question of homosexuality, often subtended by a psychologizing or apologetic discourse institutionalized in language itself, retained a shock value that interfered with intellectual dialogue. The publication of the book, with its rich variety of essays, brought the study to the fore, at least in North America; remedied the marginalized, if not repressed, status of the inquiry; and helped shape gender studies within the broader context of a flexible approach to literary study. If "gender" studies had previously been more or less interchangeable with a kind of feminism, the book by Stambolian and Marks helped bring the heterosexual model into question in the light of day.

In France and in French-speaking countries, gay liberation has remained by and large a nonacademic activity. There has been no queering of the classroom, and in France, at least, no rush toward establishing tenure-track lines in queer theory. Indeed, one would be hard-pressed to find the impact on the French university, not only of queer theory and queer studies, but even of feminism as such as an academic discipline. In Canada, of course, the situation is different: French-speaking Quebec is still (for all its "foreignness" to Anglophones) part of the North American academy and there has been an appearance of both disciplines in the academy in Quebec. For all that, it is only quite recently that gay and lesbian studies, or what we might more properly call gender studies, has reappeared as part of the academic discourse of French departments on this side of the Atlantic. Ross Chambers and Anne Herrmann have recently edited a special issue of *Canadian Review of Comparative Literature*, Michael Lucey has published a book on Gide, Kevin Kopelson has devoted several chapters of his book *Love's Litany* to a discussion of French figures, and one of the editors of this volume has published two books on the subject. These are only several of the current burgeoning of gender studies as an academic discipline relating to French literature. And we would note that the field is becoming plural in other ways as well, with the recent publication by Emilie L. Bergmann and Paul Julian Smith of the collection *¿Entiendes?*, an anthology relating gender studies to Latin American discourses and the collection *Outing Goethe and His Age*, edited by Alice A. Kuzniar.

The path is somewhat different in Anglo-American studies. In the 1980's a whole academic discipline developed in the United States that is now generally referred to variously as gay and lesbian studies, gender studies, and most recently queer studies. Despite being what some might have felt to be a natural breeding ground for gender studies, French departments were not where it occurred. Perhaps because of its increasing marginalization as a field within the academic marketplace of the American university, French studies did not develop a gender-studies component with the same force as did English departments. French departments and programs, in the United States at least, found themselves ever more frequently fighting for their basic survival and did not have the luxury, even if the interest and intent were there, to occupy a territory that might have been perceived as a marginal one.

While gay and lesbian studies might have seemed a natural outgrowth of the impact of French theory on the American academy, it is important to recognize that the institutional affiliations of gender studies were by and large in departments of English. Gender studies developed as a field relative to canons of English literature, and specifically to two historical periods more than others: the Renaissance and twentieth-century studies. Modernism itself and its precursors—in other words, the literary formations of our current cultural consciousnesses, as the work of Eve Kosofsky Sedgwick and Elaine Showalter amply demonstrates—is a hinge for the door to gender studies. Gay and lesbian studies or gender studies develop, changing names along the way, becoming most recently queer theory, in an attempt to relate this field to cultural studies—"queer," because it was once pejorative, seems less stamped with the marks of high culture.

The field has had an extraordinary impact on curricula in English departments throughout North America. The burgeoning of the field brings more works to light, canons or reading lists change, and the lenses with which works are viewed, the languages with which they are discussed, undergo startling transformation. The impact of feminism on the academy challenged the position of the male ego as a priori construct for the epitome of the model, rational, and cultured subject. Gender studies have similarly dislodged to some extent the definition of the world based on the solipsistic model of a heterosexual subject bent on reproduction or the refusal thereof. Moreover, the changing methods of inquiry over the past twenty years have moved strategies of reading away from a purely oppositional practice that saw hierarchies as being unshakeable except through reversal. With feminism, cultural studies, and poststructuralism come modes of reading and understanding that depend on series of differences, not oppositions. Thus, if social structures had, for example, codified the male/female or masculine/feminine relationship in a hierarchy, contemporary criticism has seen the need to redefine genders and to point to the artificiality of the "feminine" and the "masculine." Feminism, cultural studies, and poststructuralism have redefined, regendered, and thereby regenerated the text.

And yet the theoretical position most often enunciated for gender studies remains intertwined with the metaphors of English and American literature. In other words, as it is now constituted institutionally, Anglo-American gender studies depend on the existence of the closet and on pandemic homophobia as the transcendental signifiers to be challenged, overcome, or destroyed. In a sense, queer theory is beginning to move beyond the impoverishment of literary or textual object by the insistence of the metaphor of the closet. At the same time, even the most current work, like Lee Edelman's *Homographesis*, has not fully severed ties to those useful metaphors, though Edelman's desire to unpack representation and put its logic into question (xiv) will help to move the field away from the reinscription of its metaphors of identity. Queer theory seems to have two meanings that are somewhat in conflict with one another. On the one hand, it is a repositioning of identity politics that seeks to be inclusive of all sexual and gendered positions, whether they fit discursively or institutionally into a predefined context. This aspect of current queer theory therefore depends on the affirmation of the identity of the self as a valid queer speaker. The other face of queer theory is the final refusal of identity politics, a refusal, we believe, that represents the final sloughing off of the metaphor of the closet. In the most radical requestioning of identity found in the work of Judith Butler, not coincidentally a work that is very much in the line of Nietzsche's and Foucault's genealogical critiques, the position from which the subject speaks, writes, or desires seems to be permanently decentered. That position is constructed and deconstructed by discourse, thus revealing the artificiality of the epistemic and ontological regime on which the heterosexual matrix relies.

Theory proceeds at a different rate from its institutional incorporation. And to examine further ramifications of these points, let us look for a moment at the most recent and (by one standard) most authoritative word on the subject: *Professions of Desire: Lesbian and Gay Studies in Literature.* This collection of essays, edited by George E. Haggerty and Bonnie Zimmerman, is marked with the imprimatur of the Modern Language Association of America. This book becomes an official document because of the weight of the publisher's name. Indeed, the official acceptance of queer theory by the institution is everywhere in evidence. In the preface, Catharine Stimpson, the former president of the MLA, refers to a Modern Language Association convention meeting in Chicago—a fictional one, since the reference is to a murder mystery published a few years ago by D. J. H. Jones entitled *Murder at the MLA*. The connection is not only fictional but real as well, for in the introduction the authors tell us that the "idea for this book emerged at the [real] 1989 convention" (1). The book is not, of course, a compendium on gay and lesbian studies, queer theory, or anything of the kind. It is a symptomatic metadiscourse on the limits of the queer theory it is both officializing and universalizing. Let us look at these symptoms.

On the first page of the preface Stimpson writes that "*Professions of Desire* offers three gifts to us all." Never mind for the moment that, as Jacques Derrida has shown and Marcel Mauss before him, gifts imply obligation, the taking of the self, the dissolution of the singular identity constituted as an independent subject. Let us see what the gifts are. The first gift is that "it asks the most serious and valuable of questions about literature and culture." But what literature and culture could this be? The subtitle of the book proclaims a universal "literature." Stimpson gives us examples: "What difference does it make that Oscar Wilde was a gay man? That Gertrude Stein was a lesbian woman?" Suddenly, for us, the universal is reduced to the Anglo-American, one from each column, one man, English, but not really, because he was Irish, one woman, American, but not really, for she went to live in France. One "gay" man, one "lesbian" woman. Fortunately, Stimpson goes on to put these categories in question: "And whatever do we mean by sexuality? by sexual identity? by gender identity? by desire?" The universal "literature" is posited, but the argument seems to be based on an Anglo-American universe. The details are put into question, but only the details.

The second and third gifts are no less of a problem to the reader attuned to what one might grotesquely call a non-Anglo-American bias. The second gift is that the book "cares about pedagogy. . . . Our sexualities and their representations are the raw material of volatile syllabi and classrooms. Some teachers and students wish to stigmatize homosexuality ferociously" (xii). Indeed. But is it not also true that the world here is not even the Anglo-American classroom, whatever that might be, because that too is a fictional amalgamation that smooths out difference? For one would be hard-pressed to find some communality between a tutorial at Oxford and a French 1 class at the University of North Carolina or the University of South Alabama. No, the world here is that of the engaged classroom, the world of small classes in humanities on trendy or radicalized topics, offered at privileged sites in American colleges and universities. Such courses, undoubtedly meant to foster discussion and permit all students to speak from their valid positions of identity, are a means of countering the traditional, conservative, and stereotypical image of the classroom. It is a means of opposing the monolith of phallocentric man-and-his-books courses taught by overbearing stentorian white men lecturing on universals and not taking into consideration the other: the multicultural, the woman, the gay, the person-of-color. Does this represent a classroom at the Sorbonne? Perhaps the myth hangs on there of culture with a capital "C," but it is not the same culture: it is the culture that never forced the writings of Balzac or Proust or Colette or

Gide into a closet. The monolith may be there in the perpetuation of culture as dominant culture, but that dominant culture never excluded homosexuality. The third gift is the tone of the book, at once "playful, ironic, fearless, resolute, and angry." But why, one asks? Is this a strategy to make the universal a cultural reflection of a multiplicity of identities? Perhaps. But it is perhaps believed to be necessary because it is the only way to combat the universalization of the metaphor: the monolith that is not man-and-his-books but the purported universality of the Anglo-American closet.

The introduction to the book extends the same arguments that Stimpson implies in her preface. The editors specify that lesbian and gay studies are not "so much a field in the classic sense as a theoretical approach to literature and culture" (2) This too may give the reader pause because of the odd universals of "literature" and "culture." Indeed, whose literature and culture could these be? A clue comes on the next page: "monoculturalism no longer has a place among us." This is the era of the multicultural, but whose multiculturalism is it? Multiculturalism may be nothing more than the extension of white male heterosexual politics to a hyphenated-American set of simulacra posing as subjects. It is not until the other radically unseats the entire dichotomous performance of identity, it is not until the entire paradigm of self and other is deconstructed, that some sense of the multiplicity of a valid multicultural force of subjects arises.

In every scenario there is a bogey-man, not necessarily a scapegoat, for the latter is innocent while the first evilly haunts the subject thrown into the world. We mean the word "haunting" in its most literal sense, because, as Derrida has pointed out in his *Spectres de Marx*, this too is another way of unseating the independent subject from "his" throne, another way of deconstructing "his" sense of identity. The example of Marx could not be better chosen, for two reasons. First is the famous beginning to *The Communist Manifesto*, in which he talks about a "specter haunting the face of Europe." For Marx, of course, this specter was communism; we will soon see how that specter, *mutatis mutandis*, has undergone a change of ghostly apparatus to become the conflated and purportedly independent "Euro-American" subject, always already identical to himself. The second reason for mentioning Marx at this point is because of his insistence on a dialectic. Indeed, Marx shows, from one end of his oeuvre to the other, that reliance on some vulgar reflection (*Wiederspiegelung*) to give a sense of identity is to fall into the traps that refuse a dialectic, that refuse to see alienation as nonrecuperable. For Marx, just as for Freud, Derrida, Foucault, Deleuze, Barthes, and so many others, including Wittig, Butler, and Hocquenghem, the subject can never fully identify with himself or herself because he or she is endlessly implicated in various sets of dialectical oppositions. There is no whole subject, there is no healed ego, there is no possibility of full self-conscious identity.

So the haunting, we would say, is very real in the case of gender studies, because gender studies has been haunted by its origins, by its other, and by its attempted incorporation of that other in the name of what one can only call the rhetoric of the politically correct. Let us take these matters point by point. First of all, gender studies, for all its origins in a real activity, a revolutionary moment that one might conveniently date to the revolt of May 1968, the opposition to the Vietnam War, and indeed the Stonewall riot of June 1969, has a theoretical origin as well. The normalization of homosexuality in the United States, not in a legal sense but in a deontological one, has occurred as a gradual process over a period of a quarter-century, though with many a backlash. But the area of gender studies, at least for the literary among us, found its theoretical underpinnings in Continental, and specifically French, thought. The work of Jean-Paul Sartre emphasizing existential freedom and choice and the work of Simone de Beauvoir engaging the artifice with which the "woman" is constructed and fighting the hegemony of male dominance are two of the most important building blocks for the eventual gay liberation movement and for the development of gender studies in the academy.[3]

Closer to us is the revolution in French thought that from 1966 on, starting with the famous conference on structuralism held at Johns Hopkins University, had a massive impact on the American academy. Who are these thinkers? All French, by the sound of it: Roland Barthes (Protestant, gay), Jacques Derrida (Algerian, Jewish), Michel Foucault (gay), Claude Lévi-Strauss (Belgian, Jewish), Julia Kristeva (Bulgarian), Tzvetan Todorov (Bulgarian), Jacques Lacan, Gilles Deleuze. Whether by background, which we mention not for the purposes of categorization but to underline differences that are often silently erased, or by their intellectual bent that leads to a massive decentering, all these thinkers are situated at the margins of Western, phallocentric ideology. These critics together establish a multiple deterritorialized and decentered episteme.

This unprepossessing consciousness of the other was never reductive, was never trivialized into a sense of identity that had to be uniform. Instead, from the very beginning of this movement of thought, as is manifest in the work of Deleuze, with *Différence et répétition*, and Derrida, with *L'Ecriture*

3. In the 1980s, Wittig radicalized Beauvoir's statement into "lesbians are not," by which she means that genders are not fixed eternal categories.

et la différence, to name two works among many, the difference of difference was endlessly explored. But the difference of French thought became lost, to a great extent, as it was translated into the American academy. To return to the imprimatur of the Modern Language Association, Haggerty and Zimmerman write in their introduction: "The contributors to the volume themselves identify as lesbian, gay, or queer, and they work on writers, texts, or situations that are similarly definable, either directly, because of their overt interest in same-sex desire, or implicitly, because the issue of sexuality can be interrogated in them" (3). Needless to say, at this point in the introduction, the authors of this volume find such a crystallization of identity politics to be leagues away from the scope, focus, and intent of this anthology and would make no such claim, either political or pragmatic, for the authors whose work is contained herein. Indeed, we wholly subscribe to the final line in Judith Butler's excellent essay "Imitation and Gender Insubordination" (in Fuss), where Butler sees subversion occurring this way: "Perhaps this will be a matter of working sexuality *against* identity, even against gender, and of letting that which cannot fully appear in any performance persist in its disruptive promise" (29). We hope to continue to subvert by difference, by the insistence of these texts and their authors on difference.

We have indicated that there is another aspect to the haunting: there is a haunting by the French. Theoretical mothers and fathers, these French thinkers—even if they are not really, wholly baguette-toting, Jean Gabin–sounding, Edith Piaf–looking French people—continue to haunt gender studies in North America. It is more than a touch ironic that Eve Kosofsky Sedgwick's groundbreaking book *Between Men*, which develops the concept of the homosocial in Anglo-American literature, has Edouard Manet's *Le Déjeuner sur l'herbe* as the cover art. But we can turn to the symptomatic work of *Professions of Desire*, and specifically to an article entitled "Pedagogy and Sexuality," by Joseph Litvak. It starts, appropriately enough, with a personal memory entitled "The French Lesson," which is about a French teacher in the author's high school who was "famous at the high school for 'liking boys'" (19). The author has duly prefaced his tale with the following thought included in a parenthetical remark: "If French teachers didn't exist, American culture would no doubt have to invent them. Come to think of it, it sort of *did* invent them." The second part of this fascinating article is entitled "The Lesson of Paul de Man." The first paragraph of that part concludes with the following remark (which is also parenthetical): "Since you could still do French in comp. lit., the French connection—along with everything it stood for—wasn't exactly severed, moreover, though de Man himself was from Belgium, that status could seem at the time a sufficient metonymy for Frenchness *tout court*" (23). And *pace* the voice of Flanders (of which Paul de Man was one), de Man was said to have a "Belgian accent" (24). One day's metonymy, by which Paul de Man metonymically substitutes for "Frenchness," is matched by another day's identification of a "Belgian accent" (in English) in which de Man's Flemish accent can suddenly metamorphose and be perfect Walloon—B-movie French, as it were.

Demonizing the French while letting the text be haunted by the French and their theories has consequences, to be sure, or has had them. One wonders what queer studies would have looked like had French not been so demonized. Perhaps the word is too strong, but there are implications: identity politics might have been called a politics of difference. The differences of French thought, which include France's others and the others of Frenchness that are found in a differently articulated concept of otherness and inclusivity and include Quebec and the Maghreb, would have maintained a status wholly other from the hyphenated inclusivity of North American multiculturalism. Rather than closets, one might have spoken of public and private spaces; the closet would not have appeared to be the transcendental signifier it has often become. And we would like to think that some of these different faces and phases of gender studies are contained in this collection.

One of the goals of this book is the capitalization of these differences. In *Articulations of Difference*, we have tried to assemble an anthology for the nineties: it takes the insights of the past twenty years and presents a collection of essays that reflect the renewed approaches of questions of gender and sexuality as they relate to homosexuality and its representations. The essays rely on models that differentiate between sexuality and gender, between natural inclinations and social constructs, even within a given category of homo/hetero sexuality. There is a tacit acceptance of Simone de Beauvoir's famous observation that "One is not born a woman, but becomes a woman," as well as of the implications of Wittig's arguments about all sexual categorizations. Thus, one is not born a heterosexual or a homosexual, one becomes it. If there are innate sexual "preferences," if one's early childhood determines a path, it is nevertheless the signifiers, representations, and structures of the world that make one a homosexual or a heterosexual. And this is never clearer than in literature and other cultural artifacts.

The essays show the differential nature of the depiction of sexuality and sexual preference (itself a misnomer) as well as the results of the dedramatization associated with homosexuality over the last twenty years. Even if sodomy was decriminalized in France two centuries ago, it is with the "empowerment" associated with recent gay liberation that the subject becomes intellectually less dramatic and more interesting on both sides of the Atlantic. In a general sense, gay liberation means the liberation of the individual from the constructs of a given social order. The absorption of that liberation into the horizons of the literary and cultural critic means an increased awareness of gender-related questions and a changing perspective on the play of genders at work in the literary text and cultural object of study.

The articles collected in *Articulations of Difference* do not propose some faddish approach to works in order meretriciously to show, for example, the repression of homosexuality in the work of a given author. For such an approach would, ironically enough, renew the fateful necessity of purely heterosexual models that contemporary literary criticism has rejected. Rather, if there is a general approach, it is that both the theoretical and practical essays in this collection all bring the insights of a multiple, imbricated, redistributed sense of gender and sexuality to a study of French literature and culture.

What these essays do have in common is the willingness of each of the authors to go beyond a set of rhetorics, a set of limitations that were a defining moment in the struggle of gay liberation and in its reflection in writing, both creative and critical. It is what Renaud Camus calls the "stage of the ghetto," necessary to enable change, but which must itself be overcome. In literature, the stage of the ghetto corresponds quite neatly to a golden age of gay literature that extends roughly from the beginnings of militant homosexual liberation in the late 1960's to the age of AIDS. In critical thought, the position is slightly different. The rhetoric of rebellion and the rhetoric of liberation find their keywords in expressions like "heterocentrism" and "homophobia." Easy expressions to bandy about, especially because of the ubiquity of the former (if not necessarily the latter). As an unfounded and unexamined means of control, a reminder of limitations and yet another avatar of the Oedipus complex, heterocentrism controls discourses, practices, rhetorics, and behaviors. The initial stages of homosexual liberation in the wake of May 1968 implicitly criticize the heterosexist enterprise through a celebration of gay liberation.

Even as early as Guy Hocquenghem's study of homosexual desire, the author underlines the necessity of criticizing the heterocentric enterprise, because it has offered names, frames, and classifications for desire, which, were it free to be true to itself, would remain unclassifiable. While proclaiming gay liberation, Hocquenghem is already showing the slippage in the role of the signifiers of heterocentrism, the meanings forced on desiring subjects by the multiple institutions that heterocentric praxis sustains in its wake. Or again, Monique Wittig has denounced the artificiality of sexual difference and the finality of its politics: "The concept of difference has nothing ontological about it. It is only the way that the masters interpret a historical situation of domination" (*Straight Mind* 29). Much later—to name only one other fundamental critical point—Judith Butler questions all sexual definitions by seeing sexual practices as a praxis, a rehearsal, an ongoing set of performances.

So along with the necessary cultural critiques of heterocentrism, of homophobia, of what Adrienne Rich has called "compulsory heterosexuality," comes something astounding in the work of Hocquenghem, Wittig, and Butler, among others, as different as these works initially seem: a critique of any "slave morality" that insists on sexuality as a set of lip-synched definitions, even if those definitions are, we hasten to add, products of the most liberal and liberating thought system.

Coming from a wide variety of backgrounds, and taking an equally wide variety of critical positions, the authors in this anthology—with no coercion from the editors—have all shown that their work is the fruit of a new stage in the development of gender studies. Not gay liberation, not even queer theory, but gender studies: a look at all the genders, a recognition of the completely destabilized system of genders and sexes, a celebration of the slippages, ambiguities, and tropings among these positions. No longer content to rail against heterocentrism, the authors in this anthology have taken positions that represent some moment after heterocentrism has been deconstructed. Instead of invectives against homophobia, there are celebrations of the individually gendered text.

And it is because of that, we feel, that this anthology can address such a wide variety of discursive situations in such new and interesting lights. The articles range from studies of traditional narrative and poetry to readings of medical records, from examinations of twentieth-century narratives of gay liberation to readings of gender in the postcolonial world. For that reason we have given the collection the title it has: *Articulations of Difference*. In that title, beyond gender and genre, is the idea of new production, new worlds, and new ideas. And we thank the contributors for having participated in this complex collective process.

Canonic French writing in the last two centuries has not led to the complete marginalization of homosexuality, even when ghosted by the institutions of knowledge and language. And we would say that precisely because of this lack of marginalization, at least when compared to Anglo-

American literature, a bold step might be taken to view nonhomosexual literature through the optics furnished by gender studies. In the first essay in this volume, "Stendhal's Legacy: Jean Baudrillard on Seduction," David Bell has written on the figuration of desire in the work of Jean Baudrillard and the reflection of his insights in the straightest of novelists, Stendhal. Bell underlines difference from the beginning, and points to problems of gender uncertainty in Stendhal's writing. Passing to the mid-nineteenth century, we have included two essays on Baudelaire's complex figures of homosexuality in *Les Fleurs du mal* and other works. In "The Silent Erotic / Rhetoric of Baudelaire's Mirrors," Dominique Fisher examines the figures of gender displacement and disruption by the figuration of the lesbian as subject and object in Baudelaire's work. Indeed, for Fisher, figures of homosexuality are the strongest means of destabilizing singular identities in Baudelaire's work; they are the sign of difference *par excellence.* For John Barberet, writing "Baudelaire: Homoérotismes," the lesbian figure is allied to other disruptive figures of femininity, especially to the prostitute. Moreover, there is a generalized feminization of the male subject, the Baudelairean figure of modernity, who, to undergo the experience of the crowd, of city life, of modernity itself, must become a passive, receptive figure instead of an active phallic male.

In the next two works, the authors have chosen to look at discourses that are not directly "literary," although in both cases the discourses—one lexicographical and pathological, the other medical and testamentary—have their parallels and effects in the literary world. In "Silence, Secrecy, and Scientific Discourse in the Nineteenth Century," Nigel Smith examines the medical discourses of mid- to late-nineteenth century France, specifically Tardieu and Carlier, as well as the Larousse dictionary, to show how this supposedly neutral scientific language was used as a means of control. But he also effectively demonstrates how these discourses contain—in both senses of the word—a homoerotics of their own, tied into the fascination with the sexual other. Vernon Rosario looks at the intersection of medical, scientific, and literary discourses in "*Histoires d'inversion*: Novelizing Homosexuality at the Fin-de-Siècle." He recalls how the novelist Emile Zola was contacted by an Italian "invert" who asked the author to look at the "human documents" of his life. Rosario shows how this one moment exemplifies the dizzying and contradictory discourses surrounding sexual inversion and how these multiple discourses were fielded in the French cultural imaginary.

In "Homosexual Erotic Scripting in Verlaine's *Hombres*," Charles Minahen analyzes several poems from Verlaine's collection of homoerotic poetry. Through this close reading, he shows how the development of Verlaine's homoerotic stance is poetically intertwined with concepts of perversion and subversion of the work itself. In "Gay Incipit: Botanical Connections, Nosegays, and Bouquets," the late George Bauer offers the reader a guided tour through a gay botanical garden. In this work, Bauer shows how the language of flowers has often served both as a code for a hidden language of homosexuality and as the very visible poetics for that language.

In "The Seduction of Terror: Annhine's Annihilation in Liane de Pougy's *Idylle saphique*," Melanie Hawthorne provides a detailed reading of a fin-de-siècle autobiographical novel about a lesbian relationship between Liane de Pougy and Natalie Barney. Though the novel differs from the facts of the autobiography in significant ways, Hawthorne analyzes these differences to show how lesbianism is inscribed within the realm of the morbid and the pathological. Turning to surrealism, Garett Heysel analyzes the figure of the male body in his article entitled "René Crevel's Body Algebra," which focuses on the novel *Mon Corps et moi*, written by surrealism's only openly gay participant. Heysel analyzes the construction of the male homosexual body in Crevel's work as the locus of dualist struggles, both between body and mind and between the social constructions of the heterosexual order and the bodily desires of a homosexual individual.

In "Love Song," Alphonso Lingis has analyzed Jean Genet's rhapsodic novels, including *Our Lady of the Flowers* and *The Miracle of the Rose*, as masterful love songs to dead hoodlums, thieves, and murderers. For Lingis, these songs do not so much retell these loves; they are a recreation of that love that stands splendidly as the overcoming of the abject through the joy of the lyric. In "Beyond Feminism: Elvire Murail's *Escalier C*," Laurence Porter discusses the development of a homocentric imaginary at the heart of a French novel set in a fictive Greenwich Village. Porter analyzes the internal mechanisms of control and repression in the novel's characters and the author's simultaneous construction of a possible new Arcadia in which each character is free to follow his or her heart's desires. In "Gomorrah and the Word: But Where Are They?" Laurence Enjolras focuses on what seemed to turn into epiphenomenal literary and cultural production in the 1970's and 1980's: the appearance and subsequent disappearance of a lesbian literature in France. Enjolras follows this discussion with an analysis of Hélène de Monferrand's lesbian novel *Les Amies d'Héloïse*, a 1990 work that seems to try to revive this cultural production by a revival of traditional eighteenth-century models of narrative and love.

The three last chapters of this anthology all deal with aspects of the contemporary literary scene as well. In "The Frame of Desire in the Novel of the 1980's and 1990's," Martine Antle analyzes the interrelation of the photographic image and the written image as vehicles for desire. Concentrating on novels by Marguerite Duras and Hervé Guibert, Antle shows how the introduction of the photographic image and the concomitant gaze it demands displaces the structuring of desire, specifically homosexual desire, through the creation of models of visual simulacra. Robert Harvey's article, "Purloined Letters: Intertextuality and Intersexuality in Tahar Ben Jelloun's *The Sand Child*," focuses on the construction and deconstruction of sex and gender in a recent Maghrebin novel written in French. For Harvey, Ben Jelloun destabilizes imposed categories through a requestioning of the expression and containment of desire and specifically through the elaboration of an intertextual figure that relates his work to sexual and textual ambiguities in the work of Jorge Luís Borges. Finally, in "The National-Sexual: From the Fear of Ghettos to the Banalization of Queer Practices," Mireille Rosello analyzes a science fiction novel by the Quebecois writer Daniel Sernine. Rosello questions the imposition of categories of sexuality and gender as they relate to questions of social and national identity, and uses Sernine's novel as a means of focusing on the limitations of all such categorizations.

In a book that takes us from the construction of the space of desire in the early realist fiction of Stendhal to the consequences of sex and gender in scientific cyberspace, we have sought to include a variety of approaches, theories, ideas, and strategies. It is our hope that this book is a means of launching conversations and debate on the consequences of gender studies within the curriculum of a French department or in humanities courses in general. Simultaneously, we hope that the new set of approaches to gender studies as made manifest in *Articulations of Difference* will be an opening up of gender studies, queer theory, and other related fields to a more complicated and much more differentiated view of the interrelations between the artifacts of various cultures and the articulations of sexual identity, the constructions of gender, and the expression of desire.

A word about translations: all translations were done by the authors themselves, unless otherwise indicated.

Our thanks to Helen Tartar, Peter Kahn, and Ann Klefstad for their invaluable help in the realization of this book.

CHAPTER 1

Stendhal's Legacy: Jean Baudrillard on Seduction

DAVID F. BELL

Recent essays treating Jean Baudrillard's work have shown a great deal of reluctance to address the contents of his essay *De la séduction.* Mike Gane and Douglas Gellner, for example, are both so leery of Baudrillard's antifeminist provocation in *De la séduction* that they hastily put distance between themselves and Baudrillard. In their rush, they treat *De la séduction* cavalierly at best and unfairly at worst. It is as if they both feared so greatly to be tainted by Baudrillard's antifeminism in the historical context in which they are writing that their discussion of *De la séduction* can only be incomplete, and such partial treatment can only lead to misunderstanding. It would be worthwhile to consider Baudrillard's essay in its own context for a moment in order to highlight the dangers that Gane and Gellner perceive and feel they must skirt. Written in the wake of Luce Irigaray's two groundbreaking studies, *Speculum de l'autre femme* and *Ce sexe qui n'en est pas un,* and thus in the midst of perhaps the most active moment in French theoretical feminism, *De la séduction* takes a clear—at times ironic and even patronizing—position against two strong currents of thought formulated by feminist thinkers in the mid and late 1970s. The first was the glorification of the woman's body and the mandate issued to women to partake of *jouissance* as they had never done in the past.[1] The second was the more

1. Roland Barthes did much to move the notion of *jouissance* into the field of theoretical play with his *Le Plaisir du texte,* in which the term is deployed by him in detail for the first time. Baudrillard will set forth a series of terms that have been

general stance favoring the empowerment of women at all levels—political, economic, ideological—that became an important theme of the feminist movement in the 1970s. As Baudrillard puts it: "Promotion of the feminine as a sex in its own right (equal rights, equal *jouissance*)" (35).

To those who call for *jouissance*—a term that serves Baudrillard here as a shorthand for describing a kind of female sexuality not subservient to the masculine and thus somehow escaping the vestiges of the structure of masculine/feminine opposition—Baudrillard responds essentially that the theoretical underpinnings of such a position are broadly Freudian, and that an attempt to break out of masculine domination via Freudianism is, in fact, theoretically impossible. Within Freudian psychoanalysis, he maintains, no room exists for a feminine sexuality:

> Freud is right: there is only a single sexuality, a single libido—masculine. . . . It is useless to dream of a nonphallic sexuality, one that is not divided, not marked. It is useless, within this structure, to want to put the feminine on the other side of the equation, to mix the terms. Either the structure stays the same—all of the feminine is absorbed by the masculine—or it collapses and there is no longer a feminine or a masculine. (16)

This explicit criticism of Freudianism implies that in order to move past Freud's positions, we may well have to discard the very notion of sexuality in its Freudian incarnation and rethink gender roles entirely. To those who trumpet the political, economic, and ideological empowerment of women, Baudrillard constantly replies that power is always on the side of the Law, of production, of being and the reality principle. The empowerment of women and its anticipated result, mastery of the political and social system, takes on a decidely negative hue in Baudrillard's presentation—in fact, it is seen as nothing short of a capitulation to the system: "Strange and ferocious complicity of the feminist movement with the order of truth" (19). Clearly, *De la séduction* represents an attempt to outline a position that would be aligned against production and the Law. By searching instead to master production, feminists simply play into the game of power that has defined masculine domination and find themselves rapidly co-opted by it.

It is easy to see how these positions would be offensive to feminists. In particular, as Gellner has put it, "In view of the history of the oppression of

---

used to attempt to spell out what is meant by the notion of *jouissance*: *polyvalence, érotisme, potentialités infinies du désir, branchements, diffractions, intensités libinales*, and so forth (*De la séduction* 16–17).

women, such sophistry [arguing that women have, in fact, not been oppressed, as Baudrillard does at certain moments] might be regarded as highly offensive" (147). To invite women precisely not to play the power game, moreover, is advice that can only appear to perpetuate their victimization. But for feminists there is something even more repulsive in Baudrillard's argument than any overt theoretical positions it espouses, namely, the tone and attitude of superiority that it conveys discursively. Formulas such as "the feminine is neither . . . nor . . . " or "the specificity of the feminine is . . . " or "femininity is . . . " abound in *De la séduction.* Baudrillard gives the impression that he believes he is speaking the truth about women and thus leaves himself wide open to criticism of his right to assume that voice of truth. Now even more than when Baudrillard was writing, that is, in the present context of an almost existential American feminism that insists very heavily on the lived experience of the feminine as a necessary element of the attempt to speak the truth about women, Baudrillard's discursive strategy is tailor-made to provoke frontal attacks by feminist theorists—and to render critics such as Gane and Gellner squeamish when they have to deal with it.

Within the logic of Baudrillard's own writing, however, a certain kind of feminism is not the sole target in the crosshairs of an argument valorizing seduction. The reassessment of seduction has other ideological and political purposes as well. Beginning with his earliest major essay, *Le Système des objets*, Baudrillard had been exploring the philosophical underpinnings of the system of capitalist production—its cracks, fissures, and illusions. *De la séduction*, along with *Oublier Foucault*, which belongs essentially to the same stage in Baudrillard's career, mark the beginning of an aggressive attempt to outline a social and ideological position in opposition to Marxism. The crisis of Marxist theory, which really began in France with the invasion of Hungary in 1956, came to a head during the events of May 1968. Even if, in a curious anachronism, Althusser's work was influential for a time immediately following May 1968, the disintegration of Marxism, its progressive disappearance as an ideological center for many younger French intellectuals, was apparent during and after May 1968.[2] This led to flirtations with Maoism and Trotskyism among student groups, for example, and later

2. In reality, the popularity of Althusser's work issued in large part from the way it recast Marx in structuralist terms, in other words, from the way it undermined what was really Marxist in Marxism (in particular, any place for an active subject of history).

gave rise to what would become known as the group of *nouveaux philosophes.* In light of Baudrillard's own theoretical development, then, the notion of seduction clashes explicitly with the term "production," as a challenge issued to the ambient neo-Marxism of the period that was attempting to salvage something from the growing ruins of traditional Marxist thought (Kellner 122–24). Baudrillard seems to be saying his violent adieu to Marxism by working through a new and different ideological position, of which seduction is a centerpiece.

The choice of seduction is also an explicit attack on Freudian psychoanalysis. Baudrillard considers one of the founding moments of psychoanalysis to be Freud's decision, precisely, to treat the primal scene of seduction as a phantasm, a screen memory, instead of as an actual occurrence. This decision by Freud was a turning point, Baudrillard claims, when Freud excluded from his analysis certain insights into human behavior and thereby reduced human interaction to a political economy of sexuality:

> Seduction as an original form is reduced to the state of "original phantasm" and thus treated, according to a logic which is no longer its own, as a residue, a vestigial trace, a screen formation in the henceforth triumphant logic and structure of psychic and sexual reality. Far from considering the devalorization of seduction as a normal growth phase, we must understand that it is a crucial event with weighty consequences. As is well known, seduction will disappear from psychoanalytic discourse thereafter. (81)

To those who think they will be able to save Marxism by rescuing it with a dose of psychoanalysis, such as, for example, Jean-François Lyotard, whose *Economie libidinale* appeared in 1974, Baudrillard sends a resounding message refusing such a philosophical strategy. Moreover, to those who were working in Lacanian circles at the time to reactualize Freud's theories in still other ways, Baudrillard wanted to demonstrate that the very bases of Freudian theory inevitably led to a dead-end definition of sexuality. In the final analysis, for Baudrillard, Marxism and Freudo-Marxism are closely linked to the brand of feminism he rejects—both to the notion of *jouissance* and to the push for political and ideological empowerment—and the position taken against one is simultaneously a position taken against the other.

Putting aside for a moment the history of seduction's importance within the evolution of Baudrillard's thought as it is engaged in its own historical moment, however, there is something provocative about the notion of seduction in itself, something that inevitably makes Baudrillard's argument less than palatable on other grounds—not simply for feminists but for philosophical critics of other persuasions as well. To say that seduction has generally had an extremely bad press in Western culture in the wake of the Judeo-Christian tradition is certainly an understatement. Precisely because of that bad press, the choice to write about seduction has the potential to create a certain suspicion and distrust. Seduction has customarily been viewed in modern times from two more or less similar perspectives—the theological and the libertine—which may at first glance seem opposed to one another. The theological perspective sees in the seducer a corrupter and in the seduced person someone who has been defiled. The libertine perspective, on the other hand, sees seduction as the affirmation of a will to make oneself master of the will of the other. The act of seduction may thus be evaluated in highly antithetical terms depending upon the approach one adopts. The theologian inevitably believes that seduction is a reprehensible act, while the libertine regards it as a triumph of human will. The mechanics of seduction proposed by the two positions are clearly similar, however, at a more fundamental level: seduction is an act of will perpetrated against a being who is fooled into adhesion to the will of the seducer and who is thus viewed as the weaker of the two and as at least partially guilty (Perniola). Seduction, then, would be a project conceived prior to its moment of realization and then implemented as a strategy designed to reach a certain end. The weakness of this approach is that it situates the problem of seduction somehow within a realm which may not be the most philosophically appropriate one for analysis—the realm of truth. If one can defile or manipulate the other, that is, if one can devise a strategy for turning the other aside and into a wayward path, then a priori there must be a right or a straight path—the true path—that the victim could have followed and was too weak to pursue. The image of the atheistic Don Juan is always the first to rear its head when the notion of seduction appears on the horizon in modern Western culture.

There are, however, other traditions of seduction within Western civilization that may occasionally have been obscured and lost, but that nonetheless maintain a certain hidden existence and suggest other possible paths for analysis. Mario Perniola argues, for example, that the notion of *apate* within the tradition of the Sophists allowed a presentation of seduction that differed significantly from the analysis I just rehearsed: "This idea [*apate*] constitutes one of the pivotal points of the thought of Gorgias of Leontium, which frees the victim of all blame and all culpability, considers seduction as the entry into a *logic* which is primarily imposed on the seducer, dissolves the dimension of trickery and fraud" (2). Perniola cites the speech "In Praise of Helen" attributed to the Sophist Gorgias of Leontium as an example (in Dumont 710–14). In this discourse, Gorgias aims precisely to exculpate Helen, to demonstrate that she does not deserve the blame that has been heaped upon her by opinion as a result of her seduction by Paris. Gorgias contrasts the notion of opinion, which he considers to be uncertain, variable, and without foundation in thought, with something else, namely, *apate*—seduction—which, as Perniola puts it, "possesses the necessity of the *logos*" (2). Perniola continues: "There is a *logic of seduction*, which compels the seduced person and the seducer alike, which has a dimension totally independent of and opposed to the subjective will, which is related to the *kairos*, the occasion" (2). It is incorrect to assume that seduction is a strategy conceived beforehand and then actualized more or less independently of the circumstances. On the contrary, it is an action of the moment, the occasion, which, by definition, cannot be planned but can only be encountered and transformed in its difference (Bell, *Circumstances*). The logic of seduction is precisely the necessity to use the *logos* each time anew, on each occasion, taking into account the differing circumstances that define the occasion. Such a conception has the advantage of restoring to the seduced person an active role in the exchange. That person has as much to do with imposing a certain necessity on the exchange that takes place within the occasion as does the seducer. The seducer, moreover, can no longer be described within a logic of identity and sameness (as the possessor of an unchanging, overbearing will), but becomes instead one who is perfectly adaptable and polymorphous, as different as is the seduced person in every new occasion of confrontation.[3]

In light of Perniola's assertions about the philosophical tradition associated with the notion of seduction, it can easily be seen that in *De la séduction* Baudrillard is attempting to reactivate parts of a now marginalized strain of reflection concerning seduction. He revalorizes them in a manner akin to seventeenth- and eighteenth-century libertines. In a clear sense, then, he claims to belong to a French tradition that goes back at least as far as the libertines—purposely alluding to his own position within that tradi-

3. Certain debates about the Sophists in the Greek philosophical tradition are quite recognizable here. The Sophists maintained that it takes just as much effort and skill to defend the innocent party as to defend the guilty one. Therefore, he who assumes the responsibility of speaking in the occasion must be capable of adapting his discourse to the circumstances, to the listeners who are to be swayed, and cannot simply impose the truth by means of some inherent strength of character or some quality that, if recognized and exposed, sets the truth apart from falsehood.

tion in the title of his essay, which can be seen in particular as a rewriting of Stendhal's *De l'amour*. Before I treat this intertextual relation explicitly by exploring what Stendhal's work has to offer Baudrillard, I would like to lay out as clearly as possible the general lines of Baudrillard's description of seduction now that I have contextualized it in a preliminary way within his own work, within a certain intellectual history of the late 1960's and the 1970's, and, finally, within a larger tradition of reflection on the notion of seduction. One can see rapidly that the theory of seduction developed in *De la séduction* combines the two strains of argument I have outlined above: on the one hand, an ideological confrontation with the contemporary theories against which Baudrillard is struggling; on the other hand, an appeal to a more classical Western tradition of seduction, one that offers insights into human relations that are quite different from the analyses to which we are more accustomed.

In a general way, seduction is presented by Baudrillard first and foremost as a mastery of the symbolic as opposed to the real, "the mastery and strategy of appearances against the power of being and the real" (22). The full meaning of such mastery becomes more obvious when the argument is extended to suggest that existence is, in fact, made up of nothing but surfaces and appearances. The fundamental philosophical illusion is to believe that there is being or depth—in other words, that there are meanings more "profound" than the signs on the surface, or that there are "latent" and hidden ideas that must be read by moving past symptoms and signs, by interpreting them. What would it mean to believe that there are nothing but surfaces? (Bell, "*Thérèse*"). The wrong turn taken by psychoanalysis led to privileging interpretation over seduction ("Freud . . . had broken with seduction and chosen the side of interpretation" [80]), to a theory that sees symptoms merely as signs of some hidden meaning.

An argument could be made that this move was precisely the one that devalorized the feminine in Freudian thought. The origins of psychoanalysis historically owe much to studies of female hysteria by Charcot, Breuer, and others. To turn away from hysteria studies as Freud did and to make the decision to treat hysterical symptoms as manifestations of latent problems stemming from sexuality is precisely to consider those symptoms as secondary to their "meaning." But what if the symptoms were somehow the primary phenomenon? What if "interpretations" could be understood as attempts to control those symptoms by positing a latent source, the libido, which ultimately feeds into a theory that is phallocentric and thus antifeminine? Freudian interpretation rests on a classical Cartesian understanding of causality (the symptom has a cause), but Baudrillard argues that in the case of seduction this logic of causes turns out to be faulty. Seduction is "a raising of the stakes with respect to the equivalence of causes and effects" (195). The concatenation of appearances that is characteristic of seduction puts into question the very notion that the world is ordered along the lines of cause and effect. In his later *Les Stratégies fatales*, Baudrillard will return to this insight: "Cause *produces* effect. Causes thus always have a meaning and an end. They never lead to a catastrophe (they are only susceptible to crisis). The catastrophe is the abolition of causes. It submerges cause beneath effect. It sends causal concatenation to its death. It gives things back to pure appearance" (73–74). By operating at the level of signs, appearances, and surfaces, seduction undermines the theory of libido as cause and, by extension, the overbearing presence of the phallus as interpretive key.

What is at stake in seduction, Baudrillard suggests, is not sex, libido, domination, anatomy, nor any of the rest of the notions that define Freudian psychoanalysis. One should not therefore understand seduction simply as a subversion or an inversion of the system of relations posited by psychoanalysis and Freudo-Marxism. Baudrillard makes a crucial distinction between inversion and subversion on the one hand, and what he calls "reversion" on the other. Inversion and subversion are strategic moves within a field where sexual domination and mastery of the system of production are the operative keys. Inversion elevates what is at the bottom of a hierarchy to the top and vice versa. It is the classic utopian move, always the first attempt to imagine how one might be able to undo an otherwise rigidly organized field of domination. But inversion does nothing to put into question the fundamental hierarchies to which it is applied. It merely reorders roles and leaves the rest intact. Subversion, which has been an oppositional notion of much strategic importance in contemporary theory, imagines that some force is capable of disrupting a field of rigidly structured hierarchies. But for subversion to wreak its destructiveness there must first be such a field; in other words, subversion also posits a priori the very same hierarchical structure of truth it supposedly undoes. Reversibility, on the other hand, is described by Baudrillard as the veritable collapsing of the distinctions that permit any hierarchical system of production and truth to exist: "For all orthodoxies [seduction] continues to be a malevolent artifice, a black magic misappropriating and diverting all truths, a conspiracy of signs, an exaltation of signs in their malevolent use. Every discourse is threatened by this sudden reversibility or absorption in its own signs, with no trace of meaning" (10). Reversibility, then, is a characteristic of systems of signs detached from truth, meaning, and law. Such systems inevitably implode and begin to function in the absence of all functionality. It is no coincidence, Baudrillard suggests, that Saussure, a great proponent of systematicity in linguistics, was also haunted by anagrams, those combinations and plays of signifiers whose proliferation puts into question any linguistic system and provokes utter fascination and impossible-to-master concatenations.

The notion of reversibility has much importance, it seems to me, for the question of gender roles. Although Baudrillard calls seduction feminine and at some level sees it as the feminine principle *par excellence* ("This power of the feminine is the power of seduction" [18]), as his argument unfolds, seduction ultimately invades the whole territory of human relations, collapsing the distinctions that define the system of Freudian sexual roles and thereby becoming the principal mode of interaction. This raises the question of whether or not there can then be anything like gender roles at all. Freudian theory, a meaning-based system in the final analysis, is founded on well-defined gender roles established in binary opposition: masculine opposed to feminine. By shifting the stage away from the level of meaning and interpretation toward the level of signs and symptoms, seduction undoes binary oppositions and freely redistributes gender roles so that in the end they are no longer structurally discernible. Signs and symptoms do not prepare anything or lead anywhere (to some kind of ultimate resolution). They simply link together in perpetually reforming sequences. Polymorphous and polyvalent, the seducer and the seduced incessantly dance around one another, exchanging positions, provoking reversals.

The rules that govern seductive encounters are precisely that—rules and not laws. The artificiality of rules, the fact that it makes no sense to call them into question and to debate them—as philosophy endlessly does with laws or with truths—but only to follow them to the letter, is an absolutely fundamental element in seduction. No one ever investigates the *foundations* of rules, only their functionality: "The passion of seduction is without substance or origin. It gets its intensity not from some libidinal investment nor from some energy of desire, but rather, from the pure form of the game, from raising the stakes purely formally" (113). One plays at seduction like a game, accepting without question the formal setting the game establishes, absorbed totally in the maze of the moves (*coups*) allowed. The notions of play and of ritual return with regularity in Baudrillard's discussion, because both situations are governed by something other than law or truth, by an *artificial* system of rules that none of the players puts into question.

The ritualistic, agonistic elements of seduction are closely allied with a certain kind of time within which seduction occurs. We saw earlier in Perniola's discussion that seduction for the Sophists was closely connected with the *kairos*, the occasion. Perniola emphasizes that seduction cannot be viewed as a strategy of conquest—pre-formed, prepared, and then implemented by stages. Instead the seducer and the seduced person encounter the proper circumstances and work out their interaction in the moment. Baudrillard's description of the timing of seduction, of its time, is very much in the same vein: "[Seduction] does not dispense itself in doses like an instrumental strategy that goes through intermediary phases. It operates in an instant, in one fell swoop, and it is always its own end in itself" (112). Indeed, the instantaneous nature of the action called for by the occasion requires, in fact, a particular application of memory, since the time for reflection is absent, and one therefore has to call on a certain kind of experience culturally stored in memory, a relation studied by Michel de Certeau (125–35).

The theme of the *kairos*, the right moment that demands waiting and that must be seized when it occurs, is one that can be found in a variety of places in the tradition of courtly politics and love. Without entering into the detail of this tradition, I will simply cite a remark by Baltasar Gracián, Machiavelli's Spanish contemporary and counterpart: "There is a point of maturity even in the fruits of understanding, and it is important to know this point to profit from it" (23). In Kierkegaard's *The Seducer's Diary*, an important intertext for Baudrillard, the wait for the *kairos*—presented under the guise of a chance event—is an indispensable element without which there can be no seduction. Plans and tactics go only so far for Kierkegaard's protagonist. At the end is nonetheless the wait for the proper moment: "Cursed chance! Never have I cursed you because you made your appearance; I curse you because you do not make your appearance at all. . . . Surprise me—I am ready. No stakes—let us fight for honor" (326–27). Preparations, however meticulous, remain at the mercy of the event that surges forth in its own instantaneous time.

Baudrillard clearly appeals in his arguments to a wider tradition concerning the notion of seduction, but, as I maintained earlier, on this topic he also situates himself within a specifically French tradition. *De la séduction* must, it seems to me, be read at least partially as a rewriting of Stendhal's *De l'amour*. I would like, then, to open a series of reflections on the parallels between Baudrillard and Stendhal at which I hinted both in the title to this essay and in the allusion to *De l'amour* earlier. Stendhal's character pairs in his major novels—particularly Lucien Leuwen / Mme de Chasteller in *Lu-*

cien Leuwen and Fabrice del Dongo / Clélia Conti in *La Chartreuse de Parme*, but even Julien Sorel / Mme de Rênal / Mathilde de la Mole in *Le Rouge et le Noir* to some extent—could well be seen as models for the kind of behavior Baudrillard describes. One can point to the fact that the principal concern in all three novels is love, the term Stendhal uses to describe male/female relationships. Questions of worldly ambition assuredly occupy appreciable space in *Le Rouge et le Noir* and *Lucien Leuwen*, but in *La Chartreuse de Parme*, arguably Stendhal's greatest novel and certainly his most mature, all pretext that Stendhal is writing about the ambitions of young men in a vein somewhat similar to Balzac is dropped, and the centrality of amorous pursuit becomes manifest. One could ultimately argue cogently, however, for the centrality of love in *Le Rouge* and *Lucien Leuwen* as well. The male protagonists of the two novels do not hesitate an instant to jettison whatever worldly gains they have accumulated in order to advance the amorous relationships in which they are involved. Lucien's neglect of his military career in Nancy immediately comes to mind. His only concern in the first part of the novel is to enter into a dialogue with Mme de Chasteller, a pursuit that leads to desertion and total abandonment of his military ambitions. And, of course, Julien Sorel's abrupt surrender of all his ambitions followed by his return to Verrières at the end of *Le Rouge* is largely explainable in terms of a reversion to the amorous relationship with Mme de Rênal that was the centerpiece of his maturity—as long as we understand this relationship in all of its complexity and not in any banal way. Indeed, Mathilde de la Mole's failure in the novel, signaled by Julien's return to Verrières, can be ascribed to her desire ultimately to act from worldly motives rather than from seductive ones.

All three novels can be read as treatises on male/female relationships in a certain historical context. The fascination with such relationships leads to the development of themes within the novels that have a very familiar Baudrillardian ring. Characteristically, gender confusion is evident in the cases of the male heroes of all three major novels: Julien, Lucien, and Fabrice. They are all a curious mixture of feminine masculinity or masculine femininity—and they are therefore at odds with a society too often defined in masculine terms, a society that attempts to force them to illustrate their skill at mastery and power games, to illustrate, in short, their male virility. Though this element is often mentioned in commentaries on Stendhal's novels, a theoretical attempt to get past a mere thematic description of it is usually lacking. To analyze *Le Rouge et le Noir* and *Lucien Leuwen* as examples of the *Bildungsroman*—to concentrate, in other words, on the difficulties of social integration faced by the male protagonists in the novels—somehow misses the point that this integration is crucially linked to gender questions. Why, for example, does the narrator of *Le Rouge et le Noir* have Mme de Rênal tell Julien Sorel that he will always be protected by women and disliked and distrusted by men?

The theme of masculine/feminine confusion is certainly not unique to Stendhal's novels during the 1830s. One can find it in Balzac (Raphaël in *La Peau de chagrin* or Vautrin in *Le Père Goriot*, for example) and to some extent in writing dating from the Romantic period more generally (Waller). But I do not think that the explanation for this phenomenon can follow quite the same lines in Stendhal that it would follow, say, in Balzac. Any treatment of gender confusion and gender bending in Balzac's work has to begin with Balzac's own homosexual penchants and, it would seem, is susceptible to an analysis that could use Freudian categories as its point of departure. Take the description of Vautrin in *Le Père Goriot* as an example. The first scene of confrontation between Eugène de Rastignac and Vautrin early in the novel clearly draws together both sexual desire and desire for a certain mastery in the economic domain—or desire and production, as Baudrillard would have it. "I am good to those who do good things for me or whose hearts speak to mine," says Vautrin to Rastignac in an attempt to win him over (3:135). This remark prepares the offer of the pact Vautrin would like to sign with Rastignac: "In short, if I find you a dowry of a million, will you give me two hundred thousand francs?" (3:142). The commingling of sexuality and economics in this confrontation forces it into the domain of strategies of mastery, rather than that of rituals of seduction in the Baudrillardian sense.

In Stendhal's novels, an interpretive strategy via homosexuality structured by Freudian categories is a much less promising way to deal with the question of gender uncertainty. In the first place, Balzacian relationships such as the one between Vautrin and Rastignac, with its implicit and yet easily readable allusion to homosexual tendencies, are not so clearly present. A more likely path for exploring gender uncertainties in Stendhal is the fascination with ritualistic confrontations between masculine and feminine that is always at the bottom of his writing. This fascination with ritual shifts Stendhal's analyses of love into a domain strangely reminiscent of certain key elements of Baudrillard's description of these phenomena. What I have been calling the logic of seduction (after Perniola)—what Baudrillard calls its ritualistic aspect—entails, as we have seen, the reformulation of the space of confrontation as an agonistic structure that results in gender confusion, with both parties locked into a logic that is shared, a certain *logos* of the *kairos* in which they meet. What is at stake is not sexual conquest in the Freudian sense, but reversals, changes of position, a kind of ritualistic dance characterized by perpetual movement and slippage.

Gender confusion is part of a larger picture that connects Stendhal's writing to Baudrillard's analyses. If we look for a moment at a crucial scene in one of the novels, *Lucien Leuwen*, we will quickly see other elements that closely link the approaches taken by both. *Lucien Leuwen* is a novel about a young man in search of a career in a society where he has no real space to develop his identity. It is in some sense a reprise of *Le Rouge et le Noir*, but in this case, the young man in question is the son of a banker, not the son of a peasant. Lucien chooses a military career, a choice precluded for Julien in *Le Rouge et le Noir* by reason of his poverty. Stationed in a provincial town (Nancy) with nothing to fill his monotonous days, Lucien, a Parisian, decides to study the provincial natives and becomes fascinated by the most distinguished woman in the town, Mme de Chasteller.

In chapter 17 of the novel, a conversation between Lucien and Mme de Chasteller takes place at a ball. Lucien has succeeded in being introduced to her only shortly before this event, but he has never really had the chance to talk with her. Her arrival at the ball has the effect of paralyzing him temporarily and rendering him incapable of conversing rationally with her. But after this first missed occasion, Mme de Chasteller decides to converse with Lucien once more in order to find whether he is as exceptional as others have led her to believe. The effect of the remark she makes to him is nothing short of electrifying: "When Mme de Chasteller spoke to him, Lucien became another man" (1:923). The transformation described here is one of tone and language. We must recall Perniola's insistence upon seduction as an act of *logos* that has its own discursive logic. In this occasion, Lucien transcends the normal banalities of conversation and transports the confrontation into a different discursive realm: "In the noble simplicity of tone he dared spontaneously to assume with Mme de Chasteller, he succeeded in bringing out . . . the nuance of delicate familiarity that suits two kindred souls" (1:923).

This and other remarks made by the narrator during the passage in question demonstrate clearly that what is at stake is a certain type of discursive logic binding the interlocutors together. Mme de Chasteller's reaction to this abrupt change of level and tone, moreover, illustrates her own adherence to the structure into which she has just entered: "However frightened she was, she could not help largely approving of Lucien's ideas and responding at times in almost the same tone; but . . . she finally fell into a profound amazement" (1:924).

The progression of this scene is programmed in terms that should by now be familiar. By addressing Lucien, Mme de Chasteller imposes a discursive logic on him that she does not really expect him to understand, given what she has seen up to this point. To her surprise, Lucien responds effortlessly and comprehends at once the tone she is seeking. Her provocation, met by an agonistic equal, entraps her in turn. She is forced to assume the same tone herself and is completely astonished—amazed, mesmerized. The ebb and flow of this exchange amply demonstrates the complexity of the seductive encounter. Positions shift continually, roles are distributed and redistributed, aggressor becomes victim and vice versa. Reversals are the rule. The narrator makes absolutely clear, moreover, that Lucien's behavior cannot be ascribed to an attempt simply to play a role—his is not a calculated gesture: "It was not an effort of genius that had brought him immediately to a tone so well adapted to his ambition; he believed everything this tone seemed to say" (1:923–24). In other words, Lucien does not actively pursue a strategy, there is no separation between performance and meaning. This perfect coincidence—the absence of any doubling—is, I would claim, one of the ways of defining the seductive encounter described by Baudrillard: a perfect understanding and acceptance of the rules of a certain occasion that allows the interlocutors to maneuver familiarly within the context they have chosen. The familiarity is not born of repetition, but of a coherence and an integration of language and context. The spell is broken and the tone lost precisely at the moment when Lucien remembers rumors he has heard about a rival suitor for Mme de Chasteller, a memory that immediately reduces the situation to one of mere sexual rivalry: "His [Lucien's] features revealed the horrible pain caused by the memory of M. de Busant de Sicile, who, after having been forgotten for several hours, suddenly came back to him. Could it be? What he was obtaining was merely a banal favor, gained simply by virtue of a uniform, and by whomever might wear it!" (1:927). The charm of the moment depends precisely on the forgetting of rivalries tied to Freudian sexual desire and mastery.

A further characteristic of the encounter in question here is important to grasp. Stendhal undermines the notion that amorous relations can be reduced to a simple, unmediated relation between two parties that eliminates civilities and normal social behavior by establishing a kind of direct and immediate contact. In some ways, Stendhal could not be more antiromantic than he is here and elsewhere. The idea that there can be an unmediated relationship between parties, in other words, outside all social structures—on a windswept island in Scotland, as the clichéd Romantic imagination would have it—could not be more foreign to him. On the contrary, the encounter between Lucien Leuwen and Mme de Chasteller I have been describing takes place at the very heart of one of the most formal settings possible—a ball, with all its protocol and decorum. The ritualistic, rule-governed aspects of the situation are not present simply by chance in the description of the scene. They are, on the contrary, its essence. This remark brings us back to *De l'amour*. Published in 1822, it is a curious hybrid work that is part fiction and part treatise (Schehr *Rendering*). Stendhal's fascination with the material treated in *De l'amour* is evident—he continually returned to it, contemplating revisions and a new edition right up to his death. I cannot treat *De l'amour* in detail here, but I do want to claim in a broad sense that it contains many of the elements defining seductive encounters that are present in the later novels.

One thing is certain: the peculiar position of the seducer and the seduced person within a set of conventions is a fundamental notion developed in *De l'amour*. The contrast established in the text between France and Italy as contexts for the formation of amorous relations is built largely on a reflection concerning the nature of the rules at stake and the use of those rules. The French are described as creatures of repetition, who maneuver within a narrowly defined space and are intent upon turning an utterly familiar ground to their own advantage. In short, their approach to amorous confrontations is a strategic one. As Ann Jefferson puts it, "All acts of domination and maneuver miss the mark because they make the code into something that is well-defined, subject to iteration, and thus monotonous" (158). The approach to conventional rules in amorous confrontations in France is too narrow, too inflexible. Invariably in such situations the French miss the potential that is concealed in moments when a move not quite covered by the rules would be possible. They are afraid to permit a true coincidence between their nature and the rules, a coincidence that would put an end to strategic maneuvers and allow truly seductive encounters. "The lover never maneuvers the code in which he is caught, and this passivity turns out to be quite productive" (Jefferson 158).

Jefferson's insight is by and large correct, I think, but I would quarrel with her characterization of the lover's attitude as passive. The binary opposition between active and passive runs the risk of confining Stendhalian seduction to the perspective of mastery and victimization from which, I would argue, it constantly works to escape. Abandoning one's behavior to the decorum required by the occasion is an act situated somewhere beyond the active and the passive. It is analogous to what Stendhal constantly calls *le naturel*: "The error of most men is to want to succeed in saying something beautiful, witty, touching, instead of releasing their souls from the weight of the world to a sufficient degree of intimacy and naturalness to be able to express naïvely what they feel in the moment" (*De l'amour* 115). Stendhal is not speaking here of an immediate and primary naïveté and simplicity (which might well be equated with passivity), but of a "second-degree" naïveté—one that is the product of an extraordinarily subtle understanding of circumstances, an understanding that permits the subject to let go of pat formulas and set strategies.[4]

Often read as an early nineteenth-century writer who remained linked to Enlightenment thought, Stendhal nevertheless offers a major correction to a vulgarized notion of libertinism as it came to be expressed at the end of the Enlightenment (I have Sade in mind here). His analysis of love eschews relations of pure desire, domination, power, and production in favor of ritualized and yet paradoxically "natural" confrontations. He reactualizes a tradition that is destined to be occulted once again at the end of the nineteenth century with the rise of Freudian psychoanalysis. It is only fitting that Jean Baudrillard, in his attempt to shortcircuit Freudianism and Freudo-Marxism, would implicitly make reference to a Stendhalian (and, of course, pre-Stendhalian) tradition of seductive confrontations and ask what the importance of that tradition might be in the contemporary world.

---

4. This naturalness or second-degree naïveté sounds very much like Clément Rosset's description of the insouciance of real joy and its relation to Mozart's work: "The insouciance of joy . . . is not completely naïve, or rather, it is so only in the second degree and as a last resort, that is, once everything is known and has been felt. This is something like the 'second naïveté' which a modern interpreter of Mozart (Edwin Fisher) attributes to Mozart in the last years of his life" (18).

CHAPTER 2

The Silent Erotic / Rhetoric of Baudelaire's Mirrors

DOMINIQUE D. FISHER

Although the term "homosexual" was not yet in use in Baudelaire's time, it would seem that it was a different case for the term "lesbian." Despite Claude Pichois's affirmation that in the nineteenth century, "lesbian" conveyed a meaning other than the one we currently know, a glance at his annotations to the Pléiade edition of Baudelaire's works reveals a contradiction. Pichois specifies that nineteenth-century dictionaries ignore the use of "lesbian" as an adjective, as well as its present homosexual meaning, and refer instead to Sapphism as a poetic device (*Littré*), or define "lesbian" as "that which belongs to Lesbos or its inhabitants" (*Larousse*). However, the definition of lesbian as "the agglomeration of [Sapphic women that] could not have avoided giving birth to shameful morals . . . Sapphism: Pathology. Depravation related to that attributed to Sappho and lesbians in general" belies such an assertion (quoted in 1:793). Indeed, what these excerpts demonstrate is that dictionaries such as *Littré* and *Larousse* did not ignore the meaning of the word "lesbian" but rather tended to (homophobically) dismiss it whether by euphemization or by hypersexualization. After all, as Terry Castle points out, "*Lesbian* and *homosexual* may indeed be neologisms, but there have always been *other* words—a whole slangy mob of them—for pointing to (or taking aim at) the lover of women: *tribade, fricatrice, sapphist, roaring girl, amazon, freak, romp, dyke, bull dagger, tommy. . . .* And where there are words—even comic, taboo or salacious ones—there is identity" (9–10).

To be sure, critics by now agree that the theme of the lesbian is neither purely accidental in Baudelaire nor solely limited to the well-known poems "Lesbos" and "Femmes damnées." On the one hand, Baudelaire's expressed intention to entitle *Les Fleurs du mal, Les Lesbiennes,* is itself significant enough for the critic to give serious attention to the place the lesbian occupies in the poet's work. On the other hand, not only is the lesbian a recurrent motif that contextualizes Baudelaire's misogyny within the framework of the destabilization of the masculine subject, but she is also at the core of both his aesthetics and his poetics. Following Walter Benjamin, Christine Buci-Glucksmann has demonstrated the lesbian's importance in the Baudelairean conception of modernity. The lesbian, along with the prostitute and other *Namenlosen,* is seen as a "heroine of modernity" as she is inscribed in opposition to the dominant role of the familial structure, the reduction of love to the family, and the definition of womanhood by women's natural reproductive function. That Baudelaire challenges these conventional notions of femininity is clear as he writes in "Les Deux bonnes soeurs":

> Au poète sinistre, ennemi des familles
> Favori de l'enfer, courtisan mal renté,
> Tombeaux et lupanars montrent sous leurs charmilles
> Un lit que le remords n'a jamais fréquenté.
>
> To the sinister poet, enemy of families
> Hell's favorite, impoverished courtesan,
> Tombs and brothels show under their arbors
> A bed never frequented by remorse. (1:114)

In fact, with the rise of industrialization and urbanization and the contingent increase of women's participation in the process of mass production, the natural status of women—the feminine essence—as well as women's aura—beauty as sublimated idealization, or Beauty as Truth—had already been called into question. Both the lesbian and the prostitute irrevocably incarnate this mutation of the feminine from the natural to the cultural by contradicting the dichotomy nature/culture around which genders have been conceived. However, if the lesbian becomes the prostitute's "sister," she nevertheless, as Buci-Glucksmann stresses, remains her "exact opposite." Contrary to the prostitute, the lesbian imposes herself as a protest against industrial modernization and consequently against "the reproduction of bodies and images." It is this aspect that most concerns Baudelairean aesthetics.

The fact that both the lesbian and the prostitute haunt the Baudelairean imaginary relates directly to Baudelaire's ambivalent position toward modernism. On the one hand, Baudelairean modernity asserts itself against modernism by pointing to a nihilistic devalorization generated by the loss of meaning and aura and the subsequent experience of spleen. As Benjamin put it, Baudelaire's writing continually revolves around "a void place" or a "mimesis of death." On the other hand, Baudelairean modernity works with the "cult of images" and has recourse to the prostitute to reinvest motifs of decomposition, fragmentation, and defiguration of the sublime body—all generally associated with the prostitute's body. It does this, however, in order to proceed to the re-construction and re-idealization of that same sublime body. The Baudelairean prostitute enters the aesthetics of artifice by her "crude" use of fashion and makeup, her nomadism, her inscription in the succession of images—in short, by all that contributes to the demystification of the "order of the real." Similarly, the lesbian, as a "heroine of modernity," is conceived of in the realm of the simulacrum. For it is only under the *image* of a modern Sappho, which allegorically combines the antique with the modern, that the lesbian incarnates the dream of a pure love, and like the prostitute, fights both sedentariness and the "abominable naturalness of women," and thus bears the seal of a "new heroism."

The Baudelairean imaginary, articulated with and against modernism in both antehistorical and posthistorical fashions by means of images of prostitutes and lesbians, which do not exclude a devalorization and a *defiguration* of the feminine figure, is also symptomatic of a destabilization in the positioning of the masculine subject. Critics such as Leo Bersani, Michel Butor, and, more recently, Buci-Glucksmann have all pointed to the links existing among "Baudelaire's androgyny" and/or "shifting sexual identities," the loss of virility, and the dislocation of the writing subject in his work. However, if Baudelaire "identifies himself alternately with both the lesbian and the prostitute" (Buci-Glucksmann, 114–15), this de-centering of the subject goes beyond questions of androgyny or "shifting identities" and calls into question a phallocentric construction of desire. Indeed, critics' interest in Baudelaire's "androgyny" and/or identification with the lesbian and the prostitute reveals two interrelated trends. The homosexual paradigm in Baudelaire's work tends to be euphemized; also, desire is maintained within the framework of the other and sexual difference. Jonathan Dollimore has pointed to the ambiguity of the reference to androgyny relative to the feminized man: "androgyny typically envisages a unity ostensibly beyond sexual difference, but in fact inseparable from it; androgyny especially has too often been a genderless transcendent which leaves sexual difference in place" (262). Critics, in their commentary on Baudelaire's androgyny, participate in this ambiguity.

Michel Butor, for example, notes that Baudelaire's "symbolic castration," resulting from the 1844 legal imposition of a guardianship, reduced him to the status of a child or a woman. Moreover, "he is a woman who desires a woman. Under his man's suit, he is a lesbian" (50). Butor thus sees in "Baudelaire's lesbianism" a kind of neo-misogyny that combines an exaltation of the *mundus muliebris* with the reassertion that "virility is the very sign of creative power" (53). While emphasizing the importance of the "shifting of sexual identities" in Baudelaire and while noting the androgynous nature of the love object (for instance, a redesigning of the female body in "Les bijoux": "Antiope's hips joined to a young boy's torso"), Leo Bersani is not specifically addressing the Baudelairean erotic but "a sexual indefiniteness intrinsic to desire itself" (66). He demonstrates that Baudelaire's misogyny and sadism both operate in reaction to the threat of "psychic scattering or self-disseminations of desire" (66) generated by his "feminine side." Whence, according to Bersani, Baudelaire's attempt to freeze the love object in stillness and to "immobilize" desire. However, this mortification and petrification of desire—the "phallus of stone" in Buci-Glucksmann's terms—is not linked solely to an ambivalence toward the feminine in general, whether it be the "feminine side" of Baudelaire himself or the threat the medusal feminine symbolizes for him; rather it is the expression of an epistemic break resulting in a crisis of representation.

Buci-Glucksmann positions the structural modality of this crisis in the feminization of culture that occurred in the second half of the nineteenth century with Saint-Simon, Baudelaire, Mallarmé, and Lautréamont: "In the work of writing, the feminine as metaphor irrupts to break a certain rationality called into question, an historical and symbolic continuum, to designate a new heterogeneity, a new alterity" (33). According to Buci-Glucksmann, it is precisely this feminization of culture that generates fear and anguish for Baudelaire (34). It should be noted, though, that for Buci-Glucksmann the feminization of culture is also generative of bisexual writing, a bisexuality that maintains sexual difference. Indeed, both the erosion and hysterization of the masculine are concomitant with the abyss symbolized by femininity. The masculine is also abyssal, as images of the "*cerveau-caveau* [brain-tomb]" in the second "Spleen," the poet-Midas in "Alchimie de la douleur," and the *Journaux intimes* exemplify: "Au moral comme au physique, j'ai toujours eu la sensation du gouffre [Morally and physically, I have always had the sensation of the abyss]" (1:668).[1]

Baudelaire's fascination with images of transgressive women—whether lesbians, prostitutes, or sterile women—conceives of the feminine as cultural and thus deconstructs the entire binary logic of *ratio*: masculine/feminine; subject/object; same/other; real/imaginary. As it appears in Baudelaire's work, submitted to an incessant succession of images that duplicate themselves and, in turn, double the image of the poet, the feminine not only reveals the unfixity of sexual identity but makes both the feminine and the masculine floating signifiers, sites of what Jonathan Dollimore calls an "otherness-across-gender." Baudelaire's allegorical writing, as we will see below, functions like a mask and allows him, well before modern gender theory, to hide while revealing the arbitrariness and the artificiality of both power and conceptual boundaries delimited by the socio-symbolic order.

Bersani's discussion of Laplanche and Pontalis's definitions of the phallus precisely approaches this "otherness-across-gender," as it demonstrates that the phallus in fact had less to do with the male sexual organ and the symbol of power with which it is generally associated than with the designation of the operation of meaning. Baudelaire's "symbolic castration" is therefore understood as an anguish in the face of "the movable nature of meaning itself" (Bersani, *Baudelaire and Freud*, 127–28).

Thus like Buci-Glucksmann, Bersani links the artist's transformation into a woman to a crisis of representation as he writes that Baudelairean desire "sets into motion a kind of fantasy-machine" (45) that is a machinelike producer of images. This "fantasy-machine" is akin to a desiring-machine in the Deleuzian sense insofar as, in its heterogeneity, Baudelairean desire is subjected to an extreme deterritorialization. In effect, for Deleuze and Guattari, deterritorialization is already inscribed in the signifying system itself (the infinite self-referentiality of the sign; its redundant nature; its infinite circularity): the excess of deterritorialization inherent in language is

1. The "cerveau-caveau" of "Spleen" opens a time beyond history ("J'ai plus de souvenirs que si j'avais mille ans" [I have more memories than if I were a thousand years old) and a theater of images. This allegorical poem is constructed with a series of figures that acquire a tautological value as they repeat the first sentence. The main motif of forgetfulness is the paradigm of modernity and is found in poems such as "L'Amour du mensonge" or "A une passante." The Midas figure is present in *Les Paradis artificiels* ("Un mangeur d'opium"); it is also a double of the poet, whose melancholia and fall into the abyss is associated with the poet's "*feminine* nature" and a certain fascination with Sapphic love. See 1:444–80.

what generates abstract or diagrammatic machines. These machines establish relations of proximity between heterogeneous terms; they precede social structures and organize segments that are more complex than a simple state apparatus. The same applies to corporeal and unconscious relations. In the case of Baudelairean aesthetics and poetics, desire is constantly shifting between sexual identities and is displayed via a series of allegorical representations that are linked to the art of writing itself (a "holy prostitution"). Desire is submitted to a deterritorialization that involves as much the rejection of family and filiation structures as any anchoring in the social order.

Masks of a "Male" Sappho

In a poem addressed to Sainte-Beuve which was written at the same time as *Les Lesbiennes* and signed Baudelaire-Dufaÿs, Baudelaire writes without hesitation: "Car je suis vis-à-vis de vous comme un amant [For I am before you like a lover]" (1:118). Not only is this epistle, in Jérôme Thélot's words, "an obvious homosexual love proposition" (295), but the formulation of the address itself also undergoes several gender reversals. Thélot notes that the epistle is preceded by a preamble in which the gender of the addressee, "the praised person," is deliberately chosen as feminine. For Thélot, this feminization of Sainte-Beuve is paralleled by Baudelaire's appropriation of Stendhal's name—whom Thélot portrayed as writing for female readers only, *une douzaine d'âmes* understood as women—to address Sainte-Beuve as a woman reader of Stendhal: "Stendhal a dit quelque part—ceci, ou à peu près—*J'écris pour une dizaine d'âmes que je ne verrai peut-être jamais, mais que j'adore sans les avoir vues* [Stendhal said somewhere—this, or something close—I write for ten souls whom I may never see, but whom I love without having seen them]" (1:116). This play on gender, which is marked visually on the page, works as a "wink" and is "the sign of a postulated understanding between the two authors" (Thélot 299), the understanding being, of course, a "lesbian love" between them, staged here in a "courtly love style" (Thélot 298). Here it is interesting to note that by placing himself in the position of a courtly poet, a feminized position due to the poet's masochistic suffering in front of his *domna*, Baudelaire uses the *amour de loin* topos to cast Sainte-Beuve in the lady's role. Significantly, he uses another courtly love poetry topos—a *senhal* or textual masking device typically used to conceal the love object's identity—yet reverses it so as to highlight the address to Sainte-Beuve. In fact, the complicity between the two authors is apparent in Baudelaire's comment that immediately follows the passage cited above: "Are these words not, Sir, an excellent excuse for intruders and is it not clear that every writer is responsible for the feelings he arouses?" (1:116). The "excuse" is ironically antithetic to the "responsibility" (of the two authors; "intruders" is in the plural form), exactly as lesbian love is to Baudelaire's so-called naïveté: "these verses were written for *you* and so naïvely." It is antithetic also to what he writes in *Fusées*: "to love intelligent women is a pederast's pleasure" (1:653). Here, the irony is bound up with the gender reversal and can be read in two ways: the man, who is dominated by an intelligent woman, is feminized; and the woman is placed in the position of a homosexual man.

The poem following the preamble to Sainte-Beuve repeats the gender displacement: "la Mélancholie [Melancholia]" is an allegory of the poet, and is embedded in a second allegory, "la Religieuse [the Nun]," a literary reference to Diderot's Nun that applies to both Baudelaire and Sainte-Beuve.[2] The poem also feminizes the poet-reader—"J'ai partout feuilleté le mystère profond / De ce livre si cher aux *âmes engourdies* [I have thoroughly leafed through the deep mystery / Of this book so dear to benumbed souls; my emphasis]"—as well as the love object by means of the metaphor of the "ghost," a figure traditionally and negatively associated with the homosexual. As Diana Fuss notes, representations of "the homosexual as specter and phantom" are symptomatic of the haunting of "the insistent social pressure of (hetero)sexual conformity" that leads the homosexual to incorporate his or her negative image ("spirit and revenant, abject and undead"). Fuss specifies that

> this process of negative interiorization involves turning homosexuality inside out, exposing not the homosexual's abjected insides but the homosexual as the abject, as the contaminated and expurgated insides of the heterosexual subject. Homosexual production emerges under these inhospitable conditions as a kind of ghost-writing, a writing which is at once a recognition and a refusal of the cultural representation of the "homosexual" as phantom Other. (Fuss, *Inside/Out* 3–4)

2. Jerôme Thélot writes that "Baudelairean melancholy is an exasperation ('the eye blacker and bluer') of the Nun's desolation, which is a useless rebellion against an imposed vocation." Thélot explains that the duplicity of the nun as she pronounces her vows creates a split between words and action that generates anguish. In this her fate is similar to Baudelaire's horror and Sainte-Beuve's "aversion" for "literature." According to Thélot, the lesbian's "sterile voluptuousness" is a mirror of the poet's and the novelist's sterile literary vocations. Both authors "cherish their own image in one another's work." Aumary is a mirror for Baudelaire which in

In Baudelaire's poem addressed to Sainte-Beuve, the figure of the ghost is feminized by the sexual apparatus: the "hand" and the "vase" from which the (feminized) lover drinks:

Poëte, est-ce une injure ou bien un compliment?
Car je suis vis-à-vis de vous comme un amant,
En face du fantôme, au geste plein d'amorces,
Dont la main et dont l'oeil ont pour pomper les forces
des charmes inconnus;—Tous les êtres aimés
Sont des vases de fiel qu'on boit les yeux fermés

Poet, is this an insult or a compliment?
For I am before you like a lover
In front of a ghost, with a rehearsed initial gesture,
Whose hand and eye have for draining strength
unknown charms;—All the loved ones
Are bitter vases that one drinks with closed eyes (1:118)[3]

Gender displacement from the masculine to the feminine, as well as the reference to Diderot's nun, define the relationship as lesbian. However, the homosexual paradigm does not only involve a simple gender reversal; it is a male homosexual relation in a lesbian mode. Within this "otherness-across-gender," exposing a feminine within the masculine and vice versa, reside the very "obscene" and "painful" aspects of the history of the lesbian subject (1:118). Although noting the ambiguity of the "ghost's sex," the allegorical nature of the poem, and its literary context, Jérôme Thélot concludes that the position of the other (Sainte-Beuve) is that of a "mistress"—"Let us turn to the other image of the other: to the mistress, since the poem also represents its inspirer as a female inspirer" (317). In his reading, however, Thélot not only posits a "mother-daughter" dynamic between Baudelaire and Sainte-Beuve, but also maintains sexual difference within homosexual relations, not to mention clichés about lesbians: "One may suppose that Baudelaire stands in front of Sainte-Beuve as the latter stands in front of his

---

turn reflects to Sainte-Beuve his true face: "a girl looking at herself in writing, loving herself in her own work, and in her readers' gaze." See Thélot, *Baudelaire*, 325–26.

3. In "La Chevelure," the masculine subject is also feminized by his sexual apparatus: "ma main dans ta crinière lourde / Sèmera le rubis, la perle et le saphir [my hand in your heavy mane / Will sow ruby, pearl and sapphire]"; and by oral eroticism: "Je m'ennivre . . . / N'es-tu pas . . . la gourde / Où je hume à longs traits le vin du souvenir [I am drunk . . . / Are you not . . . the gourd / Where I deeply inhale the wine of memory]" (1:27).

mistress and that he deliberately follows the example of his elder in representing him, with the irony of the imitator, as a ghost: woman, lover, spouse, girlfriend to whom he owes the awakening of his childhood" (317).

Baudelaire's use of the "Religieuse" and of other literary referents is far more complex than a simple lesbian identification. On the one hand, the lesbian is cross-gendered; on the other, she is engendered via a series of allegorical and spectral images—images of ghosts and polyvalent images—ostentatiously negatively coded. This is what gives rise to Terry Castle's reading of the lesbian ghost in *Les Fleurs du mal* as an effort to "better drain" her "of any sensual or moral authority" so as to "exorcize" her (6). Yet if we recontextualize the specter in relation to the allegory, following Buci-Glucksmann, it becomes clear that in Baudelaire it is precisely the lesbian's status as a specter that grants her the ultimate position of authority—she is the "heroine of modernity." It is, in fact, only via a series of allegorical masks and deterritorializations that the lesbian takes on her importance as a central figure in *Les Fleurs du mal.*

When Baudelaire writes to Sainte-Beuve, for example, "this book so dear to benumbed souls," the book is an allegory of the love object: "j'en ai tout absorbé, les miasmes, les parfums, / Le doux chuchotement des souvenirs défunts, / Les doux enlacements des phrases symboliques [I have absorbed everything from it, the miasmas, the scents / The sweet whispering of dead souvenirs / The sweet embraces of symbolic sentences]" (1:118). Yet the referent of the love object remains undefined and opaque. The "voluptuous" book could be Sainte-Beuve's novel *Volupté,* as the story of Aumary—also drunk on miasmas and scents—suggests; the *Poésies of Joseph Delorme,* for "the stanzas" are also an allegorical and ambivalent drink, a philter and a poison: "Le Breuvage infiltré, lentement, goutte à goutte [the potion slowly infiltrated, drop by drop]" (1:117). It could be Chateaubriand's *René,* or the *Religieuse* (the Nun-Melancholia's foot is numb like the "souls" to whom "this book is addressed"). Moreover, the Nun's "long" or "languorous" nights originate in "the feverish nights" of "the flowering virgins" of "Lesbos:"

> . . . la Religieuse . . . Traîne un pied alourdi de précoces ennuis,
> Et son front moite encor des longueurs (langueurs) de ses nuits . . .
> Et puis venaient les soirs malsains, les nuits fiévreuses,
> Qui rendent de leur corps les filles amoureuses,
> Et les font aux miroirs—stérile volupté—
> Contempler les fruits mûrs de leur Nubilité.

> The Nun drags a foot numbed by early troubles
> And her forehead still wet from her long (languorous) nights . . .
> And then unhealthy evenings, feverish nights came,
> Which make girls fall in love with their bodies
> And make them—sterile voluptuousness—
> contemplate in mirrors the ripe fruit of their Nubility (1:17)

The allegorical "voluptuous" book fuses feminine and masculine genders, making of them the other of the feminine and the masculine in a figural network that dismisses sexual difference and reappropriates negative images of homosexuals to conjure them away. The isotopy between subject and book is motivated by a discursive context that contradicts cultural norms by pointing to the artificiality of gender distinctions and consequently to the artificiality of the heterosexual/homosexual opposition. In so doing, the image of the homosexual as abject and pathological is blocked, since negative images of desire are staged outside and beyond oppositional schemes.

Dismissal of gender difference is not specific solely to this homoerotic poem, but also to the erotic of *Les Fleurs du mal*, as is implied both in Bersani's analysis on the fluctuating nature of desire in Baudelaire and in Buci-Glucksmann's noting of the bisexual dimension of his writing. Baudelairean love objects are submitted to an extreme deterritorialization: they are both mobile and rhizomatic. They establish multiple relations of proximities between the desiring subject and the other(s) which ultimately contradict the universal system of identity and the socio-symbolic order. Love objects delimit territories of identity that dismantle traditional notions of roots and filiation, whence their ahistorical (between the pre-Christian Western world and modern times) and allegorical nature. Thus love objects are not only undifferentiated, spectral, and nomadic, but they are related to and merge with the figural network of the poem written to Sainte-Beuve. The ghost of the poem addressed to Sainte-Beuve, with his or her abyssal charms, is akin to the falling "Ombres folles [Mad Shadows]" of "Delphine et Hippolyte." Their "cantique muet [silent hymn]" opens into the unknown, into a poetic word, bearer of infinity and loss. In this respect, the ghostly lesbian is a "sister" to the "fantôme vagissant [wailing ghost]" of "La Voix," who invites the poet to the unknown and the abyss by means of the lying word.

The disembodied voice, whose origin is said to be unidentifiable, nevertheless comes from the Latin ashes and the Greek dust of an allegorical library.[4] By associating desire with both reading and drinking, the poem to Sainte-Beuve provides an intertext for poems dedicated to lesbians, as well as to poems linked to lesbian motifs: desire, thirst, and writing, leitmotiv of "Lesbos," are also found in "Le Balcon," "Le Cygne," and "La Chevelure." Indeed, the same poem to Sainte-Beuve also provides symbols for "Correspondances" and allegories for "Le Cygne." In "Correspondances," nature is a hieroglyphic text—"confuses paroles [confused words]"—to decipher. Nature ceases to be natural and becomes textual; its language is akin to the lesbians' silent hymn. The deciphering of a trace and an "echo" of a word of origin that fuses sounds with ambivalent scents ("rich" and "corrupted") mixes religiosity with sensuality and opens into the "cult" of infinity, as in the poem written to Sainte-Beuve. In "Le Cygne," where every age of poetry is found, from Virgil and Ovid to modern times, the Roman "she-wolf" that breast-feeds lovers is an allegory for Pain ("La Douleur") inflicted by a lost object under an empty and "cruelly blue sky."

The thematic of the poem addressed to Sainte-Beuve, as well as its allegorical functioning, is typical of *Les Fleurs du mal.* The allegorical space of this poem allows for Baudelaire's uncertainty concerning Sainte-Beuve's response; the ambivalence of the address ("Poet, is this an insult or a compliment? / For I am before you like a lover"); the indeterminacy of the identity of the love object (The Nun / Sappho / Sainte-Beuve); and the nature of the love object itself (the voluptuous Book / the poet). The allegorical space is undefined: "l'écho lointain d'*un* livre [the far-away echo of a book]"; "*ces* grands murs noircis [these high blackened walls]"—the demonstrative pronoun "ces," as found later in Rimbaud, is deprived of a referent, pointing to nothing but a referential trap—; "*tout* abîme mystique [any mystical abyss]"; "le doux chuchotement *des* souvenirs défunts [the sweet whispering of dead memories]"; "les longs enlacements *des* phrases symboliques [the long embrace of symbolic sentences]"; "l'éternel bercement *des* houles enivrantes [the eternal rocking of intoxicating swells]"; "*Soit* dans les lourds loisirs d'*un* jour caniculaire / *ou* dans l'oisiveté frileuse de frimaire [Either in the heavy leisures of a scorching day / or in the shivery idleness of Frimaire]"; *des* charmes inconnus [unknown charms]"; "tous les *êtres aimés* sont *des* vases de fiel [all loved ones are bitter vases]." The alle-

4. In "La Voix," the library as a "dark Babel," locus for "confused words," oxymorons, and "lies," is an allegory for the poetic word; it is inscribed moreover in the intertext of "Lesbos." In his childhood, the poet heard the Voice and was chosen and initiated by it/her to poetry. His fate is related to the spectral and protective Voice's fate: abyss and infinity.

gorical actors are also uncertain: "la *Canicule ou* le fumeux *Automne* [the dog days or smoky Autumn]"; "Livre voluptueux [voluptuous book]"; "du Doute [of Doubt]"; "un Démon [a Demon]." Allegorical space and actors are all embedded in an oversignified mise-en-scène of fall, imprisonment, or descent to an infernal or frozen locus, that of abyssal Baudelairean desire itself.

Baudelaire's poem to Sainte-Beuve is not out of keeping with the rest of his work. The position of the lover in front of the love object is another dimension of this poem that recurs in *Les Fleurs du mal.* Aside from cross-gender identities, there exists another problematic dimension of Baudelaire's work: parent/child figures. Thélot noted that in the poem to Sainte-Beuve, Baudelaire posits himself as a child, an adolescent, and Sainte-Beuve's disciple. This power structure, which indeed suits a heterocentric perception of homosexual relations, and which reappears throughout Baudelaire's poetry, is presented ironically in the poem to Sainte-Beuve. The poem to Sainte-Beuve, as Jérôme Thélot remarked, does not allow the reader to decide whether Baudelaire's address to Sainte-Beuve as a poet is an insult or a compliment. The ambiguous nature of the address itself mocks power relations inasmuch as the writing subject engages in "folle escrime [mad fencing]," which later appears in "Les Tableaux parisiens."

As an adolescent and yet a poet, and as an imaginary Stendhal, the writing subject again subverts the dichotomies of passive/active and feminine/masculine. The referential literary framework within which desire is inscribed (*La Religieuse, Joseph Delorme*) reinforces this effect. Irony and allegories are figures that operate as a veil, hiding while revealing the very nature of Baudelaire's desire for Sainte-Beuve. At the same time, by embedding desire in writing and religiosity (more precisely the "cult" of images and infinity), these figures link the polyvocal and rhizomatic nature of desire to the cross-gendered position of poetic writing. Here lie "the science" and "the lying pleasures" of both the lover and the poet; whether he or she be a "male" Sappho figure ("Qui des plaisirs menteurs révèlent la science [that reveal the science of lying pleasures]") (1:117) or Baudelaire's art ("Hypocrite lecteur,—mon semblable,—mon frère [Hypocritical reader,—my likeness,—my brother]") (1:6).

Parent/child relations are also present in "Delphine et Hippolyte." Hippolyte's naïveté, as in the poem to Sainte-Beuve, is a pseudo-naïveté that subverts power relations. If Hippolyte is presented as a "child," a "frail beauty," a "victim," and as "prey" in contrast to Delphine, the "strong beauty" who holds the knowledge of pleasures, it is Delphine and not Hippolyte who is "à genoux [kneeling]." Indeed, Delphine continually searches but never finds the "cantique muet que chante le plaisir [the silent hymn that pleasure sings]" in Hippolyte's eyes ("already troubled by storms"). While flaunting the voluptuousness and the superiority of lesbian love, Delphine is ready to let her lover experience heterosexual relations, as Sappho did in the heterosexual version of her story.

"Delphine and Hippolyte" has often been read as a condemnation of lesbian relations, since the final version of the poem concludes with a warning, "Fuyez l'infini que vous portez en vous [Flee the infinity you carry within you]" (1:155). The added stanzas are not without homophobic and misogynist clichés, such as the "l'âpre stérilité [acrid sterility]" of lesbian *jouissance* and the darkness of lesbian caverns. These clichés are also represented in "Lesbos" and in "Femmes damnées" with oxymorons such as "flowering virgins," "sterile virginity" or "nubility." They are symptomatic of the anguish of the scattering self, but it is precisely this scattering of the masculine subject that links his fate to the lesbian's while reappropriating negative lesbian images in an ironical manner. The abyssal desire that places Delphine and Hippolyte in the position of "victims" is a topos that belongs to the Baudelairean poetics of modernity.

Edouard Glissant sees in Baudelaire's experience of the abyss not a sadomasochist component but the beginning of new politics of "Relation" in which the dismantling of the sovereign subject and the reconstructing of the other point to the artificiality and fragility of the entire field of Western knowledge and its so-called transparency and universal edict:

> Vertiginous extension, not in the world, but toward the abysses one bears within oneself. That is, essentially, the occidental subject, who, at that moment, governed and rhymed the movement of modernity. Interior space is as infinite as terrestrial spaces. Just when one discovers the multiple varieties of the space one constitutes, one experiences that the claimed fixity of knowledge is a lure, and that one will know of oneself only the knowledge one will give to others. The element of romantic lyricism Baudelaire breaks is the pretension that the poet is the introspective master of his or her joys or of his or her pains; that it is in his or her power to extract lessons from them, smoothly and clearly, that are profitable for everyone. (36)

In Baudelaire the topos of the abyssal desire renders the lesbian condemnation ambiguous and colors the poet's additions, making them appear to be an ironical gesture. Furthermore, "Delphine and Hippolyte" is an allegorical poem that combines the antique and the modern, thus placing Delphine and Hippolyte outside history. In fact, Delphine's and Hippolyte's decomposition and sentencing to spectral errancy in deserts for their insatiable *jouissance* ("le vent furibond de la concupiscence / Fait claquer votre chair ainsi qu'un vieux drapeau [the furious wind of concupiscence / Makes your flesh flap like an old flag]" (1:155) mirrors the *image* of the poet as a castrated and decomposed cadaver hung from a "gibet symbolique [symbolic gallows]" in "Le Voyage à Cythère" in order to "expiate his infamous cult." In this sense, the added conclusion to "Delphine and Hippolyte," though visually separated from the first version via a typographical device (a dash), does not contradict Baudelaire's identification with the lesbian that concludes the first poem of "Femmes damnées," "Comme un bétail pensif":

> O vierges, ô démons, ô monstres, ô martyres,
> De la réalité grands esprits contempteurs,
> Chercheuses d'infini, dévotes et satyres,
> Tantôt pleines de cris, tantôt pleines de pleurs,
>
> Vous que dans votre enfer mon âme a poursuivies,
> Pauvres soeurs, je vous aime autant que je vous plains,
> Pour vos mornes douleurs, vos soifs inassouvies,
> Et les urnes d'amour dont vos grands coeurs sont pleins!
>
> O virgins, O demons, O monsters, O martyrs,
> Great spirits contemptuous of the real
> Seekers of infinity, devotees and satyrs
> Sometimes full of cries, sometimes full of tears.
>
> You whom my soul followed into your hell,
> Poor sisters I love you as much as I pity you,
> For your mournful pains, your unquenchable thirst,
> And your big hearts full from urns of love (1:114)

Significantly, "Delphine et Hippolyte" and "Comme un bétail pensif" both come under the title "Femmes damnées," inviting the ("hypocritical") reader, Baudelaire's accomplice, to read the poems as an ensemble. This poem, however, contrary to "Delphine and Hippolyte," was not censored, although it precedes "Delphine et Hippolyte." Moreover, the spectral thematic and Baudelaire's use of the present tense again represent the lesbian as an ahistorical figure, which indicates that the poem could have been a possible continuation of "Delphine and Hippolyte." The lesbians of "Comme un bétail pensif" are already in hell, as are those of "Delphine and Hippolyte"; either they wander among other specters—"à travers les rochers pleins d'apparitions [Through rocks full of apparitions]" (1:114), are confined to the darkness of the "antres païens [pagan caverns]" or belong to the "flagellés [flagellated]."

The pre-1857 version of "Delphine et Hippolyte" ends with a craving for "a sort of extinction within Delphine's embrace" (Leakey 10–11) and with another typical Baudelairean topos of burning/frozen desire—"Je veux m'anéantir dans ta gorge profonde / Et trouver sur ton sein la fraîcheur des tombeaux [I want to annihilate myself in the abyss of your bosom / And find the freshness of the tomb at your breast]" (1:154)—which is not incompatible with the fate of lesbian love in both "Femmes damnées" poems. That Baudelaire may have intended to please his "hypocritical readers" by adopting a heterosexual version suitable for censors in his later version of "Delphine and Hippolyte" seems doubtful. Not only do poems like "Une Martyre" or "La Mort des amants" invite a homosexual reading, but even the poem "Lesbos" presents a treatment of lesbian love comparable to "Delphine et Hippolyte" (Leakey 15). If Baudelaire in "Lesbos" chose the heterosexual version of Sappho as well, it is rather to defeat Venus with Sappho: "L'oeil d'azur est vaincu par l'oeil noir que tachette / Le cercle ténébreux tracé par les douleurs [The azure eye is defeated by the black eye that is marred by / The dark circle traced by pains] (1:151). Lesbos, now a deserted island, a spectral locus of desire, is also an allegory of the poet:

> Et c'est depuis ce temps que Lesbos se lamente,
> Et, malgré les honneurs que lui rend l'univers,
> S'enivre chaque nuit du cri de la tourmente
> Que poussent vers les cieux ses rivages déserts
>
> And it is since then that Lesbos laments,
> And, despite the homage the universe gives her,
> Makes herself drunk with the cry of torment
> Which her deserted shores launch to the skies (1:152)

Pierre Brunel has demonstrated that the last version of "Delphine et Hippolyte," in its condemnation of the lesbians, is related to the deploring of Sappho's blasphemy with Phaon, that is, her betrayal of the "cult" of infinity. This betrayal does not appear in "Comme un bétail pensif," whence the allegorical lesbian identification with the land in "Lesbos" and a certain distancing from a heterocentric reading of Sapphic love. Once again, irony and allegory combine to bring forth the lying character inherent in the poetic word, which constantly fuses "sincerity" with "charlatanism" (1:185). Baudelaire repeats this in a project for a foreword to *Les Fleurs du mal.*

Destabilizing Mirrors

A diversion from narcissism is another dimension of Baudelaire's homoeroticism. Bersani has already demonstrated the complexity of narcissistic appropriation of the other in "Les Tableaux parisiens." The allegorical framework of these tableaux defies any realistic readings of the Paris of modernity, as Benjamin has shown. This framework also defeats any reading of homoeroticism within an Oedipal narcissistic context. Aware of a certain challenge that Baudelairean mobile desire poses to Freudian and Lacanian criticism, Bersani argues that the Lacanian notion of the symbolic may imply "an alternative to a view of the subject constituted by a narcissistic identification with the other" (116). Referring to the "mimetic trap" Lacan writes of as involved in the notion of resemblance, Bersani writes:

> The self is still an appropriated self, but what is appropriated is language as the other, and not an ideal but an alienated *image* of an individual self [that of "Un voyage à Cythère," "Lesbos," and "Femmes damnées"]. . . . Lacan emphasizes an alternative to a view of the subject as constituted by a narcissistic identification with other. And I think that this alternative has interesting analogies with the mobility of the desiring imagination in Baudelaire. The erotic poems from *Les Fleurs du mal* . . . define the desiring subject in terms of his continuously changing representations. The poet communicates with the loved one not by trying to capture his image in her, but rather by implicating her in an image-producing process. And the images belong neither to the poet's self nor to the woman's self; instead, they define a community in which the constant substitution of one image for another is itself the activity of both the poet's and the woman's desire. The poet's desire for the woman is enacted as a process of exchange and substitution which characterizes the universal human process of desire's displacements. (*Baudelaire and Freud*, 116–17)

Multiple displacements of desire also belong to what Bersani calls the "false prostitution of the self" in Baudelaire, since the poet-prostitute "becomes a richly problematic identity, a shattered ego available to the various (and eventually sexually indeterminate) selves celebrated in the shifting tones and modes of address of Baudelaire's erotic poetry" (107). This constant shifting of desire is specific not only to "Tableaux parisiens" but to the aesthetics of modernity and the entire poetics of *Les Fleurs du mal*, since most of the poems are allegorical; they are also ironical and thereby call for a revision of homosexual love as narcissistic. Jonathan Dollimore has argued, in line with Deleuze, that narcissism—a rhizome of the Oedipal machine—serves to regard homosexuality as inferior, inadequate, and pathologic: "homosexuality is included as perversion because it is denied that 'fundamental experience' of otherness-across-gender" (Dollimore 261). This otherness-across-gender is staged, as we have seen, by Baudelaire's recourse to allegory and irony. Both allegory and irony turn mirrors into mimetic artefacts in which the sovereignty of the subject and the order of the Other are parodied and called into question. Repetition and difference perform the same function. Baudelaire writes in the poem to Sainte-Beuve:

> Et puis venaient les soirs malsains, les nuits fiévreuses,
> Qui rendent de *leur corps* les filles amoureuses
> Et les font aux miroirs—stérile volupté—
> Contempler les fruits mûrs de leur volupté.
>
> And then came the unhealthy evenings, the feverish nights,
> That make girls love their bodies
> And make them contemplate in mirrors—sterile voluptuousness—
> The ripe fruit of their voluptuousness (1:117; my emphasis)

The singular form of "leur corps" and the plural form of "aux miroirs" allow for a reading of homosexual love as narcissistic. However, "aux miroirs" is undefined and refers both to a real mirror and to the lesbian body as a mirror of the quest for infinity. The singular form is used again in the poet's identification with the lesbian, but works there as a mediator for equating lesbian (infinite) desire with the art of poetry: "leur destin marqua des mêmes maladies, / L'art cruel qu'un Démon en naissant m'a donné [their fate marked the same illnesses / Cruel art that was given to me by a Demon being born]" (1:118). Lesbian desire and fate are now mirrors for both the poet(s)—Baudelaire and Sainte-Beuve—and poetic writing. Sameness is thus fused with otherness: on the one hand, lesbian desire is displaced onto writing; on the other, the gender of both the writing subject and the addressee are constantly shifting in the epistle. Baudelaire's identification with the lesbian is again found in "Bribes" yet nuanced: "leurs corps" is in the plural form whereas "au miroir," still undefined, is now in the singular form. Here, the same is at once same ("mirror" is singular) and other(s) ("bodies" is plural and "mirror" is undefined):

> . . . cette canicule aux yeux pleins de lueurs
> Qui sur nos fronts pâlis tord ses bras en sueurs,
> Et soufflant dans la nuit ses haleines fiévreuses,
> Rend de leurs frêles corps les filles amoureuses,
> Et les fait au miroir, stérile volupté,
> Contempler les fruits mûrs de leur virginité.

. . . this dog day with eyes full of gleams
Who twists her sweaty arms on our pale foreheads,
And blowing her feverish breath in the night,
Makes girls love their frail bodies,
And makes them contemplate in the mirror, sterile
voluptuousness,
The ripe fruit of their virginity. (1:189)

In "Lesbos," "leurs corps" is still plural but "miroir" also becomes plural. "Mirrors," preceded by a possessive pronoun, are no longer undefined but refer to the lesbian body; the mirror is no longer for contemplating but for caressing. The plural form of both "mirror" and "body" transforms the love object into an object that is at once same and other:

Lesbos, terre des nuits chaudes et langoureuses,
Qui font qu'à leurs miroirs, stérile volupté!
Les filles aux yeux creux, de leurs corps amoureuses,
Caressent les fruits mûrs de leur nubilité;

Lesbos, land of hot and languorous nights,
That make, in their mirrors, sterile voluptuousness!
Girls with hollow eyes, in love with their bodies,
Caress the ripe fruits of their nubility (1:150)

Repetition and difference undo the narcissistic paradigm in a theater of writing where sameness, by means of a series of mirror images, is constantly asserted and diverted. The image of the love object undergoes multiple gender displacements and remains other/same. This other/same engenders an infinite succession of images that transgress the order of the Other, as well as the limits of the self, the body, and metaphoricity. This production of images operates like a desiring machine by destabilizing the socio-symbolic order and decoding both the natural and the cultural only to recode them within the framework of the aesthetics of artifice ("cult of images" and "infinity"). The lesbian's and the poet's mirrors are indeed ironical mirrors or artefacts: they establish multiple rhizomatic networks between femininity and masculinity; subject and object; resemblance and difference; desire and allegory; silence and writing.

CHAPTER 3

Baudelaire: Homoérotismes

JOHN R. BARBERET

Lysander: You have her father's love, Demetrius;
Let me have Hermia's: do you marry him.
—*A Midsummer Night's Dream*

Introduction

The erotic triangle was never quite as stable as folk wisdom, or for that matter René Girard, would have it: there is always more going on than two men competing for the affections of a woman, each keeping one eye on the other over his shoulder, and the other on the object of their mimetic desire. Since Hegel, this scenario of rivalry, wherein two men stare each other down until one looks away, as in the master/slave dialectic, has encouraged a confrontational notion of homosociality that Girard elevates to a status rivaling passionnate love, if not superseding it. Eve Sedgwick, in her critique of Girard in *Between Men* (21–27), points out the "gender assymmetry" implicit in his approach: male homosocial rivalry is not necessarily the same sort of "love" as heterosexual or lesbian "love," a fact that becomes quite obvious once gendered barriers are displaced. Lysander, whose requited love for Hermia is blocked by her father's endorsement of the rival Demetrius, knows this: homoeroticism is one of the trump cards that can be played against the patriarch, and the "truth" of this "love" becomes all the more demystifying when Egeus unabashedly acknowledges it: "Scornful Lysander! true, he hath my love" (I.i.95). To be sure, where patriarchal domination greatly restricts the mobility of women such a demystification seems to accomplish very little: "And what is mine my love shall render him" (I.1.96). Lysander's remark does, however, add a nuance to the patriarchal control of women by suggesting that a woman can become the vehicle of another's, and specifically a man's, love for another man. What is more, Lysander suggests that the homoeroticism linking the patriarch to his favorite would be more directly and honestly expressed if Hermia no longer served as its mediating linkage, and proposes homosexual marriage as a resolution to the patriarch's intervention into the "eternal triangle." With the rise of relations dominated by the commodity form, more desires are brought into play around the coveted object; and the more rivals there are, the more libidinal economies come into play, and the more connections are established between desiring gazes. Imagine a group of men looking at a woman on a busy street corner, then turning their gazes onto each other in a modernist version of the story of the woman taken in adultery in John 8:1–11.[1] Suddenly, homoeroticism becomes less of a trump card, and more of a generalized situation. A horizon appears wherein the vehicle of desire could be autonomized and homoeroticism could appear unmediated. Let us imagine, then, Baudelaire heading east, towards this, his Orient.

Prostitution and Homoeroticism

In mid-nineteenth-century France, the body, specifically the urban body, was being configured by the capitalist phenomenon, through the combined effects of manipulations and resistances, to such an extent that the ideological binarisms which held the body in place (production/consumption, self/other, need/desire, male/female) were beginning to be put into play or disrupted. Emergent, experimental selfhoods, including the dandy, the flâneur, and so on, first discovered on the street what utopian socialisms imagined for mankind: a social body, what Baudelaire in "Les Foules [Crowds]" calls "this universal communion" (1:291).[2] The erotics of this social body appear as fundamentally excessive and transgressive, especially with respect to the heterosexual restriction of eroticism to male/female relations: "what men call love is quite restricted and quite weak, com-

1. The reference is to the story of the woman taken in adultery, which the New English Bible gives as John 7:53–8:11. As Tony Tanner shows in his discussion of this New Testament account (18–24), Jesus "disperses the social stare that petrifies the wrong-doer" (22). It is but a short leap from this primal scene—already no longer primal, since the original scene presumably resulted in stoning—to the scene of prostitution: etymologically, the prostitute stands out in the marketplace, just as the adultress is "set in their midst" (John 8:3).

2. With the exception of "A celle qui est trop gaie," translated by James McGowan, all translations are my own.

pared to this ineffable orgy" (1:291). As a counterbalance to such a notion of "love," which restricts eroticism to heterosexual partners, Baudelaire's works are infused with homosocial forms of address and a concomitant homoerotics linking the poet to male Others. Whereas, in romanticism, the idealized woman mediated man's relationship to Nature, in Baudelaire's modernism the idealized prostitute mediates man's relationship to urban artifice. The "divine" prostitute is the communicating vessel linking the poet to other men: "The most prostituted of all beings is the ultimate being, God Himself, since for each individual he is the supreme friend; since he is the common, inexhaustible source of love" (*Mon coeur mis à nu* [My Heart Laid Bare] in 1:692). He becomes connected to other men through her, and when she loses this transparency her body becomes problematic, material, "infâme." Thus the nudity of La Fanfarlo becomes disturbing to Samuel Cramer because he can no longer see, through her stage dress, other men seeing her: her unadorned body has become interference, noise.

"Les Foules" initially describes an erotic relationship with both sexes as entertained by the poet's soul in the guise of the prostitute, whereby he identifies erotically (this ability to identify with others is a "privilege" which causes him "jouissance") with her sexual relations with "the passing stranger." The prostitute as figure—or the act of (self-)prostitution as performed under her aegis—facilitates and mediates the narrator's connection to other men, a connection that, despite the close proximity of the crowd, would otherwise involve crossing gendered barriers. Indeed, the men to whom this text is addressed (or at least who are posed as most capable of understanding it), the "founders of colonies, pastors of peoples, missionary priests," are "exiled at the edges of the world" (1:292) and lead a "very chaste life" only with respect to a restricted notion of "love," since they still experience "these mysterious intoxications" which exceed it. The figure of the prostitute is all the more powerfully a mediating one, since it is capable of retrieving their presence and their experiences from the "edges of the world."[3] The figure of the prostitute becomes the localized site of relations between men, much like the intersection of a busy street that is her defining context.

It is through the figure of the prostitute, and more literally through the prostitute's body itself, that men are brought together in what is ultimately a homoerotic situation: through her, they are entertaining homosexual rela-

3. Although I am indebted to Nathaniel Wing's discussion (*Limits of Narrative*, 39–40) of this prose poem, which he argues "is about those libidinal exchanges which disrupt opposition," I am suggesting that the prostitute is both a disruptive and a recuperative (or mediating) figure with respect to male others.

tions with each other, once removed. Yet if the debasement of the prostitute's body (the classic example is Zola's Nana) represents men's denial of this situation while revealing the patriarchal underpinnings of it, the pluralization and universalization of the prostitute's "soul" work to affirm a new form of "love" or "communion" that is more inclusive and polymorphous. Baudelaire's prostitutes are already no longer such because their venality is no longer their defining characteristic: instead, it is their "generosity" and their "charity" that define them, since no money could possibly compensate them for the gift they make of their souls. The prostitute is no longer in Baudelaire the object of an exchange, but the site of an exchange, of a communication that occurs through her: what he obtains from her signifies his connections with other men. Traces of this connection, such as syphilis, acquire a phatic function, linking the client/artist to the public at large: "The day a young writer corrects his first proof, he is as proud as a schoolboy who has just earned his first syphilitic lesion" (*Mon coeur* 1:694). The prostitute is the locus of the (male) crowd's self-eroticization because she reflects back to them the intersection of their desires; as Benjamin puts it, "only the mass [of urban inhabitants] makes it possible for the sexual object to become intoxicated with the hundred stimuli which it produces" (57). Much like the prose poem itself, she would have no existence outside of the "frequenting of enormous cities" and the "intersections of their innumerable relationships" ("Dédicace," in *Le Spleen de Paris* 1:276). Literally and figuratively, the prostitute embodies multiple male interpenetrations: she is indistinguishable from her context, the street corner. She is ostensibly a substitute for other women, but also a homoerotic alibi, whose commodified and policed existence places her on the threshold between the enforcement of compulsory heterosexuality and the homophobia inherent in partiarchy. She might vanish (she is already, in Baudelaire, traversed, transcoded, and to a certain extent transcended) once these dogmas—and the ideology that supports them—wither away.

Baudelaire Traumatophile

It is to Walter Benjamin, who read *Les Fleurs du mal* alongside Freud's *Beyond the Pleasure Principle*, that we owe our understanding of the crucial role that "shock defenses" play in Baudelaire's poetry. Eugene Holland has depicted with great insight the oscillations between an acquiescing vulnerability to shock effects, and the defensive postures intended to repel or absorb them, that regulate Baudelaire's relations to the urban masses. This dual response to urban stimuli bears a striking resemblance to the tension between homoeroticism and the compulsory heterosexuality and homophobia that make of the prostitute a homoerotic alibi. Seen in this light, the prostitute allows the performance of homoeroticism within the constraints imposed by ideology on the performance of gender in particular, and on the social distribution of power among gendered sites in general. In order to think the prostitute in this way, Baudelaire must radically reimagine anatomical differences.

Baudelaire retrospectively advances his theory of anatomy in conjunction with his theory of the "beautiful" in the 1869 version of "Morale du joujou," couching both in semiautobiographical language. The narrator/child is confronted with an expansive mother-figure, the dame Panckoucke, "the toy-fairy" ["la Fée du joujou"], which thrusts his own mother into a restrictive, mediocritizing role whereby the child is forced to accept the "happy middle" instead of his first choice, the "most bizarre toy." Fecund with an array of artificial and imaginary beings who are presumable sexed, yet described in the same gender-neutral terms (e.g. "beautiful costumes, eyes as pure as diamonds, cheeks aglow with makeup" [1:582]) that are characteristic of the descriptions of "la foule"—this expansive mother-figure possesses one unforgettable feature: "I distinctly recall that this woman was dressed in velvet and fur" (581), she is "the lady dressed in velvet and fur" (582). This simple, metonymic displacement of the fur for orifice, the fur being what conceals an orifice, eventually becomes, for "most brats," a desire to "see the soul [voir l'âme]," to open up and to penetrate the body of the other: where do you cut to find the soul? In *Fusées* we find the following: "The precocious taste for women. I confused the smell of fur with the smell of a woman" (1:661). This originary confusion, now presumably a corrected error, seems to state that in actuality the two belong to separate realms: yet read another way, it could mean that the child/narrator had assumed that only women possessed orifices or the promise of an orifice (one may recall this remark from *Le Peintre de la vie moderne*: "Woman is without a doubt . . . an invitation to happiness" [2:714]). This assumption reveals itself to be doubly false: not only is "Celle qui est trop gaie," discussed below, lacking such an orifice, but it will be the poet's goal to open up a multiplicity of orifices in those of both genders who surround him, including the reader. This is, after all, the Poet's motto in "Les Foules": "For him alone, all is vacant" (1:291). The purpose of this "orificealization" is to enter into a communicative and erotic relationship to the other—and, thanks to his epidermal sensitivity and the bustling crowds, the wounder is also wounded in turn, in the act of wounding, thereby completing the communicative circuit or, as described in "Les Foules," ultimately creating a "universal orgy" (1:291). The fact that all this bears a resemblance to the transmission of syphilis should be kept in mind, especially because Baudelaire brings it up himself in the one poem most clearly devoted to this wounding, "A celle qui est trop gaie [To One Who Is Too Cheerful]." This poem describes the urbanization of a woman who is initially described, in the first two stanzas, as too closely tied to nature's attributes:

> Ta tête, ton geste, ton air
> Sont beaux comme un beau paysage;
> Le rire joue en ton visage
> Comme un vent frais dans un ciel clair.
>
> Le passant chagrin que tu frôles
> Est ébloui par la santé
> Qui jaillit comme une clarté
> De tes bras et de tes épaules.
>
> Your head, your air, your every way
> Are scenic as the countryside;
> The smile plays on your lips and eyes
> Like fresh winds on a cloudless day.
>
> The gloomy drudge, brushed by your charms
> Is dazzled by the vibrancy
> That flashes forth so brilliantly
> Out of your shoulders and your arms. (1:156)

The final three stanzas depict one of the most violent agendas of *Les Fleurs du mal*:

> Ainsi je voudrais, une nuit,
> Quand l'heure des voluptés sonne,
> Vers les trésors de ta personne,
> Comme un lâche, ramper sans bruit,
>
> Pour châtier ta chair joyeuse,
> Pour meurtrir ton sein pardonné,
> Et faire à ton flanc étonné
> Une blessure large et creuse,
>
> Et, vertigineuse douceur!
> A travers ces lèvres nouvelles,
> Plus éclatantes et plus belles,
> T'infuser mon venin, ma soeur!

So I would wish, when you're asleep,
The time for sensuality,
Towards your body's treasury
Silently, steathily to creep,

To bruise your ever-tender breast,
And carve in your astonished side
An injury both deep and wide,
to chastize your too-joyous flesh.

And, sweetness that you dizzy me!
In these lips so red and new
My sister, I have made for you,
To slip my venom, lovingly! (157)

Ultimately, however, and despite the title, "A celle qui est trop gaie" was not (to be) addressed to a woman at all, but instead to a group of presumably male judges, as the reader learns in the "note" included in the *Epaves*:

> The judges believed they discovered a meaning both bloody and obscene in the last two stanzas. The seriousness of the Anthology excludes such *jokes.* The possibility that *venom* might signify spleen or melancholy was too simple an idea for these criminalists.
>
> May their syphilitic interpretation remain on their conscience. (*Publisher's note.*) (1:157)[4]

This addendum compels a radical rereading of the poem, which is henceforth inserted in a circuit linking a fictional "éditeur" to a group of judges, who saw in this poem "an assault on public morality." The reader is invited to judge the judges, while the "éditeur" stands in for both the prosecutor, with the judges as defendants, and the defending attorney, with the poet as defendant. Thus the original address to/of the woman turns out to be—and/or to have been—a series of addresses to many men, which is the figure of the homoerotic alibi. It is according to a chiasmus (that figure which presents two parallel structures while reversing one of them, creating a kind of intersection or street-corner which, as it were, is the locus of the prostitute) that the "injury both deep and wide" is made: for just as "the gloomy drudge, brushed by your charms / is dazzled," so the next stranger who brushes up against her will be rendered melancholic by the "spleen" she now

4. "A celle qui est trop gaie" was one of the six poems condemned for "outrage à la morale publique" in Baudelaire's trial on these charges in 1857. The "Publisher's note" was actually written by Baudelaire himself, and was appended to the poem when it was included in *Epaves* in 1866.

carries within her body. This "melancholy" arises from the "bad faith" implicit in the channeling of homoeroticism through a woman's body. The mediating figure of the prostitute appears as the emblem of this homoerotic detour: the humiliating path the poet takes toward the "body's treasury" retraces the "stealthy" or cowardly ("comme un lâche [like a coward]") passage through the money-form that this mediation entails.

Inflicting a wound, "une plaie" is indeed one of the dominant modes of interpersonal communication in *Les Fleurs du mal* and especially in *Le Spleen de Paris*: examples abound, but the theme of vampirism in the collection is especially deserving of the kind of analysis I am proposing. And whereas the curious child in "Morale du joujou" is disappointed by the end result of the wounding procedure ("Here lie the beginnings of stupor and sadness" [1:587]) because nothing is communicated to other bodies, the narrator of "A celle qui est trop gaie" is overjoyed to have attained his goal: "Et, vertigineuse douceur! / A travers ces lèvres nouvelles / . . . . / T'infuser mon venin, ma soeur!" (1:157). It is the knowledge that his "venom" will be distributed to other passers-by who brush up against her that causes his delight. Heightened epidermal sensitivity is a prerequisite to this kind of communicative agenda, which must bypass "traditional" erogenous zones in favor of those that can be stimulated by the more discrete bodily encounters that occur among a crowd. Indeed, the poet, as it turns out, is remarkably well-prepared to carry out this program, because his masculinity was tempered by the world of women, because he has become "androgynous" and "complete," because he received a special initiation into sensitivity:

> Indeed, men who have been brought up by women and among women do not completely resemble other men . . . the soothing rocking of the wet-nurse, maternal caresses, the playful attentions of sisters, especially older sisters, those diminutive mothers, all transform by kneading, as it were, the masculine dough. The man who, from his earliest infancy, was bathed in the soft atmosphere of woman . . . thereby contracted an epidermal sensitivity and a distinctive inflection, a kind of androgyny, without which the most trenchant and virile genius will remain, with respect to artistic perfection, an incomplete being. (*Un mangeur d'opium*, "Chagrins d'enfance," 1:499)

It is this "epidermal sensitivity" which characterizes the poet, be it Baudelaire, Thomas de Quincey, or Edgar Allan Poe, because this heightened sensitivity makes their wounding all the easier; the fact that this sensitivity is "contracted" from women, from the *mundi muliebris*, reveals the interpersonal and therefore "contagious" nature of erotic stances—and, further, that the stances most valuable to the Poet are those that happen (due to ideological and social constraints) to be situated under the rubric "femme" at this point in time (Wing 19–40). In a significant parallel to the role of the prostitute as communicating vessel between men, this passage describes how a man must pass through or undergo a certain feminization in order to attain the heightened sensitivity required to experience the homoerotics of the urban crowd.

The Homoeroticization of Everyday Life

Yet such a "sensitivity" can exist apart from or beyond its feminine origins, as is revealed by the excesses of hashish intoxication. In "Du vin et du hachisch [On Wine and Hashish]" (1851), the state of "kief" provokes a return to a Sadean erotics of multiplicity, which the narrator calls "a frenzied libertinage": "In this supreme state, love, for gentle and artistic minds, takes the most unusual forms and lends itself to the most baroque combinations" (1:394–95). In the version of 1860, however, this heightened sensitivity produces a more social and urban eroticism, and serves to reveal an everyday, habitually repressed homoeroticism:

> I will simply beg the reader to consider to what extent the imagination of a sensitive man, intoxicated with hashish, is extended to a prodigious degree . . . and his senses honed to a point just as difficult to define. It is thus possible to believe that a simple caress of the most innocent kind, a handshake for example, can have its value multiplied a hundredfold by the current state of the soul and the senses, and can lead them perhaps, and very quickly, to that swoon considered by vulgar mortals to be the apogee of happiness. (1:433)

Baudelaire's definition (at the fantasy level) of intense erotic experience is clearly moving beyond the erotic yet enclosed world of Sadean combination, into the more generalized erotics of the crowd as expressed in the smallest of gestures, such as brushing up against someone, or shaking someone's hand.

Paneroticism is the erotics of the crowd, although Sade described it first as the erotics of the interpersonal *combinatoire* discussed by Roland Barthes (*Sade* 33). The *combinatoire* is the sum total—if this totality can ever be reached—of the possible interpenetrations available to a human being given an admittedly limited number of orifices and/or coupling appendages (not to mention the erotic detachment of the voyeur, or the use of tools such as the whip). Sade, in his defense of sodomy, mocked those who would seek to establish a hierarchy among the bodily orifices according to which some would be "pure" and others "soiled." As Sade writes in *La Philosophie dans le boudoir*: "What crime is there in this? Surely it is not that of placing oneself in such and such a place, unless one wants to claim that all parts of the body do not resemble each other, and that some are pure while others are soiled; but . . . it is impossible to propose such absurdities" (232).

Charles Fourier, the utopian who actually read Sade, also advocated radical sexual exploration ("the exception is just as useful as the norm"), arguing that "culture cannot function according to the laws of attraction if there are not . . . all kinds of loves [des amours de tout genre]" (27–28; 203). Fourier announced an eventual "libéralisme amoureux," and even suggested that children receive an education in voluptuousness—much like the one Baudelaire, Poe, and de Quincey share—to prepare them for furthering the permutations of such a "combinatoire." Such an education would aim to "methodically refine the passions so as to render them more disposed to sample the innumerable pleasures which the new social order will offer" (43). Thus it would seem that Baudelaire is (re)enacting Fourier's program (or, as it were, taking it to the streets) in his description of the poet's childhood eroticism, as well as through his exploration of hashish effects. Yet it should be clear that, for this program to be realized, urban homoeroticism must eventually dispense with recourse to the prostitute as homoerotic alibi in favor of the more direct anatomical permutations of the Sadean combinatoire. The following anecdote, which reflects the performative nature of Baudelaire's homoeroticism and which can be read as a commentary on the erotics of the handshake, describes one way to "walk away" from the scene of prostitution:

> The brown-skinned Jeanne did not limit herself to Baudelaire's company. She had even been seen dancing at a public ball with a stranger, and leaving with another stranger.
>
> These events were brought to the attention of her lover, who merely observed, with a sigh:
>
> —Poor girl! That's her job. She has to make a living.
>
> Shortly thereafter, the same friend who brought the news to him, and received this response, overheard Baudelaire presenting himself as a man of strong passions, and ventured:
>
> —But wait! when I told you that Jeanne was carrying on . . .
>
> Baudelaire cut him off.
>
> —You see, I know how to contain myself. Listen up! and you'll see. I know how to contain myself so well, that the other night, as I prepared to enter Jeanne's apartment, as I was about to put the key into the lock, here's what I

> did when I heard two voices, one of which I knew to be Jeanne's, and one belonging to a man . . . Jeanne was with someone . . . Do your understand? with someone . . . Well! . . . I had the courage . . . to leave!
>
> And the poet, grabbing the hand of his friend, gave it a heartfelt squeeze, with an emotion he seemed willing to share.
>
> (Maillou 139–40 quoted in Bandy and Pichois 121)

Written by a man for a presumably male audience, this anecdote involves three male characters, in addition to the poet himself, and of course the prostitute (and Baudelaire's mistress) Jeanne Duval. We should note the paradoxical inclusion of two "premiers-venus" (literally, "first-comers") which suggests that there are more in the wings, or perhaps that the "friend" could have been one of them. The "ami" is, in any case, standing in for one of these "premiers venus" when he receives Baudelaire's warm handshake, which could just as well be given to the "other man" himself. This handshake is the bodily performance of the inner "courage" displayed by the poet who has managed to overcome the notion of the male Other as usurper of his "property": it acknowledges his reconciliation with male Others, with whom he can now "bond" directly without the intermediary and facilitating figure of the prostitute. In fact, he owes his ability to share his emotions with other men to the prostitute's ability to share her "love" with the "premier venu." It is in this manner that the poet internalizes the prostitute's availability: she has caused Baudelaire to share a strong emotion with another man, and through him with the many "premiers venus" that brush up against him every day in the crowd. The handshake connects two men in a homoerotic gesture all the more powerful because it is no longer blocked by the body of the prostitute. And if "la clef" never makes it into "la serrure," it is because Baudelaire has chosen to remain outside, in the crowd, where there are no locks because "tout est vacant."

Postscript

Baudelaire's homoeroticism is closely tied to his attitude toward women who stand out, as it were, from the crowd: prostitutes, actresses, and lesbians. Marcel Proust noted the important role of the latter in *Les Fleurs du mal*; in a conversation with André Gide, recorded by the same in his *Journal*, Proust draws the following conclusions:

> He spoke of his conviction that Baudelaire was a uranist. "The way he speaks about Lesbos, and even the very need to speak of it, would alone suffice to convince me," and since I protested:

> "In any case, if he was a uranist, it was almost without his knowing it; and you can't believe that he ever practiced . . . "
>
> "Say what!" he exclaimed. "I am convinced of the contrary; how can you doubt that he practiced? He, Baudelaire!"
>
> And, from the sound of his voice, it seemed that by doubting I was attacking Baudelaire. But I'm willing to believe that he is right, and that uranists are even more numerous than I had thought. (Gide, *Journal* 692)

Like Baudelaire, Proust has difficulty detaching a generalized and autonomized homoeroticism from its insertion in a mediating scenario involving women who are (posed as) the objects of a male gaze. Baudelaire's lesbians are, of course, more than that: Hippolyte, one of the "Femmes Damnées" in the poem of the same title, describes herself as ontologically evacuated: "Je sens s'élargir dans mon être / Un abîme béant; cet abîme est mon coeur! [I can feel, widening in my being, a gaping abyss; this abyss is my heart]" (1:154). And the narrator of the poem concludes with an apostrophe to them: "Et fuyez l'infini que vous portez en vous! [Flee the infinite that you carry within!]" (155). Even in Proust's and Gide's time, an intermediary and facilitating figure, coded as a vacant, ghostlike alibi, still stands in the way (and in the place) of such a generalized ("more numerous") homoeroticism.

CHAPTER 4

Gay Incipit: Botanical Connections, Nosegays, and Bouquets

GEORGE H. BAUER

> This marvelous blossoming of dark and beautiful flowers,
> I only learned in fragments.
> —Jean Genet

> Those disgusting flowers!
> —Senator Jesse Helms

In his *Michelet,* Roland Barthes writes of a Morphology of Tissues: "The corruption of bodies is a pledge of their resurrection. Hence, the goal of history is to rediscover in each piece of the past's flesh the corruptible element par excellence, not the skeleton but the tissue" (87). The conclusion that "all history depends in the last instance upon the human body" is taken back to Marx, whose assumption was that the basis of human history is "naturally the existence of individual human beings." Barthes draws on Marx's *The German Ideology* for the necessary first step: a description of the "corporeal organization of these individuals and the relations this gives them with nature" (quoted in *Michelet* 87). In *Michelet,* Barthes asks the question concerning the tissues of history: "What becomes of homogeneity when one shifts from the level of Nature to that of History?" (34). History itself becomes plant tissue. Barthes/Michelet's History as Plant finds natural history to be fundamental:

> Here, too, it is the sciences of Nature that afford an answer. History grown "uno tenore," like a plant or a species; its movement is less a succession than a continuity. Are there, strictly speaking, historical facts? No; history is rather a continuity of identities, just as the plant or the species is the extension of one and the same tissue. (35)

In this growth, there is no cause and effect relationship:

> The vegetal character of historic growth obviously excludes causality. Who would even think of saying that the jellyfish [*méduse*] is "cause" of the whale,

> or even that seed is "cause" of the flower? No; they are simply two more or less remote zones of the same substance. The same goes for the objects of history: some are not the causes of others; they are merely the different moments of the same step. (35)

The gay body as part of history has an ambiguous scent, but its fictions, depictions, and interdictions curiously fleshed out in a dialogue with natural history become natural science stem more from botany than zoology. As gay figures begin to emerge in nineteenth-century French literature, they are nosegays whose bouquets are perfumed and dandy floral offerings that flirt with a certain language of criminality and real and artificial flowers. This is hardly the "faithful and monotonous copy of inanimate nature" criticized by Sainte-Beuve (quoted in Knight 29). The flowers of flesh in Baudelaire's *incipit*, his evil Flowers, his mixed and various blossoms collected on excursions into the marasma of the Marais, are endlessly turned around his thyrsus. *Les Fleurs du mal* is a fascinating poetic nosegay whose title covers the lesbian body, object of the male gaze, with other lilies heaped on shades in limbo. *Manibus date lilia plenis.* The slip from a gay tissue of flesh to a libidinal swamp, to flowering evil, is one of displaced naming from body to *topos* to topiary: *Les Lesbiennes*; *Les Limbes*; *Les Fleurs du mal.* Baudelaire and Genet were not dry botanists, but lovers.

Nor was one of the nineteenth century's greatest illustrators, J. J. Grandville, merely a dry-as-dust scholar. His *Les Fleurs animées* was published in 1847 with an introduction by Alphonse Karr (of "Plus ça change, plus c'est la même chose" fame) and with a text by Taxile Delord, "La Fée aux fleurs." As an amateur florist, a literary horticulturalist before scented Baudelaire and his trials, Karr gaily guides us down the garden path: "We may love flowers in several ways. The naturalist flattens and dries them. He then inters them in a cemetery called a *herbarium* and below them places pompous epitaphs in a barbarous language." Before Proust and cattleyas, he addresses jealousy and the greenhouse: "Connoisseurs love only rare flowers, and these they cultivate, not so much for sight and scent, as for display. Their enjoyment consists far less in possessing certain blossoms than in knowing that others do not possess them" (quoted in Wick's introduction to Grandville, *Court* 12). In these floral tableaux, the criminal element appears only as aggressive pruners, stupid asses, or "diminutive sycophants" in the guise of butterflies and bees. The poetic places coming before Baudelaire and after Balzac's Lucien Chardon, whose name means "thistle," will have a role to play in Proust's own library and in the dialogue of the tissue of nosegays and bouquets of mauve flora. In Grandville's *Les Fleurs animées*, not in what is considered his masterwork, *Scènes de la vie privée et publique des animaux*, with its Balzac-inspired title and zoo-house tales, the smooth glide is more than a slip toward the undercutting of the acid-etched, Latin-incised natural history of Buffon. In *Animated Flowers*, flora take on a new life. Already the smell of Odilon Redon's swamp flower illustrations for *Les Fleurs du mal* is there in the vegetal and carnal humus. The pansy, the narcissus, the ranunculus, and the thistle are tentative taunts, courtly companions to tea, coffee, hemlock, nicotine, and digitalis. Belladonnas are deadly nightshades. Natural history as plant is subverted. Perversion is a garden where the ass in his proverbial stupidity eats the thistle (*L'Ane mange du chardon*) and the hawthorne (*aubépine*) hedge is clipped and floral criminality with its rosy thorns dawns.

The invert and the Uranian gaze at the floribunda, but Gide, a latter-day naturalist, is alarmed in his pastoral *Corydon*, and in that work the fauna of the Zoo compete with the flora of the Jardin des Plantes. Flowery, scented dandy Baudelaire is seen by Proust as a gay beginning. This is the *pensée*—thought and flower—Proust offers Gide: Proust "tells me of his conviction that Baudelaire was a uranist: 'The way in which he speaks of Lesbos, and before that, his need to speak of it would alone be enough to convince me of it,' and as I object: . . . What! How can you doubt that he practiced? him, Baudelaire'" (*Journal* 692). This insistence on the nature of Baudelaire's sexuality took place on May 13, 1921, when Gide came to share with him the text of his *Corydon*. Two days later, Proust's chauffeur picks up Gide. A quick read. The pastoral is returned to the frustrated naturalist and the visit is spent discussing Uranism. Proust confesses to Gide that "he reproached himself for the 'indecision' that led him to nourish the heterosexual part of his book by transposing in 'à l'ombre des jeunes filles' everything that his homosexual memories proposed to him that was gracious, tender or charming, so what remained was only the grotesque and the abject." But Gide insists that Proust "was very upset when I told him that he seems to have stigmatized Uranism, and protests" (*Journal* 694). What is missing from the shady title is "en fleur." Proust's mauve shadows are cast by Balzac's and Baudelaire's flowering, and contrast sharply with the bright sunlight of Gide's own naturalizing of the gay body and homoeroticism.

Before turning to the flowers that Proust wove into his tapestry, we should look at Gide. Already in Roland Barthes's first article published in *Existences*, in 1942, well before his reflections on the role of plants and natural history in Michelet's own poetic sorcery, Barthes insists on Gide's peculiar preferences and the natural sciences. In his article in the *Magazine littéraire*, Barthes writes the following of Gide:

> This taste permits him to cast a long, attentive gaze on the formal world. Every poet, if he probes a little, must approach the naturalist. The Natural Sciences furnished Gide numerous comparisons, indeed whole parts of his illustrations (in *Corydon*, in his attacks on the scientific writings of Maeterlinck). The fact is that nothing can better pose the ontological problem. Many great minds use Science to make the problem clearer, first to themselves, then to their readers. (27–28)

Barthes underscores his point, citing Gide's regret: "I missed my calling, it is a naturalist that I would have, should have been" (*Journal* 1305). This regret of 1938 is not new. On June 19, 1910, a year before the unsigned edition of *Corydon* that breaks off in the middle of a discussion on Darwin, Gide writes:

> I was a naturalist before being a man of letters and natural adventures have always taught me more than novels. I come to the point of loving the writing of these books which at first put me off: what Fabre says in 20 pages could often be contained in 10 lines, but in the writing you participate in his discoveries; he seems to require the same patience of the reader that he needed for his research. (*Journal* 302–3)

In *Corydon*, as the interlocutor insists, "we are entering here the domain of natural history" (*Oeuvres* 9:209), before adding, "It is as a naturalist that I speak to you, be assured." Gide's impatience with the floral is clear, perhaps because of the failure of the floral in the Virgilian pastoral seduction.

In *Corydon*, however, Gide cannot avoid the flowering of Greece. Even there, Gide sees Greece as a plant without blemish: "beautiful plant without atrophy, fully developed as no other." In this first blossoming he insists, naturally, on "a direct relation between the flower and the plant that bears it, the profound quality of its vital sap, and its behavior, and its growth" (9:297). The problem, too, surely is the floral and botanical connection to decadence and symbolism, desiccated poet: dried flower books from which the sap is gone, leaving only a rotten smell.

One can only speculate whether Genet went back to Gide, to *Corydon*, to *Paludes* (discussed by Emily Apter), as Gide went back to Baudelaire's *Fleurs du mal* before he sniffingly discounted the grotesque and abject flowers of Proust and his literary uncles. Both Gide's *Paludes* and Genet's "Lettre à Léonore Fini" poke at copied flora and invented fauna as incapable of resurrection, of erection. Proust always knew that the flower in his lapel cast a shadow on his relation with Gide and the NRF. Céleste Albaret recounts Proust's conviction that the refusal of his book and his person stemmed from "the camellia in my buttonhole" (366). The Montesquiou and his Chancellor of Flowers connection with the dominance of delicate odors and unnatural artificial couplings had their underpinnings in one of Proust's favorite botanical dilettantes, the perfumed and boutonniered Maurice de Maeterlinck.

Barthes touches on *Paludes* and flirts with Gide's *Narcisse* in his *Fragments d'un discours amoureux.* Gide strings up Maeterlinck for his floral intelligence—*L'Intelligence des fleurs*—not for his apiculture in *La Vie des abeilles.* Grandville is central to the unknotting and a proposal for floral *dénouement,* through a chemical equation: "Grandville = the wedding of hydrogen and oxygen." Gide continues: "A *naturalist* is not so much someone who deals with nature, but someone for whom things are natural, or if you prefer: who understands phenomena *naturally* (*Journal* 806). Gide turns from the animated flowers to Maeterlinck's dandelions—*dents de lion*—and their erose leaves, a flower now called *pissenlit* because of its diuretic effect: "To find the *dandelion* 'intelligent' for having easily blown seed is like finding a duck *intelligent* for having webbed feet for swimming—or admiring a bird because it wraps a shell around its egg" (*Journal* 807). These books of floral anthropomorphism must be written for "1. Poetic ignorants; 2. scientists ignorant in literature" (807). He adds, "Why not admit that the plant, it too, knows *voluptuousness*? That would shock me infinitely less than believing in its 'intelligence.'" (809).

Gide was adamant in his antipathy to floral intelligence and poetics. His natural pursuit was fauna. Fabled animals come to him from myth or La Fontaine's "Les Deux Pigeons" or the contemporary Fabre's entomological intelligence on the public and private life of the grasshopper and its song. As Patrick Pollard notes, "If they have little else in common, Gide and Proust have an engaging and sympathetic interest in natural history" (256). *Corydon* is central, but for many it has become little more than a curiosity in our literary Museum of Natural History. In his preface to his translation, Richard Howard calls it "an appallingly rigged and anthropomorphized *zoology*" wed to "literary and historical vestiges of Greek culture" (xiv).

The blossoming of men in nature and the perverted florist and botanist is quite different in Proust. In his *Proust and the Art of Love,* J. E. Rivers uses the natural presence of Darwin in *Sodome et Gomorrhe* and keys it to a hermaphroditic and "natural beauty." As Rivers writes: "The narrator is writing, then, within the best traditions of nineteenth-century natural history when he makes this appeal to the artistry and formal beauty of nature. . . . The naturalist makes us see beauty in the mating of snails, and the narrator makes us see beauty in a homosexual encounter" (240–41). Michelet finally floats to the surface in Proust, beached and florally transposed, a sight seen without cause:

> The jellyfish [*méduse*] repulsed me at Balbec, but if I knew how to observe it, like Michelet, from the point of view of *natural history* and *aesthetics*, I saw a delicious girandole of azure. Aren't they, with the transparent velvet of their petals, like mauve orchids of the sea? (3:28, my emphasis).

Natural history *and* aesthetics, but Pollard, as well as Claudette Sartiliot in her *Herbarium Verbarium*, choose to interpret the floral in terms of hermaphroditism. Sartiliot refuses any generalization about Proust's association of flowers with women: "Rather than being associated with one particular sex, flowers subvert the traditional opposition of the sexes and take Marcel back to a hermaphroditic origin" (51). I think that Proust's flowers represent something more complicated than simple hermaphroditism.

Charles Swann is an amateur botanist, an orchid fancier, well known to readers of Proust as an expert in floral arranging of cattleyas, a kind of orchid. Orchids are at the center of his seduction of Odette: "'Oh! No cattleyas this evening, then there's no chance of my indulging in my little rearrangements" (1:230). But this was the exception, since that first occasion when arranging her cattleyas ended in his possessing her:

> So that for some time there was no change in the technique he had followed on that first evening, starting with fumblings with fingers and lips at Odette's bosom, and it was thus that his caresses still began. And long afterwards, when the rearrangement (or rather the ritual pretense of a rearrangement) of her cattleyas had quite fallen into desuetude, the metaphor "do a cattleya," became a simple utterance they would use when they wished to refer to the act of physical possession. (1:230)

Swann's sensitivity to the scent of the cattleya contrasts with the repulsion experienced by him and others fascinated by the smell of another variety of orchid.

The narrator recounts a botanical conversation overheard one evening at the Guermantes' between Oriane de Guermantes and another guest, the Princesse de Parme, who is taken with the beauty of a potted orchid Oriane is cultivating. The narrator recognizes it as one Elstir had been painting:

> They are ravishing, look at their little velvet mauve necks; but as can happen to quite pretty, well-turned out young things, they have a nasty name and a bad odor. In spite of that I like them a lot. But what is sad is that they are going to die. (2:805)

This particular orchid is not documented in Darwin but is drawn from Proust's reading and fascination with Maeterlinck's *L'Intelligence des fleurs*. It is the *Loroglossum hircinum*, that is, the loroglossum that smells like a goat (*loroglosse à odeur de bouc*). Maeterlinck describes it as having the color of "those drowned—after a month in the river. On the whole they evoke the idea of the worst maladies and seem to blossom in unnamed nightmares of ironic and maleficent landscapes and emit a frightful and powerful odor of poisoned goat spreading abroad to reveal the presence of the monster" (*Intelligence* 67). In Proust's flowers, Rivers and Sartiliot see only art—formal beauty coming from natural history; but Proust is clearly attracted to this orchid he finds in Maeterlinck, not only for its malodorous smell and method of fertilization, but also as a monstrous thyrsus. Maeterlinck allows that he describes "this nauseating Orchid because it is rather common in France, easily recognized, and it lends itself because of its size and the distinctiveness of its organs to the experiments one would like to make" (*Intelligence* 80). Darwin, he reflects, may not have studied it because it may well be rare in England, but insists that of all "our indigenous orchids, it is the most remarkable, the most fantastic, the most stupefying. If it were the size of American Orchids, one could confirm that no more fantastic plant exists" (*Intelligence* 66–67). Naturally Rivers refers us to the English Darwin for the bee's encounter with the orchid incarnated as Jupien and the Baron, with references to *The Descent of Man* and *The Different Flowers of the Same Species*, but doesn't pick up Darwin's *The Various Contrivances by which Orchids are Fertilised by Insects.* Rivers also completely overlooks Maeterlinck's presence in Proust's portrait of Charles Swann as botanist and the botanical experiments of Charlus.

Palamède XV, Baron de Charlus, familiarly called Mémé, has nearly two dozen antonyms in Proust's novel, but the most important is "Fleurus" who always has a flower in his buttonhole. In November 1912, in a letter to Gallimard, Proust prepares his publisher for the shock to come:

> You will see a M. de Fleurus (or de Guercy, I have changed the names several times). . . . He is a type of character I think is rather new, the virile pederast, in love with virility, detesting effeminate young men, detesting, to tell the truth, all young men, as men who have suffered from women are misogynists. The character is so scattered through absolutely different parts so that the volume has in no way the appearance of a special monograph such as the *Lucien* of Binet-Valmer. (quoted in Rivers).

According to Rivers, the novel *Lucien*, published in 1910, "gave overt and even favorable treatment to homosexuality" (141). Rivers explains the reference to *Lucien*, noting that "Proust took due notice of the book's turbulent reception" and for that reason, he points out in his letter to Gallimard, "what should, by now, go almost without saying: that the optimistic vision of *Lu-*

cien is not the vision of *A la recherche* and that, indeed, 'nothing is more dissimilar'" (144). Binet-Valmer's Lucien is dismissed but Balzac's Lucien Chardon de Rubempré and the language of flowers is a different matter.

The thorny nosegay and prickly thyrsus were already on Marcel's mind at the tender age of seventeen when he penned two remarkable notes inscribing the crushed flower beds and uncut, unpicked blossoms with rhetorical flourishes and allusive references to Montaigne and Socrates. We owe a debt to Rivers for having given them their currency. The "two passionate schoolboy crushes," in Rivers's words, were on Jacques Bizet and Daniel Halévy, both from musical families. Two letters, one to Georges Bizet's nephew and the other to Halévy's nephew, inscribe flowers at the center of the attempted seductions. The first, a habañera, rose clenched in lionizing teeth, is written to Jacques Bizet and opens on a Pascalian note:

> But the heart—or the body—has reasons of which reason is scarcely aware. I therefore accept with admiration for you (I mean your mind, and not for the matter you refuse, for I am not [vain] enough to think my body is such a precious treasure that one needs great will power to do without it) but also with sadness the superb yet cruel yoke you impose on me. Perhaps you are right. However, I still think *it is unfortunate not to pick the delightful flower which very soon we shall no longer be able to pick.* Because by that time it will have turned into . . . *forbidden fruit.* I realize that even now you think of it as a poisonous flower. (quoted in Rivers 57, my emphasis)

Marcel learns the pain of flowers of evil, as Carlos Herrera had done before him from Lucien Chardon's suicide note in *Splendeurs et misères*: "It is the poisonous plant, rich in color, that fascinates the children in the woods. It is the poetry of evil" (6:790). Like a young Saint Sebastian, Proust accepts, even welcomes the flower-entwined arrows. Already Fleurus/Charlus's masochistic floggings are breaking into bud. Carmen gives rise to Fleurus's omnibus men, but Daniel's musical inspiration arouses the Jewess of the uncle's *La Juive*.

The second letter addressed to Daniel Halévy focuses on the "verbal spanking" Daniel has given him. But the switches, like Baudelaire's Dionysian thyrsus, are entwined with flowers with thorns, and are quickly transformed into a poet's lyre:

> You have administered to me a slight chastisement, but *your switches are so laden with flowers*, that I cannot hold it against you: the brilliance and the fragrance have so sweetly intoxicated me as to soften the cruel sting of the thorns. You have administered a beating with a lyre. And your lyre is enchanting, I would therefore be enchanted if . . . If you are delightful, if you

> have clear, beautiful eyes which reflect the fine grace of your mind so purely that it seems to me that I do not love your mind completely unless I also kiss your eyes, if your body and your eyes are, like your mind, so graceful and supple that is seems to me that I can mingle better with your mind while sitting on your lap, if, finally, it seems to me that the charm of your you, the you in which I cannot separate your lively mind from your nimble body, would refine for me, by increasing it, "the sweet joy of love," there is nothing in all that which causes me to deserve these contemptuous phrases, which would be more properly addressed to a man tired of women and seeking new pleasures in homosexuality. . . . I will gladly speak to you of two Masters possessed of refined wisdom who all their lives *picked only "the flower."* Socrates and Montaigne. . . . So don't treat me like a homosexual, that causes me pain. (quoted in Rivers 58, my emphasis).

Marcel's sylvan confession of love is one of mistaken or displaced gay seductive reading of the body and the plants. Gautier's Mémé, *Mademoiselle de Maupin*, before that other Mémé, Maurice Maeterlinck, tickles the nose of gay fanciers. When Gautier's Théophile speaks of love in this written-out dream: "Yes, that's the way I imagined love. . . . Now I feel what I dreamed. —Yes here are the charming and terrible insomnias where *roses are* thistles and thistles are roses" (194, my emphasis). He is like Phèdre: the horror crosses his red-rose lips: "Now pity me for loving, and most of all for loving whom I love. . . . I no longer know who I am nor what others are. . . . Oh! no, I can never say it to you . . . I love a man" (195). Floral confusion reigns.

Oscillation between flower and flesh, the carnal and the floral, the florid poet and his poetry. Among others, Proust will romance the *chardon* (thistle), a flower that pricks with a flourish and leaves a slight gash that the French call a boutonniere. Fencing is a duel of both flower and name. Fleurus (i.e., Charlus) is one of a bunch of horticultural names born of sexual misapprehension. The *chardon* is the heart of the nosegay to be read. In *Illusions perdues*, Lucien's bunch of sedum (5:689), held in his hand just as he meets the man who will change his fortunes for a while, Carlos Herrera, is already there in the bouquet of desire, "a symphony of flowers," concocted by Félix to send his love a message in *Le Lys dans la vallée* (9:1055). Félix and Henriette are displaced by Lucien and Carlos in *Illusions perdues*, where Balzac inserts a floral offering from Gautier. "La Tulipe" is Lucien's Sonnet "L" from his collection *Les Marguerites*: "I am the tulip, a flower of Holland / And my beauty is such that a greedy Fleming / Pays more dearly for one of my bulbs than for a diamond" (5:341).

Like Balzac's incorporation of Gautier, Proust places *Le Capitaine Fra-*

casse, and not *Mademoiselle de Maupin*, at the center of the musings of *Jean Santeuil*. But in the revision that produces the *Recherche*, Gautier loses out to George Sand, for her *François le champi* is the book finally taken to bed. Both Balzac and Baudelaire created male flowers stemming from Gautier that leave a characteristic scent. Gautier begins the undercutting of straight floral discourse in the sexual ambiguity of the not yet male mauve Maupin(e) when he inscribes eros as a thistle. In contrast to Balzac's lily of the valley, Gautier's inspired thistle is an effeminate male flower poet and a prickly flower on which the energetic virile male can dote. Lucien Chardon replaces young Rastignac as the object of desire of the best-known homosexual of French nineteenth-century fiction.

The encounter between Lucien and Carlos Herrera is a model for gay horticulture. Roger Kempf gaily shows the importance Proust attaches to Balzac's depiction of Lucien de Rubempré's encounter with Vautrin/Herrera, but he barely winks at the floral patrimony. We should not forget the importance of the bunch of sedum Lucien carries, for it reminds us of the serenade of flowers tossed at him by the youth of Angoulême with the cries of "Long live the author of the *Archer de Charles IX*! Long live the author of the *Marguerites*! Long live Lucien de Rubempré!" (5:652). The Scotch lovage and thistle is in the patronymic of this beauteous poeticule. The father of his "crush," David Séchard, twits the "disguised young lady" for the wages of his blooming sonnets: "You gave them marguerites and you get bouquets in return" (652). Lucien's career as a writer has failed, his illusions lost. In suicide, he will leave behind his sonnets, his *Easter Daisy*, his *Marguerite*, his *Camellia*, his *Tulip*. Beside a river's edge with "weeping willows all rather picturesquely placed" (689), his contemplation of death is interrupted. Not wanting to be seen, he hides in a little hollow and "began to pick flowers" (543). Once back on the road with the huge collection of sedum clutched in his hand, he is a flower that will be picked by Carlos Herrera, Vautrin in disguise.

As Charlus says to the narrator of the *Recherche*, who has asked the Baron about his preferences in Balzac,

> What! You've never read *Illusions perdues*? It is so beautiful. The moment when Carlos Herrera asks the name of the château they are passing: Rastignac! The residence of the young man he used to love. And then the abbé falling into a reverie that Swann, with a great deal of wit, calls the *Tristesse d'Olympio* of pederasty. And the death of Lucien! I forget what man of taste who, when asked what event in his life had most upset him, replied: "The death of Lucien de Rubempré in *Splendeurs et misères*" (3:437–38).

Proust's narration hints at Charles Morel's relation to Chardon and to Charlus's own as a descendant of Carlos Herrera: "When M. de Charlus was not speaking of his admiration for Morel's beauty, as if it had no relation to a taste called vice, he would refer to that vice, but as if he himself did not share it" (3:437). In French, "moreau" is the English "morel," a nightshade, especially black nightshade. The wild morel (*moreau sauvage*) is bittersweet and toxic: Belladonna. Chardon and Morel are flowers to be buttonholed, peddled by florists. In ancient Greece, the Palamedes went to barbers and florists. In the criminal world of nineteenth-century France, the suspect professions have movingly been discussed by Neil Bartlett in his work. In Wilde he scents his own connections to Huysmans and Des Esseintes's "collection of the most monstrous and expensive flowers that the florists of Paris can provide" and to Rachilde's Jacques Silvert (cousin to Lucien Chardon, the flower-poet): "Fatally pretty eponym of *Monsieur Vénus* (1884), first seen in a garret of silk flowers, engaged in his profession of florist." Jean-Paul Aron and Roger Kempf looked into the medico-botanical herbariums composed of these flowers and Latin inscriptions: "Foedissimum tamen et singulara genus libidinosorum vivido colore exprimit appellatio *renifleurs*: The most hideous and bizarre species of these debauchers is picturesquely named *sniffers*" (*Pénis* 58). These criminal types are falsely elegant: "Curled hair, tinted with powder, open-neck, provocatively tight clothes, fingers, ears, and chest dripping with jewelry, doused in heavy perfumes, and a handkerchief, needle-work or flowers in the hand, this is the repugnant and for good reason suspect physiogeny of the pederast" (*Pénis* 53). In *Who Was That Man?*, Neil Bartlett remarks: "I immediately suspect him, having read in *Etudes de Pathologie Sociale* (1889) that floristry, along with hat-making and hairdressing, was one of the professions that M. F. Carlier, Chef de Préfecture, has identified as characteristic of the queens that he sought to rout out from the boulevards and pissoirs of Paris" (44–45). Who are these men of flowers?

Charlus may forget Oscar Wilde's name or dare not speak it. The Wilde trials come after the famous satire published anonymously by Robert Hichens. *The Green Carnation*, Oscar insisted, was not his: "I invented that magnificent flower. . . . The flower is a work of art. The book is not" (quoted in Hichens vii). In his introduction to that book, Stanley Weintraub states that "the green carnation was worn as a symbol of homosexuality in Paris, and worn there to deliberately advertise the fact" (xvi). If this is true, it is not a Wilde invention, but French in origin. As I have noted, it is the flower and the buttonhole of incipient Charlus that so becomes Fleurus. Bartlett's

Wilde is elegantly buttonholed and cited for his *mot* from *Phrases and Philosophies for the Use of the Young*: "A really well-made buttonhole is the only link between Art and Nature" (243). Proust's Fleurus/Charlus out of Séchard/Chardon, out of Carlos, and out of Charles and Charlie is a creature of habit. He is a dandy lionized for his particule. De Rubempré and de Charlus may merit ribbons or rosettes, but the *oeillet*/eyelet cut in the lapel is the *fleuron* and missing link in the pre-Darwinian chain of daisies and names. If Proust was fascinated by Lucien's floral sonnets that included *La Tulipe* quilled by the rose *gilet*, infamous Gautier, he was also intrigued by the flower collaboration of Rimbaud and Verlaine in *Le Sonnet du trou du cul*. In December 1908, Proust acquired "four obscene pamphlets at the sale of a respectable Protestant banker. The two 'secret, unclean, and stupid Verlaines, of the kind of pornography that mortifies the senses,' were *Femmes* and *Hombres*: the former a shameless lyric-cycle on the poet's heterosexual orgies; the latter a sodomitic counterpart which reads like a versified prospectus for Jupien's brothel" (Painter 119–20). Their joint sonnet opens floridly:

> Obscur et froncé comme un oeillet violet
> Il respire, humblement tapi parmi la mousse,
> Humide encor d'amour qui suit la pente douce
> Des fesses blanches jusqu'au bord de son ourlet.
>
> Crumpled like a carnation, mauve and dim
> It breathes, cowering humbly in the moss
> Still wet with love which trickles down across
> The soft slope of white buttocks to its rim
> (Verlaine, ed. Eliot 128–29)

Oeillet, oculum, oculist. The green carnation turns to mauve. Disgusting flower. Not a rosebud but a place for a monocle to see that other link between art and nature in the *marais*. This slippery poetic slope from the flower in question is also behind the adolescent reading of innocent forebears. In his consideration of Baudelaire, Proust speaks of his school days: "The pupils passed around works of pure pornography they thought were by Alfred de Musset" (in Rivers 27). Rivers speculates on the fecund reflections that include the allusion to Hugo's "Puisqu'ici bas tout âme" in the union of Charlus and Jupien. Cued by Jeffrey Myers, he cites the allusive allusion and puts the whole poem in its place. It is not an innocent list of *dons* for lovers. Proust finds the prickle and the rose in the close reading of not yet gay flowers pinned to the lapel:

Puisqu'ici toute chose
Donne toujours
Son épine ou sa rose
A ses amours; . . .
Je te donne, à cette heure,
Penché sur toi,
La chose la meilleure
Que j'aie en moi!

Since here below everything
Always gives
Its thorn or its rose
To the things it loves;
I give you, in this hour,
As I bend over you
The best thing
I have within me! (in Rivers 294)

The hole and the flower are an important part in nature imitating art, in the past's flesh and corruptible history and story before Darwin, before the overlay of bees humming in orchidaceous seduction. Not only is Charlus concerned with his buttonhole from the very first, but the seductive narrator is too. In his *Contre Sainte-Beuve* nosegay, Fleurus and his flowering buttonhole create a dandy anxiety in the young man. Invited to the "fairy-tale hotel" of the Guermantes, Charlus and the boutonniere obsess him: "I wanted to order a boutonniere from the florist but my grandmother thought that a rose from the garden would be more 'natural.' After having walked a steep bed and pricked my habit with the thorns of others, I cut the most beautiful, and jumped on the omnibus" (*Contre Sainte-Beuve* 250). The result is farcical. His overcoat destroys the petals and he was left with only "the immense green stem that was indeed too 'natural'" (250).

In his next reincarnation, the flower is a war of roses. I turn from *Contre Sainte-Beuve* to the redolent sketch that stands between these incipits and the final version where Maeterlinck and Darwin displace the florist observed. With Fleurus as Guercy, Jupien is not a *giletier*, but the intermittent Borniche *fleuriste*, as Proust attempts to skirt his flower-picking reading and writing. Esquisse II takes place in a courtyard dominated by a great sophora, a papillonaceous tree with rose blossoms. The narrator-voyeur contemplates from behind jalousies the comings and goings of pollinating bees and two men in floral transaction. The boutonniere is at the center of the astonished narrator's observations. He sees M. de Guercy reach the florist's shop, pull up sharp, then continue on his way before abruptly doing an about-face. He checks his watch, ruffles the rose in his lapel, begins to hum, and is oddly changed. Borniche, too, is transformed and begins to whistle softly, then slips inside his shop: "M. de Guercy left only to return in an instant. He must have discarded his rose, he no longer had it, once again rang Mme de Guermantes's doorbell, I don't know whether he asked the *maître d'hôtel* where he could find a florist but he was pointed in the direction of Borniche's shop" (3:937). The narrator has run out and down the stairs to see what is going on. He catches the men in the shadowed doorway of the *arrière-boutique*. He missed it: "M. de Guercy who has inserted [his rose] in his buttonhole was slipping into Borniche's pocket a coin that gallantly he did not want to accept" (3:937). Furious at his client's fickle inquiry, he appears "ruffled, jealous, and dignified" when asked for other recommendations in the neighborhood. His reply is glacial: "I see that you have the heart of an artichoke," standard French for saying someone is fickle. But "l'ivresse du commérage" wins out and from that day forward "M. de Guercy changed the hour of his calling on Mlle de Villeparisis, and never went away without buying *une rose à Borniche*. . . . From that day the Guermantes always had their flowers from *chez Borniche*" (3:938).

Françoise finds both these gentlemen to be quite eligible bachelors and innocently confides to the narrator that "He and the Marquis are the same kind of people" (3:938). The narrator perversely inserts Hugo's "Puisqu'ici bas" that the narrator retains to such effect in the transformed buttonhole-maker's ruffling and pleating arts in *Sodome* (3:28). But it is Françoise, in her inherited *patois*, quite unscientific, but a born naturalist, who offers a Proustian version of the Verlaine-Rimbaud sonnet: "Qui du cul d'un chien s'amoureuse / Il lui paraît une rose [He who becomes enamored of a dog's asshole / It seems to him a rose]" (1:122).

In *Jean Santeuil*, the tension between botany and poetry is embodied in Jean and his best friend, Henri de Réveillon, "whom lovers of Proust," as André Maurois notes in his introduction, "will at once recognize as a first sketch of Saint Loup" (xxiv). Jean describes this specimen of fauna: "Henri, as has already been mentioned, was much interested in botany. The study of that science and the collecting of specimens, satisfied both his love of order, the need to do a lot of walking, and his taste for all that was charming" (261). Jean's own relation with flowers was a furtive sniffing and embrace of mauve tissue:

> As he passed he would draw towards him for a sniff the ravishing top of a lilac bush where the blossom rose from its leaves as from some silent, supple, sweet-smelling garment. He would catch sight of the delicately flowering tip of a young lilac lightly brushed with that indescribable freshness of color which its scent conjures up before the eye with an extraordinary charm of which no amount of thought can ever plumb the secret. Then, making sure that none of the gardeners could see him, he would set his foot upon the carefully tended soil, put his arm around the bush and draw its scented head towards him. But, no matter how deeply he concentrated his senses upon smelling it, he always failed to discover the secret he was seeking . . . (122)

Shortly after this scene worthy of Grandville's *La Vie animée des fleurs* and colored by the prose of Maeterlinck's *Le Double Jardin* and *L'Intelligence des fleurs*, Montesquiou's poetic cut flower displaces Jean's lilac and hawthorn, white and pink: "A memory of the white cream cheese into which, one day, he had crushed his strawberries, so that it flushed" (132). Cryptically and more revealing for concealing, he confesses:

> Gradually, and at a later date, he came to know many flowers. . . . Often when he saw a flower in Monsieur de Montesquiou's buttonhole, and remarked upon it, that consummate connoisseur of Nature could, with a word, set him on fire with passion for the moss-rose, the deep blue of the gentian, and the rich pigmentation of the cineraria. There is something in us that lies more deep than aesthetic appreciation, something that is a part of ourselves, something that is silently given back to us, embedded in a moment of the past that still lives on, intact and fresh, in some forgotten corner. (133)

The boutonniere lies between the uncut but embraced posy and the collected specimen pressed by the botanist. "La digitale dans le vallon [Digitalis in the vale]" is the enigmatic entry in the first sketches of *Sodome et Gomorrhe* and takes its place immediately after the florist's rose has been inserted in a well-made buttonhole. In this brief notation, we are returned to problems of flower picking as they are figured in *Jean Santeuil.* Together on a botanical excursion the poet is momentarily left by his charming botanist: "Alone in the sweet valley he stayed, lost in wonder at the sight of the slender stalk of a violet digitalis, a noiseless brilliant dweller in that spot, with for companions, only a few snapdragons in family groups of four or five" (263). To pluck or not to pluck? Tempted by this poisonous bloom, he oscillates:

> He gazed upon the digitalis. He would have to leave it, and it would never have anything to look at but the three snapdragons, and this little cleft be-

> tween the rocks, never having known a flower on which sea winds had blown, nor a living creature that had been in Italy. . . . He felt a sudden longing to take it away with him. What matter if it meant uprooting it? . . . But he dared not do so. One fears to touch what is so wholly itself. How could he take the digitalis without the snapdragons? (26)

He must share it with Henri: "'I want to show you a lovely digitalis, but you must promise to leave it where it is.' 'Oh! That's not worth taking!' said Henri, 'just *digitalea corrunbea*, I've got one of those already, they're common as dirt'" (263). The lonely, perishable flower has become a type and entered the botanical books: "'I, too,' he reflected, 'have often felt isolated from the rest of the world, just like this poor growing thing'" (263). And with the unpicked flower behind him, he takes Henri's arm affectionately and expresses how very wonderful it is to have him.

The provocative flowers in Montesquiou's buttonhole, like the flowers in the wild plucked by Lucien and his floral poetry, inspire perverse pastiche and cruel portraits despite the aesthetic appreciation of natural beauty and inversion. Françoise's doggerel is but one page before the narrator's recognition of what is behind Legrandin's invitation to sup:

> Like the nosegay that a traveler sends us from some land to which we can no longer go, make me sniff from the far place of your adolescence those spring blooms that I walked amidst so long ago. Come with primavera, with the buttercup, the sedum from which the Balzacian flora makes its bouquets of delectation, come with the Resurrection Day flower, the Easter daisy. (1:124)

This "Saint Sebastian of snobbery" and master of floral discourse has a disturbing *derrière*. Well before his witnessing of Jupien and Charlus in the flesh, the budding poet focuses his gaze on the flowery Legrandin:

> This quick straightening-up caused a spirited, muscular wave to ripple over Legrandin's rump, which I had not thought so fleshy; I don't know why this undulation of pure matter, this totally carnal flood lacking any spirituality, this zealous fawning whipped up a storm, suddenly awakened in my mind the possibility of a Legrandin completely different from the one we knew. (1:123)

Should he go or shouldn't he? His grandmother makes the winning point: "His simple clothes have nothing of that of a man of fashion" (1:125). Like Lucien, this tender bud comes to perfume Legrandin's moonlit terrace and hear him wax poetic:

> For hearts that are wounded, such as mine is, a novelist whom you will read one day claims there is only silence and shadow. . . . In my heart I no longer

> care for anything in the world except a few churches, two or three books, several paintings, and the moonlight when the gentle breeze of your youth brings to me the scent of flower gardens that my old pupils [*prunelles*] can no longer make out. (1:125–26)

In his confrontation with things botanical, he will not pick but will let stand in for him, the foxglove / digitalis / *gants de Notre Dame*, gazing from the narrator's closet of Darwin's natural science at the *gueule de (Saint) Loup*. In French and in English, the snapdragon—*gueule de loup*—is at once flora and fauna in name. The wolf is a flower whose heady lips dare not be embraced. His real *gueule* is unseen, but his scent is left behind in Jupien's flower shop turned brothel. Proust's pastiche of Maeterlinck breaks off in mid-inscription of the incarnation of flora and fauna, never plucked for the slash that is his buttonhole. The singular *fleur démodée* of Maeterlinck is multiplied there: "the *gueules de loup* let slip from their saffron lips the dew drop left them by dawn as a secret to be kept until high noon" (*Les Pastiches* 345).

As Mark Guenette shows, Saint-Loup is the real object of the narrator's desiring mechanism. With the help of Allan Pasco, Guenette outs Saint-Loup as *l'homme rose* that he is, but insists on the fauna, "A Wolf in Swan(n)'s Clothing." Guenette's turn to gay Tchaikovsky's *Swan Lake* distracts Guenette from smelling the flowers that may or may not provoke sickness and death, for Proust's *écoeurement* when confronted with real flowers was real. What Proust was always and already in search of was a flower that would not make him sick. Painter (1:214) recalls Proust's remark about pansies: "The only flower I can smell without getting asthma. . . . It smells like skin. This is the heartsease. Brewer notes that 'it has a host of fancy names; as the "Butterfly flower," "Kiss me quick," a "Kiss behind the garden gate," "Love in idleness," "Pansy," "Three faces under one hood," "Herba Trinitatis"' " (592). For Carlos Herrera, it is a thistle; for Charlus, it is the orchid or belladonna picked; in the end, for the rarely named Marcel growing out of Jean Santeuil, it is the snapdragon that is never plucked.

Jean Genet and Lucien Chardon open and close as names of poets and poetic inversion. Thistle and broom, the prickle and the purgative. In his *Saint Genet*, Sartre writes that "Genet once told him that he loathes flowers: it is not the rose that he likes, but its name" (438). But in his self-administered purge of floral names, Genet as papyrophogenist ingested the paper flowers and regurgitated or shat out his own pot-pourri. In his "Lettre à Léonore Fini," he means to end the history of male flowers: "What do you want? What are you in search of? Flowers, animals, you have already shown them to us *outside* their animal and flower destiny, that is to say their innocence. They all wear the mark of a voluntary crime" (*Fragments* 58). Her invented fauna and copied flora are charming, but Genet would take Fini down a new path. The descendants of floral history and botanical arts and sciences and fabrication (natural history and aesthetics) have left real flesh behind the symbolic tissues of animated flowers named.

Gide knew that already. First in *Paludes* through pastiche, then in conversation with the apprehensive Proust, and sharply in his notes on Proust's animated flowers and floral intelligence, Gide defined the displacement of men loving men in the guise of women loving women: floral displacement of the real gay tissue. Genet asks such figures to be quit of floral reincarnation and copying (Gautier, Balzac, Chardon, Baudelaire, Proust, Genet himself he does not name), to cease her charming marasmic scapegoating, and to let drop the drag of coy criminality begun in Gautier and Grandville, redressed in Baudelaire's blue delphinium, and, in short, to buzz off. One senses the excremental smell of finger flowers and miracle roses behind this appeal. Genet writes: "Criminals, the beaten, men of misfortune roam your world of fabrics and flowers: you recognized them, separated them from the rest, and have paid them special attention" (*Fragments* 54). Now one should be quit of flora or fauna, copied or invented, and turn to the flesh behind the carnation, to what is hidden behind the carnival mask of flora and fauna and papier-mâché. Gay botany? Gay zoology? What Genet has already sensed in this tradition is a new opening, a delicate bursting of a human smile or a human gaze secretly nourished, unseen, a heroic visage: "These tatters, this thorny holly cutting, these animals, these flowers, these sumptuous maladies, these personified passions; I want them to be unreadable except in the break or curve of the lines of the most readable of faces" (*Fragments* 51). Here he no longer equivocates. Confusion is gone. The lily is a lily: "I will explain myself even if it is confusing: the whole mystery of an animal-vegetal intrigue asks for resolution in a purified mien, in a face" (*Fragments* 51).

Faces, flesh, and flowers are distinct in the impish art of Robert Mapplethorpe. Inside the no longer closeted gay floral tradition, he looks out at us. He faces the problem and poses as a witness in the most recent history of floral fascination with eros. The strategy of looking away from the real issue of gay flesh ironically links Proust and Jesse Helms—digitalis and nicotiana, an American plant of the nightshade family. In his "Common Sense" musings, Mitzel does not have Proust and his French predecessors in mind although he puts a face on Greeks, and Michelangelo's fig leaf is not far behind. Mitzel writes:

> It has been reported that Neanderthal Senator Jesse Helms, the highly financed drug-pusher, while reviewing the work of the late Robert Mapplethorpe prior to Jesse's attack on the art world, pored over Mapplethorpe's photos. He flipped through books, looking at the S&M couples, the photos of a leather whip sticking out his asshole, the bevy of black men with their cocks nicely in view, the calla lilies, the roses. . . . Finally, Senator Tobacco slammed the books shut and was heard to mutter in his own quiet rage: "Those disgusting flowers!" (38)

Genêt, Maeterlinck glosses in *L'Intelligence des fleurs*, the Spanish Genet—Derrida notes the importance of the name in his pony ride on the name of the flower—as *spartium junceum*: "It is the most superb representative of this powerful family of Genêts, avid for life, poor, sober, robust; undaunted by place or trial" (56). Genet is not flora or fauna. He wants to be free from floral drag, the "layering of images from 'nature,' each with its own cluster of contradictory, moralizing-cum-scientific appeal to what is finally 'natural,'" undressed by Eve Sedgwick (*Epistemology* 221). History depends upon the human body. Spartan. A new incipit without pansy connections. Just human beings in the flesh. Without animal or floral figmentation. Without the fig leaf. Just a *fico*.

CHAPTER 5

Silence, Secrecy, and Scientific Discourse in the Nineteenth Century

NIGEL E. SMITH

> I cannot avoid soiling my pen with the infamous turpitude of pederasts!
>
> —Fodéré, *Traité de médecine légale* (1813)

> When I conduct [an examination of pederasts] in a prison . . . I never fail to explore successively the anus and the sexual organs.
>
> —Tardieu, *Etude médico-légale sur les attentats aux moeurs* (1857)

Before the likes of Benkert, Freud, Westphal, and Krafft-Ebbing transformed the homosexual into "a species," and before "homosexuality began to speak in its own behalf, to demand that its legitimacy or 'naturality' be acknowledged" (Foucault, *Sexuality* 1:101), there was the pederast. According to the majority of pseudo-scientific texts that discussed him during the nineteenth century, the pederast was not a species in his own right; he was a freak, an aberration, a criminal. His acts constituted a nonprocreative sexual anomaly that ranked alongside masturbation, bestiality, and prostitution as a threat to France's moral, political, and economic welfare.

Certain scholars have read the wealth of nineteenth-century discourses that purported to document, describe, and define pederasty as representations of institutionalized homophobia and of cultural myths that sustained empowering, heterosexist ideologies and that served to suppress homosexuality in the name of bourgeois morality and *pudeur*. In *La Bourgeoisie, le sexe et l'honneur*, Jean-Paul Aron and Roger Kempf argue convincingly that the suppression of homosexuality during the second half of the century reflected "the implementation of a nosology of transgression" (61) and "the birth of a sexual stigmatology" destined to safeguard not only public morality but also, by extension, the political and economic stability of the Second Empire, since "in order to dominate nature and submit it to the interests of emerging capitalism, it is important to eradicate uncertainty, the source of insecurity" (59). Nature was controlled, and uncertainty checked, by explaining everything scientifically and by making sure that everything and everyone fell neatly into some category.

Pierre Hahn also has remarked that the beginning of "la chasse aux pédérastes" (*Nos ancêtres* 41), which he places in the 1850's, along with an alarming spread of syphilis and a vehement antimasturbatory campaign, coincided with the apogee of Napoleon III's authority (42) and with the origins of modern homosexuality. According to these arguments, the explosion of discourses about pederasty emerges as a means to suppress and repress the act of pederasty and those who practiced it.

Michel Foucault, of course, in the first volume of *The History of Sexuality*, rejects or at least reevaluates such "repressive hypotheses," preferring instead to examine the relationship of certain realities, such as sexuality, to knowledge, power, and the creation of the subject, as Jean-Manuel de Queiroz notes in "Foucault: The Imaginary Sex" (in Mendès-Leite 43). Although Foucault discusses the "invention" of homosexuality, stating that during the nineteenth century the homosexual "became a personage, a past, a case history, and a childhood, in addition to being a type of life, a life form, and a morphology, with an indiscreet anatomy and possibly a mysterious physiology" (43), he rarely singles out homosexuality, but treats it "as an aspect or an inner part of a larger whole" (de Queiroz in Mendès-Leite 42). He asserts that during the nineteenth century "sex was driven out of hiding and constrained to lead a discursive existence" (33) that nonetheless exploited it as "the secret" (35); and he goes on to describe the nineteenth-century discourse on sex and sexuality as "a screen-discourse, a dispersion-avoidance . . . [that] never ceased to hide the thing it was speaking about" (53). Silence and secrecy are central to the relationship between power and sex, according to Foucault. Secrecy, of course, implies knowledge, and knowledge in turn implies power. A fundamental link between language and power lies in the tendency of authors of discourses on sex and sexuality to construct their own truths about the subject. The scientists selected, exaggerated, and even falsified their medical observations in order better to "prove" that pederasty constituted a dangerous deviation from the heterosexual norm, and in order to assert their power.

Dominique Fernandez concurs that the nineteenth-century homosexual represented a potentially explosive political force and a threat to the established power structure (iv), but he introduces the possibility of a different, and very intriguing, dynamic operating in certain discourses. In his brief preface to a new edition of François Carlier's *La Prostitution anti-*

physique (1887) and Ambroise Tardieu's *La Pédérastie* (1857) Fernandez suggests that the former hides "a curiosity, even a secret attraction of which even the author may have been unaware" (ii). Of the latter he asks rather tentatively, "Can we assume that such excessive anathema served as a shield against a vigorously repressed attraction?" (vi). As Guy Hocquenghem wrote in the introduction to *Homosexual Desire*, "desire is no more homosexual than heterosexual. Desire emerges in multiple form, whose components are only divisible *a posteriori* according to how we manipulate it" (50). He described also the complex knot of dread and desire evoked by a homosexual fantasy that is "more obscene than any other and at that same time more exciting" (50). So we can deny desire and we can run from it, but we cannot control it. As much as authors of nineteenth-century discourses claimed to be repulsed by pederasts and by their acts, I believe, with Fernandez, that certain texts bear the imprint of desire and that they reveal an incongruous alliance of anathema and attraction. In the texts I have chosen to examine there emerge discursive practices that, while serving ostensibly as assertions of power and as showcases of bourgeois morality, reveal also subjects apparently desirous of the homosexual object, or at least of the homosexual discourse.

Concentrating on Ambroise Tardieu's landmark *Etude médico-légale sur les attentats aux moeurs* (1857), on the definition of pederasty in Pierre Larousse's *Grand dictionnaire universel du XIXe siècle* (1866–79), and on François Carlier's *La Prostitution antiphysique* (1887), I shall first situate the texts within a context of discursive development and show that they can indeed be read as extensions of a bourgeois endeavor to suppress pederasty and so to protect society from the most dreadful ignominy. I do not seek, though, simply to redefine or to reevaluate the cultural construction of homosexuality and its evil twin, homophobia. By no stretch of the modern imagination can these discourses not be labeled homophobic, but such terminololgy and such taxonomies (hetero/homo) belong primarily to our own era, not to the France of the 1800's. I prefer to trace the development of a discourse on male homosexuality in order to reveal that subsumed within a discourse of secrecy, knowledge, power, and fear there exists also a discourse of desire. I shall look beyond the surface document and read the texts as expressions of an uncertain teratological, perhaps even sexual, attraction on the part of the "scientists." In so doing, I shall point out limitations in Foucault's discussion of the screen-discourse and demonstrate, in response to more recent critical tendencies, that not all nineteenth-century scientific discourses on homosexuality can be reduced to a simple formula that pits heterosexuality/homophobia against homosexuality and that emphasizes political correctness at the expense of cultural politics and textual analysis.

Prior to the publication in 1857 of Tardieu's *Etude médico-légale sur les attentats aux moeurs*, in which the author fetishistically reduced the pederast to a purely sexual being with either, if he was "active," a corkscrew-shaped penis or, if he was "passive," a funnel-like anus into which the doctor had to insert his finger to verify the form, discourses offered little information about the subject at hand, tending to favor an attitude of moral outrage over clinical detachment (Nye, "Sex" 169). In certain later texts, descriptions of behavior gave way to methodical studies of anatomy and physiology. However, the knowledge—or *scientia*—that all these works present is a pseudo-science based not only on observation and experiment, as their authors would have us believe, but also on speculation, judgment, and selectivity. The texts reveal several modalities of the screen-discourse, including discourses of deprecation, of avoidance, of reluctance, and of disguise, and they force us to ask just what is being screened. Is it pederasty or some other agenda that the authors hide from our view? Just as today, according to Leo Bersani, we learn from the popular press coverage of AIDS more about "heterosexual anxieties" than about AIDS research itself, when reading nineteenth-century discourses on pederasty we can learn as much about the authors' fears and desires as about the subject of their discussion ("Rectum" 202).

The deprecation-discourse makes no attempt to explain pederasty, only to condemn it. Senancour, for example, in a section of *De l'amour, considéré dans les lois réelles et dans les formes sociales de l'union des sexes* (1806) entitled "Jouissances," effectively dehumanizes homosexuals, stating that "sexual pleasure between members of the same sex is even more unnatural than bestiality. Such a fruitless union is as sterile as it is depraved" (quoted in Courrosse 234).

The avoidance-discourse does little more than acknowledge the existence of pederasty. Friedländer, in *De l'Education physique des hommes* (1815), conceded that the acts of pederasts constituted "horrors than my pen refuses to write" (Aron and Kempf, *Bourgeoisie* 50); and throughout the century authors of nonmedical texts appeared more reluctant still to describe this unnatural vice. Littré limits the "definition" of pederasty in his *Dictionnaire de la langue française* (1846–72) to three words: "Vice against nature" (5:1616). The same three words appeared in the *Dictionnaire de l'Académie Française* (2:314);[1] and while Hatzfeld and Darmesteter

1. My source is the eighth edition of the dictionary (1932). However, "pédérastie" was first admitted to the dictionary in its 1762 edition.

stretched their definition in the *Dictionnaire générale de la langue française* (1871–88) to five words—"Depraved love of young boys" (2:1702)—clearly they still offered no context or description. The entry "Pédéraste" offers no illumination: "One who practices pederasty." Proudhon claimed in his voluminous *De la Justice* (1860) that having read Tardieu's essay on pederasty, he realized that "any quotation is impossible," such commentary being "forbidden to the philosopher" (1920). Foucault's arguments apply perfectly to these edited scientific discourses that suggest knowledge of a secret and thus accord power to their authors. The keeper of the secret holds power over two distinct groups: the pederast whose own secret has been discovered; and the reader who desires a share of the author's knowledge and thus of his power. Again, power resides in language and in the ability to produce subjective truth, this time through censorship, one of the principal features in Foucault's "analytics" of power. Censorship for Foucault "links the inexistent, the illicit, and the inexpressible in such a way that each is at the same time the principle and the effect of the others" (*Sexuality* 1:84). Censorship effectively expels pederasty from reality by silencing it, and vice versa.

Fodéré preferred the reluctance-discourse. He lamented the necessity of discussing pederasty but felt it his moral duty to protect the social order from "the infamous turpitude of pederasts." Similarly, the author of an essay on prison dormitories in the *Gazette des Tribunaux* (March 23, 1836) expressed his indignation at having to report such horrors: "It is not without hesitation that we are publishing our opinion on this subject: a feeling of disgust held us back, and we feared that our readers would share this sentiment" (Aron and Kempf, *Bourgeoisie* 50–51). But, in the interest of social order, he discussed it anyway. Fourier-Pescay reluctantly described sodomy in Panckoucke's *Dictionnaire des sciences médicales* (1819), stating at the end of his article that "I have just completed a most unpleasant task, but one that is indispensable in a work such as this"; and he concluded, victoriously, that his "pen remained chaste" (Aron and Kempf, *Bourgeoisie* 50). Reydellet, in his entry "Pédérastie" in the same dictionary, maintains a tone of indignation, but like many others offers as justification the need to reveal to his public the dangers of same-sex unions. He did, however, wish to maintain some standard of propriety: "Although it is necessary to uncover this vice in all its ugliness, it is necessary also that the means employed not offend public morality; there are, in this respect, boundaries that no honest man should overstep, however praiseworthy his intentions" (quoted in Hahn 32).

What I call the disguise-discourse provided yet another means to protect the sensibility and the morality of readers, and, we can assume, to flaunt knowledge of the secret and thus assert power. This method involved the attempted concealment rather than the complete avoidance of the subject of discussion. The veil of propriety that authors sought to drape over their discourse took several forms, the most striking being the use of Latin within their otherwise French texts. A certain Dr. Moll, mentioned by Aron and Kempf (57), while discussing an intriguing text entitled "Les règlements d'un fellateur pour son amant," claimed to be so disgusted by what he read that he felt obliged to cite the text in Latin, ostensibly in order to protect his readers and to ensure that his pen remained chaste, but more likely as a means of institutionalizing the act being described by resorting to the classical language of science. But what better way to arouse the curiosity of one's readers than to offer an account of sex between men, all the more titillating for its being veiled? As Aron and Kempf have remarked with reference to a text that Tardieu cites in Latin, "Far from preventing reading, the Latin here dramatizes it" (*Bourgeoisie* 58). The same can be said of Moll's text. Although no French words appear, most of the words designating sexual organs or sexual functions are clear cognates: "erectionem," "membrum," "testiculos," "anum," "ejaculationem" (quoted in Aron and Kempf 57). Thus even a reader not schooled in Latin—and surely most readers of medical treatises would know some Latin—could grasp the meaning of the passage. In other words, the Latin text hides little if anything, but rather stresses the alterity of the acts described. The interjection of Latin phrases creates a rupture in the flow of the French text and so draws our attention to the passage. Moll's endeavor to expel nonprocreative forms of sexuality from reality by dissociating the word and the act, by distancing the sign from its referent, clearly failed. His use of Latin suggests something that we are not supposed to see, a forbidden fruit, knowledge of which becomes all the more desirable for its interdiction.

The tide turned with Ambroise Tardieu, "Professeur agrégé à la Faculté de médecine de Paris, Médecin à l'hôpital La Riboisière, Membre du Comité consultatif d'hygiène publique." The publication of his *Etude médico-légale sur les attentats aux moeurs* (1857) heralded a new chapter in the nineteenth-century discourse on pederasty, and the unnatural vice was dragged screaming out of the closet. Silence, one could say, became a mute issue for Tardieu, and his was the most extensive study to date of pederasts and their acts. The work's title at once flaunts its scientificity—*Etude médico-légale*—and announces its judgmental social agenda—*sur les attentats aux moeurs.* What first strikes the reader of the *Etude* is Tardieu's attention to detail. The first edition of the work contained 176 pages, the sixth and seventh, published in 1873 and 1878, stretched to over 300 pages. Within these 300 pages Tardieu offers a systematic study of behavior based upon observation after observation. That there were six new editions in the space of twenty years (1858–78) attests to its popularity and has led Hahn to conclude that the work was a "bestseller" of its time (68).

All the aforementioned modalities appear in Tardieu's work except the avoidance-discourse. The *médecin-légiste* deprecates his subjects at every turn and alongside "scientific" descriptions and explanations offers plenty of judgments, moral, legal, or otherwise. He speaks still of "unnatural relationships," of "these infamous practices," of "a real and unhealthy perversion of moral faculties" (24); he claims to be ashamed at having to discuss certain sexual acts; and, as already noted, he made occasional efforts to disguise his text.

Tardieu concentrates exclusively on effeminate pederasts "to whom the name *tante* applies" (29) in his description of outward appearance and claims that "[their] character is often evident in their outward appearance, in their dress, in their gait and in their tastes, which in some way reflect the unnatural perversion of their sexual preferences" (29). By describing only the limp-wristed, foppish homosexual he sustains and promulgates a constructed stereotypical image of the entire homosexual community. His portrait of the typical *tante* is a caricature with its avalanche of details, and the admission at the beginning of the passage that "this is not always the case" (29) is easily forgotten:

> Tightly curled hair, powdered complexion, open collar, waist pulled in tight so as to accentuate the shape, fingers, ears and chest covered in jewelry, the odor of heavy perfumes emanating from the whole body, and in the hand a handkerchief, some flowers, or a piece of embroidery: such is the strange, repugnant, and, it has to be said, suspect physiology that betrays pederasts. (29–30)

This image, coming early in the text, establishes the tone for the entire study even though it represents only one kind of pederast, the kind that Michael Bronski, in reference to the 1970's, has described as "the visible tip of the iceberg of an entire culture's repressed fears and desires" (3). Tardieu apparently sought to inspire ridicule and disdain with his fearful portrait in which exceptions become the norm. He went to great lengths to find isolated examples that he could then claim to be representative of all pederasts: "It is to no avail that I have examined different parts of the bodies of well-known pederasts in the hope of finding a particular tattoo, like those we find so often among prostitutes" (30). In this instance, in spite of his "observations spéciales" (30), the search proved futile. However, in reporting that he has nothing to report, Tardieu has nonetheless managed to equate homosexuality with crime and prostitution.

In his provocative analysis of responses to AIDS in "Is the Rectum a Grave?," Bersani draws the parallel between the public discourse about twentieth-century gay men and representations of nineteenth-century female prostitutes: "The realities of syphilis in the nineteenth century and of AIDS today 'legitimate' a fantasy of female sexuality as intrinsically diseased; and promiscuity in this fantasy, far from merely increasing the risk of infection, is the *sign of infection.* Women and gay men spread their legs with an unquenchable appetite for destruction" (211). The equation of homosexuality and prostitution is clearly not a new one. According to Tardieu, the homosexual body was comparable to that of the prostitute and indeed of women in general, since both represented the site of insatiable desire and of disease. The scourge of the pederast was not AIDS, of course, but rather a seemingly endless number of contagions and physical deformations that labeled him as a sexual pervert. The catalogue of maladies that Tardieu enumerates suggests to the reader what Foucault calls "an imaginary dynasty of evils destined to be passed on for generations" and which results in a "pornography of the morbid" (*Sexuality* 1:53–54). In other words, he justified ostensibly his attention to gruesome detail by insisting upon the dangers of same-sex unions. Furthermore, he employs a phallocentric discourse to stress the heterosexist categorization of sex partners into two distinct groups: passive and active, submissive and dominant, female and male.

Among the inevitable consequences of passive pederasty listed in "Des troubles généraux de la santé chez les pédérastes," we find the following: "redness, excoriation, painful burning of the anus, difficulty in walking . . . fissures, deep tears, . . . extravasation of the blood, and . . . swelling of the mucous membrane and underlying cell tissue" (34). Such are some of the signs of a recent sexual encounter. Prolonged sexual activity results in an entirely new series of notable characteristics, all of which Tardieu discusses in some detail:

> Typical signs of passive pederasty . . . are excessive development of the buttocks, the infundibuliform deformation of the anus, the relaxing of the sphincter, the smoothing of skin-folds, crests and caruncles around the anus, extreme distension of the anal orifice, incontinence, ulcerations, hemorrhoids, fistula, rectal blennorrhea, syphilis, foreign bodies introduced into the anus. (35)

He mentions also strange conformations of the mouth observed in two—just two—pederasts: "A crooked mouth, very short teeth, thick, inverted and deformed lips, completely in keeping with the infamous usage to which they are put" (44). If we have not been convinced by this litany of anal ills and disfigurations that the pederast is some kind of freak, Tardieu's scrutiny of the penis of active sexual partners leaves no doubt. He describes the active pederast as having a penis of excessive dimensions—either excessively small or excessively large, but never "normal." He likens the small pederastic penis to that of a dog—"le canum more"—and so, like Senancour, dehumanizes his subject. The bestial analogy continues in the vivid description of voluminous organs: "The head of the penis, tightly constricted at the base, is sometimes excessively elongated, giving it the appearance of the muzzle of certain animals" (48). Such disfigurements, Tardieu tells us, are the inevitable result of anal penetration. Either they match perfectly "the infundibuliform disposition of the anus onto which they mold themselves"; or they offer demonstrable evidence of "the resistance of the anal orifice proportionate to the size of the member," which necessitates on the part of the penetrator's penis "a screw-like or corkscrew-like movement" (48). Such forced classifications (passive/active, human/animal, etc.) and the discourse used to describe them (and so to define the pederast) allow Tardieu to create artificial codifications that serve his own ends and that thus accord him limitless knowledge and, subsequently, limitless power over his subject and over his reader.

However, this insistence on the sexual act and the obvious fascination with male sexual organs, besides revealing a desire to instill fear in unsuspecting readers and to stress physical difference, suggests also a curious voyeuristic attraction on Tardieu's part. He spent an inordinate amount of time observing his subjects, a point he makes frequently throughout his text: "I have observed a hundred times . . . "; "I searched in vain"; "I have noted quite a number of times" (30); "I have been able to judge for myself . . . "; "I recognized only too well . . . "; "I have seen some" (31); "I came across a curious example"; "I have often noted"; "I have seen . . . " (35); "For several years I have examined . . . " (47); and so on. Tardieu spent a lot of time examining penises and exploring anuses to determine whether they displayed the all-telling "twisted penis" or the corresponding "infundibuliform deformation." Indeed, all his arguments are based on examinations of these two body parts. The pederast is recognized and defined by his penis or his anus; he is fetishistically dismembered and reduced to a synecdochic representation of his sexual apparatus in much the same way as women were defined by their reproductive organs. Pederasty, in turn, is reduced to a sexual act. He even informs us in "De la manière de procéder à l'examen des pédérastes," that when examining incarcerated pederasts he did not reveal to his subject the object of his visit. He simply ordered the prisoner to undress, "and very often, without further ado, he adopts spontaneously the position that is most favorable to my inspection" (52). This action and the subsequent reaction lead me first to believe that Tardieu enjoyed watching men take their clothes off, and second, that they were used to doing it for prison officials. Why else would the *médecin-légiste* remain silent about the purpose of his visit? He claims, after all, that most prisoners offered no resistance to examination. His method also suggests that he went beyond the call of duty. He certainly went beyond observation, not just examining but *exploring* his subjects' genitalia: "I never fail to explore successively the anus and the sexual organs" (52–53). He knew too how to encourage a reluctant subject to open up, so to speak: "all you have to do is make them quickly change position, or have them kneel on the edge of a chair in an awkward position, or simply prolong the examination so as to tire the contracted muscles" (53). Finally, in cases where the famous "infundibuliform deformation" is only slightly noticeable or not apparent at all, "the introduction of the finger is necessary" (53). The doctor here adopts the dominant, active, male role as he penetrates his "patient" in the name of science.

Towards the end of the text we find the traditional disclaimer:

> The aim of this long and difficult study, in which I have avoided neither the image of moral degradation, nor the most distasteful aspects of the physical deformations caused by pederasty, has been simply to give the forensic doctor the means to recognize pederasts by certain signs, and to allow him to resolve with more certainty and authority than has hitherto been possible, the questions asked of him by the courts in order that they might pursue and eradicate, if that is possible, this shameful vice. (51)

The vehemence and determination of the disclaimer and its insistence on the practical, legal value of the study suggest to me that there is at work here more than science, more than heterosexist ideologies, more than the thirst for power and knowledge. An examination of Tardieu's text reveals limitations in Foucault's theory of the screen-discourse and adds new meaning to the notion of repression as a prohibitive-generative agent. There is still a secret, but a different one. The new secret is desire; not necessarily a closeted desire to engage in homosexual acts, although this is possible, but the desire to speak about pederasty, to commit it to discourse.

Tardieu's text became a primary source for many discussions of pederasty that followed, including the definition in Larousse's *Grand dictionnaire universel du XIXe siècle*, which, at first glance, seems like just another example of the deprecation-discourse or the avoidance-discourse favored by previous lexicographers. The article begins with the following alarming, but now familiar statement: "Vice against nature, shameful love of a man for a young boy, or between men" (12:491); and the euphemisms keep on coming, leading us to wonder what the author was afraid of that his comments be so defamatory. In a relatively short essay (short compared to Tardieu's text, but long compared to other dictionary entries) the author refers to the unnatural vice as "infamous vice," "the most shameful of vices," "infamous pleasure," "disturbed love," "this terrible contagion," "the most infamous turpitude," "this degrading vice," "these abominable vices," "these horrifying passions," "these monstrous unions," and "this detestable penchant." And he asks: "With all its disgusting and ignominious horrors, how is pederasty possible in an advanced civilization such as ours?" (12:491).

What is perhaps most disturbing to the modern reader about the comments, besides the obvious, is the context within which they appear; that is to say, in a dictionary. When we leaf through the pages of a dictionary, we usually hope to find the definition of a word, or perhaps to verify its etymology, its pronunciation, or its spelling. Once we have located the desired entry, we tend to accept readily what we read. Dictionaries, as supposedly impartial, scientific documents, have that kind of authority over us. Larousse apparently concurred and claimed in one of the epigraphs chosen for his 21,000-page opus that the *Grand dictionnaire*, in keeping with the spirit of *L'Encyclopédie*, represented "the truth, the whole truth, and nothing but the truth." The so-called truth that we encounter in Larousse's work is not, as its title would suggest, "universal"—rather, it is socially, racially, politically, and sexually exclusive. The dictionary is the work of an educated, European, republican, more than likely heterosexual male. Subsequently, the morality and ideologies reflected in its pages are those of an educated, European, republican, more than likely heterosexual male. The dictionary thus contributes to the perpetuation of cultural myths that serve educated, European, republican, more than likely heterosexual males by sustaining the ideological positions of those same empowered individuals.

To what extent, then, did the author of the dictionary entry "Pédérastie" seek to conceal sex, specifically homosexual sex, and to exploit it as the secret? Like Tardieu, he presents facts and descriptions as undeniable truths that portray pederasty as a disgusting, self-serving lifestyle associated often with immorality, crime, and prostitution. Taking the effeminate pederast as the norm, as did Tardieu, Larousse equates homosexuals with women by insisting upon their supposed obsession with physical appearance: "Hairstyle and dress constitute one of the most constant preoccupations of pederasts" (12:491). The insistence on vice, degradation, and genitalia throughout the essay reduces homosexuality to a sexual act, and there is no suggestion of the possibility of love between two men, only lust. The emphasis on hedonistic sexuality again implies a parallel with women, since Larousse considered women oversexed and lascivious also. The most vigorous of men, he tells us (with a hint of pride, perhaps), cannot manage more than seven or eight ejaculations per night. (They may have more erections, but without emission of semen!) Having thus produced a complex of sexual inadequacy among many a nineteenth-century male, he compares male and female prowess, comparing all women to Messalina, and concluding scientifically that "on average, in this exercise, a woman is worth two and a half men" (8:202–3). And while we perhaps like to think that times have changed, Bersani cites examples that show the contrary. Speaking of homosexual males, Professor Opendra Narayan of the Johns Hopkins Medical School is quoted as stating that "these people have sex twenty to thirty times a night" ("Rectum" 197); and Justice Richard Wallach of the New York State Supreme Court said that gay bathhouses promote "the orgiastic behavior of multiple partners, one after the other, where in five minutes you can have five contacts" ("Rectum" 199). If such supermen do indeed exist, clearly they represent the same kind of minority as Messalina represents in relation to all nineteenth-century women. Exceptions again are used to categorize entire groups of human beings, and to suggest a dangerously promiscuous substratum of society.

In an attempt to ascertain the causes of homosexuality, Larousse looks to the ancient Greeks and to their acceptance of same-sex relationships. However, rather than attribute such relationships to a cult of beauty or to an expression of natural desires, he blames these "libidinous" acts on the hot climate of Greece, further strengthening the homosexual-as-woman equation since women too, according to the entry "Femme," succumb easily to the effects of heat: "The elevated temperatures of hot countries increase the voluptuous desires of the female sex, and it is said that at Patani, their desires are so imperious that men are forced to wear a kind of belt to protect themselves against the audacious enterprises of the opposite sex" (203). This observation contradicts the claim in "Pédérastie" that "in extremely hot countries, we see violent passions, and yet women there have a harder time meeting men" (12:491). So according to one text men have to protect themselves with chastity belts against oversexed women; according to the other, women cannot meet men because they have all turned queer. In spite of such incongruities, the outrageous claims of both texts serve to ostracize those who are different, that is, not male or not straight.

It appears initially that Foucault's arguments apply to the discourse of the *Grand dictionnaire*, which appears to represent another instance of the avoidance-discourse. Larousse claims, for example, that certain homosexuals and their acts are so abhorrent as to be unmentionable: "kinds of pederasts that we dare not even make known" (12:491). The author of "Pédérastie" does refer his readers to works, notably Tardieu's, in which we can find descriptions of those unspeakable acts. Furthermore, he reiterates in gruesome detail Tardieu's descriptions of the physical consequences and visible signs of anal intercourse between men. So, subsumed within the harsh criticism and misguided conclusions, there again emerges a fascination with homosexuality that suggests on its author's part a perverse kind of pleasure not only in condemning it but also in describing it. On the one hand, homosexuality is presented as a crime and a sin, as a fearful anomaly of human (hetero-)sexual behavior; on the other hand it inspires fascination and even desire: a desire to speak of it, and so to reveal and to share its secrets, *the* secret. By telling us what he is not going to tell us, by telling us that he has a secret, the author of the entry does not condemn such acts to concealment and silence. On the contrary, he instills a curiosity in us, a desire for knowledge of what is not supposed to be known. Although Larousse's text presents a screen-discourse of sorts, the screen is a somewhat diaphanous one. He presents a veiled discourse that allows enough of what lies behind it to show through to capture our attention and arouse our curiosity and our desire for knowledge, not just our fears.

Like Larousse, François Carlier, head of the dreaded *brigades des moeurs* in Paris from 1850 to 1870, was familiar with Tardieu's work and refers to it occasionally in *La Prostitution antiphysique*. Any discussion of this text would be incomplete without a brief consideration of its title. The association of homosexuality with prostitution has already been mentioned, and Carlier's choice of title serves to strengthen the equation. His text does not deal exclusively with male prostitutes, simply with men who had sex with men. Prostitution and homosexuality were both perceived as expressions of wanton lust, and any notion of affection on the part of the pederast, or of economic necessity on the part of the prostitute, was not considered. Both fell outside the range of "normal," procreative sexuality; both were seen as threats to society; both were thus designated by the same sign. As Carlier stated, "these two things are . . . two parts of a whole" (88).

Given the continued insistence on this equation, it is not surprising that the pederast continued to be described as a feminized man; and Carlier offers a description of the attire and demeanor of the average pederast that, while very similar to Tardieu's, is even more detailed:

> Wearing tight, brightly colored trousers, a small jacket that goes no further than the small of the back, or tight-waisted clothes that accentuate the shape, a Colin tie, all of an uncertain cleanliness, ears and fingers bedecked with fake jewels, curly-haired, made-up faces, rouge on the cheeks, a handkerchief in hand, they stroll nonchalantly for hours on end, leaving behind themselves trails of musk or patchouli, holding hands, chatting quietly, emitting shrill bursts of laughter, stopping in front of the best-lighted shop fronts, flashing from one side and then the other their provocative smiles. (144)

The pederast, according to nineteenth-century thinking, fell somewhere between maleness and femaleness and was judged by how he differed from those norms. Discourses tended therefore to feminize the pederast (and to masculinize the lesbian or tribade) because the bipolar, heterosexist model was the only known frame of reference. Of course, as Brigitte Lhomond has pointed out in "Between Man and Woman: The Character of the Lesbian," "this conceptualization implies also a reinforcement of the two poles of categorisation" (in Mendès-Leite 63) and so stresses the alterity of any "intermediate" type while strengthening the "normalcy" of the writing subject. Lauvergne, in *Les Forçats considérés sous le rapport physiologique, moral et intellectuel* (1844) described the faces of passive homosexuals as "sickly, soft, feminine with their moist eyes"; his voice is "weak" and "not unlike that of a castrato," his gaze "dull and lacking virility" (Hahn 34). In other words, he was not a man at all, but rather a feminized being emasculated by the doctor's manipulation of language.

Carlier's portrait is slightly more ambiguous. The association with women is clear, but if we lift the interjected phrase "all of an uncertain cleanliness" and the adjectives "fake" and "shrill" there is little to suggest that Carlier is criticizing this dress and comportment. The insistence on body-hugging outfits and the inclusion of adjectives such as "nonchalant" and especially "provocative" would even suggest the contrary. And, after all, if heterosexual men desire women, and pederasts resemble women, we arrive at the inevitable conclusion that heterosexual men may also desire pederasts. Of course, within a strictly defined heterosexist cultural context, such desire on the part of a heterosexual male could never be admitted, and more than likely would not even be recognized as such.

We find, though, ambiguous statements throughout *La Prostitution antiphysique* that are suggestive of this imprint of desire. What are we to make, for example, of Carlier's use in his descriptions of the impersonal pronoun "on"? The pronoun, of course, is far more ambiguous than its English equivalent "one." "Everywhere that one/they/we meet, one/they/we eye each other up and down, one/they/we exchange a few offensive words" (117); or better yet: "One/they/we give a little sign . . . one/they/we head for a dark and deserted spot . . . one/they/we accost each other" (125). On the one hand, the pronoun (*on* = *ils*) appears pejorative, as a means to deprecate and infantilize pederasts and to distance the writing subject from the group he is describing. On the other hand, if we read the pronoun as *on* = *nous*, Carlier appears, perhaps inadvertently but very tellingly, to include himself in the group. He informs us also that in Paris between 1860 and 1870 "police headquarters . . . dealt with 6,342 pederasts" (203). This figure is quite remarkable in itself—it works out to about 1.7 pederasts a day for ten years! And this at a time when pederasty, theoretically, at least, was not illegal—but Carlier explains that the actual number of pederasts in Paris was far greater because "[those] who had the talent to hide themselves carefully, the luck not to be denounced and the prudence not to get arrested are not included here" (202). Is this a lament or a celebration? Carlier's choice of words again results in an ambiguous polysemy; and when he asserts that "legislation is powerless against human passions," he accords pederasty the status of a human emotion, not of some bestial crime against nature, as was the case in many earlier texts. Furthermore, he prefigures the discourse of the psychoanalysts by describing homosexuality as "a kind of madness," "a mental illness," "an erotic madness" (217, 220). A justification of pederasty? It certainly would not be long before "the love that dare not speak its name" became "the neurosis that cannot shut up" (Courousse 18). Carlier's ambiguous comments are hardly reassuring to our twentieth-century sensibility, but, whatever the author's intent, they appear quite revolutionary within their nineteenth-century context.

Carlier's work is less scientific and less systematic than that of Tardieu or Larousse. It is a kind of memoir of his days as police chief, in which anecdotes take precedence over scientific inquiry. What the texts do have in common, however, is their insistence on categorization and classification, and on description and observation: the "sovereignty of the gaze" that Foucault discussed at length in *The Birth of the Clinic*. The objectives and tone also appear the same: "We have done violence to our disgust, and we have completed our work in the interest of public safety" (88); and just as Tardieu insisted throughout his work on the scientific and moral value of his observations, Carlier also emphasizes the practical application of his text. He describes the French army as a hotbed of homosexuality, for example, but is quick to point out that "We would have kept silent about this if we had not thought that our revelations might interest the leaders of our army" (188). (Just why the higher ranks would be immune to homosexual desire, especially since presumably they were once a part of the lower ranks, is not clear.) Similarly, he only discusses prostitution in order to "call to the legislator's attention a vice that should be a crime, since it endangers morality and public safety" (202). This insistence on explaining why he has chosen to discuss such a subject reveals a fear that readers might reach the wrong conclusions and assume that the subject interests the author for reasons other than the desire to protect society. It implies also that he does in fact have something to hide. Carlier's knowledge of the homosexual community is no less startling than Tardieu's knowledge of the homosexual body. He recounts the exploits of several famous homosexuals; he describes in detail their social activities and reports their conversations; he knows where male prostitutes plied their trade and the secret signs they use to attract customers; he is familiar with all the names used to designate various kinds of pederasts; and so on.

So was Carlier, along with Tardieu and Larousse, a repressed homosexual? Fernandez has stated that "none expresses as much severity toward homosexuals or brandishes as high the standard of repression as he who is not sure about himself and who harbors in himself those tendencies that he condemns in others" (vii). Stallybrass and White also have suggested that "disgust always bears the imprint of desire" and that objects of disgust "return as the object of nostalgia, longing and fascination" (*Politics and Poetics* 191; quoted in Dollimore 247). However, since repression and homosexuality as we understand them had not yet been "invented," or at least were not an accepted part of the nineteenth-century lexicon, we find ourselves falling into the trap of anachronism. David Halperin has proposed that instead of attempting to describe the history of sexuality, we should perhaps "analyze the cultural poetics of desire"; that is, "the processes whereby sexual desires are constructed, mass-produced, and distributed among the various members of human living-groups" (in Abelove et al. 426). Tardieu, Larousse, and Carlier, perhaps in spite of themselves, constructed, distributed, and represented desire in their works. It is a veiled desire, to be sure, and a desire that battles against disgust and deprecation and hides within them, surfacing only occasionally. I believe, though, that it is a real desire. Tardieu examined his pederasts a little too closely; Larousse read Tardieu's text a little too carefully; and Carlier did both. By reading these nonliterary texts, as opposed to accepting them as documents, we uncover subtexts that lead us beyond anathema to attraction. Sexual attraction is tied up in textual attraction, in the desire to speak of pederasty. If we look closely enough at their screen-discourses, we can see right through the fear, the disgust, the deprecation, and the thirst for power, and discover their own secrets.

Whether or not we accept that homosexuality was a nineteenth-century cultural construction is not the point here. Before the integration of the word "homosexuality" into discourse, men were having sex with men and presumably falling in love with each other. Carlier's *La Prostitution antiphysique* reveals also that there was indeed in France, and in the whole of Europe, at least during his term as head of the *brigade des moeurs*, a distinct queer subculture with its own language and its own dress codes. To reduce nineteenth-century discourses on pederasty to expressions of repression is, I believe, to oversimplify an extremely complex issue. On the other hand, to dismiss the existence of such repression and to group discourses on homosexuality with all other discourses on sexuality, as does Foucault, at least in the first volume of *The History of Sexuality*, is also reductive. The texts I have read, and the way in which I have read them, reveal that complex knot of dread and desire of which Hocquenghem spoke: "Every effort to isolate, explain, reduce the contaminated homosexual simply helps to place him at the centre of waking dreams. . . . Difference may breed security, but the mere word 'pederast' turns out to be strangely seductive" (*Desire* 52). What has been read as repression hides also an expression of desire. Just as homosexuality cannot be reduced to a symbol of repression, homophobia cannot be dismissed as the vehicle of that repression. Within their nineteenth-century context, both emerge as multireferential signs suggestive of silent fears and secret fantasies.

CHAPTER 6

Histoires d'inversion: Novelizing Homosexuality at the Fin de Siècle

VERNON A. ROSARIO

Monsieur Emile Zola, Paris

> It is to you, Monsieur, who are the greatest novelist of our time and who, with the eye of the savant and the artist, capture and paint so powerfully *all* the failings, all the shame, all the ills that afflict humanity that I send these *human documents* so cherished by the cultivated people of our age.
>
> This confession, which no spiritual advisor has ever learned from my lips, will reveal to you a frightful illness of the soul, a rare case—if not, unfortunately, unique—which has been studied by learned psychologists, but which till now no novelist has dared to stage in a literary work.

So opens a truly unique "human document" of the late 1880's: a bundle of letters and postcards mailed to Emile Zola by a twenty-three-year-old Italian aristocrat.[1] In florid, raunchy detail, the young man recounts his sexual history from his early cross-dressing experiences and masturbatory addiction through to the feverish evolution of his "frightful illness": *an erotic passion for men.* He notes that Zola had briefly referred to the "horrid vice that dishonors humanity" (Invert 212) in the person of Baptiste the groom-loving

A different version of this essay appeared as "Inversion's Histories / History's Inversions: Novelizing Fin-de-Siècle Homosexuality," in Rosario, *Science and Homosexualities.*

1. Invert (212); original emphasis. As I will explain shortly, the Italian's confession (which I cite as "Invert") was published anonymously in a medical journal in 1894–95. Its date of composition is uncertain. Setz in *Der Roman eines Konträrsexuellen* estimates that it was written in 1887 or 1888, based on the Italian's references to historical events (82). Alternatively, the document can be approximately dated to 1889, since the Italian author wrote Dr. Laupts upon encountering the published version of the confession in *Tares et poisons* (1896), and Saint-Paul (*Thèmes psychologique,* 115, n. 2) notes that this was seven years after the original letters were sent to Zola. Unless otherwise noted, all translations are mine.

valet in *La Curée* (591). But, the Italian complains, that that was a matter of debauchery, not love: "it is a purely material thing, a question of conformation, which doctors have more than once observed and described. All of that is very *common* and terribly *disgusting* and has nothing to do with the confession that I send you, which may perhaps serve you in some way" (212).

The young man's aim is to provide an abundance of authentic documentation so that his unusual "deviation" might be represented more extensively and candidly by Zola, the inventor of the "experimental novel," who had declared: "The dream of the physiologist and the experimental doctor is also that of the novelist who applies [Claude Bernard's] experimental method to the natural and social study of man" ("Roman" 1188). Zola's image as paternal doctor clearly endeared him to the young Italian, for he wrote, "Please forgive my horrible scribble, but I [write] with my heart on my sleeve, as if I were confessing to a doctor or a friend, and I have not paid attention to the form or the spelling" (231).

As it turned out, Zola's mysterious correspondent was indeed confessing to a doctor, in fact, to the whole community of doctors who read the *Archives d'anthropologie criminelle, de criminologie, et de psychologie normale et pathologique* where his letters were first published in 1894–95. What was an erotic confession doing in a medical journal and how did a novelist, Zola, make such a contribution? In addressing these questions, I will show how the construction of "inversion" and "homosexuality" in fin-de-siècle France was a broad literary and cultural affair beyond the professional confines of medical texts and knowledge.

The importance of late nineteenth-century medical science in constructing "homosexuality" has been well documented (Foucault, *Histoire*; Greenberg; Chauncey; Lanteri-Laura). My essay focuses on the significant role of *belle-lettristes*—both medical professionals and scientific dilettantes—in shaping this medical discourse. Some writers, such as Marc-André Raffalovich, were engaged in more or less explicit self-representation and defense of homosexuality. Others, such as Zola and J.-K. Huysmans, were concerned with condemning the epidemic of "perversity." Apologists and censors both argued for the power of fiction in shaping disciplinary knowledges, social stereotypes, and intimate experiences of "inversion." The etiology of "homosexuality"—whether it was a supposed product of biological "degeneration" or of social decay—was of concern to these medical and nonmedical writers who, even as they argued for the congenital "nature" of "inversion of the genital sense," erected new ontological structures out of old materials and new historical experiences.[2] The oldest association was with "sodomy" (any non-phallo-vaginal sex),[3] but French neurologists of the late nineteenth century recharacterized same-sex passion within a new narrative of hysterical gender delusion and fictional excess.

Effeminate Sodomites and Novel Hysterics

Ambroise Tardieu (1818–79) made his fame in forensic medicine with the publication of his *Etude médico-légale sur les attentats aux moeurs* (1857) in which he described how to positively identify both active and passive sodomites by the anatomical peculiarities of their penises and anuses (see also Aron and Kempf 47–52). He was equally preoccupied with the behavioral deviance of pederasts or sodomites (he used the terms interchangeably). Tardieu sketched the following image to illustrate the effeminate façade and psyche of the typical pederast:

> Curled hair, made-up skin, open collar, waist tucked in to highlight the figure; fingers, ears, chest loaded with jewelry, the whole body exuding an odor of the most penetrating perfumes, and in the hand a handkerchief, flowers, or some needlework: such is the strange, revolting, and rightfully suspect physiognomy of the pederast. . . . Hairstyles and dress constitute one of the most constant preoccupations of pederasts. (216–17)

The physicians who began to describe same-sex erotic attraction in the late 1860's did not equate this *new* phenomenon with the old category of "sodomy" as Tardieu had represented it. For example, the neurologist Wilhelm Griesinger (1817–1869) published his observations under the title "On a *Little Known* Psychopathological State" (emphasis added). Other German writers scrambled for an appellation. The Hanoverian lawyer Karl Heinrich Ulrichs (1826–95), under the pseudonym Numa Numantius, suggested *Urningen* to describe those with a female soul caught in a male body. Dr. Karl

2. For a discussion of the contemporary stakes of the "essentialism" versus "social constructionism" debate regarding the appropriate historical use of the terms "gay" or "homosexual," see Stein, *Forms of Desire.*

3. The word *sodomy* was used quite loosely in eighteenth- and nineteenth-century France to refer to any variety of "unnatural" sexual acts: anal intercourse (no matter what the sex of the participants), oral sex, and penetration by dildos. *Pederasty* (etymologically, the love of boys) was frequently used interchangeably with *sodomy.* Dr. Fournier Pescay struggled to provide a precise definition in the *Dictionnaire des sciences médicales*: "SODOMY. . . . Under this name is designated the infamous coitus, for the accomplishment of which, the depraved man prefers, instead of

Westphal (1833–90), editor of the *Archiv für Psychiatrie und Nervenkrankheiten*, proposed the name *conträre Sexualempfindung* (contrary sexual sensation) in 1869. In a historical review of the condition, Dr. Richard von Krafft-Ebing (1840–1902) was only able to identify seventeen such cases in all the medical literature through 1877. Given the German dominance of the field, it is no wonder that a French medico-moral novel by Armand Dubarry was entitled *Les Invertis (Le vice allemand)*(1896). Journalist and traveler Armand Dubarry published a whole series of novels on the "Déséquilibrés de l'amour," including the volume on *Les Invertis (Le vice allemand)*. He eventually succeeded Jules Verne as the science popularizer for the magazine *Le Musée des familles.*

Not to be left out of this hot new research direction, the French entered the arena in 1882 led by two prominent neurologists: Jean-Martin Charcot (1825–93) and Valentin Magnan (1835–1916). They were the first to introduce *inversion sexuelle* into French along with their description of the first French "invert": a man whose imagination since the age of six had been inflamed by the image of naked men. Like the Italian, this French invert had no sensual interest in women but loved women's clothes and wished he were female so he might dress in ladies' garments—which he confessed he did on occasion. Charcot and Magnan exclaimed, "This patient, what is he?" (56).

They founded their answer in the dominant hereditarian, degenerationist theories of the time. These had been initially suggested by Prosper Lucas in his *Traité philosophique et physiologique de l'hérédité naturelle* (1847–50), but gained almost universal currency in France through Bénédict Morel's *Traité des dégénérescences* (1857). Morel argued that all varieties of environmental, biological, and psychological insults (from miasmas to alcohol) could be expressed in offspring through almost any form of pathology. The cumulative weight of these hereditary degenerations would eventually lead to idiocy, sterility, and the termination of family lines.[4] German neurologists such as Westphal and Krafft-Ebing had adopted this

---

the organ destined by nature to receive the fecundating liqueur of the male, that neighboring organ where the most disgusting excretion of the human body occurs. Theologians, as well as legists, define this vile action: *Sodomia, turpitudo masculum facta.* This definition is incomplete and applies only to pederasty. Sodomy is equally well exerted between a man and a person of the other sex as between two men: when it takes place between a man and a child, and even between two men, it is distinguished under the name of pederasty" (441).

4. For more on the extensive social impact of the theory of degeneration, see Pick, *Faces of Degeneration.*

hereditary degenerationist model in neuropathology by the 1860's. Charcot and Magnan, therefore, agreed with the Germans that "sexual perversion" was a product of neuropsychopathological degeneration, but they rejected the German notion that inverts suffered from a nosologically distinct gender discordancy between their psyches and their bodies (often called "psychosexual hermaphroditism"). No, Charcot and Magnan argued, inverts were neuro-degenerates of the hysterical kind and did not differ much from those with erotic penchants for boots, buttocks, or bonnets—attractions that would later be labeled "erotic fetishes" by Alfred Binet. The invert simply had a delusional attraction to *human* objects of the same sex (Charcot and Magnan 321–22).

Although Charcot and Magnan tried to portray "inversion of the genital sense" as a new nosological entity, the diagnosis was actually a new hybrid of the older medical descriptions of the sodomite and the male hysteric (Rosario in Merrick and Ragan). The construction of the hysterical male in France in the 1870's (the decade when German physicians were uncovering "contrary sexual sensation") is particularly interesting because of the numerous associations made between these patients' symptoms and perverse literary production.

Hysteria in the male (although etymologically an oxymoron) developed as a credible diagnosis in the nineteenth century because hysteria had increasingly been theorized as a neuropsychiatric disorder and not a disease of the uterus (Greek *hystera*) (see Veith; Micale). Nonetheless, hysterics of either sex were portrayed as exhibiting characteristics traditionally associated with "femininity": excessive emotionality, hyperexcitability, and impressionability. Furthermore, male hysterics were regularly found to demonstrate physical stigmata of "*féminisme*" (for example, sparse beard, delicate complexions, fine hair, weak constitutions, and underdeveloped genitals) as well as familial histories of degeneration—in particular, hysterical mothers. For example, Paul Fabre, physician at the Vaucluse Asylum, noted that "the individuals stricken by this neurosis [male hysteria] offer certain psychological and physical analogies that seem to distance them from the sex to which they belong, to direct them to a new sex, so to speak, whose neutrality [i.e., indifference to sex with women] and exaggerated impressionability are the principle attributes" (365). To illustrate this, Fabre described the case of Mr. X——, a "man of letters" whose character "resembles in many ways that of a woman; despite an entirely virile exterior appearance, he cries and laughs easily depending on the circumstances, emotions have the greatest influence on him" (363).

Mr. X——, the hysterical writer, was in good company, since Gustave Flaubert also bore the diagnosis of hysteria. Indeed, Goldstein argues that Flaubert used his hysteria to gain a subversive, androgynous gender position from which to write of women's experiences. While one can interpret hysteria to have been Flaubert's muse, Flaubert instead complained that his hysterical, feminine hypersensitivity—like masturbatory exhaustion—was the cause of his bouts of literary *impotence*: "Each attack . . . was a seminal loss of the picturesque faculty of the brain" (Flaubert to Colet in Dumesnil 430). Flaubert wrote George Sand complaining about his isolation in Croisset: "The sensibility is unduly exalted in such a milieu. I suffer palpitations for no reason, rather understandable, all told, in an old hysteric like myself. For I maintain that men are hysterical like women and that I am one. When I wrote *Salammbô*, I read 'the best authors' on the matter and I recognized all my symptoms. I have the ball [*globus hystericus*] and the nail in the occiput" (January 12–13, 1867; 1980–91, 3:592). He later wrote to Mme. Roger des Genettes, "Dr. Hardy . . . calls me a hysterical old woman. 'Doctor,' I tell him, 'you are perfectly right'" (May 1, 1874; 1926–54, 7:134). To his longtime friend Marie-Sophie Leroyer de Chantepie, he similarly wrote that he had the *nervous irritability* of a kept woman (March 18, 1857; 1980–91, 2:692).

The diagnosis of hysteria stuck to Flaubert even into the twentieth century; René Dumesnil (editor of the Pléiade edition of Flaubert's works) retrospectively examined Flaubert with the intention of dispelling persistent rumors that the novelist had been epileptic, sexually frigid, and *afraid of women* (88). Dumesnil determined—supposedly in Flaubert's defense—that the novelist's nervous crises were the product of "epileptoid hysteria with a strong neuropathic tendency" (94). Flaubert's superior literary abilities could thus be attributed to his neuro-degeneracy, since "his mania for analysis is pushed to exaggeration, and this is a trait common to all intellectual neuroses and superior mentality" (95). The excessive imaginativeness and hypersensibility of the hystero-epileptic placed Flaubert on the dangerous edge between insanity and literary genius. Fortunately, as the son of the physician-in-chief of the Rouen Hôtel-Dieu, Flaubert was endowed with a medical mentality and steely surgical literary style that prevented him from falling into the abyss (148). Reproducing Third Republic physicians' penchant for degenerationist, hereditary mechanisms of psychopathology, Dumesnil concluded that Flaubert united the ardent imagination and romantic character inherited from his mother with the superior intelligence and scientific spirit of his father the physician (317).

The image of Flaubert as doctor had been popularized since the publication of his first novel, *Madame Bovary* (1856). Inspired perhaps by Sainte-Beuve's comment in *Le Moniteur* (May 4, 1859) that Flaubert "wielded a pen as others a scalpel," A. Lemot's famous caricature in *La Parodie* (December 5–12, 1869) depicted Flaubert as a surgeon conducting an autopsy of Emma Bovary. Baudelaire, in a review of the novel that originally appeared in *l'Artiste* on October 18, 1857, had even declared that Emma was the female incarnation of Flaubert, and inversely that, "despite all his zeal as an actor, [Flaubert] was unable not to infuse virile blood into the veins of his creature, and that Madame Bovary—despite all the energy and ambition she may possess, and also her dreaminess—Madame Bovary remains a man. Like armed Pallas, springing from the brain of Zeus, that bizarre androgyne has kept all the seductions of a virile soul in a charming feminine body" (652). The representational brilliance of hysterical medical novelists to spawn fictional inverts may have struck Baudelaire as the zenith of literary genius, but contemporary physicians were far more wary of the novels of hysterics.

Dr. Ernest Lasègue (1816–83), in an article on "Les hystériques, leur perversité, leurs mensonges" (1881), warned colleagues against the willful malevolence and irresistible deceitfulness of the hysteric's imagination. Hysterics and lunatics both told untrue stories, he noted, but the great danger was that "The latter are unbelievable, whereas *the novels of hysterics* impose themselves by their verisimilitude" (114, my emphasis). The same principle could be applied more broadly, he observed: "Do we not have something analogous in the wide field of human inventions? This is the novelist who, commencing with a premise furnished by the imagination, allows himself to be led by this to the point of believing that everything he creates actually happened" (112). The novels of hysterics and hysterical novelists would seem to collapse into the same category, distinguished by hypersensibility, overimaginativeness, deceitfulness, and self-delusion. The same characteristics would hold true of the novels and lives of inverts—the literate perverts of the fin de siècle such as the Italian dandy. Echoing Lasègue's warnings concerning hysterics, physicians cautioned against the seductions of inverts' narrative productions and these stories' ability to pervert society.

Science, Inverts, and the Flaming Truth

> Whenever my nurse sees me, she always tells me that all the women she knows had named me *the little Madonna*, I was so cute and delicate. . . . I still recall the shiver of joy and pleasure that coursed

> through my little person when I went out in my little puffed-up blue piqué dress with blue bows and my big Italian straw hat.
>
> When I was four, they took away my little dresses to put me in trousers and a little jacket. Once they had dressed me as a boy, I experienced profound shame—I remember it as if it were today—and I quickly ran to my nanny's room to hide and cry; to console me, she had to dress me again as a girl. They still laugh whenever recalling my cries of despair in seeing them take away those little white dresses which were my greatest joy.
>
> It seems as if they took away something that I was always destined to wear.
>
> That was my first great sorrow.
>
> (Invert 215)

Zola was impressed by the Italian invert's confessions of effeminacy and same-sex passion, and felt that the subject was extremely important. "I was struck by the great physiological and social interest [the confession] offered," Zola wrote, "It touched me by its absolute sincerity, because one senses the flame, I would even say the eloquence of truth. . . . It is a total, naïve, spontaneous confession that very few men would dare make, qualities that render it quite precious from many points of view" ("Preface" 1). He hoped that its publication might inspire some pity for these "unfortunates," but he found it impossible to utilize the manuscript in his own writings.

"With each new novel of Zola's," the Italian later wrote, "I hoped to finally discover a character who was the reproduction of myself, but I was always disappointed and I was finally convinced that the writer had lacked the *courage* to stage so terrible a passion" (quoted in Saint-Paul 115). Zola was hardly one to shy away from controversy. Even before the Dreyfus Affair and his famous polemic "J'accuse!" (1895), his naturalist novels had been condemned for their vulgarity, sensuality, and morbidness. Some of Zola's harshest literary critics were those people he claimed as his colleagues—physicians, who nevertheless considered him a "scientific dilettante." Like Flaubert before him, Zola had been deemed a pathological writer and had been "diagnosed" as an epileptoid degenerate, a "superior degenerate," an olfactory fetishist, and a sexual psychopath (Toulouse; Nordau 2:456). Yet Zola had persisted in portraying the great spectrum of physical and moral degenerations: alcoholism, prostitution, monomania, adultery, and homicide. Therefore, Zola's literary impotence on the topic of inversion is quite revealing. He could never have edited the Italian's manuscript, he confessed, because,

> I was then in the roughest hours of my literary battle; critics treated me daily as a criminal capable of all vices and all debaucheries. . . . First of all they would have accused me of entirely *inventing* the story from personal corruption. Then I would have been duly condemned for merely having seen in the affair an occasion for base speculation on the most repugnant instincts. And what a clamor if I had permitted myself to say that no other subject is more serious or more tragic; that it is a far more common and deep wound than pretended and that still the best thing for healing wounds is to study them, to expose them, and to treat them! ("Preface" 2)

The social taint of "inversion" was clearly too much even for the scientific novelist, despite the dictum "Science, like fire, purifies everything it touches" (regularly cited in the introductions to medical works on sexuality). Privately, Zola confessed to a far more personal impediment: "I can barely overcome the instinctive repulsion I experience in shaking [an invert's] hand" (quoted in Laupts, "Mémoire" 833). And to another correspondent, Marc-André Raffalovich, in a thank-you note (April 16, 1896) for the gift of the former's book, *L'Uranisme et l'unisexualité*, Zola wrote: "If I am full of pity for those whom you call Uranists, I have no sympathy for them, no doubt because I am different" (quoted in Allen 221).

So, after pouring his heart out, the poor Italian never saw himself fictionalized by Zola. *Or did he?* Zola had become increasingly fervent over French natality—a concern most clearly voiced in *Fécondité* (1899), the first volume of his *Quatre Evangiles.* Therefore, he was extremely anxious about all forms of nonprocreative sexuality, and once moaned, "How much seed wasted in one night in Paris—what a shame that all of it does not produce human beings" (quoted in Laupts, "Mémoire" 832, n. 1). This seminal waste was of equal concern to the medical and anthropological communities, particularly after the humiliating defeat in the Franco-Prussian War (1870–71). Therefore, Zola delivered the Italian's confession to his medical friend, Dr. Laupts, who was conducting a survey in 1894 on "sexual inversion" for the prestigious French medicolegal journal *Archives d'anthropologie criminelle.*

Glancing into a bookstore window by chance some years later, the Italian discovered a book entitled *Tares et poisons. Perversions et perversités sexuelles* (1896) in which were republished his own confessions. He immediately wrote to Laupts that he was elated to find himself "printed in *living color,* although I would have much preferred to be reborn in the pages of a novel and not in a medical science treatise" (quoted in Saint-Paul 116). Indeed, the Italian dandy repeatedly suggested that he fancied himself a *belle-lettriste* and envisioned his life as a work of art: "I unloaded my soul somewhat [in my confessions to Zola] and I wrote with a retrospective voluptuousness of the abominable and ardent scenes in which I was the actor. . . . I therefore want to complete the study of my person, whom I often consider favored by nature because she made me a creature that even the most audacious poets have been unable to create" (Invert 231–32). Ironically enough, his "true" confession was printed *verbatim* but under the title, "Le *roman* d'un inverti."

Dr. Laupts, a student of the prominent forensic doctor Alexandre Lacassagne (1843–1924), introduced the "document" in a style more suited to the back cover blurb of a racy "true crime" novella: "It is the true story of a man who bore a great name, a very great name in Italy. As exact as a scientific observation, as interesting as a novel, as sincere as a confession, it is perhaps the most complete and most endearing document of this genre" ("Enquête" 212). Like most of Zola's novels, the confession was published serially, and Laupts had a knack for breaking the action at critical moments of sexual titillation. For example, in the third installment, "Youth—First Acts," we learn of the Italian's first erotic encounter with a handsome young officer during his military service:

> He was half undressed and seated on my legs right up against me. I spoke to him as if enchanted. . . . suddenly he leaned over, embraced me in his arms and applied a long kiss to my cheek; at the same time he plunged his hands under the sheets and seized my flesh with both his hands. I thought I would die and an immense joy suddenly seized me. We remained a few seconds like that, resting one head against the other, our fiery cheeks touching, my mouth in his in the warmth of the pillow. I was never so happy!!
>
> The lamp on the floor cast faint rays upon the immense dormitory where, in the distant beds, my companions were sleeping, and left in the deepest darkness the corner where we were thus ecstatic. (Invert 737)

Break! Readers had to cool off for two months before the hard-core action continued. But is it science or is it fiction? As Zola feared, some foreign writers were convinced it was entirely his own fabrication—their critiques were related by Laupts ("Mémoire" 837)—and it did not help matters that Laupts labeled it a "novel."

The second half of the title is equally important: "inversion" itself was a novel diagnosis coined just twelve years earlier. Remarkably, the young Italian never applied any label to himself, although he liked comparing himself to Greek heroes. Perhaps he felt the two traditional terms, "pederast" and "sodomite," were inappropriate in his case. Technically he was not a pederast since he was attracted to virile, adult men. "Sodomite" seemed inappropriate because he had only experienced sodomy (anal sex) quite late since he had feared it was too painful. In any case, the Italian dismissed these two designations as old matters of vice and defective genital conformation which had long been examined by doctors. He was quite convinced that his condition was rare and new, and therefore worthy of publication (212).

Physicians of the time clearly agreed, since, as we have seen, the diagnoses of "contrary sexual sensation" and "inversion of the genital sense" which sprang up in the 1870's and 1880's were considered new disease entities. After the publication of Charcot and Magnan's article introducing the terms *inversion du sens génitale* and *perversion sexuelle* into France, French medical journals were pullulating with these queer new creatures. Just three years later, Chevalier published a whole medical thesis on the matter of *Inversion de l'instinct sexuel au point de vue médico-légale* (1885). Chevalier highlighted the dizzying panoply of designations for the illness: "contrary, inverse, perverted, [or] inverted genital sense;—contrary, inverse, [or] perverted sexual attractions, impulsions, [or] sensations;—attraction of same sexes;—crossed sensation of sexual individuality; . . . —perversion, [or] interversion of the sexual instinct, [etc.]" (14). Some order needed to be brought to this field of confusions; therefore, Dr. Laupts had bravely launched a national "Enquête sur l'inversion sexuelle" with a detailed list of questions concerning the heredity, physical and psychological status, and medical and legal history of inverts. The questionnaire was published in the *Archives d'anthropologie criminelle* but was addressed to professors, lawyers, and novelists, as well as doctors (105–6). The first published response was the Italian's manuscript, which was contributed by Zola, who strongly endorsed Laupts's research.

Laupts shared Zola's natality concerns, which were the *raison d'être* of the whole project. In the introduction to his monograph *Tares et poisons*, Laupts argued for the sympathetic treatment of these "patients," but continued:

> These days, no one doubts that the number of degenerations, of cerebral derailings—expressed by the tendencies towards suicide, by phobias, etc.—result in large part from the fact that in our nation the genital functions often are not accomplished as they should be.
>
> Therefore, it is necessary from the point of view of the vitality, of the future of the race, to study the morbid causes, to discern the dangerous and evil elements, amongst which must be ranked for an appreciable part the creature stricken with sexual perversion: the pervert, the feminiform born-invert. (104–5)

For Laupts, sexual inversion was a terrifying nexus of medical, social, and moral deviations, and the "feminiform born-invert" was the embodiment of almost all fin-de-siècle social ills.

The second published response to Laupts's survey was from Marc-André Raffalovich (1864–1934), who would become the most prolific writer in French on the subject of "unisexuality" (his preferred term) and would eventually accuse Laupts and his colleagues of being far too squeamish and prejudiced to study inversion scientifically. These "fatuous" French scientists, Raffalovich declared in the pages of the *Archives*, discuss inverts "as if they were newly imported savages that had been unknown in Europe" ("Uranisme" 126). Raffalovich was in a privileged position: he kept abreast of the German, French, and English medical literature, and, most significantly, he had insider information—he was an invert. But then, so was Dr. Laupts, literally: "Laupts" was a fiction—the inversion of his real name, St.-Paul. Even better, he was a writer of fiction, under the pseudonym G. Espé de Metz—a name he started using when he discovered to his dismay that bibliographers were cataloguing "Laupts" under German authors (Saint-Paul 5).

Raffalovich was also an impostor of sorts. Although he was entrusted with writing the "Annales de l'unisexualité" within the *Archives d'anthropologie criminelle*, and was the only French writer on homosexuality that British sexologist Havelock Ellis praised, Raffalovich was in fact not a doctor. He had no degree whatsoever—he was an Oxford dropout. Raffalovich came from a wealthy Russian-Jewish family that had emigrated to France. His mother was an intimate friend of Claude Bernard, who had recommended that Marc-André become a doctor. He was shipped off to Oxford but he was too sickly to finish his studies. Instead he became a London dandy, published a few novels and collections of maudlin love poems, and established a literary salon frequented by the notable authors of the day: Henry James, Aubrey Beardsley, Stephan Mallarmé, Pierre Louÿs, and the most coveted of aesthetes, Oscar Wilde.

Raffalovich and Wilde were intimate friends until their vicious falling out in the early 1890's over an indiscreet comment by Wilde. At that time, Raffalovich was enamored of Wilde's companion, a pretty-boy and budding poet named John Henry Gray (1866–1934), whom Raffalovich had met in 1892 through a mutual friend, poet Arthur Symons. *A Portrait of Dorian Gray* was published in 1891 with its secret dedication to John, but the next year Wilde met the younger and more angelic Lord Alfred Douglas. Raffalovich got the suicidal Gray on the rebound and they became lifetime and reportedly Platonic companions (McCormack 151). The Queensbury v. Wilde Affair of 1895 perturbed Raffalovich and Gray as well as other London dandies. Raffalovich converted to Catholicism the following year, and Gray renewed his Catholic faith. In 1898, Raffalovich was admitted to the lay order of Dominicans under the name Brother Sebastian, and Gray began training for the priesthood in Rome thanks to Raffalovich's financial support. After ordination, Gray served as a curate in a poor Edinburgh parish for three years before becoming parish priest of Edinburgh's St. Peter's Church (which was constructed largely with Raffalovich's funds) (McCormack 202–3). Raffalovich moved into a house near St. Peter's in 1905, and the two met every day there for tea. Raffalovich became a great benefactor of the Dominicans, and donated funds for the construction of St. Sebastian's priory in Pendelton, Manchester. His wealth was held in a joint account with Gray. Raffalovich passed away in his sleep on St. Valentine's Day 1934; Canon Gray died four months later (Sewell 33–34, 48; Ellman; McCormack.

Perhaps it was through Arthur Symons, a close friend of John Addington Symonds and Havelock Ellis, that Raffalovich was introduced to the burgeoning scientific study of inversion and to Ellis and Symonds's groundbreaking *Sexual Inversion* (1896). But even before Ellis began to publish his series on *Studies in the Psychology of Sex*, Raffalovich had begun writing a stream of articles on homosexuality for the *Archives*, including a review of the Wilde affair with a spiteful critique of Wilde's pederasty and literary style. Raffalovich inveighed against Wilde's "flaccid" and "unoriginal" writing, which only represented "artificious, superficial, effeminate" homosexuals ("Affaire" 450). These were in the minority, Raffalovich controversially argued. Not all inverts were degenerate sodomites, and he mocked doctors who, in the tradition of Tardieu, "search, almost with desperation, for stigmata of degeneracy" ("Unisexualité" 429). Most unisexuals were virile and law-abiding, but "pseudoscience," caving in to popular prejudice, had pushed these decent homosexuals into the shadows (*Uranisme* 25–26). Given Raffalovich's conservative position condemning flamboyant "effeminates," it is not surprising that he showed even less sympathy than Laupts for the Italian invert and his "novel." "This autobiography resembles those of all effeminate Uranists who have gone public," Raffalovich warned, "This novel of an invert will teach nothing to those with experience in psychiatry. . . . Unbridled vanity and lust are especially demonstrated in the relations between the invert of the novel and the Captain [an older pederast who seduces the hero]. . . . Repugnant or dangerous acts will generally occur between people united by debauchery, vanity, or interest" ("Roman" 333). He cautioned, "It seems to me that one should not dwell on such autobiographies or attach much importance to them" ("Uranisme" 116). Furthermore, Raffalovich made the intriguing literary distinction that "ultra male, male and a half" homosexuals did not write their own *memoirs*, historians wrote their *biographies* ("Roman" 333). It was only the effeminates who penned their conceited, immoral confessions.

Echoing Lasègue on the novels of hysterics, Raffalovich exhorted doctors and the general public alike to beware of the narratives of artifice-loving, effeminate inverts not only because their "true confessions" might be deceitful novels, but, more seriously, because these novels were socially noxious. Raffalovich warned that literature reflected the true, inner moral state of its creator just as the portrait of Dorian Gray (and Wilde's novel itself) reflected the true corrupt and corrupting soul. Appropriating Wilde's dictum that "life imitates art," Raffalovich claimed that literature shaped the moral character of its readers. Artistic representations had long been criticized as dangerous to the malleable brains of women and children, but Raffalovich argued for their salubrious use in the treatment of the imagination. With poetic grandiloquence, he lectured novelists from the bully pulpit of medicine about the connection between fiction and social hygiene:

> I call upon our French novelists. . . . I would tell them: Because your readers, your admirers permit you to say anything, why not deliver them real observations? You have them. Describe then that passion of the strong for the strong, of Hercules for Colossus, of robust flesh, as they say, for robust flesh; show that it is not only the female but also the effeminate who is of no interest to these virile [homosexuals]; draw back the veils of ignorance and of falsehood . . . the clichés must be shattered. . . . We must contemplate the education of our children, of our grandchildren. ("Unisexualité" 431, n. 1)

The battle over the moral purity of France became even more feverish and nationalistic after Raffalovich drew another French novelist, J. K. Huysmans (1848–1907), into the medical literature by publishing extracts from a letter about the sordid Parisian sodomitic underworld. "It made me think of Hell," Huysmans wrote,

> Imagine this: the man who has this vice willfully *withdraws* from association with the rest of mankind. He eats in restaurants, has his hair done at a coiffeur, lives in a *hôtel* where the patrons are all old sodomites. It is a life apart, in a narrow corner, a brotherhood recognizing itself by their voice, by a fixed gaze, and that sing-song tone they all affect.

> Furthermore, that vice is the *only* one that suppresses the castes, the decent man and the rogue are equal—and speak to each other naturally, animatedly without distinction of education. . . . It is rather strange and disquieting. (April 19, 1896; Allen 216)

Raffalovich contrasted this "Sodom of Paris" with Dr. Paul Näcke's description of the gatherings of educated, bourgeois homosexuals and lesbians at a meeting of the Scientific and Philanthropic Committee (a homosexual organization started by Magnus Hirschfeld) and at other social venues in Berlin. Näcke was so moved by the narratives of these homosexuals' sufferings and their struggles with their parents, that he wondered, "Why doesn't someone write unisexual novels?" (quoted in Raffalovich, "Groupes" 931). Raffalovich hoped to indict French society for its general immorality, irreligion, and ignorance of the psychology of *healthy* unisexuals. "Heterosexuals, by their example and behavior," Raffalovich complained, "have created many [immoral] inverts" ("Groupes" 935).

Näcke promptly responded to the article complaining that it was totally unbalanced and ill-informed. He imagined that the homosexual worlds of Paris and Berlin were quite similar and that the number of homosexuals given to vice was a small minority in both cities. He estimated that Paris probably had fifty to a hundred thousand homosexuals and that, although pederasty was not the rule amongst homosexuals, he suspected there was a higher incidence of pederasty in Latin cultures than Teutonic ones ("Monde" 184). In a subsequent article in a *German* journal, Näcke further suggested that the French suffered from more degeneration than the Germans ("Einteilung").

Dr. Laupts/Saint-Paul immediately took umbrage at these aspersions against French masculinity. He shot back at both Raffalovich and Näcke that the French were no more degenerate that the Germans (Laupts, "Dégénérescence"). Furthermore, he insisted, "*I know* that homosexuality does not exist save as a *rare* exception in the entirety of continental . . . France. . . . *I know* that the vast majority of my (noncolonial) compatriots experience an undissimulated and *extreme* disgust for homosexuality" ("Lettre" 693, 696; original emphasis). (Laupts was less certain of the sexual normality of France's colonized subjects.) This was in dramatic contrast to the situation in Germany, where notable doctors, such as Westphal, Krafft-Ebing, and Näcke, had taken up the defense of homosexuals and had favored the deletion of antisodomy laws from the Penal Code. Laupts feared that homosexuality was contagious and was spreading in both France and Germany precisely "because it is studied, and spoken, and written about"

("Lettre" 694). The very fact that German doctors had done so much work on the subject was proof of (and presumably cause of) the higher incidence of homosexuality in Germany than in France ("Dégénérescence" 741). In retort to Raffalovich's insult that Laupts's work on homosexuality was in "a literary tradition," Laupts accused Raffalovich of being "a bit too literary, too inclined, in any case, to introduce into a scientific debate considerations of a moral nature which have no place there and are . . . sort of meaningless" ("Lettre" 695–96).

These accusations and counter-accusations that scientific scholarship was merely fictional "literature" continued to be flung across national boundaries thanks to essays by Eugène Wilhelm. A homosexual Alsatian lawyer, Wilhelm had already published several articles in the *Mercure de France* on German sexology and initially joined the debate under the pseudonym "Dr. Numa Praetorius." If Laupts and his French colleagues were practically ignorant of the existence of homosexuality in France, Wilhelm observed, it was because their old prejudices prevented them from broaching the subject with their patients and discovering how many of these, in fact, were homosexual (Praetorius 201). He chastised French men of science for generally neglecting sexual questions and flung Laupts's insult of "literariness" back in the face of French physicians: "They seem to want to leave this terrain to literature and superficial popularizers; one could say that a certain false shame, an ill-placed prudishness prevents them from studying these problems in detail and methodically" (Wilhelm 301). To an extent, Wilhelm was right. Men of letters, heterosexual and homosexual alike, *did* have an especially significant role in shaping the French discourse of homosexuality, but one can hardly accuse the *belle-lettristes* of having perverted science; rather, they informed the very fictions science was dedicated to spinning.

Science Fictions and Inversions

In his scathing critique of degenerate, fin-de-siècle culture, journalist Dr. Max Nordau (1849–1920) fumed: "Does [Zola] think that his novels are serious documents from which science can borrow facts? What childish folly! Science can have nothing to do with fiction" (2:437). As we have seen, however, the scientific literature on inversion was especially dedicated to fiction: both the fictions it studied and the fictions it sponsored. To label the scientific literature on inversion a "fiction" is not, however, to dismiss it as *untruthful.* Foucault has pointed out that "there is the possibility for fiction to function in truth"; indeed,

> for a fictional discourse to induce effects of truth, and for bringing it about that a true discourse engenders or "manufactures" something that does not as yet exist, that is, "fictions" it. One "fictions" history on the basis of a political reality that makes it true, one "fictions" a politics not yet in existence on the basis of a historical truth. (Foucault, *Power* 193).

The novelizing and fictioning of "homosexuality" served to advance the underlying goals of defenders and derogators of homosexuality alike: on the one hand, to reify the notion of a normal, virile homosexual; on the other hand, to fashion a monster of perversity embodying all the degenerations and insecurities that plagued the cultural imagination of fin-de-siècle France.

While perfectly consonant with the latest scientific, biomedical "truths" of the day, the medical debates on the nature of inversion were, nevertheless, also molded by the cultural and political preoccupations of the time. The nationalistic fires of Franco-German rivalries continued to burn on the terrain of science well after France's defeat in the Franco-Prussian War. The construction and counting of inverts was just one among many ideological weapons (just as it is, albeit under different scientific and political conditions, in the United States today).[5] The fictioning of what would later be called "homosexuality"—embellished as it was by associations with effeminacy, hysteria, and deceitfulness—was especially critical in bolstering na-

5. In the United States—particularly since the wave of "gay liberation" and public visibility sparked by the Stonewall Riot in 1969—fictions of homosexuality have served the nationalist cause. During the Gulf War (1990–91), Iraq's President Saddam Hussein was portrayed as a transvestite sadistic pederast (*National Examiner*, March 12, 1991). T-shirts sporting an image of a camel with Hussein's face for an anus declared patriotically, "America Will Not be Saddam-ized" (see Goldberg, *Sodometries* 1–5). Homosexualizing the enemy and protecting the U.S. nation from homosexual invasion were a unified strategy of defense. The U.S. military, quite literally, feared a homosexual invasion in 1993 when threatened by President Bill Clinton with the open admission of gays into the armed services. U.S. television viewers were treated to grainy footage of enlisted men in the showers as soldiers confessed their fears of being cruised by the impending hordes of queers clamoring to enter the services. These soldiers' anxieties (or fantasies) of homosexual objectification and scopophilic feminization clearly outweighed their concerns of flashing on millions of television screens. Given the incessant mention of AIDS throughout the debate, one imagines that these showering soldiers feared a double contagion: both AIDS and homosexuality. Their generals' paranoid fabrications of the homosexual menace strangely mirror the very neuropsychiatric unfitness for which homosexuals were originally screened out by the Selective Service in 1940 ("Medical Circular"; also see Bérubé, *Coming Out Under Fire*, 11–15).

tionalist myths of strength in which potency was always figured as masculine (see Nye, "Sex" and *Masculinity*).

In the case of the history of inversion, fiction and nonfiction were blurred on a stage bustling with novelists in medical drag, and physicians passing incognito as novelists or inverts. Inverts and homosexuals found their "true" confessions presented as scientific fictions under the fear that these narrative productions shared in the deceitfulness and self-delusion of inverts' sexual natures. Homosexuals also played an active part in the fictioning of their experience—and not just because they wrote anonymously or under pseudonyms. Like the medical researchers of "sexual perversions," homosexual correspondents found it necessary to invent a new history for themselves. Manufactured in the political cause of homosexual emancipation and decriminalization, this *histoire homosexuelle* or historical coming-out narrative advanced seemingly contradictory claims of a long tradition beginning with "the Greek vice" alongside claims of "homosexuality's" historical novelty. Likewise, the scientific *histoires* simultaneously asserted the congenital nature of homosexuality and its acquired, even contagious, nature (Laupts, "Lettre" 695 and 694, respectively).

In the promiscuous intercourse between doctors and novelists over the societal *tares et poisons* of "sexual perversion," science itself served as a potent but ambiguous elixir. As Derrida (in *Dissémination*) points out in his exegesis of the *pharmakon* (poison or elixir) in Plato's *Phaedrus* (274c–275b), symbolic language is unmasked as a dangerous supplement to "true learning": superficially, writing appears to be a technique for remembering, but ultimately it produces forgetfulness.[6] Like the female soul disguised in the male body, the mechanism of poisoning is that of inversion. Physicians and littérateurs played a similarly dangerous game with the *pharmakon* of science, which—like the novels conceived by Zola, Raffalovich, and the Italian invert—had the seductiveness of a social panacea.

---

6. In this Platonic dialogue, Socrates tells Phaedrus the following story. Theut (the god of numbers, geometry, letters, and games) offers Thamus, King of Egypt, letters (*grammata*) as a means of making Egyptians wiser and of improving their memory: it will be an elixir (*pharmakon*) of memory and wisdom, Theut promises. Thamus rejects letters, predicting that they will produce forgetfulness since people will come to rely on alien marks rather than their own memory. "You have discovered an elixir not of memory," Thamus declares, "but of reminding" (275a). Writing merely produces an appearance of learning rather than true learning. Instead of a cure for forgetfulness, the *pharmakon* of writing (*logos*) is rejected as an artifice of learning: it is rather a poison of memory and knowledge.

We have seen that the Italian invert was delighted to find his confessions represented by science, and, in his letter to Laupts, praised the doctor as a "savant . . . and a kind and indulgent man." The Italian contributed dozens more pages directly to Laupts because "like every sick person who sees in a doctor a friend . . . , I am filled with friendship and gratitude for those who occupy themselves with the odious illness that haunts me, and . . . I seek to render them service by exhibiting that which they painfully seek, and which I, on the contrary, know so well: *by innate science*" (quoted in Saint-Paul 116). Even while attempting to condemn and contain perversity, the scientific fictions of inversion were embraced by the inverts themselves who used science to defend their "naturalness," consolidate an identity, and disseminate their stories of passion and "robust flesh." Where better than in scientific journals could the Italian invert "cry my [joy] from the rooftops" for finally having been sodomized (quoted in Saint-Paul 115)?

In addition to science, there is the *pharmakon* of history itself. Of all the human technologies, none is more inherently dependent on fabricating and forgetting than history. It figured prominently in the fin-de-siècle medical analysis of homosexuality. A patient's individual case history or *anamnesis*, often printed as a confession, was connected to other family histories and anamneses of supposedly related disorders. Doctors and inverts regularly alluded to the "Greek vice" of antiquity; yet, as Raffalovich astutely noted, these historical connections were un-remembered in the convenient science fiction that "inversion" was a new syndrome of organic degeneration and social disintegration. Inverts were thus concocted as a terrible social and cultural poison through the conventions of amnesia and anamnesis: the inversions of forgetting and reminiscence, the masquerade of intolerance as sympathy, the travesty of ignorance as knowledge.

CHAPTER 7

Homosexual Erotic Scripting in Verlaine's *Hombres*

CHARLES D. MINAHEN

When, in the nineteenth century, the advent of the nineties ushered in the *fin de siècle* (as is now the case in the twentieth), Paul Verlaine was quietly assembling two groups of poems that include, as readers eventually would recognize, some of his last great works. Although clandestine versions began circulating in the early 1890's, only *Femmes* was published during his lifetime, albeit anonymously ("under cover and not for sale anywhere"). In this repressive era, *Hombres* was still too taboo and thus appeared posthumously. Despite their importance in his poetic development, their remarkable synthesis of the sacred and the profane, masterfully set, *Femmes* and *Hombres* were not included in the Pléiade edition of his *Oeuvres poétiques complètes* [*OPC*] until recently, when a supplement entitled "Oeuvres libres," including *Femmes* and *Hombres* (1387–1416), was added in 1989. In 1985, Jean-Paul Corsetti and Jean-Pierre Giusto brought out a carefully researched and annotated edition, but it is flawed by an introduction that perpetuates the attitude of condescension and indignation these poems have always elicited and relegates them to the murky status of scandalous—but poetically inconsequential—aberrations.

The editors of this introduction, who repeatedly betray their discomfort with the texts they have chosen to edit, raise a couple of important points that I feel must be addressed from the start. First, the problem of autobiography and art or, specifically, the relationship of the author to the text. Notwithstanding their own caution to the critic about being blinded by "an endless series of psychological speculations" (11) based on Verlaine's life, the editors do in effect conflate the historical poet and the textually constructed one, especially in the late erotic works. In *Femmes*, for example, they observe "the brutal irruption of autobiography" (19), although Verlaine never explicitly links himself to the speaking subject. Like many of the well-known "confessional" authors, including Augustine, Montaigne, and Rousseau, Verlaine constructs texts in the first person that draw heavily on his personal experience. But the constructed autobiographical self (even when explicit, which is not the case in Verlaine) is always a simulacrum, a figured figure. Moreover, from his Parnassian origins and throughout his career, Verlaine sought to attenuate subjective sentimentality without altogether eliminating it, and he wrote some of his most perfect poems, many would claim, in an "objective" style attributable to the influence of Rimbaud. Sometimes there is something to be gained from a juxtaposing of the life and works—in this case perhaps an exemplum of bisexuality as both a lived and figured experience—but a conflation of life and art can trigger a moral judgment that puts a negative, reprobative spin on scholarship that is otherwise factual and informative.

Corsetti and Giusto speak of a "guilty conscience" and a sense of "disenchantment in which obscenity mocks feelings" (22). They even scold Verlaine: "Even more bothersome: and that from the hand of a poet who was able to trace some of the most ethereal verses in our language" (33). Yet despite their claims to the contrary, there is actually very little evidence of disenchantment and guilt in the poetry of *Femmes* and *Hombres.* The lover/hero of the erotic fantasies is too busy openly indulging his lusts. The sincerity of sexual exuberance is in fact one of the remarkable qualities of these poems, since the lover is more often than not shamelessly expressive of his fantasies, taking great pleasure in his imagined realization of them. In *Hombres* VII, after reveling in an explicitly related act of anal sex, the lover observes,

Mais il va, riche et généreux,
Le don de ton adolescence,
Communiant de ton essence
Tout mon être ivre d'être heureux.

But it goes, rich and generous,
The gift of your adolescence,
Communicant of your essence
All my being drunk with being happy.

I detect neither guilt nor disenchantment in these lines. The significant feature of the full text is the flaunting of the twin taboos of homosexuality and pedophilia. Such shocking practices are intentionally aimed at risking scandal and humiliation, but it is the intensified libidinal charge of taking the risk, not an overwhelming sense of guilt, that motivates them. Moreover, explicitness and a readiness to shift shamelessly to the pornographic are essential factors of the perverse dynamic, which decrees, in effect, that "dirtiness" is *de rigueur.* As Robert Stoller remarks, "Dirtiness is, of course, aesthetic—also its twin, obscenity" (48).

Although *Femmes* and *Hombres* form an interrelated, if nonetheless discrete, pair that reflects the decentered bisexuality of a self-described "*homo duplex*" (Stone viii), I shall be focusing here on *Hombres* in an attempt to elucidate types of erotic scripting in which sexual deviance combined with taboo produces a particularly charged and subversive form of perversion, which Stoller defines as a "habitual, preferred aberration necessary for one's full satisfaction" (9).

A word about scripting: Stoller claims that "In the daydreams of perverse people, especially those stories concretized in pornography, I can make out the construction of a script, the principal purpose of which is to undo childhood traumas, conflicts, and frustrations by converting these earlier painful experiences to present (fantasized) triumphs" (vii). In such cases, "the particular moment of erotic excitement" is "a microdot—of scripts made up from impulses, desires, defenses, falsifications, truths avoided, and memories of past events, erotic and nonerotic, going back to infancy—a piece of theater," which, even though it "feels spontaneous, . . . is, rather, the result of years of working over the scripts in order to make them function efficiently—that is, to ensure that they produce excitement, with its end product, gratification, rather than anxiety, depression, guilt, or boredom. Like humor, it has its aesthetics, especially the requirement that it seem to be spontaneous, spare, uncomplicated, unmotivated" (viii). It is this aesthetic element that Verlaine develops in his late erotica, which transforms the personal psychological fantasy-scripts of a particular erotic imagination into carefully constructed, sensually charged, evocative, even provocative, works of art with a broader, more universal appeal.

Narrative Construct of the Erotic Consciousness

As I have suggested, the narrator of the poems and the activities described are fantasy constructs. It may amuse some readers to imagine Rimbaud as the companion masturbating alongside the poet (who is, accordingly, Verlaine) in *Hombres* XII ("In that café packed with imbeciles"), but such speculation, because unverifiable, has mostly what might be termed titillation value. Any referential interpretation of an erotic text is, in effect, a fantasy constructed on a fantasy, which by personalizing the script may indeed heighten its erotic charge, but which may be a property less of the text than of its reception. Focusing on the texts, the narrative structure involves, in most instances, an anonymous *je* or "I," a lover, who is usually but not always the narrator. *Hombres* VI ("Rendez-vous") is an interesting case in point. The poem is framed by opening and closing strophes that describe a man impatiently awaiting the arrival of a youth who has stood him up before. The intervening strophes, in quotation marks, record his anticipation and uncertainty in the first person. Here, it is clear that the narrator is an observer of the scene, although an identification of the poem's protagonist with the poet-narrator is suggested when, in the last quatrain, the former is seen writing the poem in which he has just figured:

> Du phosphore en ses yeux s'allume
> Et sa lèvre au souris pervers
> S'agace aux barbes de la plume
> Qu'il tient pour écrire ces vers . . .
>
> Phosphorus glows in his eyes
> And his lip in a perverse smile
> Is pricked by the barbs of a feather
> That he holds to write these lines . . .

Such a merging of third and first person, however, is exceptional. Most poems are narrated from one perspective or the other. Typically, a first-person lover recounts a sexual experience as it occurs, often addressing himself to a *tu* who is the all-consuming object of his attentions. There is, in these cases, very little affective distance, and the reader is drawn readily into the script and invited, as it were, to share vicariously in the action. The recurrence of this particular type of narrative structure is to be expected in erotic scripting, since participation in the fantasy is made immediate and direct. One striking example is *Hombres* VII ("Mount me like a woman"), a description of anal sex with the partner astride the lover "à cheval [horse-style]," which also conveys, by a fracturing of the verse, the straddler's swift erection and quickening ecstasy:

> Car voici que ta belle gaule,
> Jalouse aussi d'avoir son rôle,
> Vite, vite gonfle, grandit,
>
> Raidit . . . Ciel! la goutte, la perle
> Avant-courrière, vient briller
> Au méat rose. . . .

For now your handsome rod,
Jealous too to have its role,
Quickly, quickly swells, gets bigger,

Stiffens . . . Heavens! the drop, the pearl
Forerunner, comes to glisten
At the pink opening. . . .

Another example is *Hombres* XI ("Even when you don't get hard"), where the lover's detailed, doting description of the partner's flaccid phallus provokes a sudden stiffening: "Tu bandes! [You're getting hard!]."

In *Hombres* IV, the second of the two poems entitled "Balanide," a word that comes from the Greek *balanos*, meaning "glans" (Corsetti and Giusto 136), the *tu* the poet addresses is the penis itself: "Gland, point suprême de l'être / De mon maître [Glans, supreme point of the being / of my master]." Structurally, the poem displays a very original prosodic interplay of seven- and three-syllable lines, distributed symmetrically in 7–3–7 tercets through seven six-line strophes. Visually, the three-syllable verses create a rigid central shaft, rising vertically and culminating in the "point suprême" of the title word, a vertex tip that the repeated circumflex of the opening verse's *suprême/être/maître* image-cluster structurally reflects. Additionally, the "î" of "maître" also visually echoes the ithyphallic calligram formed by the poem. The poem's theme is thus graphically illustrated by this clever deployment of the signifiers.

At other times, the narrating *je* is less a participant in than an evaluator of the erotic experience, and his remarks are addressed either to the reader (at least implicitly), as in the case of *Hombres* X ("As much certainly woman gains"), where the relative merits of women and men are compared and the imperative "Admirons [Let's admire]" subtly involves the reader; or to a specifically named other, as in *Hombres* I ("O don't blaspheme, poet, and remember"), where the interlocutor is another poet or an objectified construct of the self. The lover's audience may also be a collective "you," a *vous*, as in *Hombres* II ("Mille e tre"), which depicts the lover boasting of his Don-Juanesque prowess to all thousand and three of his past, present, and future conquests ("Et vous tous . . . / Chéris sans nombre qui n'êtes jamais assez! [And all of you . . . / Countless darlings who are never enough!]"); or, as in the penultimate poem ("O my lovers," *Hombres* XIV), the plural *vous* and the *tu* may combine variously with first person to evoke the "we," the *nous* of a brotherhood of hedonists, bent on pitting an orgy of physical pleasure against the "discours tristes [sorry discourses]" of pedants and sublimators:

Ne métaphorons pas, foutons,
Pelotons-nous bien les roustons,
Rinçons nos glands, faisons ripailles
Et de foutre et de merde et de fesse et de cuisse.

No more metaphors, let's fuck,
Let's stroke our balls well,
Rinse off our dicks, and feast
on come and shit and ass and thigh.

Erotic Realism: "Taking the Side of Bodies"

The rejection of metaphor in "O mes amants" and the privileging of the concretely real highlights an important principle of eroticism. Abstraction exists in an inverse proportion to arousal. To the perverse erotic imagination, vagueness and generality have the effect of a cold shower. This is not to say that there are not lesser degrees of the erotic than the very explicit type that Verlaine more often than not exhibits in these poems. The erotic, in my view, involves a spectrum of intensities, ranging from the least explicit (teasing, titillation) to the most explicit (pornography, obscenity). Vagueness and romantic suggestiveness play a greater role in the lower range of intensities, while graphic realism and specificity predominate at the high end. In this respect, most of the poems in *Hombres* (as well as in *Femmes*) could be classified as pornographic, because of the high degree of prurient sexual explicitness and uncensored focus on detail.

In his introduction to Packard and Mitchell's translation of the Verlaine works, Hugh Harter denies that the poems of *Femmes* and *Hombres* are pornographic (he quotes Lawrence and Elizabeth Hanson to the same effect). Unbelievably, the Hansons state that "pornography they are not if by pornography is meant the deliberate excitation of sexual appetites" (8), which makes one wonder whether they missed the point of the volumes. Harter himself distinguishes the poems from (presumably inferior) "writing simply intended to arouse" (9), when it seems to me that Verlaine's intention might well have been simply that. Remembering that the term "aesthetic" refers etymologically to an appeal to the senses, when aesthetic mastery is applied to content of a prurient or lascivious nature, as is the case in *Femmes* and *Hombres*, the synthesized sensual/sexual arousal is rendered all the more potent and effective. If Verlaine's poetry here is "simply intended to arouse," and if such writing is pornography, then these verses are (brilliantly) pornographic, a term that seems all the more appropriate given the etymology of the word "pornographic" and the recurring references to prostitutes throughout *Femmes* and *Hombres.*

Verlaine's success in effecting a graphic sort of poetic realism may come as a surprise to readers who accept at face value the exclusive, clichéd view of him as an impressionistic evoker of the vague and the diffuse in bittersweet *états d'âme* and moods. There is no denying he is one of the most adept and subtle portrayers of feeling, but initiated readers will also recognize in his work a counterbalancing "desubjectified" interest in capturing objective reality that can be traced to his earliest published pieces and that finds a fuller, if still somewhat muted, expression in *Romances sans paroles* [Songs without words]. In *Femmes* and *Hombres,* the mute is off and the feeling and the reifying are *fortissimo.* That Verlaine thus shows himself capable of being an unabashed realist on the side of things, boldly expressing the object of desire in all its corporeality as well as the often intense emotion of desire and its satisfaction, seems to me to be the most revealing characteristic of these texts, which, in their suppression and dismissal, have been for a century a well-guarded and surprising secret.

The *chosiste* (thingy) representation of the body/thing is essential to the pornographic type of erotic scripting that abounds in *Hombres,* and it takes many forms. It can be as simple and playful as the poet's sensual reference, in *Hombres* I, to deploying "mes mains, mes bras aussi, mes jambes, / Mes pieds [my hands, my arms too, my legs, / My feet]" to cop a feel; or the description can be photorealistic, the object/organ rendered in minute graphic detail, like a face or a facade in a novel of Balzac or Flaubert. Such is the case in *Hombres* XI, which describes the male genitals from every conceivable angle, as well as the stages of an erection. Here, the inventory of parts combines with the increasing degrees of arousal to create a kind of suspenseful dramatic *dénouement,* a theater of pleasure and lust.

Inventories, lists, accumulations of nouns and adjectives are integral features of the overdetermined body/thing that predominates in erotic scripting. In *Hombres* II, the list of male attributes includes eyes, mouth, genitals, thighs, feet, heart, back, ear, nose, arms, sweat, breath, feet (again), toes, ankles, legs, pectorals, and chest; and this inventory adjoins a catalogue of favorite lovers, each possessing a prominent sexual asset that is adoringly praised. Although the two Charleses, Odilon, Antoine, Paul, François, Auguste, Jules, and Henri hardly add up to the 1,003 the lover brags of having had, his promiscuity and insatiable sexual appetite are undeniably worthy of Don Juan.

Lest this piling up of bodies and things imply a completely materialistic self-indulgence lacking any spiritual depth whatsoever, I must emphasize the playful, witty affection lavished upon the objects of desire. The lover is by no means a vapid lovemaking machine, an impersonal sensation slave going through the motions, a mindless libido. He is rather an Epicurean connoisseur of pleasure, a gourmand with an enormous appetite, seated at life's banquet, lustily delighting in many a delectable dish, tasting and savoring each and every delicious morsel. Indeed, the late erotic works are replete with images of nourishment, especially eating and drinking, strong appetites demanding satisfaction that share clear affinities with erotic desire.

Images of Carnal and Divine Delight

Although unsettled by the blatant eroticism of *Femmes* and *Hombres*, the critics have been even more disturbed by the fact that they were being composed at the same time Verlaine was finishing *Bonheur* (Happiness; 1891), the third panel of his Christian triptych, which, with *Sagesse* (Wisdom) and *Amour* (Love), completed "La trilogie de la Grâce" (The trilogy of grace) (Adam 157). How can one reconcile the devout spiritual yearnings of the Christian poems with the graphically explicit poems of hetero- and homosexual lust? Some readers have seen a troubled soul wracked by Faustian waverings between good and evil, heaven and hell. Others have judged the religious conversion insincere and hypocritical. Adam notes, however, that "The surest texts . . . leave no doubt. He remains a true Christian. In 1887, in 1889, his letters inform us that he regularly attends mass and Sunday vespers, and that every morning, as every evening, he kneels at the foot of his bed to say his prayers" (164). How, though, could one possibly celebrate the ecstasies of divine love one moment and revel in lascivious fantasies of carnal pleasure the next?

The title of a work conceived in the mid-eighties and published in 1889, even as he was engaged in completing the Christian trilogy, reveals Verlaine's unique response to his physical and spiritual desires. *Parallèlement* (In a parallel way), "a book," he writes in a January 5, 1888, letter to Félicien Rops, "of an extreme and, so to speak, ingenuous sensuality," is proposed as a kind of complementary expression of carnal love running "parallel" to the celebration of divine love in the trilogy (quoted in Robichez's edition of Verlaine 428). Bringing together poems from various periods, including the youthful lesbian poems, *Les Amies* (Girlfriends) (1867), modeled after Baudelaire, and the more recent *Filles* (Girls), overtly sexy verses though not legally obscene, *Parallèlement* represents, as the author admits in a Foreword to the second edition, "in a sense the *hell* of his Christian Work" (OPC 483) with its quasi-confessional focus upon what Robichez calls "eroticism, liberation, [and] disavowal of the past work" (421). The volume would thus seem to attest to Verlaine's attempt "to have . . . renounced conciliating irreconcilable elements," in keeping with his statement in *Les Poètes maudits* that "I believe, and I am a good Christian at this moment; I believe and I am a bad Christian the instant after" (in Robichez 423–24). Opposing or even contradictory desires need not be self-canceling. The solution is to give them equal, if separate and parallel, expression.

A close reading of the poems consigned to these two tracks reveals them to be parallel indeed, but not necessarily separate. There is interpenetration of the sacred and the profane. The religious verses denote at times "an almost carnal and sensible presence of God" (Adam 166), and the pleasure poems, as I hope to show (especially the sexually explicit *Femmes* and *Hombres*, which perpetuate and elaborate the eroticism of *Parallèlement*), often evince—or at least attempt to—an aura of the sacred. Adam observes that between the two levels

> the foundation is the same. It is this obscure and strong thrust, it is this will to make every greeting, every love his own. And Verlaine knows it well. Old faun on the lookout, he goes about the world, sniffing, reaching toward the beauty that offers itself, eager to take a bite of every fruit. With no remorse for that, since he would be unable to imagine joy offering itself to him without his having the right to receive it. But also ready for higher soarings, ready to be transfixed with love before the image of Christ or that of the Virgin whom he glimpses in his innermost depths, completely open to that supreme love he calls God. (167)

There is something almost naive in this view—or "ingenuous," to use Verlaine's own word. And yet it could be argued that he displays a more unfettered, fundamental appreciation of the religious than Catholic-Christian doctrine has tolerated in modern times. He has somehow been spared the guilt that the Church has reinforced for anyone who dares affirm, outside the strictures of ecclesiastically sanctioned institutions such as marriage, the concurrence of divine and earth(l)y love. In this sense, Verlaine's work testifies to a truly extraordinary intuition of the erotic, as conceptualized by thinkers like Bataille, whose ideas I propose to consider briefly, since they offer a theoretical viewpoint that may well elucidate the poet's case.

Interrelationship of the Erotic and the Religious

George Bataille's definition of "eroticism" in *L'Erotisme* as "the approbation of life unto death" (17) is as broad and ambiguous as it is perplexing, since it encompasses both an affirmation and a negation of the life-impulse. When, though, his distinction between "discontinuous" and "continuous" being is taken into consideration, its meaning becomes clearer. Life, as earthly human beings experience it, is discontinuous: "Between one being and another, there is an abyss, there is a discontinuity" (19). Since continuous being necessarily implies the annihilation of this discontinuity, it could be said that death is the abyss that separates humanity from the continuity it desires. "This abyss is deep, and I do not see any way to remove it. Still we can feel the dizziness of this abyss together. It can fascinate us. This abyss is, in a sense, death, and death is vertiginous, it is fascinating" (19). The desire for continuity thus creates a fatal attraction that conveys us to the brink of death. It is an erotic impulse, according to Bataille, which explains why he defines eroticism as "the approbation of life unto death."

From another perspective, this abyss is also what separates the "sacred" from the "profane." Although these terms are not easily defined, certain general characteristics can be discerned. The profane encompasses the world of discontinuity in which humans live and function or, more specifically, the "world of work or reason" (52); it is also the world of prohibitions, of the forbidden. The sacred includes, by contrast, the world of continuity that humans do not inhabit but nonetheless yearn to attain; it is the "world of violence" (52) and, as well, the world of transgressions.

The erotic impulse aims at continuity, at bridging the gap between the other and the self, the sacred and the profane. It can do so only through violence, the violence of death, which terminates the discontinuous state, or the violence and/or violation of sexual intrusion, which provides a fleeting experience of continuity through "the little death" of sexual union. But violence undermines the stability and well-being of the human community. Murder is an obvious threat, but sexual activity is also disruptive: "in opposition to work, sexual activity is a violence, . . . as an immediate impulse, it can disturb work" (57). Limits, in the form of prohibitions, have thus been imposed upon the violence of murder and sex, and these activities have been relegated to the domain of the sacred, since, as Bataille notes, "whatever is the object of a prohibition is sacred" (76).

But the erotic, as has been said, aims at achieving continuity, which means, in effect, transgressing the forbidden. It resists the prohibitions of "discontinuous life," challenges, questions, disturbs them: "What is at stake in eroticism is always a dissolution of constituted forms. I repeat: of these forms of regular social life, which found the discontinuous order of the defined individualities we are" (25). Transgression of the forbidden is, in fact, an inevitable consequence of prohibition (71ff). In the case of murder, the transgression takes the form of a sacrifice, a deliberate, ritualistic violation of the forbidden, aimed at making contact with the sacred or, if it involves propitiating a god, with the divine (cf. Girard, *Violence*). In the case of sex, the orgy exemplifies an officially sanctioned violation of taboos against unlawful sexual activities, and in certain cultures the violence of sexual transgression has been known to accompany the violence of the blood sacrifice. Bataille sees a fundamental relationship between the two. In addition to the stripping away of discontinuity and the particularity of the individual, he discovers another link between the sacrifice and the sex act, a very tangible, material, animal, human link: "What the love-act and the sacrifice reveal is *the flesh*. The sacrifice substitutes the blind convulsion of the organs for the ordered life of the animal. So is it too with the erotic convulsion: it liberates the excessive organs whose blind games are pursued above and beyond the reflective will of the lovers" (102). The *carnal* links the erotic and religious impulses, surely a remarkable insight, but one that should not come as all that much of a surprise, since the author affirms the interpenetration of the erotic and the religious early in the book when he declares his "intention . . . to envisage in eroticism an aspect of man's *inner life*, of his religious life, if you will" (37), after having cryptically stated at the outset that "all eroticism is sacred" (22). Bataille does not elaborate specific examples of the carnal and the sacred, but a Catholic like Verlaine would certainly recognize flesh imagery as a vivid and pervasive feature of church doctrine and iconography. One need only mention the "incarnation" (the "word made flesh"), the exposure of Christ's naked body on the cross, the brutal piercing of his flesh with nails and spear, and the symbolic consuming of his body and blood in the bread and wine of the mass, to name some obvious examples of "sacred flesh."

When Verlaine intermixes images of carnal and divine love in his own transgression of the forbidden, one could argue, he is merely expressing the erotic in its totality: not as an impious blurring of the boundaries between the sacred and the profane, but as a celebration of pure and impure facets of the sacred that, in ancient conceptions of the religious, existed side by side. Before any definitive conclusions can be drawn, however, this particular aspect of the poet's erotic scripting in *Hombres* needs to be examined in some detail.

The Poetics of Divine Eroticism

Inasmuch as certain basic hierarchies and categories of the Church are reflected in Verlaine's choice of religious imagery, I shall avail myself of them to organize the ensuing analysis. To begin with, we can follow the hierarchy of blessedness, from greater through lesser degrees, which means we start with the figure of God, certainly the most sacred image at the poet's disposal and also one of the most prevalent in the poems. My intention is to study these allusions, for now, without heed to what many may consider blasphemous connotations or contexts, although I shall address the question of blasphemy later. One notes, for example, that the exclamation "nom de Dieu" ("in God's name" / "for God's sake") rather frequently punctuates the text, as it often does in everyday speech, but the poet almost invariably juxtaposes it—sometimes quite cleverly—with a graphically carnal allusion. The comparison of the partner's testicles, one to the other, in *Hombres* XI, for example, concludes with the query "A quelles donc fins, nom de Dieu? [Indeed to what ends, for God's sake?]." In *Hombres* IX, it serves as an enjambment linking a series of rhymed, bawdy adjectives with the image of bodies rubbing together: "Soudain, mutin, malin, hutin, putain, son nom / De Dieu de cul, d'ailleurs choyé, m'entre en le ventre [Suddenly, mischievous, naughty, quarrelsome, whorish, his name- / of-God ass, pampered besides, pokes me in the stomach]."

Invariably in *Hombres*, it is the singular form of the divine name that is deployed as a metaphor to confer sacredness on the object of the lover's lust, equated, for example, with a young man's flesh in *Hombres* X ("Cette chair qui me fut un dieu [This flesh which was a god to me]") and a favorite hustler named Antoine in *Hombres* II. In this last instance, the word figures in a clever rhyme scheme that alternates feminine and masculine versions of the sound /ø/:

> Antoine, encor? proverbial quant à la queue,
> Lui, mon roi triomphal et mon suprême Dieu,
> Taraudant tout mon corps de sa prunelle bleue,
> Et tout mon cul de son épouvantable épieu.
>
> Anthony, again? proverbial for his cock,
> He, my triumphant king and my supreme God,
> Piercing my whole body with his blue eyes,
> And my entire ass with his terrifying spear.

This quatrain offers an excellent illustration of the way the poet intermingles images of spiritual and carnal love. The words "proverbial," "roi triomphal," "suprême Dieu," and "épouvantable" have biblical overtones that create a sense of awe in the presence of divine majesty, which is equated with the feeling of wonder heightened by desire that the mere thought of the love partner's erection excites. The direct link is made by the rhyme "Dieu/épieu," and the sacred connotation is transferred to the "spear/penis" of "épieu" not only by the rhyme but by the embedded "pieu," a *double entendre* that conjoins the sexual image of a "stiff rod" or "ramrod" (as in the phrase "raide comme un pieu") with a homonymic allusion to piety (*pieux*). Most striking of all, perhaps, is the guiltless sense of fun in these plays on words that is so typical of Verlaine's erotic scripting.

Notwithstanding the previous example, it is furthermore significant that *dieu*, as a metaphor, often is not capitalized, which suggests a generalized concept of deity and not necessarily or exclusively the Christian ideal. In fact, a homosexual fixation on the male organ is portrayed in *Hombres* XI as a kind of pagan cult worship, with the poet boldly and playfully severing the "te" from "culte," thrusting it as a *rejet* to the next line in order to make a bawdy rhyme, and all the while maintaining the octosyllable!

> Cependant le vit, mon idole,
> Tend, pour le rite et pour le cul-
> Te, à mes mains, ma bouche et mon cul
> Sa forme adorable d'idole.
>
> Nevertheless the cock, my idol,
> Extends, for the rite and for the cul-
> T, to my hands, my mouth and my ass
> His adorable idol form.

On the purely lexical level, it could be said, in spite of the poet's obvious intention to celebrate the phallus worship of the *culte du vit*, the text seems rather to perform a symbolic decapitation of that much adored fetish in order to shift attention to the *culte du cul*.

Coincidentally with the various references to divinity, the poet utilizes the word "divin" to imbue the subjects and objects it modifies with godlike attributes. In its sacralizing of these objects, it also denotes their capacity to fascinate. The sacred, Bataille points out, inspires two contrary reactions: fear of the forbidden (note the word "épouvantable" cited above) as well as a fascination with it that invites transgression; and "the divine is the fascinating aspect of the forbidden" (76). In the poems, "divine" is almost invariably associated with the sexualized body, as in the allusion to sperm in *Hombres* VII ("Lait suprême, divin phosphore [Supreme milk, divine phosphorus]."

That fascination is the lure to transgression of the forbidden, and the divine the emblem of such fascination, is demonstrated by the sacralizing not of abstract concepts but of specific organs, erogenous zones, body odors, and secretions that are normally concealed, camouflaged, or inaccessible. The poet's real or imagined contact with such forbidden and thus sacred objects is, in this sense, comparable to the desire to make contact with divinity, itself invisible, untouchable, unknowable, except through the violence of death and subsumption into divine continuity. On the carnal level, nowhere is the attempt to achieve continuity through transgression of the forbidden more apparent than in the sacralizing of the sexual orifices. In *Hombres* I, the male anus, as a metonym for homosexuality, is praised as sacred to ancient societies, despite its vilification in modern times:

"C'est mal", a dit l'Amour. Et la voix de l'Histoire:
"Cul de l'homme, honneur pur de l'Hellade et décor
Divin de Rome vraie et plus divin encor,
De Sodome morte, martyre pour sa gloire. . . . "

"It's evil," said Love. And the voice of History:
"Ass of man, pure honor of Hellas and ornament
Divine of true Rome and more divine yet,
Of dead Sodom, martyr for its glory. . . . "

The distinction between the "true Rome" of classical antiquity, where homosexuality was practiced and tolerated, and, by inference, the "false Rome" of the Church, where it has been condemned and persecuted (underscored by the reference to the destruction of Sodom as a martyrdom), is a clear criticism of the ecclesiastical that is echoed in other allusions. When we pass from the level of God and the divine to that of the Church and its conventions, the poetry, while continuing to dress the carnal in the trappings of the sacred, seems simultaneously to develop a teasing parody of ecclesiastical intolerance and prudery with regard to sex in general. And the entire gamut of church doctrine and liturgy is exploited, from the stood-up lover's anticipation of his young friend's arrival "comme le Messie [like the Messiah]" (*H* VI), to the poet's description of one of his "two Charleses" as "[une] Sorte d'enfant de choeur [sort of a choir boy]" (*H* II).

Although it would be impractical to cite every example, it is possible to get a sense of the range of Verlaine's religious eroticism by descending the ecclesiastical hierarchy. Saintliness (*sainteté*), because of the homonymic link, is associated with women's breasts ("Gloire et louange à vous, Seins très saints [Glory and praise to you, saintly breasts]" [*F* II]), whereas a male partner has a testicle "D'un air roublard et bon apôtre [with a crafty, sanctimonious air]" in *Hombres* XI. "O my lovers," a rare Verlainian free-verse poem, is addressed to fellow homosexuals, whom he calls

Les spéciaux, les servants de la bonne Eglise
Dont le pape serait Platon
Et Socrate un protonotaire.

The special ones, the servants of the good Church
Where Plato would be pope
And Socrates an apostolic secretary. (*H* XIV)

If the pope and a high officer of the Roman court are gay, it is only fitting that the "caudataire" (the trainbearer of the pope's robes) should be a mistress whom the poet has himself gladly served from behind (*F* XVI). The imposing demeanor of a bishop wearing his miter, moreover, is the perfect simile for the phallus, and it sparks a chain reaction of related ecclesiastical tropes:

Comme un évêque au choeur
Il est plein d'onction.
Sa bénédiction
Va de l'autel au choeur.

Il ne met que du soir
Au réveil auroral
Son anneau pastoral
D'améthyste et d'or noir.

Puis le rite accompli,
Déchargé congrûment,
De ramener dûment
Son capuce joli.

Like a bishop in the chancel
He is full of unction.
His benediction
Goes from the altar to the chancel.

He only puts on from evening
To dawn's awakening
His episcopal ring
Of amethyst and black gold.

Then the rite accomplished,
Discharged properly,
To put back duly
His pretty hood. (*H* III)

As for ordinary ministers, in Verlaine's erotic church, there is a young man whose beauty renders him a "Prêtre d'Eros ou néophyte, / D'aimer en toute nudité [Priest of Eros or neophyte / by loving in complete nudity]" (*H* X).

One could go on to disengage further examples of the religious vocabulary that suffuses these texts—signifiers such as *baptême* (baptism), *communion, bénédiction, reposoir* (altar), *dévotion, adoration, grâce, céleste, béni* (blessed), *sacré*—but I think Verlaine's rhetorical technique has been sufficiently demonstrated and that his conception of a simultaneously carnal and divine eroticism made clear. Corsetti and Giusto, then, miss the point when, in the introduction to their edition, they conclude that "In the end, Verlaine fails since he remains riveted to his solitude and does not manage to institute and live this *continuity of beings* that G. Bataille speaks of" (24). Continuity, according to Bataille, is achieved either by the violence of death or by erotic transgression (violation) of the sacred. Verlaine achieved continuity in the first sense when he died in early January 1896. But the transgressive eroticism depicted in *Femmes* and *Hombres*, not long before his death, was already aiming aesthetically at continuity in Bataille's second sense with its audacious and irreverent integration of the carnal and the divine. If Verlaine failed to "live continuous being," as the editors claim, both his life and work indicate he was on the right track, in Bataille's view, and it certainly was not for lack of trying.

Now the question of blasphemy can be addressed. Does Verlaine's erotic verse demonstrate a blasphemous mockery of the religious or, following Bataille's theory, an authentic expression of the religious through the erotic? Is his late poetic-erotic gesture, in other words, sacred or profane? The answer, it seems to me, depends on whether sex is placed within the sphere of the sacred or the profane. One way Christianity has radically altered these very ancient concepts is by associating the forbidden (and thus the erotic impulse toward the forbidden) not with the sacred but with the profane: "Eroticism," Bataille observes, "fell into the domain of the profane at the same time it was the object of a radical condemnation" (138). Whereas the sacred once embraced aspects of the pure and the impure, Christian doctrine has relegated the impure exclusively to the profane: "Apparently, for the Christian, what is sacred is necessarily pure, the impure is on the side of the profane. But the sacred for the pagan could also be unspeakably foul" (247). This leads to a curious paradox. The exclusion of the erotic from the sacred means that it can no longer be identified with the religious, but the religious, in Bataille's fundamental interpretation of the term, is a product of the interiority of human experience of which the erotic is an integral part. What bearing does this have, then, on Christianity's status as a "religion"? "It goes without saying that the development of eroticism is *in no way* exterior to the domain of *religion*, but in fact Christianity, by opposing eroticism, has condemned most religions. In a sense, the Christian religion is perhaps the least religious" (38).

Viewed from this perspective, the case of Verlaine's late erotica could be read as an attempt to fathom a more essential sense of the religious in which the erotic complements, indeed encompasses, the divine, rather than opposing or excluding it. These are not malicious poems, even if they do impertinently mock the Church's repudiation of carnal pleasure—a criticism of the ecclesiastical but not necessarily of the religious. Nor do they betray the guilt of an insincere intention or hypocritical attitude. Verlaine, as we have seen, was a practicing Catholic, even as he composed these verses. He thus situates himself in the Epicurean Christian tradition of such kindred souls as Erasmus and Rabelais, who were themselves closer to the more basically human and humanistic religious spirit of Boccaccio and Chaucer than to the view the Catholic Church would tolerate after the Reformation. Adam even imagines that Verlaine,

> [who] hates Protestantism, Jansenism, all the attitudes that, under pretext of morality, surround human life with barriers and guard-rails . . . would say willingly . . . that his Catholicism, broad, comprehensive, immense, "embraces all of human nature" and accepts descent into the double cesspool of man, into his heart, into his loins! (168)

This is not a belief that was popular in the poet's own time, a century ago, nor would it likely find many adherents among churchgoers today. And yet the image of a failing invalid confined to bed, setting erotic fantasies to verse, penning them, as he often did, on hospital stationery, is compelling in its own right and, from a purely human perspective, even tragic. A dying Aschenbach enthralled with the life-affirming youth and beauty of a Tadzio—this is an approbation of life unto death expressed in the best way a poet knows how, in poetry, and appropriately so, since, according to Bataille, "Poetry leads to the same point as each form of eroticism, to indistinction, to the confusion of distinct objects. It leads us to eternity, it leads us to death, and through death, to continuity" (32). In this respect, Verlaine's intuition of the erotic reveals, in addition to its roots in the religious, the very essence of poetry.

CHAPTER 8

The Seduction of Terror: Annhine's Annihilation in Liane de Pougy's *Idylle saphique*

MELANIE HAWTHORNE

Liane de Pougy's *Idylle saphique*, first published in 1901, is remembered as a "blatantly autobiographical" *roman à clef* describing her affair with Natalie Barney in the summer of 1899 (Waelti-Walters 20). As a novelist, Pougy had already published *L'Insaisissable* (1898), a *roman à clef* that became an instant bestseller, and *Myrrhille* (1899). She went on to publish *Ecce homo* (1903), *Les Sensations de Mademoiselle de La Bringue* (1904), *Yvée Lester* (1906) and *Yvée Jourdan* (1908). In the twenty-five chapters of *Idylle saphique*, the author recounts Annhine's (Liane's) affair with Flossie (Natalie), and includes a number of people and events readily recognizable to Pougy's contemporaries. Annhine's friendship with "Altesse" (Valtesse de La Bigne, another well-known courtesan who had served as the model for Zola's *Nana*); the courtship of Flossie (Natalie Barney), dressed as a page who brings flowers and letters; their "date" to see Sarah Bernhardt in *Hamlet* (May 22, 1899), followed by a drive in the Bois de Boulogne, are all included. The parallels with Pougy's life continue: Annhine's current lover Henri (Pougy's lover Henri Meilhac had in fact just died in 1897); a visit to a gay ball with Jack Dalsace (Jean Lorrain); Annhine's flight to Lisbon, where she meets José de Souza Mialho (Pougy rejoined her former lover, the Duke of Oporto, in Portugal in early 1900, which in reality ended the relationship with Barney); Annhine's return to France via Arcachon where she has an affair with her doctor (Pougy had had an affair with Doctor Robin, the personal physician of the Rothschilds and of writers such as Zola, beginning in

1896); and her return to Paris where she has an affair with the eighteen-year-old Maurice de Sommières (Maurice de Rothschild, who became Pougy's interim lover in 1899), before being briefly reunited with Flossie. The novel was published in late September of 1901, and the public ate it up.

The reader cannot help noticing, however, that despite the superficial similarities mentioned above, as autobiography the novel is in some ways a failure. For example, although the novel is sometimes treated as pornographic (Frappier-Mazur), Pougy is in fact reticent when it comes to sexualizing the relationship between her heroines Annhine and Flossie. Thus, even if one accepts Natalie Barney's comment on the novel—"My entire history with Liane is there, moment by moment, or almost" (Chalon, Préface 10)—one cannot help feeling that something has been left out, something is lacking. Moreover, a strictly autobiographical reading must somehow account for the fact that at the end of *Idylle saphique*, Annhine dies, whereas the relationship with Barney proved far from fatal for Liane de Pougy. Born Anne-Marie Chassaigne in 1869, already notorious as an author, stage personality and courtesan when she met Natalie Barney, Liane de Pougy went on to become first a princess (after her marriage to the Romanian émigré Georges Ghika, twelve years her junior, in 1910), then a tertiary lay sister[1] in a Dominican order a few years before her death in 1950. This is all extensively covered in Jean Chalon's biography.

This article will argue that these apparent discrepancies are not inconsistent with an autobiographical reading. Rather, by examining the representation of lack in the novel, it will reconcile the unusual trajectory of Pougy's life as recently summed up in the subtitle of Jean Chalon's biography—"courtisane, princesse et sainte"—and reveal the underlying logic of the novel. The key to this reading is provided by the very event that appears to undermine the autobiographical aspect of the novel: Annhine's death. This death could be ascribed to turn-of-the-century views that lesbianism is *ipso facto* pathological and hence morbid, in which case no further explanation of Annhine's death is necessary. It has been suggested that it is her relationships with men that are killing her. Annhine herself states that "the love of men kills" (82), and Jean Chalon concurs: "the content of *Idylle saphique* [is]

1. "Tertiaries"—or lay members of the Third Order of certain mendicants such as the Franciscans or Dominicans—follow rules adapted from their particular order. The rules were different from those followed by nonlay members of the order (for example, tertiaries could be married), but they conferred certain privileges of the order, such as the privilege of being buried in full habit.

essentially a condemnation of the love of men" (*Liane de Pougy*, 104). Each stage of Annhine's decline, however, seems to coincide with a development in the relationship with Flossie (Barney).

Certainly there is no attempt to present a medically credible account, but the fact that there is no medical etiology does not mean that there is no medical voice of authority. After Flossie's ex-lover, Jane, commits suicide in front of the couple (139), Annhine's friend Tesse decides to take her away to Italy for the winter. Before they depart, the doctor comes to examine Annhine. He enigmatically concludes "you have nothing wrong with you [vous n'avez rien], my child, and yet that is worse than anything" (144).

This pronouncement can be taken to mean (as I have translated it) "there's nothing wrong with you," as a confession that the doctors are unable to discern the cause of Annhine's illness, or in other words, as a failure to diagnose. In this reading, Annhine's illness is hysterical, the typically feminine "default" pseudo-diagnosis that prevails when other explanations have been exhausted. But I wish here to take the doctor's statement more literally. Rather than reading these words to mean "there's nothing wrong with you," we might take them to mean that there *is* something wrong: Annhine has *nothing* where implicitly there should be *something*. The doctor's words—"You have nothing"—may be restated as "you have a lack." This lack, then, is the cause of her illness. The doctor's words turn out to be a diagnosis after all, and taking the diagnosis seriously suggests a different way of understanding the novel.

The obvious reading of this diagnosis is as a statement about the psychoanalytic problem of female castration: the lack must refer to phallic lack. Annhine's illness becomes not hysterical (related to the workings of the uterus), but phallic: instead of something where medically speaking there should be nothing (the usual definition of hysterical symptoms), there is nothing where there should be something (castration). But psychoanalytically speaking, female castration is not, under most circumstances, fatal. To understand Annhine's demise, then, we must still ask what sort of castration—or lack—could account for the heroine's death.

As a clue to the direction this search must take, I wish to highlight a remark made by Annhine in the course of Flossie's courtship. Rebuffing Flossie's advances, Annhine explains: "Don't take advantage of a moment where the unreal and vague feeling of a strange terror would push me into your arms" (75–76). The statement is somewhat ambiguous: it could be that Annhine would fall into Flossie's arms to *avoid* a strange feeling of terror, but that feeling could also be construed as precisely what might lure Annhine *into* the relationship. Is the "push," in other words, a push "away from" or "toward"? Terror, rather than being something to be avoided, might here represent a temptation, might constitute part of the attraction to Flossie. Terror, the horripilating kind that makes your hair stand on end, the kind that might be associated with the threat of castration, may be sought after as something attractive, a component of seduction. An explanation of the apparent paradox might reside in a theory that can effect a conjunction of Eros with Thanatos.

One theory that posits such a conjunction of love and death can be found in Jessica Benjamin's *The Bonds of Love: Psychoanalysis, Feminism, and the Problem of Domination*, and, in a slightly different version, her article "Master and Slave." Benjamin's goal is to analyze "the interplay between love and domination" (*Bonds* 5), and her work on "erotic domination" may explain the seductive quality of terror noted in *Idylle saphique*. She accomplishes this by blending a Hegelian, metaphysical account of the master/slave dialectic of dependence and independence with a psychoanalytic account of the construction of the subject in the earliest years of infancy through a similar paradox, that of the simultaneous need for assertion (to control the other) and recognition (to be seen as a subject by the other).

According to Benjamin, in order to find out if another subject has external existence (the kind of existence powerful enough to guarantee my own existence), I try to control or destroy it. "When I act upon the other it is vital that he be affected, so that I know I exist—but not completely destroyed, so that I know he also exists" (38). For infants, and also sometimes for adults, then, objects (others) have value to the extent that they survive our attempts at destruction. Paradoxically, we do not want the objects of our destructive impulses really to be destroyed. We want them to survive, and we love them to the extent that they do, because this confirms our own subjecthood. This dynamic explains both why a subject may experience sadistic impulses and how a subject may love the object of those impulses even as s/he tries to destroy it.

To explain the complementary attraction of masochism, Benjamin invokes the work of French philosopher Georges Bataille. In Bataille's work, since life is characterized by discontinuity, the subject seeks to return to a state of continuity that transcends the human condition. This isolation of the individual can be overcome, claimed Bataille, through transgression and excess, acts that effect the loss of self. The most obvious of these is death, but Bataille also noted the transgressive possibilities of the ludic, of economic waste and sacrifice, and of linguistic waste such as poetry.

In literal death, the subject's ability to experience this state will be limited, but human sacrifice continued to haunt Bataille. In addition to his fascination with Aztec society, rumors surfaced of his desire to participate in a human sacrifice organized by Michel Leiris. Apparently, a volunteer for the sacrifice had been identified, but legal considerations prevented the realization of the plan (Torgovnick 108). Whether true or not, the rumor illustrates a persistent problem in Bataille's thought: despite his recognition of the many symbolic forms of transgression, waste, and excess, for example in potlatch rituals, in literature, and in laughter, Bataille continued to emphasize the literal over the figurative.

It is for this reason that Jessica Benjamin's work represents a useful extension of Bataille's insights. She recognizes, for example, that the state of continuous nondifferentiation is at best constructed imaginatively, and is not literally available. The adult's desire to recover this retroactively imagined state is a nostalgic project. Rather than exploring the literal death of the subject, then, her work is devoted to explicating the symbolic ways of attempting to (re-)create such a state, through simulations of death such as orgasm (called, after all, *la petite mort* in French), and sadomasochism—or, as Benjamin calls it, "death by other means" ("Master and Slave" 286)—which allow the subject to cease to exist temporarily. Liane de Pougy was not unaware of the attractions of death, especially if the experience was temporary. She attempted suicide several times by taking laudanum, beginning in 1896 (*Liane de Pougy* 125). It was while recovering from such a failed attempt to experience death in 1916 that Pougy met her future husband, Georges Ghika, who was convalescing at the same clinic for the same reason.

Similarly, Benjamin builds on Bataille's assertion that one of the ways to experience the merging offered by death is through "erotic violation": "The body stands for boundaries: discontinuity, individuality, and life. Consequently the violation of the body is a transgression of the boundary between life and death, even as it breaks through our discontinuity from the other" (Benjamin 63). Here, then, we find once again death in an erotic context, which explains why an erotic relationship might be both terrifying and seductive. As Flossie's ex-lover, Jane, puts it in *Idylle saphique*: "we kill each other and complain about each other and hate each other—but we are still attracted to each other" (95). One of the attractions of sadomasochism, then, is that it allows one partner to attempt a return to a blissful state of imagined pre-oedipal indifferentiation through psychic death enacted through a sexual relationship. In this scheme, terror is seductive precisely because it is, in some sense, fatal: the prospect of death is terrifying to the subject, but it is only through such death of the self that the subject can attain the satisfying indifferentiation.

Benjamin thus explains why both dominance and submission may be attractive in an erotic relationship, but in this account of things, there is no indication that either men or women are more disposed toward one role or the other.[2] Both presumably have a need to experience subjecthood, both may wish to return to a state of nondifferentiation. But for Bataille, the encounter between partners in erotic violation is strongly marked by gender. In Bataille's model, there is a clear division of labor by sex which Benjamin upholds and expands:

> Bataille explains that in the ritualized form of transgression known as sacrifice, the man is the actor and the woman is the victim. Still, he argues, the woman performs the function of breaking her discontinuity, of risking death, for both of them. And, I would add, the man upholds the boundaries of reason and control for both, by subjecting his violence to ritual limits. ("Master and Slave" 285)

The roles of master and slave, top and bottom, "s" and "m," are sexed: the dominant is male and subordinate female, but the question arises as to whether this is a necessary division of labor, or merely an arrangement perpetuated by conventions that have solidified into the sex/gender system. Benjamin seems to present the case for essentialism. In her analysis of *The Story of O*, "an allegory of the desire for recognition" (55), Benjamin argues that a penis is necessary to maintain clear roles. The penis represents the

---

2. Benjamin goes on to claim, following Chodorow, that boys experience a need to repudiate the feminine in order to consolidate their masculine identity, and also that girls are more likely to become submissive rather than dominant because they identify with their mothers, who are denied sexual subjecthood in our culture. But this process of either identification with or rejection of the feminine can only take place *after* the subject has established its own gender. Unless gender pre-exists the constitution of the subject, "becoming" a certain gender is part of the process of becoming a subject. Therefore, at the time when the infant first experiences the destructive impulses associated with the formation of subjectivity described above, it does not yet have a fully constituted gender. This makes it difficult to argue that either boys or girls have a different predisposition at this stage of development without invoking essentialism. To the extent, partially acknowledged by Benjamin, that the pre-oedipal state of indifferentiation is a nostalgic retrospective construction of a state that never really existed, the problem can be glossed over, but the issue continues to dog social theory, as Judith Butler has pointed out (*Gender Trouble* 16–17).

master's desire, it emphasizes difference, and it "symbolizes the master's resistance to being absorbed by the thing he is controlling: however interdependent the master and slave may become, the difference between them will be sustained" (57–58). A penis is necessary, then, "as a boundary" to ensure the clarity of roles (difference) and as a safety precaution (to sustain difference). If either participant lost sight of his or her role, the result could be disastrous: the man might forget that he is supposed to uphold certain limits, for example. The penis thus functions like a safeword. However, whereas safewords are agreed-upon, a matter of convention, Benjamin seems to suggest that the role of the penis is a given, rather as Lacan assumes the phallus is a transcendental signifier "because it is the most tangible element in the real of sexual copulation" (287). In other words, the penis not only violates boundaries in the transgressive scene of erotic domination, it creates the boundaries to be violated.

Bataille's, and Benjamin's, assumption that the erotic scene proceeds according to gendered scripts raises the question of what might happen in a relationship of erotic domination in which the roles were not so clearly preassigned, a relationship, for example, in which there was no penis. Is such a relationship necessarily doomed, as turn-of-the-century views about lesbianism suggest? If so, the lack of a penis might explain why Annhine's experiments with "death by other means" prove fatal. Since neither partner possesses a penis, there is no boundary, and since there is no boundary, what should be a controlled loss of self goes out of control, leaving the self "unprotected before the infinite, the terrifying unknown" ("Master and Slave" 291). Annhine is annihilated. Because she has nothing ("nihil"), she becomes nothing, "a nihil," virtually an anagram of her name.

But this conclusion reaffirms the homophobic discourse of pathology. To decide if Annhine's death can indeed be attributed to castration, let us examine more closely the relationship between Annhine and Flossie. It is not sadomasochistic in the traditional sense (if "traditional sadomasochism" is not an oxymoron), but it might indeed be described as a relationship of "erotic domination" since it involves a significant power imbalance.

The roles are not distributed according to the script of sadomasochism, but they do evoke the similarly asymmetrical and psychically loaded roles associated with courtly love. On her very first visit to Annhine, Flossie comes dressed as a Florentine pageboy (28), kneels, "and, with religion, she prostrated herself in front of Annhine" (28). Like the courtly lover, Flossie wants only to serve: "I ask nothing more of you than to let yourself be loved . . . adored . . . admired" (29). She insists that the page's place is at

Annhine's feet (53) and even lies there during an entire performance of *Hamlet*, starring Sarah Bernhardt, hidden from public view by the box (chapter 4).

Within the conventions of courtly love, in an echo of the master/serf structure of feudal society, the lady is viewed as the dominant figure, placed metaphorically on a pedestal, and empowered to bestow or withhold favors, while the supplicant begs for her attention and engages to carry out her slightest wish unquestioningly and slavishly. To use a Hegelian paraphrase, it would appear that the mistress is the master, while the servant is the slave. The relationship between Flossie and Annhine starts out this way. Annhine accepts Flossie as her "slave" (30), and Flossie renounces personhood: "Like the holy martyrs, I shall go bravely to my death for the glory of my religion. . . . I abdicate all personality in this blessed hour, I am nothing but your page" (30). She wants only to die at Annhine's feet (37). Annhine appears to control the relationship by withholding sexual favors and keeping the relationship on a "platonic" (45) level.

The parallel with courtly love suggests that Annhine occupies the dominant, sadist, master, and subject position, but her desire for annihilation, her vulnerability to the seduction of terror, suggests that the role she desires is that of the one who experiences the erotic violation for both partners. The position she appears to occupy should be analyzed further.

The "s" and "m" roles are not as stable as they at first appear. "S" may stand for "sadist," but it also stands for "slave," while the masochist may in fact be the master of the situation, as Hegel's master/slave paradox illustrates. In the case of Barney/Flossie and Pougy/Annhine, the roles may appear equally confusing. As Jean Chalon writes:

> The page and the queen see each other, like each other and come to a perfect agreement. . . . When she recalled this meeting in an almost incantatory way Natalie would repeat to me: "Ah, Liane, she is my most voluptuous memory, she taught me everything." Imagine my stupefaction when, in 1977, five years after Natalie's death, *Mes cahiers bleus* [trans. as *My Blue Notebooks*] was published in which the author [Pougy], speaking of Florence who became Flossie, declared: "Although she was younger than me, she was my exquisite master and opened new horizons for me." So whom to believe? Who was the master, or the mistress, of whom? (*Liane de Pougy* 88)

Thanks to the absence of the penis, the roles are not predetermined, and confusion remains, as Chalon's hesitation between the gendered terms of "master" and "mistress" indicates. In this particular relationship, the lines of dominance are not as obvious as they appear.

Jessica Benjamin notes a similarly deceptive tendency in relationships involving domination. In the child-parent relationship, for example, the infant is usually viewed as helpless and dependent while the parent is powerful, but in the construction of the subject, the infant places itself in the position of subject while the parent is cast as the other to be attacked and challenged. Thus, in *Idylle saphique*, Flossie is consistently described as a child, even though there is little difference in age between her and Annhine—Flossie is 20 (Barney was 23), while Annhine is 23 (Pougy was 30)—but this does not mean that she remains in a submissive role.

Similarly, the courtly love script can obscure the way power may circulate beneath the surface: the Lady, supposedly the powerful figure, can be seen as the "m/bottom/femme" partner because of her passive and reactive position, while the Lover plays the "s/top/butch" role, controlling the development of the relationship. Just as the Hegelian dialectic disrupts the clear separation between master and slave, scenes of erotic domination may become complicated in parallel ways: the mistress takes on something of the slave while the page takes on something of the master. Thus, in *Idylle saphique*, Annhine is in some ways dominated by Flossie, despite appearances. Thanks to Flossie's violations, Annhine has new experiences: "I feel myself to be other. You make me glimpse so many things which I never suspected before" (72). The role of dominant seemed to fit Barney's inclinations. In her journal, Pougy described Barney as controlling: "she adores directing love's revels, leading them on, halting them, starting them up again" (*My Blue Notebooks* 203).

The position of Annhine as the one seeking indifferentiation is consistent with the religious experience of both Annhine and her real-life counterpart, Pougy. According to Bataille, the ritual transcendence associated with erotic violation can also be achieved through religious experience. As Benjamin notes, "Erotic masochism or submission expresses the same need for transcendence of self—the same flight from separation and discontinuity—formerly satisfied and expressed by religion. Love is the new religion" ("Master and Slave" 296). It is therefore not surprising to find religious overtones in Flossie's relationship with Annhine. At one point, they go into a church where they talk about "things of gothic paleness" and imagine Christ descending from the crucifix and apologizing for having replaced the beautiful Greek gods (71).

The parallel between sexual and religious experience can also be found in Liane de Pougy's life. If religious and erotic experience are indeed similar, it would appear consistent, rather than puzzlingly contradictory, that Pougy should move from the abjection of prostitution and the terrors of lesbianism to monastic life's renunciation in her later years. This religious script was, moreover, laid out for Pougy from childhood. Writing in her journal on her fiftieth birthday (July 2, 1919), Pougy noted that the Virgin Mary had appeared to her mother just before her birth and told her that she would have a daughter called Marie who, "After an eventful life . . . will end up in Paradise as a great saint" (*My Blue Notebooks* 23). No doubt this story was repeated to Anne-Marie (alias Liane) by her mother often enough that it became something of a self-fulfilling prophecy. The theme of the eroticization of death is also present elsewhere in Pougy's fiction. The eponymous autobiographical heroine of *Yvée Lester* (1906), for example, exclaims: "Lord, hear the beating of my heart, send me into the void and leave me without life. . . . Take my being which offers itself, destroy it, absorb it, crush it and reduce it in a holocaust, . . . and so doing, make me die many times over, die atrociously, Lord" (*Liane de Pougy* 141).

Annhine, then, is the submissive one. The model of erotic domination provided by Benjamin accounts for the seductiveness of terror she experiences. In her sadomasochistic relationship with Flossie, Annhine succumbs to the terrifying but irresistible desire for indifferentiation. Flossie even recommends it as a cure for depression: "When one is sad, it is so salutary to lose one's individuality. It is like a short death, better and more interesting than sleep" (68). After Tesse takes Annhine away for health reasons, Annhine wants Flossie more and more, and she desires increasingly to be dominated: "she felt an imperious need to give herself, to be taken, brutalized, violated" (180). The desire leads to nymphomania, and Annhine throws herself at the nearest man (180), but her desire is never satisfied. When she returns to Paris, she is capricious, she calms her fever by keeping a skull on her bedside table, she tries writing, and has an affair with an eighteen-year-old man (188–89), but nothing slows the progress of the illness. When Annhine is reunited with Flossie, she offers herself with the words "make me die of ecstasy" (210). Flossie contemplates the possibilities, simultaneously outraged and enchanted by the idea of "killing" the "angel" who had ceased to resist her (211). Although it is not clear that the relationship with Flossie is ever consummated, Annhine's desire for indifferentiation is finally satisfied through her literal physical death. As her condition deteriorates, she suffers "about three deaths per day" (234) until she finally succumbs (252). Does Annhine's experience prove the necessity of a penis for successful "death by other means"? For in Benjamin's analysis, erotic dominance functions only in a heterosexual context in which the roles of dominance and submission are distributed according to sex. The woman risks death, while the man "upholds the boundaries of reason and control." In this light, the textual stress on Annhine's and Flossie's "lack" appears to refer less to a failure to imagine sexual relations without a penis but, on a more complex plane, to a failure to provide a way of making death temporary.

The relationship with Flossie did not work for Annhine as a model of erotic domination, but what conditions might have made such a controlled loss of self possible? If Annhine were the submissive partner, as I have argued, Flossie, as dominant, would have to have some sustained differentiating mark. For Benjamin's model to work properly, Flossie should possess a penis. Since there is no evidence to suggest that Flossie/Natalie is a hermaphrodite, we must look to some symbolic phallic substitution. One method Flossie uses is that of cross-dressing, substituting male clothing for male anatomy. Flossie assumes the male role when she cross-dresses as a page: "She was so sweet and tiny. Her stiff long jacket opened to reveal black breeches, very short, which clung to her thighs, a little white shirt of masculine cut could just be seen covering the elegant and rounded chest, big yellow boots cut across the calves, while on her head there perched proudly a large grey felt hat" (78). Flossie's transgressive role-playing thus signals a willingness to assume responsibility for the boundaries of reason and control, but Annhine seems unable to "read" or accept Flossie's performative masculinity.

Flossie's provisional masculinity and symbolic difference is underscored by an embedded narrative that thematizes phallic presence and lack and shows how phallic difference may be discursively constituted. Flossie and Annhine cross-dress to go to a masked ball, Flossie as a Louis XV marquis and Annhine as an *abbé*. The transvestism (which pervades the entire novel) produces what Marjorie Garber has called a "category crisis," in this case a breakdown in the clear distinction between the dominant and subordinate roles linked to the illusion of the presence of the phallus. Before they go to the ball, Flossie and Annhine dine together and amuse each other by telling bawdy tales in the voice of their assumed personae. Flossie, speaking as a marquis, recounts an embarrassing incident at court, when his (her) ex-mistress draws his attention to "something white, something fine, something dainty, which was sticking out . . . at the place where the satin breeches closed" (127). The marquis had not buttoned the flap of his pants properly, and while the offending protuberance turns out to be only the marquis's shirttail, the positioning of the shirt, hanging out of the fly, presents the shirttail as a phallic substitute.

The marquis discreetly tries to rectify the situation, leaving only "just a little end, perceptible only to those in the know" (128), but the mistress compounds the trouble. She asks to borrow the handkerchief of a baronne, who is proceeding to look for one when the mistress exclaims "Never mind! . . . Your handkerchief is in the gentleman's pants!" (128). The marquis thus becomes embroiled in a duel in which he is injured thanks to the ex-mistress's clever manipulation of his sartorial mistake, but Flossie's story also has another function. In the embedded narrative, things that protrude from a carelessly buttoned fly, such as shirttails and handkerchiefs, are allowed to give the illusion of a hidden phallic presence. Flossie, the narrator, draws attention to the existence of a category of objects linked by their shared status as "things that can hang out of pants." Speaking in a male voice, s/he suggests that shirttails and handkerchiefs are less offensive to modesty than other things which, by implication, might have been revealed. The narrative masquerade evokes relief in the reader that it was *only* a shirttail, and makes the reader forget that, given the narrator's "true" sex, there *was* no more to be revealed. Shirttails and handkerchiefs, used in other narratives to supplement male insufficiency, here disguise lack and displace the anxiety of castration onto the anxiety of impropriety.

While at first it seems, then, that Annhine dies because Flossie lacks a penis, perhaps it is not phallic lack but some other kind that proves fatal. To understand this, we must return to the question of the need for a penis. A boundary is necessary, but must it be grounded in biology, as Bataille and even Benjamin seem to suggest, or could it be symbolic? Are the paradigms of dominant/subordinate, master/slave, subject/other always isomorphic with that of male/female? Is a penis really necessary for casting the erotic scene, or could a shirttail or a handkerchief in the pants do the job?

Flossie's story suggests that clothing can substitute for the phallus. But while "l'habit fait le moine" (clothes make the man), or in Annhine's case "l'habit fait l'abbé," clothes do not make Flossie a man for Annhine, since the latter is unable to translate the *mise en abyme* and see costume as a sustainable mark of difference in her relationship with Flossie. Literal-minded Annhine refuses to think discursively and persists in seeing through the clothes to the literal anatomy beneath, just as Garber suggests readers/viewers persist in looking *through* rather than *at* transvestism. In a word, it is not a phallus that Annhine lacks, but imagination.

For Annhine, the lack of imagination seems an insurmountable barrier, but for Flossie (Barney), costume and performativity seem to have offered alternative ways of structuring relationships that required clear and sustained roles.[3] There are numerous other examples of the successful use of clothing as a marker of difference. Barney played the page on several occasions that have been recorded in photographs.[4] While some photos seem to be from the same sitting, as they depict Barney in the same costume (as Hamlet, a homage to Sarah Bernhardt), others clearly show Barney on different occasions (Chalon, *Portrait*), suggesting that it was indeed a recurrent alter ago for her.

Martha Vicinus has noted the importance, at the turn of the century, for the lesbian imagination of the adolescent boy figure, suggesting that the "protean nature" displayed by the adolescent facilitated the expression of "a double desire—to love a boy [when the boy was really a woman underneath] and to be a boy" (Vicinus 91). But why does the cross-dressing so frequently take the form of imitating a page or a marquis (the two cross-dressing roles Barney assumes in *Idylle saphique*)? The answer may be, in part, that for lesbians these were the images widely available in operatic trouser roles. Unlike the Shakespearean tradition for men, in which men dressed as girls and made love to other men—a fin-de-siècle example of this being Oscar Wilde's "The Portrait of Mr. W. H."—the operatic tradition, as both Terry Castle and Jeanette Winterson have suggested, gave women a voice and allowed the staging of lesbian desire, the "delicious and disturbing pleasure of watching a woman disguised as a man and hearing her woo another woman with a voice unmistakably female."[5]

One of the most well-known trouser roles remains that of Cherubino, Countess Almaviva's page in Mozart's *Le Nozze de Figaro*. (Mozart created a number of other trouser roles, too, including Idamante in *Idomeneo* and Sextus in *La Clemenza di Tito*.) The end of the nineteenth century saw sev-

3. See, for example, Sue-Ellen Case, *Feminism and Theatre*, 50–53. Case suggests that "inter-subjectivity, domestic space and personal friends were the essential elements of Barney's theatre" (50), but only later mentions costume. Also, Case treats both Barney and Pougy as equally aware of the role playing involved in their affair: "Barney and Pougy developed an exciting narrative of seduction. . . . Their public performances continued at operas and other events, scandalizing Parisian society" (51).

4. See, for example, "Natalie Barney en petit page" reproduced in the Des Femmes edition of Pougy's *Idylle Saphique*, "Natalie Clifford Barney à l'âge de 18 ans" in Causse's *Berthe*, and "Pale as Ophelia, grave as Hamlet" in Wickes's *The Amazon of Letters*.

5. Jeanette Winterson, *Art [Objects]*, 107. See also Terry Castle, "In Praise of Brigitte Fassbaender (A Musical Emanation)" in *The Apparitional Lesbian*; Wayne Koestenbaum, *The Queen's Throat*, for the importance of opera in lesbian subcul-

eral additions to the Cherubino story. To begin with, the figure of Cherubino was revived in a three-act play, *Le Chérubin*, by Francis de Croisset. The composer Jules Massenet saw the play at the Théâtre Français, and turned the play into an opera called simply *Chérubin*, first produced in Monte Carlo in 1903.

Chérubin was not Massenet's only venture into erotically charged and ambiguously gendered operas. He also wrote an opera (based on the work of Anatole France) about a courtesan who joins a convent (*Thaïs*, first produced in 1894), anticipating the life story of Liane de Pougy, as well as an operatic adaptation of Daudet's novel *Sapho* (first produced in 1897), about an artist's model. Massenet's world also overlapped considerably with that of Pougy. His pupils included Reynaldo Hahn, whom Pougy attempted to seduce away from Proust (Chalon *Liane de Pougy* 111), and his lovers were reputed to include Mata Hari, who frequented Barney's salon.[6] Alfred Bruneau has suggested that Massenet was obsessed by "the confrontation of courtesan and priest" (in Irvine 192), a confrontation that forms the narrative core of *Idylle saphique* also.

But to return to Cherubino. Mozart's role had allowed the staging of female homoerotic desire, creating a situation where one woman could sing a love song to another with public approval, but Cherubino was a relatively minor role. Massenet's opera revived the character, giving him/her new life and making him/her the central character, an acknowledgment of the character's persistent role in the imagination of some opera-goers. Massenet's opera goes one step further than Mozart, however, by presenting Cherubino as a Don Juan. At seventeen, Cherubino has received his military commission, historically a popular career choice for cross-dressing women (Wheel-

ture; Corinne E. Blackmer and Patricia Juliana Smith, eds., *En Travesti*; Sam Abel, *Opera in the Flesh*, especially chapter 10, "Women-as-Men in Opera," for the discussion of Cherubino as Foucauldian "masturbating child" and of Octavian's sword as detachable phallus; and Elizabeth Wood, "Sapphonics," for some of the lesbian connections between turn-of-the-century opera and Barney's circle.

6. Massenet's most recent biographer, Demar Irvine, has written: "From the evidence available, we must conclude that [Massenet] enjoyed a rare domestic serenity and happiness. . . . The conscientious biographer must dismiss all hearsay evidence as rubbish. Thus, Massenet's supposed 'affairs' with named correspondents—typically prima donnas—are probably sheer fabrications of mischievous minds. . . . That the man had a warm heart we can be sure, and also that he was friendly and urbane. But as far as we are concerned here, his only mistress was the lyric theater, to which he was utterly devoted." *Massenet: A Chronicle of His Life and Times*, 47. I beg to differ. For references to Mata Hari, see 262.

wright), but he/she simultaneously courts the Countess, a Baroness, "L'Ensoleillad" (a dancer and the King's mistress), and the Count's ward Nina, who finally wins his heart. Massenet insisted on a trouser role for the lead in the face of considerable opposition: right up until the dress rehearsal, Croisset, author of the play and one of the librettists for the opera, maintained that the role should be performed by a man. But Massenet held out, and in the première of *Chérubin* (on St. Valentine's day, 1903), the lead role was sung by Mary Garden, one of the great divas who, according to Terry Castle, "have always excited ardor in their female fans as well as male" (Castle, *The Apparitional Lesbian* 202). Another diva on Castle's list—Frederica von Stade—takes the role of Chérubin on the most recent recording of Massenet's work. Whatever Massenet's intentions in insisting on a trouser role, *Chérubin* seems consistently to be appropriated as a vehicle for lesbian desire.

Indeed, this seems no less true today than at the turn of the last century. Although Massenet did not delve into Cherubino's affair with the Countess, this aspect of the character's life has been recently revived in (gay) composer John Corigliano's *The Ghosts of Versailles* (an opera commissioned from Corigliano and librettist William M. Hoffman by the Metropolitan Opera of New York and first performed in 1991). Here, the Countess and Cherubino sing a love duet, and the fact that the relationship has been consummated is represented, albeit heterosexually, by the fact that the Countess has had a child by Cherubino. The reappearance of Cherubino in Corigliano's postmodern tribute suggests not only the enduring popularity of Mozart's characters, but also the persistence of the audience's pleasure in the multiple levels of meaning created by trouser roles.

"The Ghosts of Versailles" has yet another lesbian subtext, though, this time one that sends us back to the turn of the century, specifically to the year 1901, in which *Idylle saphique* was published. For Corigliano's title also evokes the "ghosts" purportedly seen at Versailles by two lesbian Oxford dons on a visit to the palace in 1901 and described in their pseudonymous joint work *The Adventure*. First published in 1911, this book became a bestseller and attracted numerous responses, rejoinders, and republications.[7]

The shared paranormal experience—seeing ghosts in the gardens of Versailles—was, it seems, the foundational moment in the lifelong relationship of Charlotte Anne Moberly and Eleanor Frances Jourdain, principal

7. I am telescoping a long and complex series of events here, but for a fuller account of these sightings, the background, the publications, responses and consequences, see Terry Castle, "Contagious Folly: *An Adventure* and Its Skeptics" as well as "Marie Antoinette Obsession" in *The Apparitional Lesbian.*

and vice-principal respectively of St. Hugh's College, Oxford. Yet it was not just the fact that the vision was shared that bound them together, but the subject of the vision: Marie Antoinette. As Terry Castle has suggested, the figure of Marie-Antoinette (the heroine of Corigliano's opera) has served as a kind of lesbian code, "a kind of lesbian Oscar Wilde," and references to her and her court could function "as a kind of proleptic hint to the reader—as the cipher, or symbolic intimation, of Antoinette's own emerging lesbian desires." Moreover, although the ghost of Marie Antoinette appeared to Moberly and Jourdain on August 10, the anniversary of the sacking of the Tuileries, the two women came to believe that their vision of an *ancien régime* version of Versailles came from the queen's recollections of an earlier moment, October 5, 1789, Marie Antoinette's last day at the Trianon, where she received the news that a mob was on its way from Paris. In other words, Marie Antoinette was "channeling" an earlier time, when her court was still intact, a court at which Beaumarchais's play *The Marriage of Figaro*—the play on which Mozart based his opera, the opera which gave us the trousers role of Cherubino—was first performed.

Within a few years of Massenet's revival of Cherubino, another memorable trousers role was created, once again using the figure of the *ancien régime* marquis, though this time a marquis not from the French court but from the Austrian one (the court of Marie Antoinette before she married Louis XVI). The figure of Count Octavian, from Strauss's *Der Rosenkavalier*, became available on the operatic stage for lesbian appropriation in 1911 (the year in which Moberly and Jourdain's *The Adventure* appeared), and has been part of the operatic lesbian repertoire ever since. (Not uncoincidentally, this role too has been famously incarnated by Frederica von Stade, though Terry Castle prefers to focus on Brigitte Fassbaender's film version.)

While Massenet and Strauss may merely have been, shall we say, "attuned" to gay desire at the turn of the century, Pougy herself was more than passingly acquainted with the world of opera (though not always as a music lover): in 1894, Henri Meilhac—librettist of Massenet's *Manon*, Bizet's *Carmen*, and Offenbach's *La vie parisienne*, among other works—paid 80,000 francs to see Pougy in the nude; in *Idylle saphique* this role is played by Flossie's American fiancé Will, though he pays only 25,000 francs for the honor (103). Meilhac and Pougy had an affair in which Pougy's rival was Geneviève Straus, Bizet's widow. Meilhac had worked with Massenet—the former as one of the librettists, the latter as orchestrator—of Debussy's *Kassya*, an opera based on a story by Leopold von Sacher-Masoch and performed in 1893 (Irvine 186). Pougy's best friend, Valtesse de La Bigne ("Altesse" in *Idylle saphique*), was the mistress of Offenbach, one of the many artistic conquests that earned her the nickname "l'union des artistes." The same year that Pougy revealed herself to Meilhac, she revealed herself in another way to the public at large through her debut at the Folies-Bergère, where she carried on a much-talked-about lesbian affair with Emilienne d'Alençon. The worlds of opera and Lesbos-sur-Seine were thus never very far apart for Pougy, continuing a tradition reputedly begun, not uncoincidentally, in the late eighteenth century (Bonnet 11, 65, 113–14).

The appeal of the page and the marquis seems to continue into the present, as a recent series of photographs entitled "The Knight's Move" by Tessa Boffin illustrates (Boffin and Fraser, *Stolen Glances* 42–50). This series offers a narrative journey of re(dis)covery, framed parenthetically by photographs of a dark wooded path leading past an angel-capped monument of the kind often seen in cemeteries. In between are five photographs depicting images of lesbians lost to history, including those of an eighteenth-century Octavian-like marquis described as "Casanova" and a "lady-in-waiting" who looks for all the world like Marie-Antoinette.

Barney was at home as the page or the lady, and numerous photos depict her in feminine poses such as a "lady with her page" and as a nymph (Wickes), underscoring the performance *qua* performance of all the roles she played, something that can also be seen in the photographs in the *Album secret*, in which she mimics the seductive poses of stereotypical pornographic pictures of women. This flexibility was not unique to Barney, since others in her circle seem to have enjoyed a similar performative playfulness, including Romaine Brooks, but especially Renée Vivien (who, like Pougy, portrayed Barney as a page in her novels, see *Une femme m'apparut* [A woman appeared to me], 1904). A series of photographs depicts Vivien in costume that evokes *both* the cross-dressing roles Barney plays in *Idylle saphique* (Chalon, *Portrait*; Jay; Wickes): it is at once that of a page (as suggested by the juxtaposition of cover photo and title of Karla Jay's biography *The Amazon* [Barney] *and the Page* [Vivien])[8] and also that of a marquis (in satin pants and lacy sleeves), as identified by Romaine Brooks, who recalled seeing Vivien "dressed in a masculine Louis XVI costume" (Werner 180). Indeed, the roles circulate so freely that in one photo they are misattributed. In one illustration of Jean Chalon's *Portrait of a Seductress*, Vivien and Barney are posed together in the same costumes as on the cover of Jay's book.

8. In addition to the roles depicted on the cover (Natalie as lady and Vivien as page) and the linguistic parallel of title and subtitle (Amazon:page::Barney:Vivien), Jay's title evokes George Wickes's biography of Barney, *The Amazon of Letters*.

The caption reads "Natalie (the little page) and Renée," but it is of course Vivien, not Barney, who is dressed as the page in this picture. The slippage indicates that Barney is still somehow the page even when she is dressed as the lady. For Barney/Flossie, roles are fluid and performative (so much so that entire identities are confused), but there seems little or no evidence that Liane/Annhine participated in this kind of role-playing, with the notable exception of the intriguing photograph of Pougy with Régina Badet in a ballet by Jean Lorrain entitled "Le Rêve de Noël" from 1896 in *Mes cahiers bleus* (note this is one of several illustrations omitted from the English translation).

The role of "lady" is the only role we ever seem to see Liane play (the reclining portrait, which Barney kept by her bed until her death, is reproduced on the cover of *Idylle saphique*). She never seems to want to play the page. In fact, the desire to cross-dress (though not to dress up) seems to have been unknown to her. In 1920, Liane de Pougy, then Princess Ghika, wrote in her journal: "I shall never understand that kind of deviation: wanting to look like a man, sacrificing feminine grace, charm and sweetness" (*My Blue Notebooks*, 111). At about the same time, Princess Ghika received the same diagnosis as her heroine Annhine had gotten some twenty years earlier. In the 1920s, Pougy began to suffer increasingly from depression. Her doctor, Dr. Hayem, prescribed injections of radium every other day, but the depression, compounded by deaths in the family, mysteriously failed to respond to his treatment. Pougy switched to Dr. Clément, who could find nothing wrong with her:

> "*You have absolutely nothing wrong with you* [Vous n'avez rien, rien, rien]." The princess bursts into tears. The doctor is surprised at this: "*What, I tell you there is nothing wrong, and you cry? —Doctor, I so much wanted to have something* [j'aurais tant voulu avoir quelque chose]," *and for you to cure me*," answers Liane. (*Liane de Pougy*, 208)[9]

Like Annhine, Pougy is unable to confront and overcome lack, but looks to medical authority to supply what is missing. She is reduced to tears by the fact that her condition has no medical cure, but as I shall suggest below, failed to realize that the cure was not something a doctor could simply prescribe.

At the time of this depression, in the 1920's, Pougy was still seeing Natalie Barney. In *Idylle saphique*, Annhine's death put an end to the relationship with Flossie, but in real life things were more ambiguous. Although the

---

9. In this biography, Chalon uses italics to indicate quotations from previously unpublished letters, diary entries and other papers.

affair ended, the friendship between Barney and Pougy continued, amorously at times. When Georges Ghika left Pougy (temporarily, as it turned out) on July 4, 1926, Barney was Pougy's support. She introduced Pougy to Mimy Franchetti, who by September 23 had become Pougy's "consolation." In October, Natalie called on Pougy in Paris in the middle of the night, with Mimy Franchetti and a violinist named Pola in tow, and set about comforting Pougy: "It was like a lovely dream. Nathalie [sic] on one side, stroking and caressing me; Mimy on the other, her lips on mine; Pola playing for us in the next room" (*My Blue Notebooks* 203).

Pougy's "lack" continued, then, to cause depression, a narrative interwoven with her relationship with Barney, but it would not continue much longer. Barney's jealousy of Pougy's relationship with Franchetti during a trip the three took to Venice in late 1926, not long after the episode described above, led to a rupture. Pougy and Barney saw each other again only once, by accident. In 1934, Pougy was shopping in Toulon when she caught sight unexpectedly of Barney. Barney smiled, "half-ironic, half-amused" (*My Blue Notebooks*, 258); Pougy fled, took refuge in a cafe, and reassured herself in her usual narcissistic way, by contemplating her own beauty. They would never see one another again, despite Barney's attempts at reconciliation. In the words of Jean Chalon, "How sad, this separation, in Toulon, on a sidewalk, of two women who once loved one another and who, in avoiding each other, nevertheless cannot forget what brought them together" (325).

Perhaps finally it is not so much phallic lack as lack of imagination that proves fatal for Annhine. Flossie credits her with the "gift" of imagination, and extols its virtues: "If at my christening the fairies had offered me a treasure, that is the one I would have chosen as the best of all" (49). While Flossie appreciates the advantages of this gift, it is not clear that Annhine does. Similarly, despite his emphasis on symbolic forms of excess, Bataille seems unable to appreciate the role of imagination to supply what may be missing in life, and falls back on a literal-mindedness that dismisses the rich wastefulness of representation. Despite the transgressive possibilities of the ludic, as Sartre puts it, "[Bataille] tells us he is laughing, but he does not make *us* laugh" (*Situations I* 158). Like Annhine, Bataille has imagination, the best of all gifts, but lacks the ability to use it. And as the doctor in *Idylle saphique* correctly diagnoses, "that is worse than anything."[10]

10. I am greatly indebted to Harriette Andreadis, Samuel Gladden, Pamela Matthews, Krista May, Mary Ann O'Farrell, Martha Vicinus, and Margaret Waller for their help with this article, an earlier version of which was presented at the Nineteenth Century French Studies Colloquium in Lawrence, Kansas in October, 1993.

CHAPTER 9

René Crevel's Body Algebra

GARETT R. HEYSEL

> Psychoanalysis helped us to see things clearly. . . . That said, I do not believe that it is possible to reform sexual life, in the context of a bourgeois world, with the help of philosophy.
>
> —René Crevel

In his preface to Deleuze and Guattari's *Anti-Oedipus*, Michel Foucault characterizes the France of the 1920's and 1930's as dreamy and utopian. Certainly these two terms apply to the surrealists. In 1924, Breton himself locates "sur-reality" at the intersection of dreams and reality—an absolute and pure state of reality—a point, for Foucault, at which Freud and Marx meet. Breton's reading of Freud posits great possibilities for desire and the unconscious as a revolutionary mechanism (Breton, *Manifestes* 24). To unveil unconscious thoughts and desires and perhaps even to act them out was for Breton the ultimate surrealist act. René Crevel, a surrealist writer, at first intimately associated with Breton's group, also saw the potential of desire, both for himself and for his writing. Crevel's form of desire, however, distinguished him from his surrealist contemporaries. Although credited with introducing the surrealists to hypnosis and to automatic writing, René Crevel is often cited in anthologies, yet he is quickly dismissed and almost always categorized as the openly homosexual member of the group. His oeuvre has suffered an even worse fate, since it remains largely unknown and even more rarely studied.

Given the recent critical attention paid to the role and figure of the human body in literature and culture, along with a growing interest in gender studies, the overlooking of Crevel's work seems curious (Beizer; Brooks; Fuss 205–88; Rivers). This is especially true in the case of *Mon corps et moi* of 1925, which unequivocally engages the questions of desire and the body. What is more important, *Mon corps et moi* develops a philosophical explanation of desire and foregrounds the role of the body in the process. Crevel's writing attempts to liberate his own desire, rejecting the ideological bivalent categories of heterosexuality and homosexuality, while striving for a novel expression of his unique longing for corporal pleasure (Schehr, *Alcibiades* 23–67). One focus of this study will be to evaluate the possibilities for desire suggested in *Mon corps et moi* through an investigation of the figure of the body—its representations and its manipulations—as the site of desire.

In the most basic terms, *Mon corps et moi* may be considered as a collection of memories. Seeking solitude, the narrator retreats to a room in the mountains to reflect upon his life's experiences. Like many of Crevel's texts, this one reveals much about his life and vice versa. Crevel sought solitude and rest at a mountain clinic as he suffered from the effects of tuberculosis. Referring to another novel, *Détours*, written shortly before *Mon corps*, Crevel wrote to Paul Eluard:

> This manuscript of *Détours* which is hardly embellished with correction stars, nevertheless took a very long time to write, since if a couple of weeks were necessary for me to edit this first novel, I must admit that I spent a number of years not living it but thinking it. I will add that I continue to do so.
>
> So, *Mon corps et moi*, which follows it, is only the reprise for a longer analysis, a longer meditation, of diverse ideas, hallucinations, dreams, regrets, of which *Détours* holds in itself the promises or the threats, whichever you please. (quoted in Rochester 35)

Crevel's tortured prose reflects a less than ideal existence accentuated by disappointment and solitude. Throughout most of his memories, however, the body plays a repeated and central role. It is possible to distinguish the various representations of the body in *Mon corps* into three groups: the body re-membered, the reflected body, and the body in nature. I do not wish to consider these categories as exclusive; rather, my goal is to clarify the various forms the body takes in Crevel's text so as to flesh out the relationship between the body and desire. By examining the different textual manipulations of the Crevelian body I hope to draw some larger conclusions as to what may be Crevel's philosophy of desire.

As an integrated unit, the body makes few appearances in the text. In fact, the male body is almost always partial, fragmented, or cut up. Crevel's body-cutting differs from the familiar mutilation and degradation of women's lips, eyelids, and hands found in many other surrealists' texts, in that he dismembers and then re-members male bodies. The first body reference in *Mon corps* is to the skin. He writes: "Each time, however, before it could even wonder at its plantlike softness, my late afternoon skin remembered a carnation" (21–22).[1] From the very beginning, the skin's importance to the body is foregrounded in two curious ways. First, the skin enjoys an immediate association with nature in its comparison to a plant; second, the skin remembers. Yet the latter is less surprising given that memory is as partial as the body. For Crevel, memory is suspicious: "From that time onwards, how not to wish for the minute when, free from all thought, I could get rid of the memory itself" (31). The mere thought of some "complete" memory, just like some "complete body," is absurd for Crevel. Coherent and total memory in *Mon corps* belongs to the dubious realm of representation, which Crevel disdains, preferring partial dreamlike recall, where all parts of the dream deny closure and synthesis. At issue also from the very beginning in *Mon corps* lies the metaphysical duality of the body versus the mind. Crevel's narrator distinguishes between two types of bodies: "minds wearing bodies" and "bodies wearing minds." He wonders whether the body wears the mind, like it wears a suit or a dress, for example, or does the mind wear the body? (23). The difference is important since only "minds wearing bodies" experience desire directly on the surface of the body. Such immediate body pleasure distinguishes the *je* from the *autre* at the very onset of the text: the narrator proclaims himself a "mind wearing a body," distinct from all others who will allow the cognitive filter of the mind to rob them of their pleasure. Crevel vows "not to give up on happiness but to live, act and get off with thoughts [jouir avec des pensées]" (23). In order to combat the other's pretension of wearing the mind, Crevel's writing isolates the body of the other by dissection—singling out and valorizing their body parts—while ignoring their minds. For example, on one occasion the narrator seeks the company of a particularly well-made man, Pepo, to whom he refers as "l'homme le mieux fait du monde."

And yet, as handsome and pretty as the most well-built man in the world may be, he cannot remain whole. Pepo's tanned thighs, torso, abdomen, and varnished skin are enough to make the scopophilic narrator nervous: "I worry: a curious jersey, funny dough. I do not understand anything about this polished chest and stomach. . . . I like the color of well-done skin, the attire of sunbathing, but all these ostentatious displays of brown greases, rouges on a body" (78). In memory, even the most well-made man is as easily unmade as he is undressed. Pepo's problem is that he wears his mind instead of his body. Specifically, Pepo too is hypocritical in pleasuring his clingy older female friend, while secretly eyeing male cyclists'

1. I thank Philippe C. Dubois for his help with the translations of Crevel's writings.

posteriors and thighs. The visitor to the lodge loses interest when he discovers Pepo's vain insecurity and theatrics. "L'homme le mieux fait du monde" is not true to himself.

Men as easily dis-membered as Pepo will not satisfy Crevel's desire. An evening at the boxing ring, where he can watch some true men-on-men contact, might offer a more pleasurable memory. The memory quest for "real" men, however, falls short as the narrator recalls a pseudo dandy/artiste named Jojo, who is dressed in butch military gear and who is squaring off with the he-man Zo. Like the promise at the lodge, body parts suffice to titillate the narration, but not the narrator: "[H]eavy neck, fingers that are too fat, and so one could forget the neck and fingers, legs" (87). But the desired brawl between "real" men becomes just another silly spectacle. "What, more affectation . . . ?" he asks, more "art like at the home of the dancer of the best-made man in the world? I hoped boys would be true all the way to their blood" (87). A show will not suffice. The sight of thick appendages and manly chests in this boxing ring fade to art and artifice. Zo, however, is more desirable in his raw and natural appearance. As the narrator describes him: "Vegetable, or mineral. Not animal. His muscles inhabit an insensitive skin. Protected from pain, he must know nothing of sensual pleasure" (88). Nevertheless, Zo has a skin problem. It is beautiful to look at, but too hard to touch: "As for the body, it seems of varnished precious wood. He is very handsome and yet I do not feel like touching him" (88). What the narrator really wants to see and feel is the real thing—a struggle to the death—or a spectacle devoid of fiction.

Re-membering bodies for Crevel involves violence, whether that violence be directed toward the self as he wonders if he will have "the strength to try a few times if I did not catch a glimpse of the solution in the definitive, ultimate gesture?" (102). Or that violence may be directed toward someone else: "I would like, with the point of a knife, to trace drawings over all his body" (88). Even as a child, the narrator fantasized over the plight of an infamous murderess most notable for her neck. He lovingly called her "la dame au cou nu," or the lady with the naked neck. Like Pepo and the boxers, she too falls prey to the cutting edge of his memory; her identity has been reduced to her most precious body part. Besides the intrigue she provokes as someone who killed her own husband and mother, desire for "la dame au cou nu" works differently than desire for men. First, the recalled fantasy is only possible through the intermediary of Rémy, an older local boy who supplies his younger friends with magazines depicting the plight of the infamous killer. The exotic *dame* is desired for no other reason than her most salient feature: "The lady with a naked neck is the lady with a naked neck" (26). In his memory, however, her unique symmetry quickly unravels: "So, she that I believed the only one, she whom I wished would live always identical to oneself [soi-même], in my memory already, it's no longer like the egg in its shell" (27–28). At the very least, the choice of the disjunctive pronoun *soi* instead of *elle* seems curious. The "dame au cou nu" surpasses and transgresses her own identity, since in his memory she becomes equal to the neuter and impersonal subject. Moreover, her ambiguous reflexive identity mimics the narrator's cry to be sufficient unto himself: "But this evening, my wish finally realized, I find myself available to myself" (21). For him a desire to be alone to seek self-availability translates into risk of both complete disengagement and loss of gender for her.

Being available to oneself involves another representation of the Crevelian body—the body in the mirror. For example, most striking in the narrator's recollection of his sexual experience as a soldier is the role of the mirror. Unsuccessful in reaching orgasm with a gloved lady, the soldier throws her off to finish "the business" himself. His glance in her mirror recalls childhood masturbation in front of his family's mirrors in the hallway. In front of her, he becomes self-available through his own recollected reflection. Certainly, for Crevel, autoeroticism in front of a mirror has advantages over sex with a woman. Looking back at himself, as a soldier or as a young boy, most closely resembles a state where the body is equal to itself. In the mirror, the desperate woman's body disappears while the reflected self appears along with another self and the soldier seems to finally enjoy his "mind dressed with a body [esprit habillé d'un corps]." The reflected image allows the loss of the self: "And then, in front of a mirror, my eyes would not know how to learn to know this body to which they belong" (129). A vision of the same produces another. If autoeroticism offers one definition of self-availability, then masturbation in front of a mirror offers a greater pleasure that risks self-effacement. Unrecognizable and yet the same, the reflected body disallows knowledge, forcing the mind inside the skin while focusing pleasure on the body. As a boy in a hall of mirrors, he feels the pleasure process increase, as do the bodies:

> Thanks to the indulgence of that mirror, I loved myself as I did at twelve years old, when, my family asleep, I would go to the hallway, turn on the lights and with the complacency of the mirrors which multiplied me, got off on a body that my hands loved to caress without moreover knowing which way to use it for a specific pleasure. (124–25)

At the age of twelve, he has already become a *bricoleur*, tinkering with his body, processing desire, without making products. For Crevel, desire—whether reflected or re-membered—is always a process. In the mirror, desire as process centers on one's own body, while recalled desire targets the other's body. Both processes transgress the body's unity, either through multiplication or division, although neither process allows the body's autonomy from the mind. Inevitably the soldier, like the voyeur at ringside, finds little satisfaction in his sexual adventures. In fact, in watching sex or being watched having sex by another, he feels "the same sort of pleasure arranging my library once a year" (127).

It would seem that the problem with desire reflected and desire remembered lies in the fact that both processes are ultimately subordinate to the conscious mind. In a hierarchical fashion, reason, guilt, and conscience disallow the pleasure of one's own body and especially one's own skin. Crevel's narrator turns to nature, seeking a novel desiring adventure in the mountains where all pleasure centers on the skin: "At this altitude all skin must be well-cooked and offer to breathe in a little closer, a surprise more appealing than that of hot bread" (117). The skin's baked surface, the hoped-for locus of ultimate pleasure, connects with nature and desires nature, unlike any other surface. Nudity is critical to a natural body adventure. The body and the body's surface must be free of clothing in order to permit maximum connections between skin and nature.

> I will open my shirt to the belt. The breeze will try a funny game around my torso. Each caress will imprint itself in sweet circles. Beautiful parallels will add up to give me the contemptuous vivacity of the zebra and my epidermis become a sheath of happiness, my chest will enlarge and strain a thousand little elastic unsuspected muscles. (117–18)

In a frenzy of half-sheathed bodily pleasure in nature, the body threatens to open itself—to offer itself up like a flower: "my chest will it open itself up, hive finally submitted to the bees of happiness?" (118). Here the body waits calmly passive and ready to be stung by nature. Each body part waits, ready to cede and become free:

> One must be docile. In the cities, my feet imprisoned by leather, insist on some vengeance. All my skin exiled, incensed to the point of no longer knowing, after days of waiting, how to use for the greatness nocturnal happiness some other skin whose search had complicated the hours. But today the flesh is free, my feet no longer remember the shoes, or the socks. (118)

Memory and knowledge become temporarily impossible as the body willingly succumbs to nature. The flesh too finds a freedom it could not enjoy in the city. With every surface, every fold of the skin exposed and open, and every trace of the flesh set free, the body becomes curious, processing pleasure directly while bypassing the intermediary of the mind: "What honey are you going to bring me, desires, that I let the swarm scatter? I am curious about all flowers" (119). Even more liberating than reciprocal nature/body contact and curiosity is the potential for nature to make man more than himself. Whereas in the city, man is belittled, pushed aside and alone, in nature lost in naked bliss he becomes *M*an: "I was a lost man. I have found myself again. At last I am Man. I believe in my grandeur because I walked naked in the sun" (119). Only now, and through striking Rousseauist imagery, can Crevel explore the possibilities of what he considers Man's full desire ("plein désir") (119).[2]

Not only does a single desperate *m*an become something greater than himself, perhaps even a symbol for all humanity—"je suis l'Homme"—but he becomes lost, found, and forgotten all in the same day. Later, Man becomes Earth as his body changes into a pleasure-giving terrain: "My fingers barely reaching let them go. And by the top of their small sensitive tips, learn to know the vibrations of a creature that one forces to love, to happiness. And how not to want to get lost in the heart of countries that offer a voluptuous atlas" (120). On the skin-map surface, the neck becomes an isthmus, while the shoulders turn to plateaus. This image of the skin as a sensual exploring envelope seems to anticipate Didier Anzieu's metaphor of the Skin Ego: the body's surface functions as the boundary, interface, and site of inscription for nature, heightening the process of unfettered desire (40).

Although at the beginning of the experience the narrator believes himself a "sensual" rather than a "sentimental" individual, the mountain adventure reveals neither category to be wholly appropriate. In fact, from now on, the body and the pleasure it seeks and produces are only classifiable in their multiplicity: "So many adjectives are necessary to describe me that I can brag—or accuse myself—of belonging to no single category but to all of them" (122). Plural and universal, everywhere and nowhere, the body and the self get lost. The mountain adventure disperses and decodes the body and the self, leaving them neither categorical nor recognizable: "From one

2. The return of Rousseauism is especially evident in the ninth chapter of *Mon corps et moi.* Rochester indicates that after his death many pages of Crevel's reading notes on Rousseau's *Confessions* were found in a suitcase. (157)

minute to the next I no longer recognize myself. I no longer recognize myself in my body" (122).

On the mountain and caressed in nature, the Crevelian body has broken free from traditional desiring relationships. Triangular and structured desire—described by Freudian psychoanalysis and venerated by men such as Breton—remains insufficient to describe Crevel's body experience.[3] A more useful model of understanding desire in nature comes from Deleuze and Guattari's notion of desiring-production. In the *Anti-Oedipus*, Deleuze and Guattari propose that the schizophrenic out on a stroll is a better model of desiring-production than a neurotic lying on the analyst's couch. For them, schizophrenic desiring-production involves an immediate connection to nature. Such a connection allows multiple and endless contact with all life. The polarity between man and nature fades away, and eventually becomes false and untenable. The same holds true for Crevel on the mountain where oppositions such as body/nature, self/other, outside/inside, and the like, lose all meaning.

Nevertheless, Crevel's desire in nature cannot last. Ultimately memory, prohibitive and oedipalized, robs the body of its place in the process of pleasure. Memory also reminds the narrator of his loneliness. Even the skin in nature, touching and connecting with the grass, opening before a flower, finally succumbs to the mind that will lead the way off the mountain. The reader and the writer come to learn of the shared limitlessness of the skin, with the body and the mind acting independently. A tortured tone marks the realization that after all, the body and the mind are not so separate: "In truth, the mystery remains. The skin revealed nothing to me. I ultimately learned that the contours of the flesh mark no borders at all, and that the bodies yield themselves in vain; appeasement will not at all be a thing of the mind" (137). For a moment, there seems to be no hope for the body or the mind to desire in peace. Alone, the subject is sad and condemned to suffer the body/mind conflict. With another, the subject will only be disappointed by false representations and ersatz eroticism. On the mountain, the body's solitary pleasure is interrupted by the mind that needs to participate. Far from abandoning hope in his search for pleasure, the narrator adapts the concrete mountain body experience to the abstract, effectively involving the mind in the desiring process. However promising such a transformation may be, it remains unattainable with real bodies. Crevel hopes that an algebraic equation may offer solutions to his form of desire.

3. Crevel's own interest in Freud's work was somewhat cautious. See for example: "Freud. De l'alchimiste à l'hygiéniste" also in *Mon corps et moi*.

Proposing that "everything turns to algebra [tout se fait algèbre]" (138), Crevel seeks to manipulate bodies as variables and objects in his very own equation of desire. At first, the central equation seems rather simple:

$$\frac{\text{JE} + \text{X}}{\text{Y}} = \text{jolie partouse}$$

or, in longer terms: "I" plus a variable "X," on top of variable "Y" equal a nice orgy. We may be tempted to interpret the equation as a clever declaration of the author's preference for groups of three: himself, "la danseuse," and "l'homme le mieux fait du monde," or himself and his male and female friends at the train station, or the two boxers and himself at the boxing match. Such an interpretation underestimates the primordial task that preoccupies Crevel from the very start, which is nothing short of figuring his own unique desire—rejecting any individual or societal categorization of his sexuality—and participating in a desiring-process that is universal and multiple. In other words, Crevel's final algebraic equation not only combines but also goes beyond all previous manifestations of body desire in the text.

Shortly before introducing the equation, Crevel ponders what would happen if his project of reducing the other (body and mind) to an object were successful:

> Unhappiness undoubtedly came from the fact that I accepted the belief that everything would be simplified if, I would manage to turn those to whom I was attracted into objects. Thus, stubbornly and in vain, a transubstantiation was attempted, by which, by the way, had it been perfect, I would not have been able to make myself happy. (137)

Algebra offers Crevel the possibility to think beyond mind and body, to play and manipulate the two at once, to tinker (*bricoler*) with their different possibilities: "Therefore everything turns to algebra, even for my senses. Equation of skin on the couches, human letters and numbers joining together, changes of place, looking for notions of equality, without even appearing to amuse themselves much" (138). Bodies as objects may be manipulated, joined, and equated algebraically. Instead of just talking about love and desire, instead of just writing and representing it, the author now needs to figure it out and investigate its possibilities. Moreover, in abstract mathematical terms desire achieves, at the same time, what individual encounters and actions could not: the combination of self-reflexivity and multiplicity.

At the textual level, Crevel's writing of desire offers three axioms concerning desire: desire is multiple and varied; desire is enhanced through reflection or when it focuses on one's own body; and finally, in order to be fulfilling, desire must directly engage the body first and the mind second. Examining Crevel's equation from a purely mathematical perspective and borrowing from group and field theory in mathematics, we discover that "je+x / y = jolie partouse" defines a group.[4] According to group theory (and in the most basic terms), a group is a set with an operation subject to three axioms. First, the operation is associative, in other words, order does not matter. Second, the operation has an identity element. For example: 1 is an identity element under the operation of multiplication because every number multiplied by 1 equals itself. Third, each member of the set has an inverse element (a and -a, or 4 and 1/4). All three axioms must be met in order to define a group. In many ways, the writing of desire in *Mon corps et moi* demonstrates all three axioms necessary to define a group.

The case of the "dame au cou nu," for example, who is desirable as long as she is equal to herself, demonstrates the identity axiom. If we had to identify a symbolic identity element in the text, it would be the body, or the body of the self, as the site of self-reflexive desire. Just like the recurrent request to be alone ("tout seul") or to be available to oneself ("disponible à moi-même"), the body of the self willingly and uniquely serves as the locus of desire. The desire of the soldier who can find pleasure only in his own hand and in his own self-reflection, pivots on his body, bringing back the other to itself. Yet also necessary to the self-reflexive pleasure of the body is the inverse image created by the mirror. As we have seen, the mirror image of the self produces the same body, one that is not fully recognizable to the self. The mirror fools only the body, and it is the mind that desires and recognizes the image as the inverse, or as the "not" body: "And yet, it was not my body but my mind that asked for a mirror" (143). By asking for the mirror, the mind corrects or perhaps punishes the body, denying true self-sufficiency, or solitude.

It seems that for Crevel, sexuality and desire are as variable as the elements in his equation. *Mon corps et moi* barrages us with various combinations of desire and preference: bestiality (116, 129), transvestism (62), homosexuality (59), and heterosexuality (123–24). Although any variables work in Crevel's equation, just as desire has value as a process rather than as a reproduction, homosexual desire is preferred over heterosexual sex. For example, Crevel considers the act of human reproduction more as a form of photographic duplication than as some expression of love: "And to say that

4. I am grateful to Renée J. Miller for her help and suggestions regarding group and field theory.

this passer-by could give me my photograph: a son. I'm afraid. Two coins in the slot. And in nine months, my portrait in miniature" (80). Process supersedes product. He considers, however, that friendship between people of the same sex expresses "the highest point of love itself" (135). The final equation, in light of his text and philosophy of desire, breaks sexuality and preference free from categorization. Desire is liberated, free to pursue and focus on anything and everything. Here too, the anti-oedipal and the Crevelian conception of desire share many commonalties: "Besides, who carries in himself universal desire, indifferent to details and small profits, dreams less to satisfy that desire than of wanting that nothing triumphs over the thirst that it has of everything" (149). Calls for such nonterritorialized desire, ready at all times to move on and reconnect to something else, only foreshadow what Crevel prophetically terms "a first rainbow dream [premier rêve d'arc-en-ciel]" (149), an image that today symbolizes diversity for many people. Crevel's dream of an unquenchable and universal thirst, anchored in the relationship between the body and desire, rebukes any form of structuring or categorization. Interest and profit have no role in Crevelian body desire, since for him sex and sexuality must remain variable, solely seeking pleasure. As a surrealist, Crevel believed in resistance. Like his sexuality, his writings resisted traditional conventions. Most unique, however, is that he envisioned resistance at the level of the body and for that reason Crevel's body algebra foreshadows an appeal developed by Foucault in *The History of Sexuality*:

> It is the agency of sex that we must break away from, if we aim—through a tactical reversal of the various mechanisms of sexuality—to counter the grips of power with the claims of bodies, pleasures and knowledges, in their multiplicity and their possibility of resistance. The rallying point for the counterattack against the deployment of sexuality ought not to be sex-desire, but bodies and pleasures. (1:157)

For Crevel, Foucault, and Deleuze and Guattari, bodies and pleasures (in the plural), are the terms of resistance. Crevel writes: "But what multiplication since catechism when I was ten! It was not two nor three, but a multitude I feel in me. Which one should I overcome? There are too many enemies for me to be victorious over any one" (157). To resist the social constructions of sexuality and desire would be less preferable, since both are invested in our bodies from without. Resistance is in multiplicity: in rejecting such singular and pigeonholed categories as homosexual, or heterosexual, and adopting the pursuit of pleasure*s* and bodie*s*, and bodies in pleasure. Likewise, with all four authors, resistance to power begins and proceeds at the level of the body, since pleasures, and the pleasures of the body/bodies, belong to us. Our pleasures are what allow us to resist the mechanisms of power that otherwise dominate our bodies. As in Crevel's dream of a rainbow, Foucault concludes *The History of Sexuality* dreaming of a "someday" or of a "one day" when our bodies and our pleasures will no longer be subjugated to sex and its powerful grip (159). As long as our bodies continue to both contribute and yield to the discursive powers of sex, and until our bodies are no longer the subjects to everyone and everything except our own pleasures, then both author's "somedays" remain a future, perhaps not impossible, yet difficult to imagine.

CHAPTER 10

Love Song

ALPHONSO LINGIS

At the age of fourteen Jean Genet was placed by the Paris Agency for Wards of the State to work as guide and secretary for a blind composer of popular songs, René de Buxeuil. It was to be the only time in his life he had regular employment, and it ended after seven months when Buxeuil had Genet arrested for theft and inaugurated his long criminal record. During those seven months, Sartre reports, Genet learned the rules of prosody and rhyme. How did Genet, who had received but six years of grade school education, and whose recently discovered and published letters to Ann Bloch written when Genet was twenty-seven show him incapable of narrating an incident or sustaining a thought in writing (or even of writing correctly spelled and grammatically coherent French), four years later compose one of the masterpieces of the French language, *Our Lady of the Flowers*?[1] Literary historians will speculate. What is essential is that the five books he wrote are nothing but love songs.

Love songs—the love song that Gil, in *Querelle*, sings to Paulette through the intermediary of Roger—invoke the presence of the beloved, and seduce that presence. Their words, charged with more glamour than meaning, express the poverty of meaning and craving, and hollow out longing in the one that sings them. By song one does not recount love, but pro-

1. References to Genet's works will be to the translations and abbreviated in the body of the text as follows: *Our Lady of the Flowers* (*L*); *Miracle of the Rose* (*M*); *Funeral Rites* (*F*); *The Thief's Journal* (*T*); *Querelle* (*Q*).

duces it. The love song *Our Lady of the Flowers* Genet wrote for the transvestite Divine, the love song *The Miracle of the Rose* he wrote for the convicts Harcamone and Bulkaen, and the love song *Funeral Rites* he wrote for the dead communist résistant Jean D. were written for men who were dead and who did not love Genet: "I now confess to you: that I have never felt anything but the appearance of warm caresses, something like a look full of a deep tenderness which, directed to some handsome young creature standing behind me, passed through me and overwhelmed me" (*L* 338–39).

Genet wrote *The Thief's Journal* in the presence of Lucien Sénémaud, who did love him in return, but he wrote this song for the pimp and crook Stilitano who had left him, and wrote it in order to leave Lucien. *Querelle* is the stanzas Genet adds to Lieutenant Seblon's love song to the sailor Jo Querelle. Seblon fills the pages of his journal with chants to Querelle, which Querelle, though he searches his cabin and steals his watch and his gun, does not read. *Querelle* is also the stanzas Genet sings for the bordello owner Madame Lysiane, who makes love to Jo Querelle and to his brother Robert, but finds herself excluded from their presence by their extreme presence to, and fratricidal love for, one another. Genet's songs are produced by the consuming storms of his love, which did not produce love and did not require it in return; in no wise means of seduction, they are ballads and threnodies of a profligate adoration.

Love songs are sung with voices wet with kisses and semen. Genet's throat does not simply pump in the semen of prodigious males in order to discharge in his own pleasure, leaving them stretched out stiff on the flat bed, like coffins on the sea: "At the climax, you were lit up with a quiet ecstasy, which enveloped your blessed body in a supernatural nimbus, like a cloak that you pierced with your head and feet" (*L* 54). This supernatural nimbus is the song of Genet's sexual climax.

No more than love songs in general, Genet's writings are not masturbation scripts (if this cliché of psychagogy even means anything) turned into art, that is, addressed to others. Lyrical stanzas added to epics, love songs exalt as heroes lovers that have departed, have died or been killed. To adorn one's beloved with the attributes of a hero, a love song could only lift from the common language the lustrous words with which the community adorns one that has died for its existence and common glory. And the love song itself enshrines one's beloved in the words and the survival of that community. Genet's love songs could only be banned in every society where a significant minority would begin to take them seriously.

Love of Murder and of Murderers

The dead men Genet loves he loves by singing love songs to murderers. As, alone in his prison cell in Fresnes awaiting sentence to life imprisonment, he begins to write his songs, the swallowed jism of Weidmann, Angel Sun, and Maurice Pilorge, three executed murderers with empty faces and pale and motionless bodies, make it possible to compose his love song to Divine, dead of consumption, by becoming a love song to Adrien Baillon, Our Lady of the Flowers, the sixteen-year-old murderer who had taken Divine's lover from her. From life imprisonment in Fontevrault Genet is able to write his love song to Bulkaen, whom he had known in the juvenile reformatory of Mettray and who died in an escape attempt, by writing *Miracle of the Rose* to the murderer Harcamone during the days Harcamone was in a death cell until his execution. It was watching the gypsy Pépé plunging a knife into a Spaniard's heart immediately in front of him that made Genet hear the first grandiose stanza of *The Thief's Journal* he composed for Stilitano. *Funeral Rites* can only be a love song to the dead Jean D. by becoming a love song to his killer Riton. By writing "The Glory of Querelle," a multiple murderer, Genet is able to write his love song too to the undercover police agent Bernardini (Mario in *Querelle*), whose sex slave he became and for whom he ratted on his underworld friends in Marseilles.

Love songs sing of men who killed in war, of bandits who killed for their outcast band, of men maddened by jealousy or revenge who killed the man who killed their love. Genet's lyrics sing of outcasts who, unlike the jealous or demented whose violence is not their own, kill consciously and cynically: "I want to sing murder, for I love murderers" (*L* 120). The murderer has not, as does a warrior or soldier, killed fellow humans for the sake of a nation or a people. A murder frees the murderer from the hundred great roles a hero may play in society, a hundred great roles that possess him. The chance to free oneself from the hundred great roles that possessed her is what motivated Ernestine to murder her son Louis Culafroy, called Divine (*L* 61).

The murderer does not polarize all Genet's love because he arrogates to himself a godlike power over the life and death of others, nor because, isolating in himself pure revolt, he pits himself against the order of carceral society. Although Genet takes pleasure in the fear that Wiedmann's face, multiplied by the presses, strikes into the depths of the most out-of-the-way villages, in castles and cabins, his love is kindled by Wiedmann's mumbled words, "I'm already beyond that."

Genet's songs do not celebrate, in the hoodlum, the instincts and loyalties of a higher community, bolder and stronger, than that protected by the community of the police. Although Jean D., for whom Genet's grief composes funeral rites, was a communist and a résistant, Genet loves as much the sixteen- to twenty-year-old crooks and little rats of the collaborationist militia who terrorized France for three years, and the Nazi soldiers themselves. He chants his love for Jean D. by loving Riton, the militia hoodlum who had killed Jean D., leading Riton into the arms of Erik, the Nazi soldier Genet himself had loved. Genet chants his love for this Nazi who got separated from the evacuating German army and hid out with the mother of a communist résistant, and he chants his love for this collaborationist who kills this Nazi after physically uniting with him in love on the rooftops.

Querelle has to leave the policed city of Brest, where he cannot continue as an opium smuggler and murderer. On his ship Querelle will depart not with his own community, that of the fighting navy, but alone, torn from his friends Mario, Nono, Robert, and Gil, to be taken to ports where he has murdered and will murder. But the detective Mario has the same physical splendor and cunning Genet chants in Querelle, the same courage and cowardice, and Querelle will come to love Mario as Genet does. Mario knew it was Querelle who had killed the sailor Vic, and protected him to order to himself rejoin the underworld. For it was not the threat to his life from the docker pals of the convict Tony he had unjustly sent to prison that Mario feared, but rather their contempt for him. That is what made him Querelle's accomplice. But outlaws and police, though they resemble one another like brothers, and fuck one another, form no community: "Certain that his lover rejoiced in cowering on his knees in front of a cop, Mario exhaled all his own ignominy. Teeth clenched, face tuned up into the fog, he murmured: . . . 'I've screwed a lot of guys! And they're all in the joint now, doing time! I love that, you know'" (*Q* 256).

Genet's love is not directed to the superhuman force that in turning against a human life breaks all the bonds of value and prohibition the human community can forge. As he had left his cigarette lighter with the corpse of Vic, each time Querelle had left some sign by which the crime could be traced to him. Afterwards, he always perceived the mistakes, and convinced himself that he had made them on purpose (*Q* 138). The killer Genet sings does not enrich himself with his crimes; he only succeeds in becoming a murderer—empty of everything but the corpse of his victim and his own imminent execution. Harcamone has no idea why he killed a ten-year-old girl and a prison guard who had always befriended him. Riton killed Jean D., whom Genet loved, by shooting at random from the rooftops. Querelle's first victim was a young Russian he had killed accidentally in Shanghai; seeing that the sweep with his knife he had made in response to the other's insult had taken out his eye, he cut his throat to get rid of the horrible sight.

The murderous force achieves nothing, and empties the murderer of everything but the corpse of his victim and the death he awaits in murder by another or execution by society. Our Lady of the Flowers retches, trying to vomit out the taste and smell of the carcass. It is the physical disgust of the first hour, of the murderer for the murdered, of which a number of murderers have spoken to Genet: "Your dead man is inside you; mingled with your blood, he flows in your veins, oozes out through your pores, and your heart lives on him, as cemetery flowers sprout from corpses. . . . He emerges from you through your eyes, your ears, your mouth" (*L* 119). The murderer can rid himself of the corpse that possesses him only by being occupied by the void of death (*L* 62). Genet chants his love song to Harcamone, the forty-seven days he spent in chains buried in the death cell, before his execution. Around Genet's chained heroes there is only "a pure, deserted, desolate field, a field of azure or sand, a dumb, dry, magnetic field."

To deliver himself of the corpse of Vic, Querelle executes the murderer he has become. Bending over to be penetrated by Nono, finding himself groaning in confession of pleasure, he makes himself a faggot. It is not the substitution of one nature for another. He is nowise thus seeking the community of men who love men; Nono "had no tender feelings for him whatsoever, nor would it ever have entered his head that a man could kiss another" (*Q* 75). It is the substitution, for himself as a living substance who retains the continuity of his acts in the community memory, of a void from which the community has withdrawn. When Nono came to show pleasure in fucking him, Querelle came to detest it, and to feel attached to the gestures, jewels, looks of Madame Lysiane, and her repeated words "my dear." But he used her in order to vengefully cuckold his brother.

It is true that Querelle escapes the guillotine in Brest, where he killed not his enemies but his friends—his accomplice Vic, and Gil whom he will deliver to the police and the guillotine only when he has really come to love him. He remembers his past victims as friends—the Russian danseuse in Indo-China, his English sailor accomplice in Cairo, his German docker accomplice in Spain, the gentle Armenian pederast he had strangled in Beirut—and he grieves too over them. What he stole from them became mystically inhabited with their lives and their friendship, such that "anyone who tried to make him 'cough up the stuff again' would commit an act of grave desecration" (*Q* 241). This also means that "Querelle metamorphosed his friends into bracelets, necklaces, gold watches, earrings" (*Q* 240–41), which he buried in secret places across the planet. The world has become for him the graveyard of friendship.

Monstrous Beauty

Not admiration of nor friendship for murderers, but love for them Genet sings—because love is the unconditioned miracle that reaches another when every bond of trust and collaboration, always conditional, is no longer possible. Consummate beauty is the apparition that produces this prodigy, this fatality, this love.

Beauty closes in upon itself, depending on nothing from its surroundings, which dissolve into darkness or pure light about it. The erotic hero whose figure and deeds are perfect rises to this pure darkness or pure light of death. "These heroes . . . must have reached such a state of perfection that I no longer wish to see them live, so that their lives may be climaxed by a brazen destiny. If they have achieved perfection, behold them at the brink of death" (*T* 113).

The core of the murderer is not character or will, but death—the corpse he has afflicted himself with and which fills him with disgust, the life that henceforth is under death sentence. Empty at the core, such individuals are nothing but their organs and their acts, and their singularity is in the matter of their bodies:

> The soul appeared to be only the harmonious unfolding, the extension, in fine and shaded scrolls, of secret labor, of the movements of algae and waves, of organs living a strange life in its deep darkness, of those organs themselves, the liver, the spleen, the green coating of the stomach, the humors, the blood, the chyle, the coral canals, a vermillion sea, the blue intestines. . . . It taught me the secret of the matter that makes up the star which emits it, and that the shit amassed in Jean's intestine, his slow, heavy blood, his sperm, his tears, his mud, were not your shit, your blood, your sperm. (*F* 62)

The somber gestures and acts that flare like stars are not born of reflection and decision (*L* 60). And they have no efficacy. Genet is enthralled by a virility that does not succeed in pitting itself against prison walls, that does not escape capture, punishment, and the death sentence—virility of pimps and cowards. Lieutenant Seblon, imagining a shipwreck, knows he would try to save Querelle, but he would rather try to make Querelle save him. But he knows that Querelle would first of all save his own beauty, even if Seblon should die (*Q* 96).

Ravishing gestures have the incoherent gratuity of mortuary objects—white gloves, a lampion, an artilleryman's jacket (*L* 61). They are in fact instigated by objects. Ernestine's murderous impulse was dictated by the presence of a huge army revolver at the back of a drawer—which must alone bear the fearful, though light, responsibility for the crime. Body contours and gestures, separated from the intentions of those who make them, gleam like radiant garb over wounded males. Bulkaen responds so immediately that Genet thinks that all his gestures were the direct expression of his feelings. But when he is kicked off his feet as by a bruiser's fist by Genet's words, he bursts out laughing; the harm done to him was expressed on his face by ripplings of light (*M* 183–84).

The beauty is not only in the radiance but in the intensity of contours and movements, where the whole constellation of surrounding objects in which they materialize is condensed. The ladder Genet sees Harcamone carrying on his shoulder is a ladder carrying him—"the ladder of escape, of kidnappings, of serenades, of a circus, of a boat, it was scales and arpeggios: it was the murderer's wings" (*M* 192–93). The radiance and intensity of sovereign gestures give them, disconnected as they are from intention as from efficacy, an appropriateness that reasoned, practical, or moral justification could never give them:

> My gaze is filled with love and does not perceive, nor did it then, the striking features which cause individuals to be regarded as objects. . . . I was unable, and still am, to make fun of people. Every remark I hear, even the most absurd, seems to me to come just at the right moment. I have gone through reformatories and prisons, known low dives, bars, and highways without being astonished. The most unaccountable gesture or attitude seemed to me to correspond to an inner necessity. (*T* 101)

It is not a programming and executing power originating in the agent himself that makes a perfectly executed act be not simply a movement conforming to the material layout. Beauty has its own power. The beauty of that act is magically transmitted from another agent:

> Approaching the altar on tiptoe, in silence, [the abbé] had picked the lock of the tabernacle, parted the veil like someone who at midnight parts the double curtains of an alcove, held his breath, seized the ciborium with the caution of an ungloved burglar, and finally, having broken it, swallowed a questionable host. (*L* 68)

The one who is able to make the splendid gesture has found himself imbued with the virtue not of the symbol but of the first executant: "the priest who, at Divine's funeral mass, imitated the sly gestures of burglary and theft, was adorning himself with the gestures, *spolia opima*, of a guillotined second-story man" (*L* 172). A hoodlum opening his fly and showing off his black penis in erection gave its power to the splendor of the Black Virgin of the abbey of Montserrat proffering her child (*Prisoner* 33). The sublime gesture in turn will eject its power into the intestines, the slow, heavy blood, the sperm, tears, and mud of another, that matter that emits the shooting stars of beauty.

These fatal gestures executed without will by the monsters, are fateful. Those who gaze spellbound at them offer themselves over to them in order to be devoured by them tenderly as by the night (*L* 75).

Abject Lover

From the beginning, an abandoned bastard child, incarcerated at the age of fifteen in the juvenile penal colony of Mettray, reincarcerated some twenty times before being sentenced to life imprisonment, Genet knew nothing but exile from the community. Absence of education, harsh penal conditions, enforced silence, solitary confinements, and especially hunger isolated him in the suffering substance of his body. For Genet to discover his own voice and sing was in no wise for him to set forth his own existence as a dignity and an inalienable right over the oppressive force of the carceral archipelago, to cry forth rejection and denial of and malediction on the order that organizes the world. Genet pursued abjection and plunged into shame as the evidence that he was making his way into his own substance.

Separated in his suffering from the physical sustenance of life, Genet separates himself from humanity, to find himself already in the realm of death. The world withdraws from him and his kind, such that the only real thing that remains of him on it is his grave. Genet accepts living in prison as he would accept, were he dead, living in a cemetery, provided that he lived there as if he were really dead (*L* 188–89).

The murderer makes himself the grave of his victim; he will live a dead man's existence in his own body. But the blood he has shed, the constant danger of being executed or murdered in turn, the way he defies the laws of life, and the most easily imagined attributes of exceptional strength, prevent people from despising the criminal. Genet chooses to reach the subterranean world of abjection through crimes that are more degrading: theft, prostitution, begging, betrayal of friends and treason against the community or nation (*T* 107).

Abjection is a protection. Like Harcamone, Genet built his life at Mettray minute by minute, one might almost say stone by stone, in order to bring to completion the fortress most insensitive to men's blows (*M* 69). Abjection is also a mire in which anyone who provokes it is caught in turn (*T* 61). And actively pursued as abnegation, abjection becomes the exercise of free acts:

> One evening, he took from his pocket something hard and dry and put it into his mouth. The warmth and moisture quickly restored the softness of the shriveled worm which had remained in the pocket where it had dried and which the darkness had prevented the boy from recognizing. . . . He made his tongue and palate knowingly and patiently suffer the hideous contact. This willfulness was his first poet's attitude, an attitude governed by pride. He was ten years old. (*F* 103)

The audacity to live enchanted and commanded by hierophanies of beauty within a world whose only outlet is death has the beauty of the great maledictions. Sacred history recounts the willed and disciplined abjection of a mankind that had been expelled from Heaven. Genet's life is a sacred history, for sanctity is to live according to Heaven, in spite of God (*M* 46).

The attributes of sanctity, and first of all pride, do not derive from a core substantiality, nor are they the result of deeds and achievements. They are instigated by objects:

> Inland, I went through landscapes of sharp rocks that gnawed the sky and ripped the azure. This rigid, dry, malicious indigence flouted my own and my human tenderness. Yet it incited me to hardness. I was less alone upon discovering in nature one of my essential qualities: pride. I wanted to be a rock among rocks. I was happy to be one, and proud. Thus did I hold to the soil. I had my companions. I knew what the mineral kingdom was. (*T* 76)

Miraculous Love

Born an outcast from the community, Genet finds pride in the pursuit of abjection. But it was not to become a rock among rocks; it was to exist entirely in the physical attachment to a solitary monster: "By this shipwreck, sunk by all the woes of the world in an ocean of despair, I still knew the sweetness of being able to cling to the strong, terrible prick of a negro. It was stronger than all the currents of the world, more certain, more consoling, and by a single one of my sighs more worthy than all your continents" (*T* 73).

This love, ignited by terrible and cruel beauty, among the abject, is not camaraderie woven out of mutual aid; it is physical love realized in sucking the prick, swallowing its jism, penetrating and being penetrated. That the starving Bulkaen showed affection for Genet in order to receive bread and cigarettes from him would have proven there was no camaraderie at all: "In prison the word friendship means nothing when it does not imply love. Therefore nothing obliged him to be faithful to me, except one thing: physical possession. I want to possess Bulkaen. Is possession the right word? Our revels so merge our bodies" (*M* 242–43).

Love occurs wholly outside the world, in those who are imprisoned within themselves, when their bodies exist not in the midst of the luminous space where "everything is only what it is: useful, without overtones, without aura" (*M* 32), but in dream landscapes. Darling, half asleep still, asks Divine what she is doing. She answers "I'm doing the wash basin." Using her mother's expression, she meant "I'm doing the wash." He takes her to mean "I'm being the wash basin" (like "I'm doing a choo-choo train"). Still in his dream that he was entering the wash basin his mother used to bathe him in, he dreams Divine is now dreaming of being that wash basin. In the embrace of the two dreams he gets an erection. "Darling has 'fallen' in love" (*L* 88). Love is the debauch of sexual penetration between dreamers whose dreams penetrate one another.

How does love emerge from abjection? By miracle:

> If the simple precept of Jesus, "Love," was to give birth to the most extraordinary pack of monsters: metamorphoses into flowers, escapes by angels, tortures on the rack, resurrection, dances with pagan animals, devoured ribs, cured lepers, kissed lepers, canonized guts, flowers condemned mirthlessly by notorious councils, in short an entire legend which is called Golden, the even more overwhelming miracles with which our families teemed were bound in the end to unite, merge, mingle, cook, boil in cauldrons so as to make visible in the depths of my heart the most scintillating of crystals: Love. (*M* 280)

Love enters through "the flaw on the hip, the beauty mark on the thigh whereby my friend showed that he was himself, irreplaceable, and that he was wounded" (*M* 76). For love is a tenderness in the midst of adoration. Love enters into the wounds and abjection of the one inhabited only by death, as "so many traps along our path that you can't help going where [God] leads you" (*M* 342), and holy and miraculous, envelops them in a supernatural nimbus: "Love makes use of the worst traps. The least noble. The rarest. It exploits coincidence" (*L* 88).

Over-weary of loving, Genet followed and spied on men who quivered with grace, waiting for the moment, the glance, the angle that would bring the speck of the ugliness into view, the line or volume that destroyed the beauty. But too often it happened that then the multiplied facets made their beauty sparkle with a thousand other lights and ensnared him in their mingled charms. He found he adored a man who had flat ears, another a slight stammer, a third who had lost three fingers, Stilitano with his severed hand: "Splendid depravity, sweet and kindly, which makes it possible to love those who are ugly, dirty and disfigured!" (*T* 91). He will come to love convicts in the cells where, no longer able to recognize his own farts in the tangle of mingled odors, he came to accept and then to relish indiscriminately those which came from the pimps. He is carried along in a descent from the world, into prison, that is, into foulness, scatophagy, perhaps into madness, and hell, which will finally land him in a garden of saintliness where roses bloom, roses whose beauty is composed of the rims of the petals, their folds, gashes, tips, spots, insect holes, blushes, and even their mossy stems with thorns (*M* 236–37).

Love is the spell enchanted not only with the specks of physical ugliness, the foulness, the excrement of the other, but also with the black splendor of the very hatred in the other borne unto oneself. Divine, pursued by kids screaming "Maricona" and throwing stones at her, climbed into an empty train. She crouched under a seat, cursing the horde of brats, rattling with hatred for them. It was impossible to devour the kids, to rip them to pieces with her teeth and nails, as she would have liked; abruptly from her excess of rage and hatred, which fell into the absurd grandeur of their hatred, love for them burst forth (*L* 220). Genet's love for the dead Jean D. is so extreme that it cannot but find ravishing his very corpse, and the sorry grandeur of a French militiaman who, during the insurrection of Paris against the German army in August 1944, took to the rooftops with the Germans and for several days fired to the last bullet—or next-to-last—on the French populace that had mounted the barricades (*F* 54).

Loving Betrayal

Every love of another is betrayal of the last one loved, because one still loves her or him. One casts her or him outside of love, into society, that is, one delivers her or him over to the police. But Genet finds that love, in the extremities of its abjection and tenderness, does not cling to the strong, terrible prick of a negro, but betrays what the beloved one black with the night of death takes to be strong, certain, and consoling in one's love of him.

"Dehumanizing myself is my own most fundamental tendency"(*L* 82). To attack one's enemies is to affirm solidarity with one's friends. To betray one's lovers is to separate oneself entirely from humankind. The strength to betray shows that one has broken the stoutest of bonds, the bonds of love; this evidence of strength makes Genet admire traitors and love them (*T* 46). But Genet obscurely knows that there is an extremity of love liberated by breaking the bonds of love. Love separates itself entirely from the craving to possess another, and even from the will that the other be and live.

Genet early found in Mettray that it was the knights, the noblest, the haughtiest, and not the creeps, who were capable of betrayal: "I took pleasure in imagining their granite-like mass undermined by a deep-winding network of molehills" (*M* 306). Indeed,

> Evil, like good, is attained gradually by means of an inspired insight that makes you glide vertically away from human being, but most often by daily careful, slow, disappointing labor. . . . Of the tasks involved in this particular ascesis, it was betrayal that was hardest for me. (*F* 80)

Genet thus prizes especially having, when still in the army, stolen from a soldier in his own barracks: "I had just violently detached myself from an unclean comradeship to which my affectionate nature had been leading me, and I was astonished at thereby feeling great strength. I had just broken with the army, had just shattered the bonds of friendship" (*T* 47). But he also felt tenderness over the stupid ingenuousness of his victim, and discovered that betrayal brings the beloved closer to the abjection of a lover. At Fontevrault Genet tries, out of a malice composed of love, to have Bulkaen sent to the disciplinary cell, not in order to be near him, but because a lover lures his friends to prison in order to sanctify it by their presence: "It was thus one of the usual mechanisms of love that made me a rat" (*M* 40).

The male who while giving himself over to homosexual acts despises and preys on homosexuals—virtually all the personages of Genet's books—is the incarnate figure of the traitor. Genet began his career as a prostitute stealing the cape of a customs officer he had serviced and giving it to Stilitano, and in Antwerp he attached himself to Stilitano by prostituting himself and robbing his clients for Stilitano. When Genet submitted to the lusts of a coast guardsman on the coast of Spain, he smothered with his lovemaking the sounds of the passing smugglers and made the coast guardsman a traitor (*T* 170–71). It was then that he came to see the relationship between betrayal and homosexuality. Querelle, Genet's most fully explored figure of a murderer, turns from murder to homosexuality, whereas in Genet it is his homosexuality that turns him to love of murder.

The four nights before Harcamone's execution, Genet exhausts himself in directing all the forces of his love to produce Harcamone's escape. He has taken Harcamone's death upon himself; he is as one dead himself, when Divers comes to love him in his cell. It was Divers who had ratted on Harcamone; because of him Harcamone was waiting to have his head cut off (*M* 121). At Mettray the inmates said that Divers and Genet resembled one another physically, and, as no mirrors were allowed, Genet had tried to know what his own face looked like by looking at Divers. Himself betraying Harcamone, Genet gives his own corpselike body to Divers. (In making love with him, he calls him Riton—who will figure as the collaborationist rat who killed Jean D. in *Funeral Rites* [*M* 332]).

If betrayal was the most difficult task in the ascesis of love for Genet to learn, it was also the most difficult to understand. Genet's most intolerable love song, *Funeral Rites*, celebrates, after the Liberation, Genet's love for the fallen résistant Jean D. in a love song to the collaborationist assassin Riton who killed him and the Nazi soldier Erik Genet had loved. *Funeral Rites* is itself a long anguished effort to understand the necessity with which love itself engenders betrayal: "At a time when the death of Jean D. ravages me, destroying everything within me or leaving undamaged only the images that enable me to pursue doomed adventures, I want to derive incomparable joy from the spectacle of the love of a militiaman and a German soldier"(*F* 78). The joy is not at all a compensation he seeks in another lover; it is the disconsolate joy of a love between two doomed men. In order to extend love over the specks of physical ugliness, the excrement, the corpse of Jean D., Genet must pour the same rivers of love over the act that killed him and the killer himself. Then the mindless killing of Jean from the rooftops by Riton shooting at random will become the kind of almost involuntary death that may occur in a war dance—or better, in an orgy carried to bloodshed (*F* 58). "I gave him to you, Riton. Love him dearly" (*F* 58). Genet pours love over Riton by giving Riton his own Nazi lover, Erik, and by giving him also the strength, on the rooftops, immediately after Erik had consummated their love—white roses flowing out slowly with each quick but regular pulsation of his prick, to be held in the trellis of Riton's thorax—to betray him mortally.

Lieutenant Seblon dreams of such a love (but love is the debauch of sexual penetration between dreamers whose dreams penetrate one another):

> The victim—innocent—despite his atrocious suffering, helped the murderer. He showed him where to strike. He took part in the drama, despite the desolate expression of reproach in his eyes. I also note the beauty of the murderer, and the sense of his being wrapped in garments of malediction. (*Q* 144)

As Genet grieves the death of Jean D. by loving his murderer, Juliette, Jean D.'s lover, grieves his death in the death of her child, not Jean's child but that of a captain of the collaborationist militia. *Funeral Rites* is a love song Genet sings to Jean D., doubled with the love song Juliette sings, in silent steps, in the funeral cortege bearing her dead child. Genet, who had in love penetrated Jean D., and Juliette, who had been penetrated by him, are so alike in the intensity of their love and in the desolation of their grief that they look like one another. This intensity that joins them in love for one man makes Genet write the cruel and beautiful song in which he keeps torturing her (*F* 164). It is not jealousy, but the extreme identification with her in his grief—his own grief wholly felt in the calvary she walks to the cemetery—that unleashes his betrayal of her into the hands of the rapist-grave-diggers.

Genet follows Juliette to the cemetery which has sealed from him the body of Jean D. He craves to make his own body that grave; he craves to cannibalize Jean's body: "A man you have killed is more alive than the living. And more dangerous, by not being one of the living" (*Q* 153). As a murderer is filled with the corpse of the one he murdered, it is to make his body as empty of everything but the corpse of Jean D. that Genet conjoins himself in the revelous mergings of love with Riton who had killed Jean D.

Solar Sacrifice

> Because I envisage theft, murder, and even betrayal as emanating from a bronzed, muscular, and always naked body that moves in the sun and waves, they transcend this ignominious tone (which was an attraction for me) and find a nobler one, which is, more closely related to solar sacrifice. (*F* 80–81)

Betrayal produced in love is not an act of appropriation and self-appropriation. It is sacrificial: "I make of sacrifice, rather than of solitude, the highest virtue. It is the creative virtue par excellence. There must be damnation in it" (*T* 215). The sacrifice does not consist in taking on the crimes, or the misery, of another in order to immolate them in one's own person and deliver the other, but in loving the other by taking on oneself his misery and his criminality. Sanctity is recognized by the evidence that it proceeds to Heaven by way of sin (*M* 45).

At Mettray Genet is led by seven of the most important big shots to a wall concealed by the latrines in the back field. They have no grief against him; he is but the occasion of a game. Ordering him to hold open his mouth, they from fifty feet away compete with one another to spit into his mouth. Divers is among them, as excited as the others, taking his turn. Like Divine unable to devour her tormentors, to rip them to pieces with her teeth and nails, Genet prays destiny to alter the game just a little, to make a false movement—it would have taken so little for love to enter their hearts instead of hate—so that they would be hurling not spit but flowers upon him. Abruptly, from his excess of impotence and shame, love for them spurts forth. As hilarity overtakes them, they move closer and closer and their aim gets worse and worse; it is no longer a competition but a collective orgy. His face and head covered with slime becomes an erect prick discharging. And his prick in his pants too is discharging (*M* 314–16).

But it was Bulkaen who had thus been plunged into abjection; Genet takes this ignominy upon himself. The substitution, out of love, of Genet for Bulkaen brings with it the reversal of the game, from that of hurling spit to spurting out the white roses of their semen. It is not that they would have loved Genet; rather, Genet's love for Bulkaen is the factor that reverses fate, that changes a random death into a death in a war game or an orgy.

Making love, the night of Harcamone's execution, with Divers who had betrayed Harcamone to the police, Genet dreams of committing a murder with Divers and laying the blame on some big shot of matchless moral rigor and physical beauty who would be sentenced instead of them, in order to take Divers' betrayal upon himself (*M* 123).

In *Querelle*, Genet writes that Lieutenant Seblon is not in the book (*Q* 79). Pages from his journal are incorporated bodily into it; he alone writes with the lyricism for which Genet has to substitute himself to recount the glamorous transports of the other personages. In fact Genet's love for Querelle is wholly Seblon's—a sacrificial love. Seblon has known intimately the path of betrayal; he was on the point of turning Querelle over to Mario. Imagining a shipwreck, he knows he would try to save Querelle. Seblon does save Querelle at the end of the book, not from the police but from a crowd of men outraged to have witnessed Querelle strike a woman. He returns to the ship *Le Vengeur* with Querelle under his arm. But the next day, confessing himself guilty of the theft Gil perpetrated on him, Seblon sacrifices himself: "I shall not know peace until he makes love to me, but only when he enters me and then lets me stretch out on my side across his thighs, holding me the way the dead Jesus is held in a Pietà" (*Q* 275). He will go to prison, wishing it was for Querelle, and without saving Gil, who remains condemned for the murder he committed and also for the murder Querelle committed.

Songs that Die Away

The lovers themselves vanish; Genet's love songs greet lovers with passionate kisses of parting. These songs of death do not subsist in the community.

With words of love Genet recorded the shooting stars of beauty ejected from the intestines, slow, heavy blood, sperm, tears, and mud of Bulkaen's life. Language—words of love—made it possible to discover and fix on paper the beauties of his friend. But the more Genet writes about Bulkaen, the less attractive he finds him. Bulkaen whose grace and whose ugliness, whose bravado and whose cowardice, the rims of whose wounds, the folds, gashes, tips, spots, insect holes, blushes, and thorns, had taken leave under the iridescence of the figure composed by Genet's words: "In the heat of writing, I wanted to magnify feelings, attitudes and objects that were honored by some splendid boy before whose beauty I bowed low; but today, as I reread what I have written, I have forgotten those boys: all that remains of them is the attribute which I have sung" (*T* 109).

He turned then to singing with the most splendid lyrics the other men who are entombed alive in his books, so as to let Bulkaen carry on without the help of magic words, living with his own life and Genet's too, a physical being whom Genet had loved with his gratified flesh (*M* 243–44). But he will have to silence those lyrics too, so as to free his lovers to live the malediction of their own lives, far from him and far from us. Harcamone's escape, which Genet had so feverishly tried to effect with the magic of thought, would have been such a departure, as would have been Querelle's departure from all his friends, including Genet, on the ship *Le Vengeur*:

> In embellishing what you hold in contempt, my mind, weary of the game that consists of naming with a glamorous name that which stirred my heart, refuses any qualification. Without confusing them, it accepts them all, beings and things, in their equal nakedness. It then refuses to clothe them. Thus I no longer want to write; I am dead to Letters. (*T* 109–10)

For himself his love songs have had their uses. Writing is an abjection and an ascesis, and the more Genet persisted in the rigor of composition—of the chapters, of the sentences, of the book itself—the more he feels himself hardening in the will to utilize, for virtuous ends, his former hardships, and the more he feels their power (*T* 62). "I am planning for the near future a perilous outlaw's life in the most dissolute quarters of the most dissolute of ports. I shall go away. I shall go to Barcelona, to Rio or elsewhere, but first to prison" (*T* 234).

But on the last page of *The Thief's Journal*, Genet wrote that the surrounding presence of wounded males is a blessing granted him not only in prison festivals but also in the army and in sport. In Lieutenant Seblon he had found again the surrounding presence of wounded male he had known in his own six years in the French army. He will seek and find it in the high-wire acrobat Abdallah Bentaga, irreparably injured in a fall, and in Jacky Maglia, injured in a racing-car crash. Then he did go to prison—to the Palestinian refugee camps in which a whole people are imprisoned.

Genet's songs then were a betrayal, although not to us; his songs have not delivered these gilded and jeweled mummies to the community. In writing of Genet, one tends to write "we"; including oneself in a community, one writes to help the community assimilate the "writer" of such singular love songs. Our love songs are incantations that summon the presence of the one we love: siren songs. Our love songs exalt our beloved with the noble words with which we celebrate the heros of our community. Our love songs enshrine those who have killed, for our community, that of policed society or of outlaws. Our love songs appropriate them and maintain them in our hearts as our lovers. Our love songs communicate our solitary love, which survives the death of our lovers and our own deaths, to others in the community. We can understand betrayal only by deciding that "treachery" is Genet's code word for the incorrigible subjective voice that can never be factored into the consensus, as Edmund White notes in his introduction to *Prisoner of Love* (xiii). Our betrayals are literary.

Lover and beloved in Genet bear too terrible a resemblance to each other to permit our affection for them. Madame Lysiane, in *Querelle*, is us—opulent, generous, so ready to give them all we have and are. But we cannot enter into the couple Robert and Jo Querelle form.

Madame Lysiane is in love with Robert and makes love with his brother Jo, in order to find in him some physical detail that would permit her to separate him from Robert. Although Robert and Jo do not actually join in the physical act of love, their physical resemblance always joins them when Madame Lysiane tries to see and touch and be penetrated by one of them apart. When Robert, who has become Madame Lysiane's lover, learns that his brother Jo has become her husband Nono's lover, he feels himself fucked by Nono along with Jo: "Dragging me through your shit!" (*Q* 121). On the street each brother pulls a knife on the other; their love is that dreamt of in the dream of Lieutenant Seblon, each wishing to be killed by the other: " 'I'm crossing a stream covered with lace. . . . Help me, I'm approaching your side . . . ' 'Jump up, onto my smile. Hang onto it. Forget your pain. Jump.' 'Don't lose heart' " (*Q* 124).

As Jo Querelle is about to leave on *Le Vengeur* to the earth become the graveyard of friendship, Madame Lysiane knows that Robert is leaving her with him: "If his brother goes to sea, Robert's face will always be turned to the west" (*Q* 275). She murders Querelle. Filled with his corpse, filled with death, she sets fire to La Féria and Robert and hangs herself. As Querelle had found his death in the hands of Nono, Madame Lysiane's husband but also her employee, who had made him into a faggot, she finds her death at the hands of this faggot she murdered. Realizing she would hang herself, "she was breathing so hard that her chest, in expanding, seemed to raise her entire body upward, and she looked like someone about to begin her Ascension" (*Q* 275). In setting fire to La Féria which had welcomed us, she takes leave of us, and ascends to the state of a monster only another monster can love. Filled with Querelle's corpse, she is also filled with that of Robert.

To dare to write about Genet, apparently only collating his texts and organizing their themes, requires having accompanied him into one's own abjection, betrayals, and sacrifice: "By my guilt I further gained the right to intelligence. Too many people think, I said to myself, who don't have the right to. They have not paid for it by the kind of undertaking which makes thinking indispensable to *your salvation*" (*T* 21).

CHAPTER 11

The Frame of Desire in the Novel of the 1980's and 1990's

MARTINE ANTLE

The folding of writing over photography is a leitmotif of French literature of the eighties. A photograph, for instance, is the starting point of the search for identity in Michel Tournier's *La Goutte d'or*; Marguerite Duras's *L'Amant* is constructed from the absence of a photograph that "could have been taken"; in *Aden*, by Anne-Marie Garat, a yellowed photograph hung on the wall remains the only vestige of the history of Europe and of the main character. In *L'Appareil-photo* by Jean-Philippe Toussaint, an ID photo is the only missing piece of a file compiled for driving school. This text, as Maryse Fauvel has demonstrated, could even be read from a specific division of space: the closed and obscure space of a camera and the tridimensional space of photographic representation.

Photography, as it is exploited in writing since the 1980's, is characterized by its absence or by its unreadability. In most cases, as Barthes would have stated, it displays the death of the subject and serves as a pre-text for the narrative. In Hervé Guibert's *L'Homme au chapeau rouge*, the photographs announce the death of the subject in the literal sense of the term. They are dreadful to the point that "there was no way to redo them so that they'd be more presentable . . . I would have this frightful, ghastly skull" (107). In the same perspective, Guibert's work *L'Image fantôme*, taken as the "beginning of a new roll of film" (17), is also written around the absence of a photograph: "This text would not have existed if the image had been taken . . . this text is the despair of the image, and worse than a blurred or veiled image: a phantom image" (18).

In *L'Image fantôme*, the eroticism of a photograph of Claudia Cardinale entirely nude, lying flat on her stomach on an animal skin, and later, one of Burt Reynolds in the same pose, nude on a fur in *L'Express*, arises from what is not shown: "it is the chest, and especially, it is imagining the contact of the chest with the fur" (26). The cliché of photographic fantasy during adolescence lacks *jouissance* in Guibert; he admits having confused *bander* (to have a hard-on) and *branler* (to jerk off) when he was that age. And thus the play of photographs from the film *Satyricon*, among which there is one of Hiram Keller, entirely nude and prepubescent, his sex existing only in the form of a gold shell, annuls all *jouissance* and leads the subject to lassitude: "And I remain then for a long time with a hard-on, without doing anything, above the photograph, as if hypnotized, until lassitude" (27).

Similarly, painting points to the disappearance of the subject in the writing of the 1980's. The portrait Yannis paints of the narrator in *L'Homme au chapeau rouge*, and more specifically the action of painting the subject—here placed in the position of object—is initially the only instance of erotic pleasure in the work. Eroticism, arising from circulations of desire via the exchange of gazes, is immediately displaced onto pictorial representation in which the subject's corporeality escapes the order of representation. Painting, in fact, dissolves corporeal attributes and the "flight of flesh into painting" reveals only a "progressive bleeding of [his] soul onto canvas" (108).

The impact of both the photographic and the pictorial media in the writing of the 1980's is allied in other respects with techniques particular to cinematography. More precisely, as desire furtively emerges in the writing of that decade, it begins to show itself through a system of framing, as will be seen below in Marguerite Duras's *Blue Eyes, Black Hair* (1986) and Guibert's *L'Homme au chapeau rouge* (1992).

Before examining the framing of desire, let us first briefly recall some basic principles of the filmic image. Like the photographic image, the filmic image is by definition divisible. The frame of the screen "assures a deterritorialization of the image" (Deleuze, *Cinéma I* 27). Any shot implies a system of framing, so that an apparently closed system necessarily refers to the out-of-field. The framing always functions then, as Bazin has already pointed out, as a mask. If what is framed is visible, underlying it is a larger set that belongs to the out-of-field, which designates what "exists elsewhere, to one side or around; in the other case, the out-of-field testifies to a more disturbing presence, one that cannot even be said to exist, but rather to 'insist' or 'subsist,' a more radical Elsewhere, outside homogeneous space and time (Deleuze, *Cinéma I* 17).

The framing is also a signifier from the point of view of the narrative instance and of enunciation. In *Blue Eyes, Black Hair*, the principal scene around which the text is articulated is presented as follows:

> Among those watching the scene in the lounge from the road behind the hotel is a man. He makes up his mind, crosses the road, and goes toward an open window. . . . Soon after the scream, a young stranger comes in through the door, the woman is watching now, the one leading to the upper floors of the hotel. A young stranger with blue eyes, black hair. . . . Outside on the grounds, as soon as the young stranger appeared, the man unconsciously drew nearer the window. His hands clutched at the sill as if stricken lifeless, shattered by the strain of watching, the shock of seeing. . . . The man remains by the open window. . . . Then he leaves the grounds by way of the beach. . . . shouting and weeping like a character in a melodramatic film. (3–5)

The appearance of the young stranger with blue eyes, black hair is framed in a particular manner by the window: the window here divides the image seen—the young man with blue eyes, black hair and the woman—from the out-of-field—the people in the lounge of the hotel. The scream that reverberates at the precise moment of the framing of the image transgresses all the divisions of space imposed by this framing. This initial image generates an infinite series of images of the young man with blue eyes, black hair in the text. One can even say that from this initial shot, the text itself functions as an out-of-field and testifies to, in Deleuzian terms, a "presence." As in film, the frame here centers the representation "where the imaginary is concentrated; it is the reserve of the imaginary" (Aumont 29).

The signs composing the framing of the young stranger's appearance persist in affirming this presence, without, however, reconstructing the initial image. The frame of the door of the hotel room, the blindfold, the khol, the blue of the eyes, and the woman, all taken as synecdoches, as they are perceived outside the initial framing, are false indices that cannot recreate the set of the initial framing. They are signs that bear the presence and the absence of the other: "He doesn't recognize her. He could only have recognized her if she'd come into the café with the young stranger with blue eyes, black hair" (5).

If the signs present in the framing can function as false indices, they still retain their value as stimuli. The presence of the woman, for example, is necessary to provoke the man's crying; tears, says Barthes, in *Fragments d'un discours amoureux*, tell a story and produce "a myth of pain" (215). As Duras writes, "He weeps over a distant image of the summer night. He needs her, needs her there in the room, so he can weep for the young stranger with blue eyes, black hair" (46).

From a cinematographic viewpoint, this framing of the initial image corresponds to four types of viewpoints established in cinema, according to Jacques Aumont. First, there is the point of view, the site from which one looks, and therefore the point of view from outside, the park, to the inside, the lounge, in *Blue Eyes, Black Hair.* Second, there is the point seen, the view itself, as taken from a particular point of view: the young man with blue eyes, black hair and the woman in the lounge. Third is the narrative point of view: the representation of a gaze, or in other words, the narrative instance and the internal ocularization, be it of the author or of a character. The narrative point of view in *Blue Eyes, Black Hair* is oriented and interiorized from the point of view of the man who is looking. Finally there is the predicative point of view, where the syntagmatic point of view is taken in a metaphorical sense.

It is this last type of point of view that interests me here. The framing of the window scene as a metaphor engenders a multiplicity of figures and projections that construct the motifs of the text, and which repeat the text infinitely by way of transfers of meaning, displacements, and substitutions: "She gives him her lips to kiss. Tells him he's embracing the other, the stranger. She says, 'You're kissing his naked body, his lips, his skin all over, his eyes'" (11).

The imaginary reconstruction of the initial framing is orchestrated around a repetitive gesture: "she would seem to be doing it . . . she seems to be doing it." This gesture seeks to approach the sexual act in order to alienate itself at the frontiers or limit points that separate heterosexuality from homosexuality. The mental projections in the text and the multiple rapprochements of the man and woman can subsist only in the space of language. Any corporeal exchange is condemned to fail. Thus, as Barthes has expressed, the subject can "do anything with his or her language but not with his or her body" (*Fragments* 54). In *Blue Eyes, Black Hair,* this gesture marks for the subject the impossibility of engaging in a heterosexual sexuality: "He says, 'I can't touch your body. That's all I can say—I just can't. There's nothing I can do about it'" (16).

The subject's desire can subsist only in the memory of the gaze of the young man with blue eyes, black hair, and all movement, corporeal or in language, toward the woman remains forever subordinated to this memory. One could also say, as does Dominique Fisher, that the text disrupts all notions of genre and gender, and that

> the man with blue eyes, black hair of the beginning of the book dissipates into the anonymity of another *feminine and/or masculine* figure with blue eyes, black hair. This neutral figure, a true scenic object, comes into being under the multiple reflections of blue and black that traverse the text. ("L'écrit" 83, my emphasis)

As Duras writes: "She says again, smiling, 'Never felt any desire for me.' 'Never. Except'—he hesitates—'except in the café, when you were talking about the man you loved, about his eyes. While you were saying that, I did desire you'" (18).

Bound to one another by "a contract" (32), the man and the woman are submitted to the contingencies of a corporeal choreography similar to a veritable ritual of simulation, a ritual without end that the characters cannot interrupt; it is mutual masturbation as a substitute for a sexual relation that itself is doomed to fail: "She asks him if he could do it with his hand, but without coming close to her, without even looking. He says he couldn't. He can't do anything like that with a woman" (31). Or again: "It's as if desire disappeared as soon as I came near you" (32).

Through its repetitions, the text marks the successive advances and retreats of two bodies, one toward the other and one away from the other. The woman's sex remains the ultimate site of interdiction, of "unworthy 'jouissance'" and blocks all satisfaction of desire: "it's something horrible, criminal, like murky water, dirty, bloody. She says that one day he'll have to, even if only once" (36). Or a few pages later: "He must sometimes have wanted to make use of her, to enter, just to see, into the warm cavity of the blood, to enjoy her with an unseemly, unworthy pleasure" (42). The corporeal gesture in the text oscillates in the interval of the "nearly" and the "to be mistaken" (26): "almost touching each other" (53); "in breaths of cries . . . without touching at all . . . almost against the skin" (111). The distant memory, emanating from the framing of the young man with blue eyes, black hair, affirms its presence and manifests itself through corporeal gesture and through the immobility of the man's gaze that scrutinizes every trace of the young stranger on the woman's sleeping face. The sleeping face engenders in turn another type of gesture: to remove the square of black silk in order to unveil the face and perhaps to reveal the face of the loved one. But, as Alain Finkielkraut notes, "the loved faced monopolizes faces" (73) and love here turns into a "religion of the face that prohibits its representation" (Finkielkraut 75). As Duras writes, "He watches her sleep, the woman who was penetrated by the young stranger with blue eyes, black hair" (73).

Desire and love remain forever frozen in the act of seeing—"He slides the silk away to rediscover the face of the other"—while the memory of the summer light becomes confused with the blinding light of the hotel room—"He says he sees the lounge again in the summer light" (92). The dynamic of desire calls for a process of blinding, and to see here implies the closing of the gaze, or what Duras calls the "blind-gaze [*non-regard*]" (38). This "in-sight," *voyure*, implies "not sight from the outside, like the others, the contour of a body that one inhabits, but especially to be seen by the other, to emigrate, *to be seduced, alienated by the phantom*" (Ponty 163; my emphasis).

In *Blue Eyes, Black Hair* the representation of the young stranger relies on the man's point of view, and the young stranger stays forever frozen in the decor of the initial framing. Evolving out of this decor, the text is only a pretext, an out-of-field of the "phantom image," and finally, a visual and auditory poetic space in which the "fading" of voices is orchestrated and in which the relation to the other is spatialized. The "fading" of the other takes place in the voice: "The phantom being of voice is inflection. Inflection, by which all voices are denied, is what is being silenced; it is that auditory grain that breaks away and fades out" (Barthes, *Fragments* 131).

Absence in *Blue Eyes, Black Hair* becomes a practice of language in which, as Barthes puts it, "manipulating absence is stretching out the moment, delaying as long as possible the moment when the other could tip over into the absence of death" (*Fragments* 22). The relation to the Other is similarly theatricalized through the structure of the text that is presented as a didascalic text punctuated by the actors' comments: "The scene, says the actor, is a kind of reception room" (11); "She seems to be sleeping, says the actor. That's what she looks as if she's doing—sleeping" (12). Or again, "They are blinded by the light, naked, their sexes bare; *mere creatures without sight*, exposed" (45; my emphasis).

These comments, made in the conditional mood, insist again on the potentiality of a representation in the state of becoming or of immanence, and point to the subject's subordination, the subject who remains the "prey of the other," according to Finkielkraut: "We see the world today as a theater of a multiform conflict between freedom and power. *There is nothing for us except free consciousness or enslaved consciousness, independent subjects or subjects as prey of the other*" (74; my emphasis). In this perspective, we understand why only the image from the initial framing subsists: "the Other comes to you from the outside, installs himself/herself in you, and remains foreign to you" (Finkielkraut 67). From that moment on, the text, a project of representation in the theatrical sense of the initial framing, belongs to a ritual I will call the ritual of framing.

In *L'Homme au chapeau rouge*, desire is again problematized by way of a framing, but a framing that will be the blurred framing of a painting or of a video screen. At first glance, the pursuit in this work seems to be centered on the question of the authenticity of the works of art that proliferate in the text. The paintings assert themselves by their "foggy and earthy" presence (25) from behind the shop windows, independent of the influence of the gaze. These paintings, both false and authentic, falsified by forgers or the art mafia or by the artists themselves, are the object of displacements and multiple denunciations: "Aïvasovski had painted six thousand paintings in his life, and there must be as many forged ones done in the nineteenth century or in the twentieth, first by his students, then by forgers" (23).

In this universe of the fake, where artists have their work signed by forgers and assure for themselves the falsification of their work, the authenticity of art and of information is put into question. From this moment on, we are in the universe of simulation and the simulacrum. In this perspective, art is placed at the stage of an ultra-rapid circulation and of an impossible exchange. As Jean Baudrillard puts it in *La Transparence du mal*: "The 'works' are no longer exchanged, neither between themselves nor in referential value. They no longer have that secret complicity that makes the strength of a culture. We no longer read them, we decode them according to more and more contradictory criteria" (23).

The paintings, invisible or unreadable, generate nonetheless atoms of traces of desire that are infinitely displaced across the text, and in such a manner that the subject must appropriate them from the first glance, even when this glance, as is often the case, is obstructed by a windowpane.[1] The rare canvasses such as the "suicidal lovers" (27) are hidden in the text "by this imperious movement of quasi-madness" (33) and allow glimpses of blurred seascapes and portraits of young boys with closed eyes, sleeping or with their backs turned. These figures, with unrecognizable or indiscernible traits, engage in no direct communication via the gaze. They place the spectator at a distance. Certain young men function as childhood memories that escape the subject; others, to the contrary, produce an effect of pleasure or

1. The mediation of the real by a screen or a window is one characteristic of the novel of the 1980's. Dominique Fisher points out how, in the work of Jean-Philippe Toussaint, "the window is the double site of the subject's and the object's disappearance. Seen through the rain from the apartment window in *La Salle de bain*, or from the office window in *Monsieur*, the mass of people moving around is always the image of a shapeless mass in an aquarium" ("Les non-lieux" 4).

displeasure, such as the blond boy with the birthmark (52). Certain paintings are smudged to such an extent that they are comparable to ancient fossilized photographs. It is the invisibility or the inaccessibility of these paintings, whose frames are sometimes only an antique dealer's or a bookseller's makeshift construction, which makes them desirable:

> Discovered from far away, behind windowpane effects, and in a movement that prohibited me from arresting my gaze on them in order to understand them well, I was sitting on the bus, looking at the street from the window. . . . The painting conquered my desire like a whiplash. I recognized it as a familiar object, a possession of forever. (25)

It is when the negotiations are not satisfying and the narrator delays the deal for twenty-four hours at the risk of losing it that he finds himself facing his own image, the one of the "too skinny man in the red hat." To delay a deal at the risk of losing it by means of bartering is the equivalent then to playing out a confrontation with one's own death, as the bad deals are compared to "bad moments," *mauvaises passes* (31). Or again: "After having voluntarily allowed twenty-four hours to pass, at the risk of not finding the painting, I was the tall man, too skinny, in the red hat (which will later become 'the skeleton in his red hat')" (30).

The back-and-forth movement vis-à-vis the canvasses engenders an extremely complex problematic of desire. The subject simultaneously juggles the acquisition and selling of paintings in several cities and in several countries, but in this compulsion to possess a work of art, he also struggles against love at first sight. Thus this compulsion to buy and sell aims not at satisfying a desire but rather at delaying the desire of possession, to allow "time to pass between things and their desire" (33).

The endless pursuit of paintings in the text accelerates at the same pace as the advance of the virus. The framing of the artistic image, unreadable or invisible, functions as a mirror of subjectivity: an opaque mirror, as I have already pointed out, since the paintings are often seen through a windowpane, but also a distorting mirror when, at the end of a bad deal, the subject becomes aware of his own body in decomposition, as the skeleton in the red hat.

Carnal desire, or any other projection of desire, participates in the same dynamic. Just as the works of art are seen through shop or bus windows, the desiring subject is separated from the object by an invisible mirror. AIDS, the ultimate frontier between life and death, signified by the window, brings with it "a sexual decomposition through general infiltration into life's every domain" (Baudrillard *Transparence* 16). For Donna Wilkerson, this constitutes the "theater of death":

> Photographic writing and the body-with-AIDS permit Hervé Guibert to suspend time—immobilize it—so as to modulate it, in order to control the fear of death. However, the figure of death—the spectral image—is always present; it is the leitmotif that haunts the text. What is remarkable about Guibert is that the production of texts ends up replacing the dead body according to a principle of fractal representation. This new body-of-writing, composed of objects, fetishes, images, paintings, photos, and videos, becomes more real than the real; it is the primitive theater of death. (36)

From this perspective, we may now better understand the narrator as he observes the young waiter: "I myself was looking at him furtively, I really wanted to lick his ass. But each of us was already in another world for the other; separated by an invisible mirror that is the passage from life to death, and that knows death from life" (40–41).

The constant questioning of the goal and the means of a work of art weaves a labyrinth where the real and the fake are mixed up and in which the framing of the pictorial image serves as a mask for the subject. The continual proliferation of works of art and of artists, both dead and alive, in fact leaves hardly any respite for the subject. Launched into their pursuit, the brief intervals of negotiation that permit him to confront the development of his desire are his only remedy. What is framed here is unreadable (in opposition to *Blue Eyes, Black Hair*) and the multiple framings of works of art remain indiscernible or falsified. If, as in cinema, any framing implies a mask, we can say here that the framing of art functions as a pure mask. From that moment, the text, as a phantom out-of-field, becomes a false informational trail of misinformation, juxtaposing and mixing discourses on art and on disease. As in *Blue Eyes, Black Hair*, the subject's dynamic inscribes itself within a system of framing. But this time it pertains to the search of childhood images, to the search of a self-image already lost, to movements toward and away from the image of death. Framed art in the universe of the real and the fake reflects only a smudged image of another image, that of the skeleton in the red hat.

On several occasions, the fake invalidates the real. In the same manner that a fake painting—authentic, however, to certain eyes—evokes a deliriously higher bid, false confessions in amorous relations can momentarily revive lost ties: "Last night I confessed to Jules that I was screwing with Yannis. It is not true. Suddenly we screwed again, Jules and I, even though we hadn't been screwing for at least six months" (114). The proliferation of art also affects the information propagated by the "falsifying" doctors about the narrator's condition. The acquisition of a work of art as an escape from the disease is confirmed moreover as a practice by several artists, as well as by the English writer, Bruce Chatwin (32).

Another means that enables the narrator to follow the development of the disease, and to complete the fantasmatic visions of the man in the red hat, which appear furtively through the "bad moments" [*mauvaises passes*], is the filming of progressive stages of the disease and of the surgical operations, an action that occurs without the surgeon's knowledge. But the accumulating video cassettes are of no interest to the narrator, who does not even watch them. Moreover, the camera, carefully positioned and adjusted before the onset of the anaesthetic, is diverted from its functions and dissimulates the subject again. The video image, much like the Hitchcockian image, inserts itself into an intricate system of masks "improvised by the smocks of the nurses that stood between the viewing angle and what one really wanted to see" (42). This dissimulation of the image makes it even more frightful and, again, the subject finds himself unrepresented. The subject, in front of the "metallic, blue" and "unreal" image, notices that the operating room on the screen is "abstract and incandescent" (42). The image in fact "censors itself" (42) and the subject finds himself in front of a blank screen. This vision of a subject sitting alone, contemplating a blank screen, constitutes, according to Baudrillard, one of the fundamental images of twentieth-century anthropology (*Transparence* 21). Similarly, according to Marc Augé, "It is in the anonymity of a 'no place' [*non lieu*] that a solitary community of human destiny is experienced. . . . There will then be room tomorrow—perhaps there is already room today—despite the apparent contradiction in terms, for an ethnology of solitude" (150).

The framing of desire from which the texts presented here arise remains doomed to failure. In both cases, the desire inscribed in the frame escapes the subject. In *Blue Eyes, Black Hair*, a distant memory is the only thing that subsists from the desire, a memory of the summer night whose dispersed signs are lost in the text. In *L'Homme au chapeau rouge*, the framing of both the pictorial image and the video image sets up a system of masks from which accelerated death drives are orchestrated and diffused. Moreover, light obliterates the image in both texts. This is the case with the yellow light that fuses with the summer light in *Blue Eyes, Black Hair*, and the image of the operating table in *L'Homme au chapeau rouge*. In both works, the framing of the image refers to what is unrepresentable; the set-up of the framing testifies to the justification of writing.

A fundamental difference, however, separates the two works in terms of the functioning of desire. In *Blue Eyes, Black Hair*, desire still enters into an imaginary and is the object of a series of mental projections characteristic of the pre-AIDS era. In fact, in Duras, as in Proust, the real still consists in establishing "a relation with what forever remains other, with the other as absence and mystery" (Lévinas 155–56). In *Blue Eyes, Black Hair*, however, the imaginary, absorbed by the image, has already tipped over into a ritual of simulation—simulation of a sexuality that inevitably fails because of the difference in sexual orientation.

In contrast, in *L'Homme au chapeau rouge*, the image is literally contaminated, and we are in the universe of the hyperreal. Any projection of desire is blocked and mediated by the "invisible mirror" of the virus. According to Baudrillard's analysis, we could even say that with *Blue Eyes, Black hair*, we were still in an era where "the body is the metaphor of the soul" (15). Yet with *L'Homme au chapeau rouge*, the body "is no longer the metaphor of anything at all" (15). Thus we retain today, according to Baudrillard, "the imprint of a sexuality without a face, infinitely diluted in the bouillon of culture, politics, mass-media communication, and finally, in the viral unleashing of AIDS" (17).

CHAPTER 12

Beyond Feminism: Elvire Murail's *Escalier C*

LAURENCE M. PORTER

Banished from the collective, teleological, transcendent grand narrative of history to the "petits récits" they share with children, fools, and primitives; banished from the political limelight to the shadows of the household; banished from the teleological drama of culture to "the repetitious burden of nurture and reproduction": from the beginning "feminist" authors have tended to react either by glorifying difference or by rejecting it.[1] Separatists, eco-feminists, and practitioners of "l'écriture féminine" have asserted that they are in some ways superior to men—indeed, that their wisdom, social solidarity, and moral sense may become necessary to save the world from the pathological destructiveness of men. In contrast, gender feminists and equity feminists have attributed the perceived inferiorities of women to acculturation, systematically engineered by male exploiters to perpetuate their domination. Although these tactics are necessary for social reform, both autonomy and assimilation bind female identity in opposite ways to a defining ground of maleness. There is a third path, however, that eludes the constraining dichotomy of female and male. Unfashionable today because it does not lend itself to overt social action, this path has nevertheless been taken by great women authors in every period. It entails the implicit recognition of androgyny as polymorphous yet not "perverse"; as opening creative spaces for artistic play.

In the twelfth century, for example, Marie de France's *lais* find a third

1. For "petits récits," see Lyotard, *Le Condition postmoderne*, "Introduction"; for "repetitious burden" see Benh`abib 157.

space of Celtic legend ("male" because warlike; "female" because belonging to the vanquished substrate) outside the classical/Christian dichotomy that defined the literary tradition in her times. (Male writers' use of the Celtic "matière de Bretagne" came later.) Regarding androgyny, Marie de France's most famous hero, Guigemar, must mature by coming to recognize his inner "femininity," to accept a mutual dependence without loss of integrity. More obviously, women authors on the third path can affirm their creative autonomy and transcend the polarities of gender stereotypes by appropriating the gay male imagination. Marguerite Yourcenar, the first woman member of the Académie Française, did so in her masterpiece *Mémoires d'Hadrien*, a fictive autobiography of the Roman emperor. In this tradition Elvire Murail moves decisively past the polarities of feminist separatism and *l'écriture féminine* in her classic male "coming-out" novel, *Escalier C*. It won the Prix du Premier Roman in 1983, and the Prix George Sand in 1984, and was translated as *Stairway C* in 1986. Jean-Charles Tacchella, the director of *Cousin, Cousine*, made it into a film.

By inventing a protagonist who putatively would neither sexually desire nor be desired by the implied author, Murail suggests that she is not a woman writer, but a writer. Avoiding a self-conscious display of her gender, she instead extends a therapeutic hand to those doubly "other," to troubled latent homosexual males.[2] Their aggressiveness toward women, the author

2. At present, gay theory lags far behind feminist theory. In 1948, Kinsey, Pomeroy, and Martin laid the groundwork for future empirical studies with their survey *Sexual Behavior in the Human Male*, which rejected the simple dichotomy of gay/straight in favor of a seven-sectioned continuum. The *Journal of Homosexuality*, founded in 1974, is to be commended for continuing the tradition of empirical studies, although the force of conviction of their articles is in general weakened because of 1) their small samples; 2) their absence of information regarding the criteria by which the subjects were selected and approached; and 3) their lack of control studies comparing behavior of the same subjects in gay, straight, and mixed social settings. Of particular interest in connection with the present study are their volumes 9–11 (1983–85) on gay and bisexual identity, social sex roles, and homophobia; and Troiden's "The Formation of Homosexual Identities." For a classic overview, see Churchill, *Homosexual Behavior*. As a benchmark in cultural history, note the changes in successive editions of the *Diagnostic and Statistical Manual of Mental Illness* produced by the American Psychiatric Association, which provides the basis for justifying medical insurance payments (formulations mine): "All homosexuality is pathological" (*DSM–II*, 1968); "Some homosexuality is pathological" (*DSM–III*, 1980); "Homosexuality per se is not pathological" (*DSM–IIIR*, 1989). *DSM–IV* appeared in 1994.

suggests, may in part derive from their rage against the social imperative that they must desire women, and from their unconscious experience of women as competitors. If they learned to free themselves from what they experience as the constraints of heterosexuality, Murail implies, if they allowed themselves consciously to desire men, they might also become able to enjoy women as friends.

Murail's classical (Anna) Freudian unmasking of ego-defenses[3] attempts to breach the heterosexual dialogue of the deaf that crops up everywhere in literature—from Elizabeth and Casaubon in George Eliot's *Middlemarch* to Antoinette and Rochester in Jean Rhys's *Wide Sargasso Sea*—whenever men force themselves or are forced into sexual relationships with women without really desiring them, or without really respecting them, or both. By emphasizing inner obstacles to free sexual expression and by minimizing external, societal obstacles, Murail adopts an optimistic position that also emphasizes individual choice and responsibility: we have more power to change ourselves than to change others or society.

In the Arcadian era just before the discovery of AIDS, and in the relatively unprejudiced milieu—also Arcadian—of a fictive Greenwich Village (a place the author had not yet visited when she wrote the book),[4] Murail presents a textbook illustration of the delusions that debar the hero Forster Tuncurry from self-understanding, self-acceptance, and creativity. While the title alludes to a "third path" of sexual choice (not A or B, but C, neither heterosexual male nor heterosexual female), Murail normalizes all

3. See Anna Freud; Laughlin; Fenichel (chaps. 8–10, 12, and 19 ("The Motives of Defense"; "The Mechanisms of Defense"; "The Direct Clinical Symptoms of the Neurotic Conflict"; "Conversion"; and "Defenses Against Symptoms, and Secondary Gains"). For me to adopt some Freudian concepts by no means implies an acceptance of all Freud's positions, such as his views on female sexuality and superego morality; but his concepts of a dynamic unconscious, and of mental defenses and symbolic behavior, remain of great value to this day. For a balanced appraisal of his contribution to psychoanalysis, see Porter, "*The Interpretation of Dreams*," chap. 11, "Challenges to Freud," 109–15.

4. For a suggestive fourfold typology of gay fiction, see Kellogg, "Introduction: The Uses of Homosexuality in Literature." 1) The Arcadian narrative conveys dreams of a secret world where a homosexual can be free, safe, and innocent. 2) The political narrative pleads for acceptance (Kellogg *dixit*) in an attempt to influence society. 3) The sociological novel presents the keen observations of the detached social outcast who must read others well so as to avoid detection. 4) The psychological narrative scrutinizes one's own homosexual feelings. *Stairway C* appears to combine the Arcadian and the psychological.

nonviolent, consensual sexuality by presenting both homosexuality and heterosexuality sympathetically and without preference. She depicts sexual relations as neither a necessary nor a sufficient condition for human relationships. According to her, a diversity of sexual choice among individuals need not preclude an overarching social solidarity. Rather than using women as sexual objects to reaffirm his own specious heterosexual identity, the hero, Forster Tuncurry, learns ultimately to care about women as human beings.

In contrast, French male authors' treatment of lesbianism appears curiously limited and even stifled in its imaginative scope, if we consider such examples as Balzac, Gautier, Baudelaire, or Proust. Mystified and scandalized by a woman who does not respond to their desire, protagonists in such writings observe her from the outside. More often than not, the implied author appears to endorse the protagonists' frustration by erasing the lesbian Other, staging her disappearance, her destruction, or both. Since my desire is ultimate reality, these fictions imply, the lesbian who does not respond to it must be deranged: she appears under the signs of pathology and secrecy. In Balzac, Gautier, and Proust, indeed, it is the moment when the woman is revealed as lesbian that she is elided, that she slips from the field of observation and disappears. In other words, the lesbian as a social being is impossible in the works of the French realists: their fictions conform to the tenets of a naïve mimesis that limits the implied author's descriptions to situations where he can imagine himself as a participant. Proust, in contrast, uses such feigned naïveté as a masterful subterfuge.

Avoiding the choice of many another author to represent sexual difference to the second power (homosexual desire among members of the other gender) as an impenetrable secret, Murail treats it with dramatic irony, going Yourcenar's omniscience one better. The sexual orientation of her protagonist, Forster Tuncurry, is a secret only from himself. He has casual heterosexual affairs, but lives alone. His psychic defenses motivate the action. He gradually works through them, with panic attacks and hysterical collapse, until he achieves self-acceptance.

Escalier C tells of the inhabitants of one entry in a Manhattan apartment building. A divorced alcoholic typesetter, Josh Hardy, and a black Jewish widow, Mrs. Bernhardt, live alone opposite each other on the top floor. Their situation dramatizes the threat of isolation and loneliness, whether self-imposed (by alcoholic withdrawal) or inflicted by circumstance (prejudice, plus the untimely loss of one's entire family). The remaining residents are thirtyish or just a bit younger. On the fifth floor, Bruce Conway lives with his cat, Agamemnon. On the fourth floor, above the protagonist, a gay male couple, Coleen and Hal, struggle with an abusive relationship. Coleen, although beaten, pities Hal: "He couldn't bear to be homosexual. . . . He was suffering. He took it out on me as best he could [because I was indecent enough to be a happy homosexual]"; 25, 31–32). When Hal flees, Coleen is freed to pursue his nascent love for Forster (Murail has chosen a sexually ambiguous name, halfway between the man's name "Colin" and the woman's name "Colleen," from the Irish diminutive form *cailin*, "girl"). On the third floor opposite the protagonist is Virgil Sparks, in his late twenties. He has a conflictual heterosexual relationship with Béatrix Holt, below him on the second floor. Sharon Dowd, divorced and with her daughter Anita, will move in opposite her and end in a harmonious relationship with Bruce, to whom Forster has been unknowingly attracted. Murail brackets the remaining major possibility, a lesbian relationship (I shall refrain from speculation). The vacant apartments on the upper floors represent places of indeterminacy in the social network. The entryway creates the potential for a community that includes and accepts a variety of sexual expressions; the bonds of this community are enhanced when Forster learns to see Mrs. Bernhardt (posthumously, in an act of memorialization) and Coleen no longer as Other.

As described here, the community provides an important vehicle for Murail's didactic purposes: its members live within the same structure, not in detached houses. Having no children (Anita Dowd is the exception), the adult characters are free to concentrate their emotional energies on relationships with each other; compulsion to conform to one sexual code or another is largely absent. (This is the great fear of any sexual minority, and of any sexual majority confronted by a militant or even by an assertive minority.) The one person, Hal, who uses force in his sexual relationship is expelled by the collective action of three other members of his community when he seriously injures his partner. Although marriage seems a prospect for the two heterosexual couples, nobody in the entryway is married: their relationships lack legal and contractual constraints. The pair bond is, however, validated (Forster is criticized for his promiscuity) to add stability to the social nexus. And heterosexual readers are not threatened with the notion that they are actually all essentially bisexuals, or latent homosexuals, repressed or acting in bad faith.[5] Nor are they challenged through the de-

5. Concerning the limitations of the concept of community, and self-segregationism, in the gay male novel, see, for example, Buchen's "Introduction" to his *Perverse Imagination*, 3–38, and Hoffman, "The Cities of Night," in Buchen 165–78. On

piction of a homosexual subculture, within or outside the apartment building. The gay males will be limited to one token, or if you prefer, to one illustrative couple, just about to be formed by the end of the novel. The belated conversion of Forster to a new sexual practice thanks to Coleen's encouragement and understanding leaves open the question whether "life-long, exclusive homosexuality" derives from nature, "an innate biological disposition"; from seduction; or from acculturation (see Meijer, 125). In other texts, anthropological studies, cultural history, and personal testimony suggest that any or all of these influences may play a role. Forster's sexual maturation, like that of most other fictional protagonists, is artificially delayed so that Murail can simultaneously depict adult society and the drama of sexual maturation.

At the outset, during the first three months after Hal and Coleen have moved into the entry, the community experiences radical disjunction between homosexual and heterosexual: "most of the tenants strongly disapproved of having two homosexuals living among them"(12, 13).[6] Forster's own stance is at first ambiguous; we do not know whether he as narrator shares the viewpoint of "most of the tenants." However, he has already been more open than the others to a possible friendship with Coleen. His prior friendships with other residents of Escalier C will predispose them eventually to accept both his and Coleen's homosexuality.

Initially, Forster's profession—art critic—suggests a mental life mediated by images created by others, as his sexual life has been mediated by the normative social expectations of heterosexuality. As the story begins, Forster

---

the menacing concept of universal bisexuality, see Buchen 12, and Vidal, "Notes on Pornography" in Buchen 125–38.

Murail's position appears to be close to that of Judith Butler in *Gender Trouble*: "There are structures of psychic homosexuality within heterosexual relations, and structures of psychic heterosexuality within gay and lesbian sexuality and relationships" (121). See also Butler, *Bodies That Matter.*

6. Translations mine. Two page references will be given for each quotation: the first to the English, and the second to the French edition. The sentence in question here has been omitted from the English version. This particular omission helps correct a weakness of Elvire's original version, where the homophobia of the other tenants of C Entry quickly and almost magically gives way to a sympathetic acceptance of Foster and Coleen ("Colin" in the English version) as a couple, well before Foster himself has accepted his repressed gay sexuality. The revision removes ambiguity through clarification: the tenants are horrified not by Coleen's sexuality, but by the behavior of his original partner, Hal, who batters and tortures him.

feels drained of spontaneity. He asks Coleen to make suggestions for a restorative trip to the country (with a hint of a homosexual Arcadia). Forster's repressed sense of being monstrous has been projected onto the images of Breughel's *Garden of Earthly Delights*—he has recently written a book about Breughel. When Bruce Conway's large, ugly black cat, Agamemnon, shows an unexpected affinity for him, the symbolism recurs. The cat turns everything topsy-turvy in Forster's apartment:

> Since that first encounter, Agamemnon and I have enjoyed an idyllic love: nothing and no one can stop him from coming into my apartment. . . . Strangely enough, he's very fond of me, and I am still the only human whose lap he is willing to sit in. There are mysteries everywhere. (17, 21)

Forster has already admitted to himself and others that he has "no intention of marrying anyone" (10, 10). Béatrix diagnoses his attitude toward women—"you're a lousy misogynist"—as fundamentally hostile because he treats them as disposable (14, 16–17). His promiscuity limits him to shallow relationships, and it masks repressed homosexual feelings with their exaggerated contrary (see Ferenczi, and Rivière). "I *have* women, thank you" says Forster, "Women, maybe, but not *one* woman," Virgil retorts. "That makes all the difference, you poor guy. It's plain to see that you don't know what love is" (18, 22). Once alone, Forster is distressed to feel that his friends' mockeries are "only too true" (19, 23).

Meanwhile, he does not feel repelled by Coleen but only by the latter's brutish roommate, Hal (11–12; 13–14). Forster makes a first tentative step away from homophobia when he sees Coleen not as a threat, but as a victim deserving of sympathy and help. Returning home with his girlfriend of the moment, Suzy, Forster meets Coleen running downstairs, bleeding from a split eyebrow. He asks whether he can help, but Coleen replies sadly that Forster can do nothing for him. Then Hal peremptorily summons Coleen upstairs. The psychic significance of this encounter for Forster is suggested by a parenthetical flash-forward concerning Suzy that immediately precedes the encounter with Coleen: "I dropped her the day Conway [the heterosexual male to whom Forster is initially, unconsciously attracted] told me she looked dumb, and when I was hit with the realization that it was more than just a look" (12, 13). The choice of a heterosexual object who seems stupid suggests that Forster is more concerned with sexual release than with a human relationship. "Fucking is like eating," he later observes, "you have to do it, but it's seldom very good" (40, 50). Alternatively, his disinterest in Suzy as a person may blind to him to what *is* interesting in her. Until he can become consciously interested in a serious relationship with Coleen, his latent sexual preference is repeatedly signaled by the author's descriptions of Forster's narcissism, of his careful choice of elegant clothes and his admiring himself in the mirror. It is as if Forster had remained fixated at the pre-objectal Mirror Phase of development.

The beginning of his move toward Coleen is revealed the next day by his humane attitude, which contrasts with that of his two male friends when they discuss the issue.

> —Frankly, Tuncurry, those two queers' problems are none of our business! Sparks answered with a shrug of his shoulders.
>
> —Wait a minute! I exclaimed. If a man was beating his wife hard enough to split her head open, you'd stand up for principles and demand justice! But because Colin is gay, you probably think it's [that his masochism is] part of his perversions. (12, 14)

Béatrix applauds, but when Forster proposes encouraging Coleen to assert himself and to expel his abusive partner, no one will help him, and Bruce Conway implies that he still holds the essentialist attitude just denounced by Forster.

Encountering Coleen in a grocery store, Forster feels sympathy and advises him to get rid of Hal (14–16, 12–13). A while later, the three men do rescue Coleen, repeatedly slashed by Hal, who then attempted to scalp him. Hal pulls a gun, but is frightened off for good. The others find Coleen unconscious in a bathtub of cold water, which Hal seems to have been using to try to revive him. After that, Coleen repeatedly allows his bathtub to overflow, so that the water drips down into Forster's apartment below. Thus he memorializes the scene of his rescue, and suggests a flow of libido directed toward Forster. He thereby attracts negative attention, like the acting-out child, for Forster comes upstairs to complain, as he does when Coleen repeatedly plays Stravinsky's "Rite of Spring" (an expression of joyous release) too loud.

Parallels in the text hint at Forster's deeply repressed fantasy of taking Hal's place. Forster says of Coleen in a moment of irritation that "sometimes I really feel like hitting him!" (11, 13) just as the abusive Hal has been doing. Much later, horrified at the idea that Bruce might end up living with Sharon Dowd, Forster observes:

> I suddenly became aware of my dependence on him. Colin Shepherd and Hal came to my mind. To some extent, we [Bruce and I] had recreated the same pattern. Conway had used me, had used my money, and often he'd cuffed me, or even struck me, something I wouldn't have taken from anyone else. (78, 103)

For the childlike Conway, such rough physical contact represents a sanctioned homosocial interaction, like that of boys wrestling. But for Forster, roughhousing vents his disguised masochistic submission, combining desire with its punishment.

Once the external obstacle of Hal has been removed, meaning that Forster could be free to draw closer to Coleen, he raises the internal defense of psychic projection: "I don't desire him: he desires me." This phenomenon first appears during a visit when Forster accepts a set of duplicate keys from Coleen, who uses the pretext that he would like Forster to check the apartment while he is away. Then Forster notices that Coleen has no shirt on. "I felt more and more uncomfortable. Strange ideas were running through my head. For example, that I was locked up alone with a homosexual and that nobody was in the building. Even if I called for help" (21, 25; compare 80–81 and 85, 107 and 113). Coleen being smaller and weaker than Forster (108, 227) and distinctly nonviolent, the latter's apprehension seems irrational. Coleen reads his mind:

> What's bothering you? Do you think I'm going to jump on you? The first thing you learn when you're gay is that most other people aren't, that they're free to choose. That's why you don't have anything to be afraid of. I've never forced myself on anyone. (24, 29)

But then Forster's fascination with Coleen finds an acceptable channel through the latter's ink and wash drawings. These represent Stairway C itself, envisioned as a community that includes them both.

Forster's repressed homosexual desire remains diffuse. He still is attracted to Bruce Conway. He manages to avoid recognizing his feelings for both Coleen and Bruce through a variant form of projection: "I don't desire him [Bruce]; *he* [Coleen] desires him." A little later, the young people of Escalier C gather to share a dinner. There Bruce Conway engages in a partial striptease to show off his muscles, and shortly after, in an unconscious act of quasi prostitution, asks Forster to lend him money for rent. Coleen offers to lend it instead, and to reimburse Forster for the sum Bruce already owes him. The shortcoming of the first type of projection, the simple reversal, is that it can inspire fear. The shortcoming of the second type, attributing one's own desire to a third party, is that it can elicit jealousy:

> I began to suspect Coleen of being in love with Bruce Conway. That bugged me and disturbed me without my really knowing why. Especially if Bruce came to owe money to Coleen Shepherd, and was unable to pay him back,

> Shepherd might try to obtain a *moral* hold over Bruce's *physical* person (43, 55; emphases in original).

As repression lifts in Forster, psychic projection modulates into a third, less fully displaced form, the King David phenomenon. There one feels indignation at another person for feeling, thinking, or doing what one is ashamed of in oneself (see Laughlin, "King David"). The reading of the other person's motivations may be accurate, but where Forster is concerned it is imaginary. He ascribes an attempt at seduction with unworthy motives to Sharon Dowd because he is ashamed of his own attraction to Bruce.

Reaction-formation, the unconscious act of opposing an inadmissible feeling with its exaggerated contrary (see Laughlin, 279–95), appears strikingly as the motivation for the two reported occasions when Forster goes to bed with women. Soon after observing Coleen's possessive smile when he asks him to take a walk, Forster has sex with Vanessa Poretski, a young painter he has just met. Some time later, after Bruce observes to him that "Coleen is in love with you . . . you make a nice couple" (157–58, 211), Forster promptly sleeps with the gallery publicist Florence Fairchild. Between these two episodes, Forster's repressed desire for Coleen is disguised by ostensible scorn and vehement insults; when Coleen shows that he understands Forster nevertheless, the latter has dramatic hysterical conversion symptoms. "When the ego and its modes of adaptation fail, two things occur: (1) the ego is overwhelmed and symptoms beyond the ego occur, which are experienced passively; (2) the ego as soon as possible tries to reestablish its control even to the extent of applying more archaic principles of mastery—by regressing, if necessary" (Fenichel, 121), even into sleep or into unconsciousness.

> —You're a drowning man and you're trying to fight the person who wants to bring you help. When you've overcome your fear, you'll let yourself get out of the water.
> —Fear? Fear of what?
> —Of loving. Like everybody who does harm.
> I burst out laughing.
> —That's a hot one!
> —Yes, it's funny, isn't it?
> I made an effort to keep on laughing. In fact, I was completely hysterical. I brought my hands up to my face and hid my eyes. I gasped for a moment, then groaned, seeking the oxygen I could no longer find. (82, 109–10).

Conversion symptoms appear in Forster at other moments as well, as does the defense of psychic regression, when he falls asleep in order to retreat from life during the day. To ascribe hysteria to a male is to question homophobic characterizations of gender. According to such stereotypes, a gay male may act hysterical because he is "really a woman." But to depict the *latent* homosexual as hysterical and the gay male who has *accepted* his sexuality as self-controlled is to deconstruct the assumption that nonaggressive, openly gay behavior must be a display of "womanish" psychic weakness—of "acting out."

As the psychic pressure becomes more intense, Forster resorts to the counter-phobic act of literally shoving Coleen away to avoid even emotional intimacy. "Coleen," he protests when the former tries to squeeze through the closing door of Forster's apartment, "I don't feel like talking to you." Coleen replies, "You never feel like anything." He pushes Coleen outside, making him stumble and cut his knee. But then Forster's overreaction yields to its secretly desired contrary: he submits to Coleen's plaintive demands to be bandaged and helped to walk back to his apartment, hand in hand and arm in arm (122–24, 162–65).

Lest we doubt the author's lucid understanding of defense mechanisms, she places an informal but penetrating diagnosis of Forster's psychic projections in the mouth of one of her other characters, the painter Grindling Conrad. He has been characterized by Forster as an eccentric, but he replies:

> —You're the nut. But in your mind, it's the other guy.
> I shook my head in vehement denial.
> —Oh yes you are, he declared. —You're using me as a surrogate, as a safety valve for your anguish. Accept yourself. Don't call your neighbor by your own name.
> —My neighbor? I echoed sharply.
> —It's just a figure of speech. I wasn't thinking of anyone in particular. On the other hand, I think it's interesting that that harmless word gets such a strong reaction from you.
> I shrugged a shoulder, trying to seem nonchalant. . . . Despite myself, I tried to think of the name I called Coleen Shepherd. Of course . . . [ellipsis in original]. The homosexual—that was the other guy. (150–51, 201–2)

As Forster is an art critic, paintings provide the images through which his unconscious is mediated. They offer the potential for self-discovery, one that can integrate his friends' observations with his revised self-image. Forster's initial fascination with Hieronymus Bosch appears to spring from his repressed sense of his own monstrousness as a homosexual. Much later, as he contemplates Coleen, Forster unconsciously attempts to sublimate physical attraction by transmuting it into aesthetic appreciation: he finds that Coleen's

> face looked like one of Renoir's little girls. I didn't like that idea at all. Then Fragonard's little boy with a white dog came to mind. I decided that it was stupid to compare him with anything whatever [by moving this sentence to the end of the paragraph, the English version loses the idea of an inescapable obsession]. Yet Leonardo's portraits of Saint John the Baptist had that same gentle tenderness around their lips, and Gainsborough's "Blue Boy" had Coleen's dignity . . . (144, 192; ellipsis in original).

Forster's comparisons help him to incorporate a mental image of Coleen as Coleen has incorporated his. The vacillation between comparison and the renunciation of comparison in this passage represents a struggle between the ego-defense of sublimation (transforming desire for Coleen into aesthetic appreciation of a work of art) and the abandonment of the defense: "in a certain sense, every artistic fixation of a natural process is a 'killing' of this process" (Fenichel, 142). Later, Forster fully registers Coleen's attraction to him when he discovers an imaginary nude portrait of himself in Coleen's apartment (168, 225–26).

For Murail, influenced here by Jungian instead of Lacanian psychology, the critical inward evolution of Forster appears in his gradual acceptance of the little girl within, a representation of his feminine side and of his hidden vulnerability. As the novel begins, Forster can no longer appreciate his favorite painting, Renoir's "Petite Fille avec un arrosoir" (the pictorial suggestion of pouring water as an expression of instinctive desire has been transferred in the text from Renoir's watering-can to Coleen's chronically overflowing bathtub in the room above Forster's, e.g., 7, 7). Later, Forster, unlike anyone else, notices and is enthralled by the "parfum" (odor) of a little girl, Anita, who has just moved into the building (50 and 57, 64 and 74). The suicide of Mrs. Bernhardt, coincidentally occurring just after Forster has indulged in an unconsciously jealous outburst against Sharon Dowd for taking Bruce Conway from him (a feeling recognized as such by both Sharon and Bruce, 78 and 79, 103 and 105), implies the risk of the death of the inner feminine side of the self through repression. Discovering the body, Forster faints in an unwitting sympathetic identification with the widow, like himself abandoned (92, 123). When he comes to and covertly recovers the keys dropped by the suicide, exactly at the mid-point of the novel, he gains both literal and symbolic access to her world, and begins the process of self-recognition (95, 127). Even then, the mere mention of Renoir's little girls in conversation gives Forster a chill (108, 144).

But after he has secretly explored Mrs. Bernhardt's empty flat, and realized that she has lost both her children as well as her job and her husband, he makes a private promise to Rachel (the daughter crushed by a school bus at age four) to fulfill Mrs. Bernhardt's wish of being buried in Jerusalem (114, 152). Via this private commission to the vulnerable side of himself that he will reveal to no one (142–43 and 172–73, 189–91 and 231), he internalizes the little girl. More accurately, he acknowledges her not as an external image but as a part of his intimate intentionality. The connection between the inner girl child and a homosexual preference is jokingly and unwittingly made by Bruce, when Forster takes him and Anita to a gallery show: "Queers and little girls, that's all he wants" (133, 177). Shortly after that remark, predictably, Forster has another fainting spell (134, 179), a strategic withdrawal from a still too threatening self-awareness:

> The state of being flooded with excitation [gives] rise to the need for blocking acceptance of further stimulation; perception and other ego functions [are] blocked or diminished by forceful countercathexes. These types of "defenses," especially their climax—fainting—may be regarded as the pattern according to which all other pathogenic defenses are formed: fainting is a complete cessation of the functions of the ego. (Fenichel, 144)

On his return home, for a week Forster isolates himself from the world, living only on tea (143, 183). "The refusal of food by depressed persons," Fenichel observes, "generally expresses the idea that pressure from internalized objects should not be increased by incorporating other objects" (136).

When he emerges, he will have accomplished enough unconscious working through that he can resume friendly relations with Sharon and Bruce; he helps the latter find the job that will allow the couple to live together (138 and 152–56, 185–86 and 203–10). As he confesses to Coleen at this point, he feels annihilated ("I'm no good for anything"). He has fantasies of suicide as he abandons his former self, but simultaneously senses a beginning: "I felt that I was real" (141–42, 189–90). Finally, Grindling Conrad presciently leads him to the Renoir painting of the "Little Girl with a Watering Can," on loan from the National Gallery. Forster had "scorned that painting for ten years of my life" (189, 252—the French, more energetically, says "j'ai craché dessus," i.e., "I spat on it"). This time he contemplates it rapturously for three-quarters of an hour, until interrupted: "I didn't feel cold anymore" (178–79, 238–39). This incident occurs just after he has told Coleen that he needs time to reflect before deciding whether to live with him.

To internalize the image of the little girl allows him for the first time to "come out" in a phone conversation with Florence Fairchild. He links the girl within to the object without when he openly describes Coleen to her as "halfway between Botticelli's 'Spring' and Renoir's little girls" (180, 240). Then his defenses can dissolve: "I've lived only for Art . . . there's something more than Art. . . . And then I'd forged such a fine shell of indifference for myself. With a protective helmet, made entirely of meanness . . . of the fear of being hurt" (181, 241). He still feels too vulnerable to take Coleen with him to see the painting (189, 253). But he adopts for himself the story of another little girl, Alice in Wonderland, when he writes Coleen from Jerusalem to accept his love (191, 254).

Coleen himself sensitively employs images for mediation—in the following example, superficially he compares himself, the homosexual, to other ostracized, suffering beings. On a deeper plane his imagery portrays Forster's own despised self as deserving of the rescue of psychic integration. Rather than appealing to Forster's sympathy, Coleen tries to encourage him to empathy; he draws his attention to a case of social isolation more serious than that of the gay male: "Haven't you ever realized that Mrs. Bernhardt is black? That she's old? Sick? A widow? Alone? A Jew? And what's more, she's a woman! Seven reasons for being rejected, overlooked, condemned, judged, punished" (24, 29). Once alerted in this way, Forster feels an instinctive psychic bond to her. After her suicide, he is unaccountably impelled to search through her effects. He learns of her tragic losses and her wish to have her ashes scattered over Jerusalem. Symbolically like Forster if he were to become openly and exclusively homosexual, she has lost her heterosexual object (her husband died some years ago) and her children (her son died in Vietnam; her daughter had been crushed by a school bus). Only after Forster has symbolically identified with her by granting her last wish can he accept Coleen's offer of love.

Forster cannot at first disclose this identification. When Coleen nearly discovers Mrs. Bernhardt's effects in Forster's apartment, the latter feels vaguely but powerfully threatened and conceals them promptly. To reveal his psychic affinity with her would make him feel too vulnerable. But her image provides an essential transition. Initially, Forster's self-image is split between the handsome reflection in the mirror and the despised homosexual self that fascinates him in his book on Breughel's monsters. As a physically unattractive old woman, Mrs. Bernhardt allows Forster to combine his self-image as womanly with the defense of repulsion. Repression weakens when Forster indirectly discloses his bond with Mrs. Bernhardt: he allows Coleen to listen to his phone conversation with his father, during which

Forster makes plans to smuggle Mrs. Bernhardt's ashes into Israel in a diplomatic pouch (172–73, 231–32). In the last scene of the novel, Forster symbolically releases the despised self and puts it to rest, by scattering Mrs. Bernhardt's ashes and those of her daughter's photograph over the Jewish cemetery outside Jerusalem. Freed from the unacknowledged feelings that were haunting him, he now can be at peace. This interpretation is suggested by a final descriptive notation: olive branches waving in the breeze.

Murail uses three main strategies to avoid threatening the reader. She does not advocate homosexuality, but rather the lifting of repression. For her, homosexuality represents only one of a gamut of possibilities in love relationships. Nor are Forster and Coleen emotionally privileged over the heterosexual couples. From the perspective of the typology of strategies for interpersonal behavior elaborated by Karen Horney,[7] Forster illustrates the withdrawn solution, suggested from the outset by his inability to make lasting commitments. Virgil Sparks and Béatrix illustrate Horney's expansive strategy of aggressive, conflictual interaction. Bruce Conway illustrates the compliant strategy in his relationship with Sharon Dowd. Near the end, however, the two artists Grindling Conrad and Vanessa Poretski imply the possibility of the Horneyan ideal: a balanced, flexible relationship between two freely creative people, not skewed by the neurotic preponderance of one of the three interactive strategies mentioned above. This heterosexual couple represents an emotional maturity toward which Coleen and Forster presumably will move.

Second, Murail scarcely ever refers to any particular sexual practices, either heterosexual or homosexual, except when Béatrix calls Virgil an "enculé" (the gay man playing the passive role in anal intercourse; inappositely translated "dickhead" in the English edition) for feeling hesitant to live with her (55–56, 72), and again when Forster is most vehemently defending himself against his attraction to Coleen by trying to alienate him: "What was the name of the first one you butt-fucked? Was he younger than you? I suppose you overpowered him?" (82, 109). Despite Forster's vehemence, the specter of anal intercourse and of homosexual rape, the most repellent of possibilities for most heterosexuals, has already been laid to rest by the mimetic realities of the novel and by Murail's third strategy of dissociating sexual practices from morality and associating them with personal taste. Moreover, she has repeatedly reminded us that in other domains, Coleen

7. (1885–1952). In *Our Inner Conflicts*, and more fully in *Neurosis and Human Growth*; Horney's theories, unduly neglected by literary critics, have recently been definitively analyzed by Bernard J. Paris.

and Forster have similar tastes: both dislike peas; they love buttered scones with raisins; they spontaneously break into laughter when they simultaneously imagine Bruce as a chauffeur; Forster admires Coleen's art (in the English, 13 and 175, 21, 45, 168; in the French, 15 and 234, 25–26, 57, 225–26).

The transparency of Murail's psychosexual universe may prevent her novel from achieving the status of a masterpiece (that it was made into a bad movie did not help it either). Knowing and following one's bliss, she seems to say, is all one needs to do. Disease and pregnancy do not exist in her world. Society is not an actor, not an obstacle. All the other characters, including Forster's father, accept his homosexuality without disapproval.

Forster's mother, described as alive although absent from the text, may provide an early clue to the origins of his ultimate choice of homosexuality. Her being bracketed suggests encryptment in Forster's mind as an imago, the focus of an unconscious fixation. In the most conventional psychological interpretation of male homosexuality, such mother-fixation would preclude his becoming seriously interested in another woman. One could reasonably object, however, that fictional characters have no unconscious, and that the hypothesis of mother-fixation does not clarify why Forster more than another male would be susceptible to making a homosexual object-choice. I would propose as an explanation a different suggestion from recent gay theory, also based, admittedly, on the unconscious. Its argument runs as follows: in resolving the oedipal conflict,

> the identification with the father involves love for the father. The heterosexual resolution of the oedipal conflict is bought at the price of the homosexual resolution which, however, is not completely surrendered. The homophobia of heterosexual males . . . is the result of remnants of homosexuality in the heterosexual resolution of the oedipal conflict (de Kuyper, 137).

Now, Forster's father is the only parent of any of the characters to be discussed in any detail or to appear on the scene. He visits just in time to announce that Forster's promise to Mrs. Bernhardt can be fulfilled, and to approve Forster's choice of Coleen. His presence, a symbolic reconciliation, coincides with Forster's triumph over homophobia, his renunciation of the heterosexual solution, and therefore the end of oedipal rivalry with the father. In this conclusion characters function less as mimetic than as psychic archetypes.

Beyond the purely interpersonal sphere, Murail transcends her nationality as well as her gender through a gesture of international appropriation similar to those enacted by other and greater metafeminist authors such as Marie de France, Madame de Staël, or Marguerite Yourcenar. She depicts a drama in New York City, a place she had not yet visited, rather than in France. Before the Hitler era, Paris had been the center of the international art world. After the flight of artists and intellectuals during World War II, that center moved to New York. For a French person, imaginatively to depict the art world in New York means to recapture her lost cultural heritage. The mark of Frenchness recurs frequently in the text, like the implied author's signature, like her demarcation of her territory. The mention of a Renoir painting associated with a lost innocence opens the text; Forster, we learn, had lived for fifteen years in France with his diplomat father; Coleen claims he can make an excellent stew "French style, of course" (22, 26).

As one might have expected, the expression of French cultural dominance engineered by the novel is overdetermined; it recurs in the second of two major privileged moments in the work, when Forster, ecstatically contemplating the Renoir painting, thereby comes to know himself better. In Murail's fictional world of 1980, revelation still originates in France. More pointedly, it originates in the Impressionism of the late nineteenth century, which thus comes to represent a timeless value, a *kairos*, beside which the achievements of postmodernist New York must pale. Murail's aesthetic conservatism is evident in her rejection of post-figurative art, notably when she contrasts the inept sculpture exhibit on the main floor of the Schmidt Gallery with the mosaic of realistic citations that display the genius of Grindling Conrad. She deplores in the former the same feature she extols in the latter, a combination of familiar elements and of allusions to the past.

In the descriptions of modern art objects, as Forster sees them, we also find a subtext of allusions to his unconscious homosexuality: on a second reading homosexuality serves, as it does in Proust, as an interpretant (see Sedgwick, *Epistemology* 213–51). Thus the inept heteroclite compositions of the sculptors in the Schmidt Gallery, with their involuntary imitations of tradition, evoke the psychic repetition compulsion, the essential dynamic of ego-defense:

> We penetrated into something like the main hall of a railway station, filled with gizmos. I recoiled involuntarily, especially when I saw some bicycle wheels . . . a jam pot set on a pressure cooker . . . a chair painted green and a pink radiator . . . a statue of the Venus of Milo poised on a heap of garbage (62, 80–81).[8]

8. The whole text is suggestive. The bicycle wheels recall Marcel Duchamp, but are also associated with "pédale," a slang word for male homosexual used elsewhere

In contrast, Conrad's art reflects a free, creative synthesis of familiar elements; the ability to move from one medium to another; and a way of transcending the familiar by looking at it differently:

> a little pink watercolor representing a carnation. . . . There too, the petals concealed strange creations. The third work was half-painting and half-sculpture. Everything was set in motion, with hollows and reliefs. The fourth was woven, a sort of abstract medieval tapestry with a wooden clown hanging from it, artfully and knowingly integrated into the geometrical composition. (64, 84)

In the descriptions of the paintings in Conrad's studio, the artist's connections with the past become more clear:

> I was immediately drawn to a canvas in the depths of the studio. I read "Homage to Breughel," and recognized a modern version of "The Fall of Icarus." . . . I scanned the other paintings with their evocative names, and then I stopped short in front of the last, rather perplexed: "After Renoir." Indeed, you could discover Renoir there, but analyzed, as it were, reconceptualized, recreated. (108, 143)

Forster has felt from the beginning of the novel that he had to choose between Breughel's "Garden of Earthly Delights" and the garden with Renoir's little girl, between pleasure and innocence: Conrad's vision encompasses them both, and through appreciating Conrad's art, Forster will learn to recuperate innocence in pleasure.

Murail's conservative tastes appear most patently in her choice of a conventional literary genre, a psychological novel focused on character depiction. Like other gestures of appropriation, her appropriation of the gay male imagination is retrospective in terms of general literary history (referring to such great novelists as Gide, Proust, and Tournier). Owing to its immediacy and clarity, however, the psychological novel also serves as an effective vehicle for her didactic intentions. On the other hand, to make such a choice also affirms that you do not need to be avant-garde or parodic (in

---

in the text by Murail. The juxtaposition of the jam pot and the pressure cooker ("cocotte minute" in French) evokes the anus as a container of pleasure juxtaposed with a pun on coquetry and brief encounters. The atypical paint colors of the chair and radiator suggest objects in drag, just as the oddly positioned Venus de Milo recalls the same Duchamp transvestite mustached Mona Lisa image, *L.H.O.O.Q.*, i.e., "elle a chaud au cul," or "she has hot pants." This same Venus de Milo suggests repressed contents of Forster's unconscious, where he feels himself to be a woman obsessed by illegitimate desires. The name "Forster" itself is a nod to the gay British novelist.

either sense, *Beigesang* or *Gegengesang*, derivation or opposition), and therefore, self-marginalized, to be a successful woman writer.

As mentioned above, Murail's greatest precursor in her act of cross-gender appropriation is Marguerite Yourcenar in the *Mémoires d'Hadrien*. The example of this precursor allows Murail to go a step further, to dispense with Yourcenar's tacit justification for drawing her subject from the grand narrative of history. Set in history, paradoxically, the gay male emperor appears both real (portraying him is not a prurient invention) and exceptional (because he ruled his age). We don't need to worry that anything said about him might apply to us; by virtue of his rank and times, he remains a curious spectacle. By depicting her gay male protagonist as an ordinary (although gifted) person among other ordinary fictive people, Murail implies that his sexual choices as well can be considered ordinary, not monstrous or exceptional. After accepting himself, the author implies, Forster can better accept others: in his relationship to his community, "coming out" leads to a move that is centripetal, not centrifugal; integrative, not separatist.

Murail, in short, depicts an idealized libertarian community where individualism and solidarity are miraculously balanced. Despite the urban setting, her story of learning to love by lifting repression places her in the tradition of the idealistic novel of George Sand (see Schor, *George Sand* 4, 10–22, 27–32, 39–41, and 53), one that depicts a movement toward a "utopian fraternal community" and where "the quest for the love ideal is inseparable from an aspiration toward an ideal world" (Schor, 21 and 53). Coleen's drawings of Stairway C, a community he describes as "my beating heart" (25, 31), emblematize this ideal community, where the sublimation of art and the expression of love can be harmoniously combined.

CHAPTER 13

Gomorrah and the Word: But Where Are They?

LAURENCE ENJOLRAS

Contexts

In a special issue of the magazine *Masques* (spring/summer 1985) published under the title "The 1980's: Myth or Liberation?" Jean-Pierre Joecker, the founder of the quarterly, opens his editorial on the gayest of notes, declaring: "If the 1970's were the coming out years, the years during which shame was put an end to, the 1980's are the years when homosexuality establishes itself as an irrefutable fact of everyday life. These are the years of visibility, a time for the gay media and a gay life style" (6). Indeed, a brief return to key moments allows for corroboration of such legitimate euphoria and for the recognition that, in every domain, be it media-linked or commercial, political or juridical, cultural or literary, after multiple tribulations, gay liberation is akin to a revolution.

As a matter of fact, when taking stock of the situation in 1985, one cannot but notice that magazines and journals abound; that Fréquence Gaie, "la radio qui bande FM," has been broadcasting twenty-four hours a day for more than two years; that parades have replaced demonstrations; that life is spent in pleasure rather than in protest; that homosexuality has ceased to be discriminated against in the Penal Code; that bars, discos, restaurants, cafés, and saunas are no longer solely housed in the Parisian rue Sainte-Anne but open up everywhere in provincial cities; that summer universities flourish and that movie festivals multiply. As for literature, it prospers out in the open at Les Mots à la Bouche, the Parisian bookstore specializing in gay and lesbian material, all the more so since it has received institutional consecration in the form of two Goncourt prizes and one Fémina prize, awarded respectively to Yves Navarre's *Le Jardin d'acclimatation* in 1980, Dominique Fernandez's *Dans la main de l'ange* in 1983, and Jocelyne François's *Joue-nous España* in 1982.

With regard to what is at stake here, that is to say the lesbian side of the matter, political action committees, international coordinations, groups engaged in reflection or in artistic expression, radio programs, summer camps, and even a project for a lesbian village in early 1981 attest to the ever-growing activity and visibility of lesbians. Publications like *Désormais, Espaces, Quand les femmes s'aiment* or *Vlasta* open sporadic or ephemeral columns for lesbians, but should not be considered failures because they were short-lived: such a phenomenon shows a steadfast concern with making theoretical stances and practical diversities coincide, coupled with the laudable courage to constantly call everything into question. Studies on lesbianism by Françoise d'Eaubonne, Evelyne Le Garrec, and Geneviève Pastre, and the first university thesis on the topic, defended by Marie-Jo Bonnet, complement fiction by Mireille Best, Gisèle Bienne, or Jocelyne François, all in the wake of Monique Wittig's theoretical and formal texts and Elula Perrin's pulp fiction in the 1970's. Indeed, to her credit, Perrin did just as much for lesbianism in her time with the 250 hurried pages of *Les Femmes préfèrent les femmes* as writers before her had in their own epoch, from Sappho to Renée Vivien, from Colette to Liane de Pougy, from Violette Leduc to Jeanne Galzy. In short, in 1985, the year of Joecker's assessment, it is clear that lesbians are also enjoying their own victory, even if it is smaller than that of their male homologues.

More than ten years later, where are they, how far have they gotten? If historical distance enables us to assert indisputably that the 1970's were the years of militancy and the 1980's the years of enjoyment, are we really to believe, following *L'Evénement du jeudi* which published a special dossier on female homosexuality in October 1991, that the 1990's will be, yet again, at least for lesbians, the years of silence (Gozlan and Lévy)? One would do well to consult *L'Annuaire*, a most useful guidebook, unique in France, and published by Les Archives, Recherches et Cultures Lesbiennes (ARCL). It lists places, groups, and activities for "lesbians, feminists and female homosexuals." Numerous entries attest to the multiplicity, diversity, and vitality of current initiatives, some of them having held firm against all odds for almost a decade, others born more recently, all of them responding to the upheavals of the times, be it through inner transformations or with new creations.

Deletions and additions between 1990 and 1996 show that changes are continuous and that they are a direct response to changes in the larger social group. This alone demonstrates that lesbians intend to be accounted for in every way.

Yet the proportion of written material available has considerably diminished. Quality concerns and financial constraints reduced the numbers of publications whose instant creation throughout the 1980's had benefited from the urge to express everything *hic et nunc*, offsetting with immediacy a lack of financial support and media skills. Today, lesbian periodicals total one monthly, *Lesbia Magazine*, started in December 1982, and one journal, *La Grimoire*, a literary, political, and artistic periodical whose publication seems chancy, given the fact that it runs material sent now and then by a few stray contributors. To these should be added the sundry newsletters that voice the concerns and list the activities of all kinds of groups: that of the Archives, of the lesbian health group, and of diverse groups meeting in Paris or in the larger provincial cities. These newsletters are not the only media outlets in which lesbians can express or inform themselves, for there are, to a greater or lesser extent, venues in certain feminist or queer newspapers. All the same, the number of publications whose content is exclusively lesbian has drastically decreased, along with their influence.

In criticism and theory, Wittig's provocative articles from the early 1980's, collected in *The Straight Mind*, seem distant indeed. In December 1989, an international colloquium titled "Homosexuality and Lesbianism: Myths, Memories, and Historiography" took place at the Sorbonne (*Cahiers Gai-Kitsch-Camp*). This endeavor was apparently the first of this magnitude in the field since the demise of summer universities. It was organized by the Groupe de Recherches et d'Etudes sur l'Homosocialité et les Homosexualités (GREH) affiliated with the Centre d'Etudes sur L'Actuel et le Quotidien (CEAQ/Paris V), in conjunction with the Groupe de Sociologie Politique et Morale (EHESS/CNRS) and the Fondation Mémoire des Sexualités (FMS). It aimed at giving the French university, which had proven rather recalcitrant about these issues, the shock necessary to help raise consciousness about them, if not to legitimize them. Despite an apparent concern for equity, however, there were fewer papers read concerning lesbians than concerning gay men. Ironically, Christiane Jouve's article titled "Invisibilities and Invisibilizations of Lesbians" echoes this disproportion. The proceedings of the three subsequent colloquia are even more skewed. And scanning other publications, such as *Nouvelles Questions féministes*, produces similar results: one article in the March 1981 issue, one in the triple issue published in 1991, and one in an issue published in 1993. Theoretical analyses from a lesbian perspective in university-accredited publications and courses on lesbian literature remain rare in France. But there is nothing astonishing about that, since within the very departments likely to have an interest in lesbian literature, such as the Centre d'Etudes Féminines / Paris VIII for instance, lesbian literature as such is not part of the programs for one simple reason: "the concept does not exist," *dixit* Hélène Cixous—founder and director of the Center—in an informal postlecture exchange at Harvard University in October 1991. This contention probably explains the fact that there was no session on lesbianism at the colloquium titled "Readings of Sexual Difference" organized by the Center in October 1990. Given the title of the colloquium, one could be perplexed by so unexpected an absence; the Centre d'Etudes Féminines evidently advocates a strict—exclusive? all-inclusive?—definition of "feminine," at any rate, one that, by making its lesbian component irrelevant, is akin to making it nonexistent.[1]

Although Cixous's opinion may reflect the French consensus that favors universalism over communitarianism, not everyone shares her opinion with regard to the concept of lesbian literature—or its lack of pertinence. For many, to conceive a course on lesbian literature is not a utopian enterprise. As a matter of fact, there are more and more courses of the sort offered in North American universities, which in recent years have pushed for the recognition and legitimation of gay and lesbian studies programs. Between primary and secondary texts in French, one could find enough material to study for a full academic year, given the traditional method of detailed analysis prevailing in French universities.

One can offer a course on lesbian literature only if the primary material exists, but a review of bookstores and publishers' catalogues shows that new

1. It would be both useful and revealing to interrogate every center and university group which promotes feminist and/or feminine research and studies on the availability—or lack thereof—of courses, seminars, or colloquia centered partially or exclusively on lesbian literature and lesbian issues. Among these groups and centers are: ANEF, Association Nationale des Etudes Féministes; CEDREF, Centre d'enseignement, de documentation et de recherche pour les études féministes, Paris VII, Jussieu; Centre d'Etudes Féminines, Paris VIII, St Denis; CRIF, Centre de recherches interdisciplinaires sur les femmes, Bordeaux III; GRIEF, Toulouse Le Mirail; Groupe Simone, Toulouse Le Mirail; Centre de recherche sur les femmes, Faculté de Droit et Sciences Politiques, Nantes; CEFUP, Centre d'études féministes de l'Université de Provence, Aix-en-Provence; CLEF, Centre Lyonnais d'études féministes, Lyon II.

titles are hard to find. And the Editions Geneviève Pastre, the only lesbian publishing house in France today, which would be more aptly described as a pushcart press, cannot fill the void alone. As word would have it, contemporary French literature is undergoing a crisis: it is a victim of its own proliferation and subsequent mediocrity. Using an opportunistic form of logic, could we conversely deduct that the scarcity of *one* particular literary category guarantees its value? As a consequence, rather than being disheartened by the shortage of lesbian novels, should we be galvanized by titles published only begrudgingly?

Anyone wanting to constitute a home library of contemporary lesbian literary works by metropolitan French women writers could do so with ease. One would collect about one hundred novels at best, including the most obscure items and counting those that require a solid dose of insiders' knowledge to spot the lesbian characters; a few collections of poems; one or two plays; and a few biographies. More than ever before, publishing houses are sparing of paper when it comes to lesbian writing and seem to believe that anyone who wrote a lesbian text in the past is outmoded, and that anyone writing one today is unreadable. In one case or the other: invisible. Pierre Assouline, who investigated homosexual literature in the November 1992 issue of *Lire*, garnered the following explanation concerning women from "a press attachée in the publishing business, who has been observing the lesbian literary milieu for years." He quotes her as saying: "Among us, it has always been more clandestine than among men. One finds a certain voluptuous delight in it. It adds a plus to pleasure, just as secrecy adds a plus to writing" (26). Discretion? Modesty? Mere alibi? No. Rather, pure ambrosia. As a result, when a lesbian novel manages to appear in the Sapphic literary desert of our contemporary times, such a phenomenon dictates that one rush for it forthwith.

Texts

In 1990 Hélène de Monferrand published *Les Amies d'Héloïse*, an epistolary novel that was immediately awarded the first Goncourt prize for a first novel, not, as one might be inclined to think, because of the audacious nature of its content, but because it is indeed well constructed and well written, and stands out as an erudite, ingenious work. As François Nourissier, of the Goncourt Academy, remarks in an advertising blurb: "One finds in this novel a certain amount of disrespect, and a kind of merry intrepidity in the avowal that makes its singularity. This novel could have been sulfurous, provocative; it is natural. One is inclined to say: innocent." Its title, its format, its composition, and its themes echo illustrious classics: the medieval abbess (born around 1101) who was Abelard's lover and their famous correspondence; Rousseau's 1761 novel, *La Nouvelle Héloïse*; Laclos's 1782 novel, *Les Liaisons dangereuses*. Indeed, the intertextuality is multiple: Rousseau's title pays homage to love as much as to God. Laclos invokes Rousseau on the flyleaf of his work. In turn, Hélène de Monferrand chooses Laclos's Merteuil as godmother: "And Suzanne herself was tricked by the skillfulness of Héloïse whom I helped, thinking I was la Merteuil" (*Amies* 243). And Valmont becomes godfather: "She seemed too young to me to play Valmont" (*Journal* 266).

If Rousseau and Laclos indebted themselves by the mere borrowing of a few forms or themes, eager as they were to deliver a countermessage about a situation they were refuting, Monferrand, a modernist who laughs at virtue, goes back directly to the original: to the Héloïse who did not burden herself with questions of sin. While perverting the works of her two male predecessors in order to serve her purpose, Monferrand plays with allusions and multiplies references to them in her own version of what one may call her new *Liaisons* or her new *Nouvelle Héloïse*, that is to say simply *Héloïse*, in the style characteristic of the late twentieth century. In Monferrand's novel one finds love, passion, friendship, and solidarity, as in the work of Rousseau; there are intrigues, seduction, astuteness, and games, as in Laclos. In sum, everything is present that gave charm, strength, and scope to these notorious classics. But there is much more: exuberant love affairs between women, something that neither Rousseau, the puritan, nor even Laclos, the libertine, had the audacity to envisage, and who knows, something that the abbess herself perhaps never had the leisure to confess. In Monferrand's work, one discovers what made Héloïse so attractive a character and turned her into a symbol: the aspiration, and in the book under scrutiny here, the firm determination to live a passion fully as well as freely. Similar to the ardent Héloïse who lived in the twelfth century, Monferrand's Héloïse is a woman in love who intends to live her passions as she thinks best, coupled with an intellectual who transgresses hampering conventions. The whole thing is executed with spirit, narrated by the author in a lively, witty, and playful tone, something that cannot prejudice the project. To summarize is to maim, but let us nonetheless reveal the minimum, through Jean-Louis Ezine's 1990 review of the novel for *Le Nouvel Observateur*:

> Young ladies born in respectable families, and even in higher ranks of society, exchange intimate confessions after experiences that are for the most part ho-

> mosexual in nature and leave them *astonished* (using the word in its seventeenth-century meaning, naturally). They know the beginning of the fourth Canto of the Aeneid inside out, can expatiate upon the role of the Princess des Ursins in the Spanish war of succession. At age fifteen, they are able to win a prize in Latin translation at the Concours Général, to seat a bishop or a prefect at a dinner table, and even to tell apart at a glance a wineglass for burgundy from one for bordeaux. They pass each other on their way from Onasbrück to Saint-Gall, part in Crest-Voland, take up with one another again where they are due at some tea party in London(they will bring back from there a collection of proper cashmere garments). They have cousins in all of Prussia and even in Duchies, often have a father who is an ambassador in Stockholm, sometimes a grandfather who had to work hard to earn his caviar (for instance, it is not uncommon for him to have invented the famous mustard gas in 1914–18). (71)

Enough for the background. Now, the framework: fifteen-year-old Héloïse has a love affair with thirty-year-old Erika, who, at fifteen, had a love affair with Suzanne, aged thirty at the time. Suzanne swipes Héloïse from Erika. A few years after Suzanne's death, Héloïse, almost thirty, and Erika, soon to be forty-five, get back together for a new beginning.

Whereas the eighteenth century and Laclos himself would recognize only wit and skillfulness in embittered adults who diabolically deceived the innocence and naïveté of young and budding lovebirds, conversely, Monferrand leaves the full initiative of the machination to the expert undertakings of two fifteen-year-olds. They are the ones who, between two siestas in Girl Scout camps in the case of Claire, Héloïse's best friend—whose first name is the same as Julie's best friend in Rousseau's work—or two receptions at the embassy in the case of Héloïse, plot their precocious sexual and amorous futures, on the pretense that one is never better armed to face life than when one precipitates its events oneself. A slew of young companions, each one more resourceful than the next, serve as alibis and go-betweens. In this novel peppered with erudite references as well as with Latin and Greek quotations, the elders are the ones who must bear the brunt of the scheming—they quickly and most willingly do so. They are tricked, by the very ones supposed to lose their purity in the enterprise, into ravishing from these young girls in bloom a most apparent virtue. Writing a joyful hymn to love, the author gave her three heroines symbolic first names: Héloïse, a direct reference to the abbess in love; Erika, which in German means heather, the flower of robust love; Suzanne, reminiscent of black-eyed Susans, or yellow daisies, which lovers pluck while saying "she-loves-me, she-loves-me-not." The book, conceived as an epistolary exchange, covers a period of sixteen years, from June 1964 to June 1980, and is coupled with occasional incursions into the diaries of some of the protagonists.

The two essential parameters constitutive of the story—one thematic, the other formal—are omnipresent: love, flanked with the whole apparatus of seduction and desire, that is, passion between women, naturally, of which the author speaks with a casual liberty, as if it were evident. This alone would suffice to give the book merit. But there is also a game at the core of its composition that intensifies its appeal, a system echoing that of the double-or-nothing bets to which the protagonists devote themselves in their spare time. Every element in the narrative is more or less strictly linked to these two conventions, which greatly increases the pleasure of reading, for as soon as one has understood this double configuration—humanist and mathematical—one will not rest until its effects have been anticipated. An example, to illustrate the playfulness of the novel: every descendant bearing the same patronymic as Héloïse must be given a first name starting with the letter H, an imperative hereditary system resulting from an ancestral family law; this first system which reproduces the letter H *ad infinitum* refers to a second system, that of the heroes of Greek mythology, since for the most part, they are the ones who provide the necessary forenames—Hector, Hippolyte, Hécube, Hélène, Héraclès, Hermione. In turn the second system refers to a third one, that of tragedy in general; in particular, it is a reference to the tragedies of Euripides, who staged the heroes whose names Monferrand gave to some of her characters, and whom Jacqueline de Romilly classifies as the tragedian of passions.

Tragedy often means ill-fortune. However, as Romilly reminds us, tragedy is far from being only that, especially if we look at works by Euripides, who first modified the laws of the genre, thereby giving tragedy a structure that she considers akin to modernity: "He developed actions, enhanced effects, expanded music, multiplied characters, took heroes down from their pedestal, played with a thousand and one reversals of situation, some of which border on melodrama" (115). A tragedy strikes us with the character of its heroes as much as it does with its action, and if Euripides "likes to take them down from their legendary heights" (Romilly 124), that is to say, if he renders heroes more human, "closer to us than heroes staged by other tragic dramatists, but also more unyielding when it comes to their passions" (Romilly 115), they remain nonetheless unparalleled beings. As for the gods who arrange fate, frightfully powerful in the plays of Aeschylus, whom Romilly designates as the tragedian of divine justice, and still highly menacing in the plays of Sophocles, whom she labels as the tragedian of the solitary hero, in Euripides, "they are no longer the ever-present, responsible agents of what happens in the world. . . . The action unfolds naturally: as a matter of fact, it unfolds alongside the passions that determine it" (144).

Monferrand knows the Greek classics well. Donning the hat of a modernist tragedian of prose, she draws blithely and freely from the genre, favoring what makes its greatness and interest, resolutely leaving doom and gloom aside, staging heroines and characters who are out of the ordinary, among other things because of their birth in society's élite. Names with particles abound in the novel: Héloïse's parents are a count and countess. After all, did not Laclos stage a marquess and a viscount, Rousseau a lord? And was not Héloïse herself, brought up by her uncle who was a canon, also part of the élite? Besides, tragedians are not known to have cast yokels as heroes. Conforming to the genre, Monferrand in turn casts "aspiring hearts" to whom, as Corneille writes in *Le Cid*, "valor is not measured by the count of years." Their culture, erudition, manners, behavior, choices, destiny equate them with the best, the literary élite who breathe and exude ingrained nobleness—if not the virtue and abnegation that Rousseau favored. Taking as her background contemporary historical and political events, such as May 1968, she gives love intrigues more than their due, multiplying sudden developments, unexpected episodes, ruses, surprises, confusions, recognitions, reunions, and, as does Euripides himself, makes her characters move about in a closed world (Romilly 44). It is a world in which they are all bound to one another in one way or another, be it because of blood ties or because of shared social privileges, the latter being just as tenacious as the former.

Eventually their paths cross and their destinies unite: Suzanne happens to be an old friend of Anne de Marèges, Héloïse's mother, of whom she had lost sight for thirty years and whom she finds again thanks to her liaison with her friend's daughter. Erika is the older sister of one of Héloïse's classmates. Melitta is a lover and friend of Erika's, and after an interval of a few years, she becomes the lover and friend of Héloïse. Marriages occur between brothers, sisters, and cousins of one or another. Borders are sieves, favoring apparent coincidences or improbable reversals of situation. Just as in Euripides' tragedies, then, a seclusion from the trivia of the world, a self-sufficient isolation in a privileged world in which, as Anouilh contends in his *Antigone*, "one can rest easy. In the first place, one is among equals" (54).

A demiurge in turn, Monferrand offhandedly pushes fate in the right direction, takes many liberties with the fearsome ancient gods whom she changes into goddesses presiding over a favorable fate. In her novel, everything is arranged most gaily: tempests end in conquests, battles are resolved after expert reconciliations. And if, in order not to depart totally from the rules of the tragic genre, she scatters a few deaths here and there, such as that of Suzanne, as well as aborted attempts at murder (that of Héloïse by Erika) and suicide (Erika), these dramatic elements have nothing really fatal about them. In the case of Suzanne, who dies nobly, the purpose is obviously to facilitate the return of the action to its point of origin: after fifteen years of sundry peripeteiae during which the heroines have matured, the novel closes on the reuniting of Héloïse and Erika, both ready to embrace a new start in life together. We have then come full circle, after four hundred pages teeming with euphoric reversals of situation narrated by an alert pen in the thousand and one letters exchanged between the most forward of protagonists.

Theirs is a self-sufficient world, a closed structure where nothing is left to occur haphazardly: just as in ancient myths or tragedies, each element in the action constitutes a potential springboard for an internal, sudden revival of the story, an episode that can assume more or less lengthy narrative proportions depending on specific needs, and this *ad infinitum.* Exploiting one of the possibilities she has deftly secured, and adopting the technique of composition dear to Aeschylus who offered tragedies in trilogies, Monferrand published the *Journal de Suzanne* in 1991, adding to her first novel a hefty complement that inserts itself temporally in the preceding work, inscribing in it a mirror image of the story. This diary, started by Suzanne on May 4, 1971, comes to an end on July 15 of that same year, one day before her death. Containing multiple flashbacks, it sheds light on shadowy areas of otherwise familiar situations described in the first novel, reveals Suzanne's own motives, and confirms or invalidates some of the speculations made by other protagonists. In each novel, the aim is to focus the narrative on one particular heroine in order to unfold further facets of her story as well as the consequences for the different members of this gigantic saga.

From one work to the next one recognizes familiar characters and events, though they are set in a new light, and above all, Monferrand's playfulness. Each novel is dotted with embryonic figures that can be developed later; this artifice once adopted, it is exploited throughout its multiple possibilities. The way lies open and is potentially inexhaustible. It demands that Monferrand deliver a third work, for which we are prepared, that is, the missing volume of her unfinished trilogy. We await "Erika's novel," which will complete the triptych devoted to her three heroines. Moreover, nothing prevents her readers from hoping that once this trilogy is completed, Monferrand will write a second trilogy, for having scattered quite a few budding lesbian heroines in her first two novels, she has enough at hand to compose more. Did she not already toy with the exercise, publishing in *Lesbia Magazine* a short narrative in four episodes entitled "La femme de l'exode," a reference to a particular incident contained in the *Journal de Suzanne*?

We do not tire of these Sapphic adventures, especially as they unfold under the most favorable of omens. The odds are that among the challenges that she included in the rules of her own game, Monferrand first and foremost bet on the reiterated pleasure offered by a playful text conceived along the principle of an everlasting return to itself. A boisterous contemporary tragedian, could she thus be nursing the unavowed—though easily surmised—desire to ensure singlehandedly, if not the permanence, at least the flourishing interim of the lesbian novel? In the present state of affairs, the last thing to do is to reproach her for her impetuous dash of excess.

To be continued . . . [2]

2. As this book was going to press, Hélène de Monferrand published *Les Enfants d'Héloïse.*

CHAPTER 14

Purloined Letters: Intertextuality and Intersexuality in Tahar Ben Jelloun's *The Sand Child*

ROBERT HARVEY

No one makes love lovingly without constituting a body without organs with the other or with others.
—Gilles Deleuze and Félix Guattari, *Mille plateaux*

Demonstration of phonological pertinence: a young bazaar vendor says, engagingly, "Do you [*tu/ti*] (non pertinent) want carpet [*tapis/taper*] (pertinent)?"
—Roland Barthes, *Incidents*

For the first time in its history the Prix Goncourt was awarded in 1987 to a North African born outside the *métropole*. The book that swayed the jury was Tahar Ben Jelloun's *The Sacred Night*, a sequel to the Moroccan writer's 1985 novel, *The Sand Child*. The two novels have in common a certain disruption of Eurocentric literary conventions by narrative structures traversed by Maghrebin oral traditions as well as their focus on the same female character raised as a man. But whereas the narrative voice in *The Sacred Night* is unitary, in *The Sand Child* several voices convene and often compete in telling the tale, which consists of unveiling some truth at its origin. And while the protagonist-narrator in *The Sacred Night* speaks from the position of an adult woman about her present state conditioned by her coerced past, neither gender nor sexuality nor voice nor time nor identity—absolutely nothing—in *The Sand Child* is stable. By 1987, in other words, Ben Jelloun (perhaps yielding to his market) had honed this story into a prize-winning, euphonic, and seamless parody of Arabic narrative traditions. *The Sand Child*, on the other hand, boldly presents itself as a generalized intertext on the verge of cacophony; its character struggles with the instability of intersexuality.

Desire is something to which Tahar Ben Jelloun's "sand child" cannot attribute any proper noun.[1] (Nor, for that matter, is the sand child—here

1. For all quotes and allusions to specific passages in *L'Enfant de sable*, I provide the page reference to the French edition, followed in brackets by the page in the

Ahmed, there Zahra—properly named by any narrative voice.) Ahmed marries his lame cousin, Fatima, who, anxious to have sex with her new husband, contents herself with cuddling him and sucking her own thumb. Growing impatient, however, Fatima reaches to caress Ahmed's genitals and confirms what she has already half guessed: she has been given in marriage to a female spouse (75). Later, befuddled "himself" by "his" female body, Ahmed is pressed by a crone to reveal his identity. A name being laughably insufficient, the creature forces him to strip and then thrusts her toothless mouth to his small breasts (112–15 [84–86]). Acts, in lesbian encounters, correspond to Ahmed's body but not to his gender.

When in a dream Zahra subverts the power of a judge by seducing him, she does so as a man enticing a man who anticipates the disrobing of another male body (97). The antecedent for Zahra's fantasm is the legend of Antar, the warrior and marabout of wanderers: a woman who, disguised as a man, simulated sodomy on her outraged male lover (83). Zahra's own wanderings bring her to a circus, where her side show consists of performing in masculine drag. Her boss, Abbas, feels authorized to sodomize her as he would a male because his mother, Oum Abbas (the sole woman to whom he has sworn fidelity), has identified Zahra as an "old queen [*vieille tapette*]" (148). Acts, in gay encounters, correspond to Zahra's gender but not to her body.

All sexualities between bodies homomorphic or heteromorphic are dysfunctional in *The Sand Child* because they are ordeals subordinated to a quest for stable identity against the force of an implacable nomadism. Just as erotic acts with the other fail to deliver pleasure to the "sand child," no gender is certain in this rhizomatic novel-machine designed to inveigle its readers into a state of generalized uncertainty. By exploring the intercultural dynamics and literary devices (especially intertextuality) that Ben Jelloun mobilizes to render nomadism and elicit uncertainty, I will, aided by Deleuze and Guattari, convey my understanding of what Ben Jelloun has tried to have this enigmatic text do.

A Child Is Stamped

Hajji Ahmed, a devout Muslim, considers himself cursed because his wife has given birth to daughters only. With seven so far, he moves to dictate, somehow, if not the sex then at least the gender of his eighth child be-

---

translation. Because numerous entire sentences—including many of those that are essential to my reading—were inexplicably deleted from the Sheridan translation, all passages from *L'Enfant de sable* here are translated by me.

fore its birth. Patriarchal coercion will deny this eighth daughter her gender: named Ahmed, *son* of Hajji Ahmed, *she* will be refused all linguistic markers of her female body. In a public square, a storyteller takes charge of narrating the ensuing travesty. Tradition with regard to boys is strictly followed: a (fake) circumcision, an initiation to the hammam by the mother, then, when "decency" commands, a transfer under the father's tutelage to the men's hammam, a man child's education. The sand child's body cannot, however, forget, and inevitably with adolescence comes ovulation. To the narrator's bafflement, Ahmed's menstruation coincides with his sudden stubborn commitment to assume unflaggingly the societal roles (except that of appearing in public) imposed upon his gendered being. Yet, while Ahmed reaps benefits reserved for men, an unnameable and irrepressible desire transports him elsewhere in his private ruminations. An anonymous admirer exhorts him, through an exchange of letters, to pass out of his house as a woman. The critique of this anonymous admirer demonstrates that an infamous condition foisted upon Muslim women has taken on radical proportions: the architectural enclosure to which patriarchal law confines a woman has been shrunken to the dimensions of the djellaba dissimulating what Ahmed's body, denuded, would affirm.

Initially confident, the narrator grows weary of his storytelling charge and abdicates to a succession of secondary narrators who contribute bits and pieces to a fantastic tale that everyone in the public square seems to know but no one knows how to finish. Suggestions abound that Ahmed's gender uncertainty may be the projection of *every* narrator's own ambivalence: the first narrator's confusion may have had roots in a libidinal economy reorganized or "straightened out" by religion.

Incongruously, the scene of the Rashomon-like narrative braid shifts, in its penultimate sequence, from Marrakesh to Buenos Aires, then back across the Atlantic to Andalusia. A new narrator, referred to as the "blind troubadour," attempts not so much to unravel the enigma that Ahmed embodies than to present an experience of his own with elements he considers analogous to that enigma. Just before lapsing into total blindness, the troubadour was handed a coin by an alluring woman with a manly voice reminiscent of Tawaddud, one of the most prominent among prominent female characters in *1001 Nights*.[2] Addressing his audience with erudite detail and

2. This passing of a coin from hand to hand has value equivalent to the gesture which, in Chaplin's *City Lights*, allowed the blind girl to finally "see" the tramp, thus proving, according to Slavoj Žižek, the Lacanian thesis that the letter always arrives at its destination (3–7).

still transfixed years later by the woman and her puzzling gesture, the native of Buenos Aires describes the coin:

> It was a *bâttène*, a fifty-centime piece, a rare coin that circulated for a short time in Egypt around 1852. The coin I had in my hand was well worn. With my fingers I tried to reconstruct the effigies engraved on each side of it. . . . On the front was a man's face with a delicate mustache, long hair, and rather large eyes. On the obverse was the same design, except that the man no longer had a mustache but a female appearance. I later learned that the coin had been struck by the father of twins, a boy and a girl, for whom he felt a fierce passion. (175–76 [138])

This shift—with its obscure talismanic coin and coming so very late in the work—will bring us closest to unlocking the enigma of Ben Jelloun's "sand child."

The Coinage Fades

> I still think that everything is given to the writer for him to use.
> (185 [145])

> I believed that the spring from which I drew my stories would never dry up . . . I stole stories from others.
> (207 [163–64])

While Ahmed, as we shall soon see, grapples with a surfeit of names, Jorge Luis Borges, arguably as essential to this novel as the hero, is never named. Instead, as Ben Jelloun studs the text with allusions to Borgesian literary practices, the author of *The Book of Sand* appears in the guise of the blind troubadour. Previous commentators have identified an impressive number of references to Borges's works in *The Sand Child*—names of characters, quotations, plots, and situations (Erickson 114–16; Gontard 112–15). In the crucial instance from which I have just quoted and which I will now analyze, Ben Jelloun comes as close as he can to plagiarizing Borges. Borges is not just *any* author to steal from, since most of his work questions the concept of originality in literature, the significance of the signature, and the very notion of authorship. Only by the manner—illustrated by the above epigraphs—in which Ben Jelloun's blind troubadour unmistakably characterizes his philosophy and writing technique as that of Borges does the novel restore a parodic credit to the Argentinian storyteller for the unavowed literary borrowing.

Ben Jelloun's intertextual deviation *imitates* (as the content of the text deviated *explains*) the nomadic survival tactics that the intersexual sand child adopts. Receiving the *bâttène* from the hands of the unnamed woman with Tawaddud's masculine voice puts the blind troubadour in mind of another ancient coin—the *zahir*. Although he never states what design the *zahir* bore, he performs two curious operations. First he explains to the audience that before being attributed to coins, *bâttène* and *zahir* were names for fundamental concepts: "You are well aware of what the word [*zahir*] means: the apparent, the visible. It is the opposite of the *bâttène*, which means the inner, that which is buried in the belly" (176 [138]). Then, in the section that Ben Jelloun lifted from Borges's story, "The Zahir," the blind troubadour provides details of the *zahir*'s history that have the effect of turning its symbolism back toward that of the *bâttène*: "the *zahir* is the bottom of a well in Tetuan and was, according to Zotenberg, a vein in the marble of one of the thousand two hundred pillars of the mosque in Córdoba" (176 [138]). (This section, which admittedly strains the limits of conventional logic, was inexplicably cut from the English translation.) It should be apparent that while Ahmed is not nominally present in the scene, because these coins allude to androgyny and ambiguity they are symbolic objects of exchange that circulate to or from the person of the main character.

On the surface, what appears to be a binary of opposites turns out, according to Ben Jelloun through Borges, to be a concatenation of the notion of the invisible (*bâttène*) with a physical token of visibility (*zahir*) which, on further examination, has invisible characteristics as well. Islamic historians employ the conceptually dichotomous adjectives of *batin* and *zahir* to group disparate sects of scholars into Batinites (*batiniya*), or those who in the Koran and Sunna seek an inner or hidden meaning, and the literalist Zahirites (*zahiriya*). Edward Said has examined the assaults of a group of Zahirites on the esoterism of Batinites in eleventh-century Andalusia (*Word, Text, Critic*, 36–39). Although Said admits that the theory may have had negligible influence on the West since the Renaissance, he extols as prophetic for structuralism the Cordovan Zahirite insistence that "words had only a . . . meaning . . . anchored to a particular usage, circumstance, historical and religious situation" (36). *The Sand Child*, however, is the product of a contemporary Moroccan writing mainly for a European readership who appears determined to maintain a middle ground, or even, at times, to favor a Batinite approach to signs in their relation to being.

By lifting this key passage from Borges's "The Zahir" and inserting it into *The Sand Child*, Ben Jelloun fits the body of his text with an intertextual prosthesis. With the possible exception of the book's English-language translator and publisher,[3] nobody seems thus far to have measured the import of this conspicuous example of intertextuality in the narrowest sense that Gérard Genette (8) lends the term: quotation, plagiarism, and/or allusion (see Kristeva, *Sèméiôtikè*). Without quotation marks or offset margins, Ben Jelloun's prosthetic passage of purloined letters disappears in its textual underbrush. Even so, it casts a light on an obscure sector of Islamic history that in turn illuminates the ontological enigma of the sand child. Like the palimpsests hiding Michel's egotism in Gide's *L'Immoraliste*, lifting the veil of mystery over this passage reveals the irreducible multiplicity of Ahmed's being.

As the sand child, represented by the *bâttène* and the *zahir*, resists unitary and definitive characterization, so Ben Jelloun's narrators clothe that selfsame female body alternately in the gender-inflected names "Ahmed" and "Zahra." Such undecidability justifies, as I deconstruct Ben Jelloun's means for weaving such a tale, my employing the combined form "Ahmed/Zahra" and the portmanteau pronoun "s/he" to designate the intersexed child of the desert.

Pitfalls and Verdigris

> One of the most important characteristics of the rhizome is that it has multiple entries.
>
> Deleuze and Guattari, *Mille plateaux*

Ahmed/Zahra's sensual certainty of self evolves, without resolution, through space as well as time. Ben Jelloun underscores the inextricable link between movement and change by forging the dual parameters into a single image: Ahmed/Zahra passes through seven symbolic city gates, marking successive developmental stages. Seven chapters of the nineteen in the novel—six at the beginning and one at the conclusion—bear the names of these gates. Surrounded by a wall punctuated by these gates, a labyrinthine Arab medina is the public space in which Ahmed/Zahra will take his/her first steps. Like the intolerable secret that Hajji Ahmed concocted to keep everyone including his "son" from knowing the body, these gates call for keys or magic words to open them.

3. If, as I suspect, Alan Sheridan and his publisher did not overlook this passage, then they omitted it for the wrong reasons: either they thought they were protecting themselves and/or Ben Jelloun from accusations of plagiarism (which I demonstrate are impossible to maintain) or they judged the passage too tedious for most readers. An article by Ben Jelloun may suggest, however, that he may later have become apprehensive about the way his debt to Borges might appear: "C'est dans un rêve . . . "

Points at which deterritorialization and reterritorialization occur, the seven gates into Ahmed/Zahra's ontological medina equal, among other things, the number of our bodily orifices. Representing the inevitability of adolescence, the Saturday gate (chapter 4) is paradigmatic of the irradicable multiplicity crucial to the sand child's being. As it reminds us that gates belong to the class of objects never definitively closed or open, Ahmed/Zahra's pubescence problematizes the notion that mutations in identity are ever either avoidable or inevitable. Passing through the Saturday gate, Ahmed/Zahra's body becomes "perplexed" and the journal in which s/he has been trying to sort out the puzzle of existence renders up a hiatus of blank pages. Writing itself with breast development and menstruation, Ahmed/Zahra's body demonstrates that to incarnate the social role for which his/her father groomed him/her "leads nowhere" (41 [27]). "I imagine him torn between the evolution of his body and his father's will to make him a man through and through," ventures the storyteller (42 [28]). Here, as at each of the seven gates of life, Ahmed/Zahra reaches the threshold of a stable identity only to succumb to aphasia before the impossible transcendence of undecidability. His/her epistemological exploration of self reverts to the virginity of the blank page—a symbol of that which is simultaneously all and nothing—which so obsessed Mallarmé. That exploration encounters as well the undeconstructable limits of conjoining and separation that Derrida recognized in the concept of hymen (both nuptials and maidenhead) and which he employed ("La double séance" in *La Dissémination*) in order to better read Mallarmé's *Mimique* in light of Plato's *Philebus.*

Veil of Complicity

The Algerian writer Assia Djébar has conducted a poetic campaign by repeatedly writing that when a Muslim woman sheds the veil, goes out into the street, thereby flaunting her commitment to a nontraditional role, she incurs repudiation, shame, imprisonment, torture, even death. Among several examples from this great writer's *oeuvre* where courageous women find companionship with each other in their common struggle against patriarchal oppression are *Les Alouettes naïves*, the lead story in *Femmes d'Alger dans leur appartement*, and *L'Amour, la fantasia.* The expression "coming out," by which homosexuals in the English-speaking world denote a public act of defiant self-identification, bears figurative resemblance to the literal egress by which some Muslim women risk their lives to challenge a mainstay of patriarchal tradition. Composed of both the homosexual's *transition* and the Muslim woman's *transit*, Ahmed/Zahra's "coming out" entails risk redoubled. Before breaking out of the concentric prisons of house and veil, s/he must first shed his/her man's clothing, cast off the social masquerade, and reclaim the gender his/her body indicates. When Ahmed/Zahra decides to follow his/her anonymous correspondent's exhortation to "go out into the street, abandoning masks and fear" (86 [63]), Ben Jelloun's narrators and audience, women and men, presumably all Muslim, express dread at the ominously familiar consequences. While "coming out" may promise Ahmed/Zahra a rebirth into existential authenticity—less a metamorphosis, we are told, than a return to what s/he is (111)—some episodes are composed to foreshadow that living out this truth could lead Ahmed/Zahra to the ultimate price paid by his/her brother/sister in enigma, Herculine Barbin, the nineteenth-century hermaphrodite whose memoirs were recovered and edited by Michel Foucault.

Despite this menace, Ahmed/Zahra does forswear the double shell of isolation. Having largely avoided mirrors during his/her masquerade as a man, Ahmed/Zahra will now seek them out in a grotesquely belated mirror stage. Autoerotic narcissism quickly supersedes specular wonderment. But even this is not enough: s/he must *be seen* by others. As an initial step in reeducating emotions and rejecting old habits, s/he naïvely longs for encounters of any nature. Out in the open, Ahmed/Zahra is immediately assaulted by male scopophilia, yet s/he accepts this perpetual violation with fascination, as if it were an initiation rite for "becoming-woman" ("I was intrigued as I emerged slowly—but with fits and starts—toward the being that I had to become"). Ultimately, however, Ahmed/Zahra heeds the advice of Abbas (one of his/her most violent oppressors) that "in this country, you oppress others or they oppress you" as s/he reclaims gender ambiguity in self-defense (121 [92]).

The most sensually exalted passage of *The Sand Child* is a long portion of Ahmed/Zahra's journal read to an audience so awestruck that it refrains from its usual interruptions (152–58 [70–79]). A residual benefit of the male privilege of education, Ahmed/Zahra's knowledge of art and literature lends a cultural dimension to the expansion of his/her erotic horizons. Ben Jelloun takes this opportunity to extol the unbridled sensuality in poetry and miniature painting, forgotten since Islam's first centuries. With repetition of the verb *sortir* lending a haunting rhythm to his/her journal, the hero/ine describes a longing to be touched by innumerable, anonymous, wayward hands. This erotic encounter, neither quite with or without others, devoid of commitment or even knowledge of the others' identity, is the nomadic sexuality to which Ahmed/Zahra aspired from the moment s/he found it evoked in travel accounts by European writers (156 [122]). Texts by André Gide, Isabelle Eberhardt, Jean Genet, Paul Bowles, William Burroughs, Roland Barthes, and others come immediately to mind in this remark, yet another passage deleted from the Sheridan translation of *The Sand Child.* For Ben Jelloun to credit Europeans for perpetuating a tradition of erotic freedom is tantamount to taking a final jab at Islam for having betrayed its sensuous past.

Although Winifred Woodhull, in her well-wrought *Transfigurations of the Maghreb*, has shown *The Sand Child* to be a "nomadic text," I would suggest further that, as a testimonial to the erotic intensities defining its nomadic hero/ine, the novel works to establish an equation wherein *medina = text = body (= being)* by extending all the interconnections among these variables. *Being* is marked with a cautionary parenthesis because Ahmed/Zahra never definitively opts for one gender to the exclusion of the other. S/he stabilizes him/herself as an ontological androgyne, a social epicene, a multiplicity at the threshold of many pseudo-unities. Although reaping advantages to the end from appearing in public disguised as a man, s/he knows that unbridled libidinal scanning is less akin to the legendary travels of Ibn Battuta than to the inner, vicarious tourism of Des Esseintes, "the nomadism of those who no longer budge and no longer imitate anything but just fit things together" (Deleuze and Guattari, *Mille plateaux* 35): "I made up those journeys, those nights without dawns. . . . If I had been a man I would have said, '*I* am Ibn Battuta!' But I'm only a woman" (164 [128]).

As if enacting Gide's lessons to Nathanaël in *Les Nourritures terrestres*, Ahmed/Zahra repudiated the family before it could repudiate her. S/he also dismissed epistemologies from psychology to Islam which "claim to know and explain why a woman is a woman and a man a man" (89). Yet "going from myself to myself" (99 [74]), s/he knew that the experience of "coming out" leads to nothing definitive and would leave him/her eternally at a threshold: the "threshold of complicity" (91 [68]) where Ahmed/Zahra resorbs the anonymous correspondent who falls silent. Ahmed/Zahra's movement becomes a virtual oscillation where intense emotions of the *here and now* count infinitely more than any future remembrance of having been there.

Molten Flux

> It is time I knew who I am. I know I have a woman's body . . . that is to say, I have a woman's genitals, though they were never used.
> (152 [118])

The hymen—Ahmed/Zahra's physical (and metaphysical) threshold—is intact. Until menstruation, no blood had flowed from his/her body. Conversely, from that moment on, this was the only blood that flowed. In accordance with Islamic tradition, Hajji Ahmed brought his sand child to the barber for ritual circumcision. The former placing his thumb where the penis would have been, the blood that gushed was thus that of the father and not the "son." The appearance of menstrual blood inspires Ahmed/Zahra to reflect upon the binaries that s/he embodies and that patriarchal metaphysics divaricates: "I am the architect and the house, the tree and the sap, a man and a woman." With that revelation comes the understanding that the embodiment of dualities can become a weapon for abrogating them. S/he declares war on the name/no [*nom/non*] of the father (Lacan): "It was certainly blood. The resistance of the body to the name—the splash from a belated circumcision" (46 [30–31]). To keep his/her clothing from stain, s/he will, like Jean Genet, become a petty thief. Disorder in patriarchy, borne by the menstrual blood flowing from the "forgotten gate" (chapter 6) of Ahmed/Zahra's body, will avenge the outrageous law of gender imposed by the father.

Ben Jelloun's choice of the term "resistance" to describe the defense of our vulnerable bodies against the strength of the law corroborates Lyotard's thesis (in analyzing Kafka's "Penal Colony") that "death is jealous of birth [as] the law is jealous of the body [as] ethics is jealous of aesthetics" (Lyotard, "Prescription" 184). "My body still bears the imprint of my father," writes Ahmed/Zahra, "He may be dead, but I know he will come back. That imprint is my blood: the path I must follow without losing my way. . . . My innocence is stained by a bit of pus. I see myself smeared with this yellowish liquid, which reminds me of the time and place of death" (66 [46]). Even with its blood flowing out at regular periods, Ahmed/Zahra's body can hope to do no more than maintain its position at the threshold between life and death.

The Well-Tomb

> For me, their birth gave me reason to mourn. . . . It goes without saying that you will be the well and the tomb of this secret.
> (22–23 [13–14])

For a father with Hajji Ahmed's beliefs, each birth of a daughter is tantamount to a death in the family: "Each of their births gave me reason to mourn" (22 [13; deleted]). With the birth of his eighth daughter, he tried to transform just one of those "deaths" into a "life" with the result that Ahmed/Zahra remained one and the other. Rather than settle upon a definitive identity, Ahmed/Zahra learns to oscillate on the verge of several. When Hajji Ahmed evokes *mourning* to describe how the birth of successive daughters made him feel and chooses the metaphors of *well* and *tomb* to characterize his wife's body when pregnant with Ahmed/Zahra, he consigns his dark secret to her and unwittingly condemns her to ontological undecidability.

How are these terms of *well* and *tomb* interconnected? We know from Freud and (later) Kristeva (see *Soleil noir*) that when the mourning process cannot be arrested the lost love object cannot psychologically be "laid to rest" and the living death of melancholy ensues. To fall (or be pushed) into a well alongside which one normally toils to quench thirst transforms the source of life-giving water into a tomb. The numismatic research of the blind troubadour permitted him to locate the *zahir* (a coin whose significance was reputed to be antithetical to that which is "within," *bâttène*) at the bottom of a well. We recall also that it was deep in some figurative well that Ahmed/Zahra located Fatima's thoughts. Using the well, the belly, and, more ominously, the tomb to connote female genital anatomy, Samuel Beckett illustrated the poverty of our existence in a graphic passage of *Waiting for Godot* that, to my mind, concisely figures Ahmed/Zahra's precarious ontological balancing act: "one day we were born, one day we shall die, the same day, the same second, is that not enough for you? They give birth astride of a grave, the light gleams an instant, then it's night once more" (58). This statement is delivered, I hasten to add, by Pozzo (Italian for "well"), the blind master suddenly furious at those who would meddle with Lucky, his slave (in Latin, *plagiarius*). Pozzo's aphorism captures the time of existence that—through the sand child—Ben Jelloun attributes to all of us. That time is an instant that we experience as an eternity: the cinematic threshold dividing as it joins the frame of childbirth and the blackout frame of the tomb.

The Coin: The Rub

> My hand tried to stem the flow. I looked at my fingers, spread out, linked by a bubble of that translucent blood, and through them I could see the garden, the motionless trees, and the sky broken by the highest branches. My heart pounded.
>
> (47 [31])

The lyricism of Ahmed/Zahra's entranced look at menstrual blood; his/her realization that no more than a man's does a woman's anatomy result from some primordial castration; *The Sand Child*'s exhaustive exploration of the Muslim woman's condition no matter what her tie to other women or men—mother, daughter, sister, wife, lover, loner. Can these products of a male writer's pen qualify as some sort of *écriture féminine*?

Ahmed/Zahra's initial opinion of women was formed by the adulteration of his/her gender through lessons imposed by patriarchy which are in turn rooted in the notion (to which psychoanalysis, moreover, is not immune) that girls are *garçons manqués*, that women are truncated men. For Hajji Ahmed, blaming his wife for bearing him none, the only *truly* human baby is a man child (26–27): "when you had your seventh daughter, I realized that you carry some infirmity within you" (22 [12–13]). So long have the seven sisters and their mother been treated as subhumans by their father and "brother" that blood runs sluggishly through their veins (66 [46]). Choosing later to identify with the "subhuman" gender s/he was trained to loathe, Ahmed/Zahra describes his/her mother's body as an "indistinct, half-living, half-dead matter" (131 [101]).

Autoeroticism brings Ahmed/Zahra closest to realizing him/herself as woman: "In the aching arms of my body I hold myself . . . I fall asleep, entwined in my arms" (54 [37]). In his/her ecstasy, Ahmed/Zahra composes another list of images of the being s/he might embody. Most of these images were omitted from the English translation and it is worth citing all of them not only because they attest to Ahmed/Zahra's ultimate solidarity with the womanhood-as-handicap lived by his/her sisters and mother, but also to appreciate the beauty of Ben Jelloun's dense imagery: "Who am I? And who is the other? . . . A swamp visited by desperate men? A window overlooking a precipice? A garden beyond the night? An old coin? A shirt covering up a dead man? A bit of blood smeared on half-opened lips?" (55 [38]).

Ahmed/Zahra marries his/her lame and epileptic cousin, Fatima, in order to offend family, society, and existence and to push the logic of travesty to its limits. Ahmed/Zahra's first proximity to another woman awakens his/her curiosity about a body so similar to his/hers. What Ahmed/Zahra *expects* to discover in examining Fatima's genitals while she sleeps is even more peculiar than what s/he *does* find. While Fatima wears a daunting "armored" chastity undergarment (77), as we might infer from the chapter's title, "The Walled-Up Gate," Ahmed/Zahra reports that she has not excised herself or sewn together her labia (76). Not only is female genital mutilation alien to Moroccan mores but the notion that infibulation could be practiced on oneself is nothing short of grotesque.

Once this monstrous marriage has sufficiently outraged everyone, Ahmed/Zahra begins to neglect Fatima's special physical needs, treating her (as any "real man" should) as an expendable commodity, perpetuating the deterioration of her health. But Fatima harbors a hidden fortitude, a tenacity born of her infirmities (including womanhood) that, to Ahmed/Zahra's amazement, places her on par with the resilience society nurtures in males. In revealing to Ahmed/Zahra that she has known all along that his/her genitals are female, Fatima declares: "We are women before being sick, or perhaps we are sick because we are women . . . I know our wound; we share it." With unbound tenderness, Fatima is the only character to signify to Ahmed/Zahra that she recognizes their shared intersex: "she slipped into my bed as I slept and began gently to stroke my belly" (80 [58]). As the leper at the conclusion of Flaubert's "Légende de Saint-Julien l'Hospitalier" did, so Fatima insists on identity through infirmity by fusing herself to Ahmed/Zahra as she dies: "She wanted not only to die but to drag me down with her as well" (79 [58]).[4]

From the moment s/he avows empirical familiarity with both genders, Ahmed/Zahra aspires to be neither: "To be a man is an illusion, an act of violence that requires no justification. Simply to be is a challenge. I am weary [*las et lasse*]" (94 [70]). The true ontological deformity, then, would be existence as either gender to the exclusion of the other: a deformity that Ahmed/Zahra can elude by remaining at a threshold between man "becoming-woman" and woman "becoming-man."

Alloy

Abdelkébir Khatibi writes the Maghreb in terms of an incontrovertible plurality—in its peoples, tribes, nations, and especially in its simultaneous linguistic cultures. The body is plural too, as Tahar Ben Jelloun (after Barthes) is adamant about showing. A node among others in the rhizome of desire, the corporeal machine's profusion of parts extends out, its openings connecting it to other bodies. These multiple bodily negotiations are so often the focus of Ben Jelloun's narrative that the sand child's body could be more accurately identified as the novel's main character with Ahmed/Zahra positioned as the body's perplexed conductor.

4. Written as a quasi epitaph for Fatima, the following words (absent from the translation) close the chapter: "Beaucoup plus tard, une voix venue d'ailleurs dira: 'Remange-moi, accueille ma difformité dans ton gouffre compatissant'" (81 [59]). In her final moments, Fatima says and does, albeit with more tenderness, what the leper in Flaubert's story "La Légende de Saint Julien l'Hospitalier" says and does in his (2:648).

The conflicting signals received by Ahmed/Zahra's body only serve to orient it further toward the multiple connections offered in the rhizome of desire. The clash between the two-day ceremony during which her/his eyes were made up with khôl and Ahmed/Zahra's traumatic first haircut (31) underlines gender ambiguity. Indeed, body shaving is so intrinsic to the ritual grooming of both sexes in Islam that Ahmed/Zahra's later neurotic face-shaving and trichotillomania (the obsessive plucking of one's hair) are unreliable as repetitive behaviors that tend to mark gender (see 90, 96, 98, 115). This scene finds an unexpected parallel in Sartre's description of the sudden and irrevocable loss of his childish gender ambiguity when his locks were sheared. In his autobiographical *The Words,* Sartre recounts how his mother, possibly compensating for her own "sad childhood," "would have liked [him] to be a girl really and truly," and thus did her best to raise him with "the sex of angels, indeterminate, but feminine around the edges." Her plan fizzled when his grandfather brought him to the barbershop where young Sartre watched his "curls roll down the white sheet around [his] neck and fall to the floor, inexplicably tarnished"(103–4 ff). Like the pubescent girl who passes as a queer boy in Hallström's film *My Life as a Dog,* Ahmed/Zahra binds his/her chest to impede the growth of breasts (36). Ahmed/Zahra's desire to henna his/her hair and impulse to shed tears are deemed "feminine" and harshly repressed. As a woman trained to be a man, Ahmed/Zahra's ruses to surreptitiously locate and employ cloth needed for stanching the body's menstrual flow further skews him/her by transforming him/her into a thief.

But the erasure of Ahmed/Zahra's gender ambiguity is not as conclusive as Sartre describes his as being in *The Words.* Although cross-dressing or masquerade dissimulates his/her body to him/herself (as to others), Ahmed/Zahra manages to *decipher* that body with increasing efficiency. From using a small mirror to compare his/her sex with those she saw in the women's hammam to the tireless efforts to read desire through rereading his/her journal entries (that is, literary deterritorializations of his/her body), Ben Jelloun causes us to consider that "the veil of flesh that maintained the necessary distance between himself and others" (7 [1]) is in fact the support of all writing and the source of all speech. Without this correlation of the body to the imbricated acts of writing, reading, and speaking, it would be impossible to understand the bizarre relationship between the black silk wrapping that envelops the mysterious journals and the silky black hair of the woman with Tawaddud's voice who haunts the blind troubadour during his Andalusian night.

The Spun Spinning

Storytelling is *The Sand Child*'s principal narrative device. In large part, however, the stories told rely on the authority of the intradiegetic written text: Ahmed/Zahra's journals themselves contain his/her correspondence with an unnamed individual. It is because Ahmed/Zahra is an omnivorous reader, we are told, that s/he emits a steady flow of writing. So much of his/her time is devoted to producing the written word that s/he becomes indistinguishable from those blackened pages. His/her writing is interrupted ("I would write before and after these sessions" [116 (87)]) only by masturbation before a mirror—a ritual pact between body and image. The form of the written word enhances its erogenous instrumentality: although Ben Jelloun writes the novel in French, the sentences read and written by his hero/ine are rendered, he tells us, in the cadenced calligraphy of Arabic (109), whose cursive letters harbor the power to reanimate bodily sensations anesthetized by the law of the father. Rereading his/her correspondent's letters, Ahmed/Zahra quivers: "It is as if his sentences were stroking my skin, touching me at the most sensitive points of my body" (96 [72]).

We have seen how the perplexities unleashed by adolescence cause a suspension of Ahmed/Zahra's writing: "I sometimes spent hours in front of the blank page." But while in most cases the white page is the virginal product of a writer's stupor, for the indeterminate Ahmed/Zahra it is none other than him/herself: "My body was that page and that book" [87]. And while s/he may give free reign to a body desperately writing itself to parry the law's vengeful violence, the guilty innocence of the body remains a blank page, free to be embellished by others ("J'ai perdu la langue de mon corps" (96 [71–72]). In coming to terms with the limitations of writing as resistance to the law, Ahmed/Zahra is not alone. After musing that reading leads him far *inside* books (172), the blind troubadour also realizes that he *is* but a book—one among thousands (177–78). Besides contributing to Ben Jelloun's intertextual play with Borges, this reiteration of the *(medina =) text = body = being* equation echoes one of the most memorable tropes that Sartre forged to describe the hermaphroditic organicity of being.[5]

5. The proof of Sartre's equation *my being = books* is irrefutable. It is in his description of books, then, that the hermaphroditism of his being becomes apparent: in his eyes, they possess the characteristics of both genders. *Male*: "I revered those standing stones: upright or leaning over, close together like bricks on the book-shelves or spaced out nobly in lanes of menhirs. I felt that our family's prosperity depended on them. . . . I would touch them secretly to honor my hands with their dust." *Female*: "I would draw near to observe those boxes which slit open like oysters, and I would

The storytellers' audience is repeatedly warned about a seductive power inherent to the written base upon which Ahmed/Zahra's story is founded. From a safe, disengaged, aloof, extradiegetic position, they too are at constant risk of being sucked into the intradiegetic vortex. Under the sway of the intertext, we readers as well are liable to becoming one with the intersex: "Now the story is in you. It will occupy your days and nights, dig its bed in your body and your mind" (208 [164–65]). None can escape the ambiguities of Ahmed/Zahra who, like the carafe Marcel plunged into the Vivonne, both contains and is contained by all life and all bodies.

"Sing O nightingale, sing, don't lower your voice" Moroccan proverb

> Speech is not neutral.
> —Luce Irigaray

While Ahmed/Zahra's writing falters, then halts altogether, his/her voice*s* hold forth. The insistence of intertextuality in Ben Jelloun's novel results less from postmodern paralogism or metafiction than from the author's incorporation of the Berber oral tradition of his native Morocco and from the intertwining of speaking and writing in Islamic culture.[6] Thus the Koran and the *1001 Nights*—two paradigmatic Islamic texts of the voice—have massive presence in *The Sand Child*. Both have origins in oral transmission and the perpetuation of both is heavily dependent on orality: the very word "koran" means (and demands) recitation; the yarns of the *Nights* are often repeated aloud.

The voice and the insinuations that society draws from its timbre unite three women in Ben Jelloun's novel: Ahmed/Zahra, Fatouma, and Tawaddud. Through her recounting of dreams deemed pertinent to the hero/ine, the identity of Fatouma (one of the book's last narrators) converges with that of Ahmed/Zahra. A bizarre complicity arises, as I will show in a moment, from the near onomastic relation between the name "Fatouma" and

---

see the nudity of their inner organs, pale, fusty leaves, slightly bloated, covered with black veinlets, which drank ink and smelled of mushrooms" (*Words* 40–41).

6. Erickson (118) identifies Ben Jelloun's intent as paralogism. Mustapha Marrouchi (72) notes the metafictional move by which Ben Jelloun returns, in *The Sacred Night*, to the same narrative space of the public square. On the Berber oral tradition, see Sarra Gaillard. There is also evidence, in this text as in Ben Jelloun's *Harrouda*, that the poetry of hetaera living in the remote High Atlas of Morocco has influenced him. For an immersion in this fascinating folk poetry, see Mririda N'Aït Attik.

that of Ahmed/Zahra's deceased wife. Tawaddud, who along with Scheherezade surpasses by far the intelligence of men, stands out among all the female characters of the 1001 Nights. A slave girl, Tawaddud managed to save her master from ruin by responding with flawless virtuosity to questions eliciting the quasi totality of Islamic knowledge and posed by Harun Al-Rachid's wise men. Her ordeal is Scheherezade's *en abyme.*

While one might argue that the masculine voice that Ben Jelloun attributes to Tawaddud may result from a male author's projective revision of a woman's encyclopedic knowledge, that voice allows us to associate her with the woman who handed the *bâttène* to the blind troubadour: "I have rarely heard a voice at once so deep and so shrill. Was it the voice of a man who had undergone an operation on his vocal cords? Or the voice of a woman wounded in her life?" (174 [137]).[7] And, far from Buenos Aires, during a night spent in the gardens of the Alhambra, the blind troubadour will once again hear "a woman's voice, deep and mocking . . . : a woman's voice in a man's body" (195 [154]). Is this voice Tawaddud's? Does the mysterious gift-giver still shadow him? Is it Ahmed/Zahra's voice? . . . or perhaps our own?

For Ahmed/Zahra, yearning "to recover the natural rustle" of his/her voice means looking for a mitigated chord: some voice quality allowing him/her to disappear into anonymity. Detecting a feminine quality in his/her correspondent's voice, s/he envisions her future, authentic *self* as simply a "voice upon which an acrobat would walk" (98 [73]). This aspiration to selfhood is a tightrope precariously bridging masculinity and femininity but never reaching either; it anticipates an ideal expressed by Fatouma: "In life one should carry two faces. It would be good to have a spare face—or, better still, no face at all. We would just be voices, as if we were all blind" (162 [126]).

On a pilgrimage to Mecca, a cry with supernatural force swells within Fatouma's breast. Intuitively, she comprehends that to release it would avenge a dead woman's suffering. Repressing that cry, however, she wonders: "Why did that cry find refuge in me and not in a man, for example? An inner voice answered that the cry should have been in a man's breast and there had been a mistake—or, rather, the young woman had preferred to give it to a woman capable of feeling the same suffering as herself" (165 [129]). Fatima's deathbed fusion with Ahmed/Zahra has thus borne its fruit

7. Scheherezade tells the story of "Abu al-Husn and His Slave-Girl Tawaddud" from the 436th through the 461st *Night* (see *Thousand Nights and a Night* 5: 189–245. Nowhere does Tawaddud mention the sound of her voice. Tawaddud's tale should be read in conjunction with "The Man's Dispute with the Learned Woman Concerning the Relative Excellence of Male and Female" (154–63).

après coup in a foreclosed cry of loving solidarity between women. That shrillest manifestation of voice reveals to us that Fatouma *is* Ahmed/Zahra pregnant with an internalized Fatima as it triggers the novel's climactic canceling of ontological differences, equating everybody with the sand child.

"Y" Name

Naming Zahra "Ahmed" was Hajji Ahmed's compensatory act for failure to *will* the transmission of the Y chromosome. The prerogative of fathers in patriarchal societies, the implacable logic of naming was ingrained in Ahmed/Zahra. Hajji Ahmed's enactment of Lacan's *nom du père* theory is truly impeccable: ignoring the existence of his first seven daughters by declining to name them (17), he imposed that unbearable weight on his eighth by giving her his name. In a dream following Hajji Ahmed's death, Ahmed/Zahra hears him say: "Ahmed, my son, the man I formed, is dead. You, woman, are merely a usurper" (130 [100]). The paternal specter then buries him/her alive.

Although the weighty attribution of names gives Ben Jelloun a pretext to engage in a vigorous *external* critique of patriarchy, by linking the role of an author to that of father, a critique of naming can be turned back on Tahar Ben Jelloun. What does he try to accomplish through his *own* nominalism? Given the importance of mirrors in *The Sand Child* and the author's close affiliations with Parisian literati, it is likely that the mirroring or "graphic inversion" that transforms an *S* into *Z*, "the letter of mutilation and deviance," was on the author's mind in choosing Zahra.[8] Amar, in a gesture of obvious identification with the hero/ine, refuses to refer to him/her by *any* name—least of all Zahra—because s/he signs her manuscripts with the initial *A*. More precisely, this initial would be *alif*: not only the first letter of the Arabic alphabet but certainly another reference to Borges and his 1949 story, "El Aleph."

Once out in the world, several other names or sobriquets are attributed to Ahmed/Zahra. While Oum Abbas lends him/her the stage name of "Ami-

8. Roland Barthes's abiding fascination with the relationship between these letters is well known: see his reading of Balzac's "Sarrasine" in *S/Z*. The forms of *S* and *Z* recur in the pronunciation of *sarrasin* (from the Arabic *charkîyîn*, meaning "Orientals"), the noun Europeans used for Muslims from Asia, Africa, and Spain in the Middle Ages. Raymond Queneau's legendary Zazie, a pubescent girl superbly perched between childhood and adulthood, masculinity and femininity, grappled with the multiple identities of Aroun Arachide (*sic*) ("Harun Peanut"). Given Queneau's encyclopedic knowledge and wild imagination, one cannot dismiss the possibility of an allusion here to the androgynous Peter Pan who adorns one of the most famous brands of peanut butter.

rat Lhob," some narrators prefix "Lalla" to Zahra. Perhaps after all, though, as Amar insisted, her name is simply *alif* since, just as in mathematics where the letter represents the power of infinite sets, Ahmed/Zahra is everyone at once and everyone is Ahmed/Zahra. The point is that once one welcomes the multiplicity of being, a plethora of names is no more bothersome than the plurality of the body or the polyphony of the text. As Deleuze and Guattari wrote in *Mille Plateaux*: "The individual acquires his/her veritable proper name when s/he opens her/himself to the multiplicities that pass through him/her everywhere at the conclusion of the most severe exercise of depersonalization" (51). In the end, Ahmed/Zahra attains a state of consciousness that one might call, after Blanchot, *le pas au-delà*: a state of consciousness in which, if one has "known the disturbance of name and the duplicity of body," one feels both here and not, already beyond rescue and contemptuous of it (151 [117]).

Paratactic Intensities

> "The end of what? Circular streets have no end!"
> (21 [12])

> So we are in Marrakesh, in the heart of Buenos Aires, whose streets, I once remarked, "are like the entrails of my soul."
> (174 [136])

> A rhizome neither begins nor ends. It's always in the middle, between things, inter-being, *intermezzo*. . . . The tree imposes the verb "to be" but the rhizome's tissue is the conjunction "and . . . and . . . and . . . " There's enough force in this conjunction to shake and uproot the verb "to be."
> —Deleuze and Guattari, *Mille plateaux*

With its shifting storytellers, discursive and epistolary exchanges, quotations, parodies, pseudo-plagiarisms, the generalized intertextuality of Ben Jelloun's *Sand Child*—regardless of whether it is the apotheosis of modernism or an exemplum of the postmodern—stretches the limits of decipherability. While the layout of an Arab medina is frequently likened to a labyrinth, the multiple openings in the novel's principal topology more closely conform to those in Deleuze's and Guattari's model of the rhizome.[9]

9. See Deleuze and Guattari (*Kafka* 3): "How can we enter into Kafka's work? This work is a rhizome, a burrow. The castle has multiple entrances whose rules of usage and whose locations aren't very well known. The hotel in *Amerika* has innu-

Unlike a labyrinth, there is no teleology of escape built into the sand child's rhizomatic ontological maze. Ahmed/Zahra must learn the pleasures of travel within an infinite network of libidinal intensities.

Deleuze and Guattari developed their theory of how minor literatures function vis-à-vis dominant cultures by invoking the infinitely knotted structure of stops and starts that is a rhizome. Ben Jelloun's work, written by a Moroccan Muslim in French, conforms to some of the criteria that contribute to the subversiveness of minor literature. But form is never so much the issue for "minoritary" writers, concerning whom I will add one final comment here. Because of his birth within the economically privileged class, Jorge Luis Borges has been identified with the "high" culture or elitist aesthetics of modernist Europe. Purely formalistic readings of Borges are usually intended to confirm this identification. But when Ben Jelloun shunts his blind troubadour "from an Argentinian shanty town into an Arab medina" (192 [151]), or—even more outlandish—when he declares that Marrakesh is at the heart of Buenos Aires, he reclaims Borges for the decentering project of minor literature. By shunning—at least in this one instance—the genealogy of culture fostered and nurtured in the salons of European capitals, Ben Jelloun transplants Borges into the rhizome where his Morocco can easily connect with the *criollo* quarters of Latin American medinas.

Ben Jelloun's intertext about an intersexed "enigma who oscillates between darkness and an excess of light" (85 [62]) is designed to implicate everyone. His mapping of the threshold that defines our being-with-others begins at Bab El Had—the "limit" or "border" gate—and culminates at the Gate of the Sands. He lures us in and sets us into motion like grains of sand in an ever-shifting Sahara. Wherever and however it is displaced, no grain eludes the proximity of others—ultimately all others: "We exchange our syllables until our hands may touch" (105 [78]). Any limit to encroachment while we ineluctably approach and intertwine with others demands a becoming-other at her/his threshold.

---

merable main doors and side doors that innumerable guards watch over; it even has entrances and exits without doors." Deleuze and Guattari share with Lyotard a sense of the importance of this notion. The formers' description of how intensities work in Kafka's writings could be said of Ben Jelloun: "Kafka's animals never refer to a mythology or to archetypes but correspond solely to new levels, zones of liberated intensities where contents free themselves from their forms as well as from their expressions, from the signifier that formalized them. There is no longer anything but movements, vibrations, thresholds in a deserted matter . . . underground intensities" (*Kafka* 13).

CHAPTER 15

The National-Sexual: From the Fear of Ghettos to the Banalization of Queer Practices

MIREILLE ROSELLO

This article is slightly schizophrenic: it oscillates between two utopian desires, each perceived as the ideal and unrealized logical consequence of two cultural discourses about sexuality. Let's oversimplify grossly. The French tend to think we are all equal in a "République une et indivisible" and that what you do in bed is nobody's business (I said I would simplify). The United States has long practiced the art of creating nurturing communities, and often it is possible to treat sexuality as a relevant political problem, so why not "out" hypocritical politicians? One principle pushes toward banalization, the other pushes toward identity. In the meantime, individuals maneuver within discursive systems that accuse each other of having it all wrong. This article interrogates the imaginary and theoretical repercussions of the "in-between": Is it possible to bridge the gap by creating multinational discourses, nationally and sexually hybrid fictions?[1]

The "national-sexual" is a code, a set of linguistic and cultural reflexes, a collection of myths, images, metaphors, and clichés by which each national entity defines the realm of the sexual, including the opposition between dominant and marginalized sexual preferences and practices. By national entity, I do not mean a strictly political category: "national" does not exclude ambiguous cases like Quebec or Corsica. "National" here refers to a certain level of national consciousness that may or may not be officialized

1. I would like to thank Thomas Spear and Russell King for a meticulous reading of a first draft of this article and for their most helpful suggestions.

by the existence of a passport. The national-sexual is a specific case of intersection between what Homi Bhabha calls "nations and narrations." It is the limit put by national discourses on our imagination when we seek to define our sexual desires and sexual categories. It is the often invisible interaction between the way in which we culturally inscribe our sexual practices or preferences, and the values promoted by national discourses. The national-sexual is historically unstable and it does not have the same significance for each individual.

Even if we think that our cultures share certain dominant narratives about sexualities, it is as impossible to assume that there is intercomprehension between national-sexual codes as it is silly to expect people who do not speak the same language to understand each other.[2] For instance, most people would agree that certain types of sexualities (same-sex attraction or the large spectrum of practices known as queer sexualities) share the sad international privilege of being marginalized or singled out as problematic and controversial. And yet it is illusory and perhaps countereffective to conceptualize the existence of an international gay community, if only because even the idea of community is dependent on distinct national-sexual contexts. I am not suggesting that we cannot imagine an international queer continuum. In practice, we do it all the time. Yet the idea that there could exist an international queer community is either a case of wishful thinking or an example of hysterical heterosexual panic. It may be that same-sex attraction cuts across race, gender and class, but I am not sure queers can talk to each other across national borders. For one thing, we would have to agree on one internationally accepted word, and the recently emerged and still rather controversial "queer" will certainly not play that role even if we choose the approximation of other words in target languages.

Rather than creating solid threads of international solidarity, our national-sexual codes tend to make differently queer national subjects violently intolerant of each other's definition, sometimes hostile, often sarcastic, and ready to make fun of how the other community imagines itself. Because I often miss the American way of being queer when I am in France, and because I am often surprised and offended by certain Americans' reactions to the so-called French way of being gay, the position I adopt in this

2. For an analysis of the advantages and disadvantages involved in assuming that being gay can be defined as political position or as a form of belonging to an "ethnic" minority, see Epstein's "Gay Politics, Ethnic Identity: The Limits of Social Constructionism" (in Stein, *Forms of Desire* 239–93).

article will probably sound quite defensive if not downright irritating to readers on both sides of the Atlantic. I should point out, however, that I make no claim to be representative and that totalizing gestures (such as sentences starting with "the French" or "the Americans") should definitely be taken with a grain of salt. I have deliberately focused on those moments of the national-sexual encounter that tend to be most stereotypically ignorant of the other culture. I hope that such in-betweenness is not so much an uncomfortable sitting-on-the-fence exercise as a critical attention to what, in my own discourse, is transparently governed by the myopic vision of some national-sexual syndrome.

Each national-sexual mental and ideological galaxy generates moments of puzzlement and moments of ignorant hostility of which I am alternately guilty as I move back and forth across the Atlantic. But I don't think the problem is limited to my own territories of temporary hybridity. By emphasizing the national element in sexual constructions, I would like to invite others to help me maintain a hybrid dialogue rather than a no-man's-land populated by mutually hostile national subjects.

Since each culture treats issues of identities in radically different ways, I don't know how to listen, within one language, to the multilingual dialogue, or noise, or complex harmonies, produced by the encounter between, say, a "gay male" living in a North American urban capital, or a Parisian male who may refuse to even entertain the idea that his sexuality is defined in terms of "homo-" or "bi-" or "hetero-" sexuality. And I wonder if a Québécois writer would be more likely to identify with a Francophone Parisian gay male, or if he would be closer to the national-sexual discourse of an English-speaking Canadian. Where would a British activist fit in as an English-speaking European? How do all the national-sexual codes crisscross in the expression of sexual preferences, sexual ethics, and above all, in the definition of collective sexual identities?

Consider the following quotation from *Le Magazine Littéraire*, arguably one of the most popular literary magazines distributed in France and in Francophone countries. This paragraph appears in the middle of an interview granted to Guy Cloutier by Michel Tremblay, the occasion being the publication of the Québécois author's novel *Le Coeur éclaté*, a sequel to his successful *Le Coeur découvert*. After stating that he would have been a feminist if he had been born a woman, Tremblay goes on to say:

> But since I am gay, I found myself in a different family, a family in search of its identity too, within a world that continues, despite its claims, to justify the ghettoization of gay people. Whatever I do, I am always a member of some mi-

> nority, as a Québécois first, then as a gay male. That said, my books were never about gayness. I talked about gays, which is a completely different matter.[3] (68)

Some time has passed since the publication of the interview and I realize that the author's remarks still puzzle and intrigue me. I don't recall being particularly attracted to or annoyed by Tremblay's formulation when I first read it, I don't remember recognizing this remark as one of those dense passages that can immobilize the reader and act as a mental stumbling block for weeks or months on end. In all simplicity, I thought I had "understood," understood what the author meant, or perhaps understood that he had chosen to exaggerate a little bit for the sake of the interview situation, for the benefit of his mainstream audience. It did not seem to me that it was urgent to either adhere to, or immediately oppose, the proposition. The almost unconscious impression I had kept of this passage was that the author's stance was rather obvious, probably strategically necessary in its simplicity, even if theoretically debatable. In other words, I don't think I was willing to listen to whatever dialogue was going on between this text and its publics, I thought this discourse was not news to me (that is, was not addressed to me). The key words here were familiarity and banality.

Yet I am not so sure what to make of, or how to deal with, Tremblay's strange movement back and forth between sexuality and nationality. He defines himself as "québécois" and as "homosexuel" in a journal addressed to an audience that we (and the editorial board of the journal) can safely assume to be both straight and French. Consequently, a dialogue is already taking shape in a context where the doubly minoritized individual is addressing an imagined majority. But the fact that Tremblay chooses to describe himself in terms of a double Québécois and queer minority identity is quite significant in itself. There is a tautological aspect to such a defini-

3. The beginning of the paragraph reads: "Aurais-je été une femme, j'aurais été féministe [Had I been a woman, I would have been a feminist]" (Tremblay, "Un affaire" 68). It is fair to say that, in another context, I could have reacted strongly to that first hypothesis which could be seen as a rather careless equation between "woman" and "feminism": although Tremblay's remark implicitly rejects the idea that all women are necessarily feminists and that all feminists must be women ("Had I been a woman," the author implies, "I might have chosen not to be a feminist"), the formulation finally leaves us with the impression that feminism is women's business and no one else's. But the fact is that I was not willing to devote too much energy to that part of the quotation because I decided that it was easy to neutralize its absentmindedly sexist premise. I was more intrigued by the remarks about "homosexuality" and "homosexual characters."

tion if we accept that the possibility to *use* such concepts is already predetermined by Tremblay's *belonging* to a culture (Québécois culture) and to a community (the gay community) that authorizes certain individuals to claim their membership. This double belonging is what legitimizes the thought that Tremblay can be gay and Québécois in comparable ways.

If Tremblay addressed a strictly Québécois audience, I assume that the notion and formulation of a "double minority" (the sexual and cultural minority) would be so familiar as to render its existence (as an ideological definition of identities) completely transparent. But the publication of this passage in the *Magazine Littéraire* creates a transcultural conversation, one that may defamiliarize the transparent links between national culture and the definition of same-sex attractions, what Eve Sedgwick calls "the difference between the precisely contestable status of gay definition and the completely uncontestable current status of national definition" (*Tendencies* 145).[4]

For if it is quite understandable, almost banal, to call oneself "québécois" and "homosexuel," I am almost sure that there would be no simple counterpart to the formulation in a Parisian milieu: I don't think it is easy to *call* oneself "parisien *et* homosexuel" even if one *is* both from Paris and gay, as Simon Watney notes in his article in *Gay Times*.[5] The construction of a double identity cannot be exported as is, and such discrepancies are what makes crosscultural dialogues interestingly challenging as well as frustrating. A metropolitan reader of *Le Magazine Littéraire* would certainly "understand" Tremblay's remark, but a process of translation would take place to which we normally pay no attention.

For instance, it may be worth wondering whether Tremblay meant the interview as a moment of international coming out, and whether the sentence would reach such an objective: for it to function as a proper coming-out moment, we must assume that the readers of the *Magazine Littéraire*

4. During a conference, Sedgwick had noticed that even when most papers sought to redefine the boundaries of their own discipline, one category was left intact: that of the national paradigm. The borders of "America" remained transparent. Sedgwick then goes on to cite articles published the next day about the conference: while "any mention whatever of so alarming a subject as homophobia or gay and lesbian culture" (145) had been edited out, it was assumed that the main issue had been the definition of America. Sedgwick herself was misquoted as having said: "What we're really talking about is America, our vision of what the country is, what the country should be" (Lee A. Daniels cited in *Tendencies*, 144).

5. See also Watney's *Practices of Freedom*, especially "Missionary Positions: AIDS, 'Africa,' and Race" (109–30), for constant references to the ways in which queerness is discursively inscribed across nations as the result of the AIDS crisis.

not only did not "know" (that the author is gay and Québécois) but are also able to express at least a minimal amount of interest in such discoveries. Would they be able to conceptualize the two adjectives as relevant and interpretable pieces of information? I am not sure that it is the case: for even if readers had not "known" about Tremblay being gay and/or Québécois, I strongly suspect that the revelation would have been a nonevent because the French cultural landscape seems relatively impervious to the rhetoric of "coming out." The coming-out narrative does not really have an equivalent label, the model is not named, it is not part of the list of (even marginally) accepted literary genres that members of a given culture seem to internalize as part of their intellectual heritage. And if Tremblay's "revelation" was not immediately greeted by readers' comments (whether positive or negative), I would still hesitate to conclude that this lack of intensity is comparable to the form of mental violence Eve Sedgwick expects as a response to a coming-out attempt in a North American context: "That's fine, but why did you think I'd want to know about it?" (in Abelove 48).

What fascinates me in this interview is not what the author says (neither the position he takes nor the definition of "queer" and "Quebec" he implicitly adopts). It is the imperceptible hybrid space created between Tremblay's discourse and that of its public. This interview is a hybrid text because, on the one hand, it is written in the "same" language that its public uses, which means that the level of exoticism and foreignness is relatively low (I think I understand what Tremblay says in my own language). Yet, at the same time, this text written in French in a journal read by French people cultivates a sort of ambivalence, an illusory site of transparency where the meaning of each word is saturated with a heavy dose of fruitful opacity. By going back to this apparently clear and simple passage, I have tried to understand why this text had remained so present in my memory, so active and militant, as it were, while requiring practically no effort, no resistance at first sight.

I am now suggesting that Tremblay's remarks about being queer and being Québécois produce some kind of discrete disturbance, a turbulent flow running deep below the surface of our theoretical waters, because he redefines the category of what is *debatable* in the sense that the critic's work could be characterized as the urgent need to enter into a spontaneous and yet thoughtful debate. Depending on what side of the Atlantic the reader is found, different definitions of what is obvious, what is banal, what is unacceptable will be deployed, a difference that the text, written in one language, will carefully pretend to ignore. Discourses on (homo)sexuality could thus be said to inhabit the realm of the *debatable*, a hybrid place of speaking and listening where what is most banal, what goes unnoticed, what is most invisible, coincides with what is most vividly remembered, what remains most significant and incomprehensible.

If we start paying attention to those moments when the familiar and the completely unknown meet inconspicuously, we may find ourselves listening to hitherto inaudible hybrid dialogues between texts or discursive universes that are usually thought to be indifferent to each other because we tend to put them in radically different categories. In the second part of this article, I will suggest, for example, that reading queer discourses and science fiction in parallel produces a new and hybrid dialogue occurring at the intersection between the banal and the intensely memorable. But first, I would like to go back to Tremblay's quotation, to try and understand why it makes me think of a strange conversation between two people who think they speak the same language when it is obvious to everyone else that they don't. The French would say, "un dialogue de sourds," a dialogue between two deaf people.

For example, the word "ghetto," as used by Tremblay, deserves attention and interpretive vigilance: the word is very likely to provoke a knee-jerk mental reaction among the *Magazine Littéraire*'s (typical) metropolitan readers. Like a well-oiled ideological machine, I think I would myself be somewhat recruited, pleased, by the implicit denunciation of all the evils of "ghettoization" (a concept that the author does not even dignify with any sort of definition here). I am not sure, however, that my reaction would be as individually thought through as I would like it to be: there is a national-sexual element involved in a certain French rejection of the ghetto, and it crops up in my own mental structure even as I insist on dissociating myself from a certain French discourse that pretends to believe that the "ghetto" is a typically American phenomenon. The "ghetto" is the undesirable result of social tensions and discrimination—whether ethnic, cultural, economic, or sexual. The "ghetto" is as fashionably foreign and as exotic as the "politiquement correct," and to criticize it is to show that one is well-traveled, multiculturally literate. No one knows what the ghetto really is except that it is an American fad and that it is acceptable to make fun of it: it must be slightly silly, bad for you, tasteless, and responsible both for high unemployment and sexual frustration. Let's be reasonable now, it is sheer common sense to oppose a "ghetto homosexuel."

Stereotypes call for stereotypical examples: "Triste à écrire, mais la seule culture homo, c'est le sida" writes David Jones, a young Parisian interviewed in an issue of *Gay Défi*. And he vehemently insists that there is no such thing as a queer culture: "For culture is everything but the ghetto. Culture is about sharing, about knowledge, about transmission (to all). As a homo, you don't share your tastes, you don't know about them, you don't transmit them. To know Cadinot and the back-room, that is not homo culture" (33). The formulation may sound crude to whoever disagrees but the lack of nuance is also a sign that Jones need not justify his position because he knows that he is on safely hegemonic ground. He is obviously confident that he is on the side of common sense. As a result, it would be a serious error to dismiss such statements for lack of finesse: more or less sophisticated versions of this remark pervade French culture. If Flaubert's *Dictionnaire des idées reçues* could be updated, "ghetto" would be an obvious entry: "ghetto: do not define, oppose strongly. American mistake."

Unfortunately, the critique of American ghettos is often a convenient way of ignoring that our own concept of what constitutes an acceptable definition of communities, sexual or other, is influenced by an increasingly nationalistic and xenophobic national—French—context. In the meantime, the emergence of what is more and more often automatically referred to as "queer studies" in the United States does not have any equivalent in French academe. And even if queer studies developed and gathered enough social and intellectual momentum to be noticed by the media and sociologists, I wonder if it is not too late for a "French" movement to emerge: the word "queer," like "reality shows" and "sitcoms," may well never be translated. Although I have no ambition as a linguistic prophet, I would venture to predict that "queer" is one of those words that end up "passing" rather than being translated. As the French phrase goes, some words can "passer" into a language like illegal immigrants who cross national borders, sometimes with the help of "passeurs." And such words could also be said to "pass" in the English sense, because their margin of foreignness eventually becomes imperceptible at least to most native speakers (who remembers that "magasin" comes from the Arabic?). The only manifestation of their foreignness is a vague sense of having heard them somewhere else. At the risk of greatly offending every Québécois I know or do not know, I suggest that Tremblay's interview itself would probably "pass" (for French) simply because his article is written in a language called French. But the fact that he implicitly defends values that would be more immediately recognized and accepted in North America leaves an imperceptible gray area in the legibility of his remarks.

I suspect, by the way, that even if the word "queer" crosses the Atlantic, its acclimatization will not be immediately successful. Queer culture might be accepted only as a newfangled theory from America. Its exoticism would explain both enthusiastic gestures of adoption and strong negative reactions. After all, I wonder if I should impatiently look forward to the moment when grammarians and academicians will insist on coining a suitably legitimate "French" translation to the word "queer." Of course, even if the formidable obstacles raised by the lack of direct link between literal and connotative meaning were solved, queer culture would probably still suffer from its original "passing" act: its status as imitation, as plagiarized Americanism, would continue to jeopardize any legitimate positioning as an object of study. Like American sitcoms or TV series, departments of "études kwir" would probably be viewed as doubly tasteless: once for being a secondhand version, and a second time for being imported from a mythic and culturally underdeveloped country known as "Amérique."

Tremblay's formulation might therefore bring water to a typically French anti-queer theoretical mill. But even if I fear that this interview may inadvertently push a dangerous antighetto button, I cannot conclude that the author was pandering to his French audience's preconceived ideas: it is very difficult to ascertain (and may be not so useful to wonder) whether or not Tremblay was consciously echoing a stereotypically French position. I have no reason to believe that Tremblay wanted to ingratiate himself with a French public by adopting hegemonic ideological premises.[6] Could it be instead, that Tremblay's antighetto statement is an original, unexpected, and difficult point to make within his own national-sexual context? Could it be that this antighetto declaration is dissident within a Québécois context?

Most remarkable in what I call the rhetoric of the ghetto is not so much the originality of the arguments as the intensity of the opinions, reactions, and gut feelings the word triggers. In France, the refusal to be confined within a "ghetto" asserts itself as a grand and noble gesture, when in fact the choice of words has already marked the end rather than the beginning of a debate. Often, by criticizing ghettos, we do not so much reject a specific form of collective identity as indulge in the expression of a stereotype: by reciting a number of antighetto formulas in a certain order, it is possible to create a certain paradoxical effect: that of belonging to a community. By proclaiming myself anti-(queer)-ghetto, I immediately become a member of the antighetto community. And if antighetto positions are so devoid of nuances, it must mean that they function like highly recognizable flags, it

6. I am tempted to say "quite the contrary" given the history of relationships between the Québécois and the "maudits Français" except that this opposite expectation is not less stereotypical for being a more plausible generalization.

must mean that it is possible to confuse "ghettos" and "communities" and "families" and "groups" without being taken to task at dinner parties or conferences, without losing one's credibility as a reasonably valid interlocutor.

I originally wondered if Europeans in general were more sensitive to the historical implications of "ghetto" situations, if their first-hand experience of what a Jewish ghetto could mean made them more careful not to overuse the word. But I think the opposite is happening. Inflationary use has blurred historical memories of what the Warsaw ghetto was in the same way as the American use of the pink triangle may have nothing to do with the memory of death camp victims. The "ghetto" is now a synonym for an American countermodel, it is a negative mirror held up to a supposedly French way of dealing with difference. By repeating the word in all kinds of different contexts, I forget that there is a crucial distinction between (queer) ghettos and (queer) cultures (or "famille" as Tremblay puts it), and "ghetto" becomes a password: if I use it, I am sure to capture the immediate attention of an audience who speaks my language.

Naturally, a symmetrical situation is to be expected in a context where "communities" are valorized. It is quite acceptable to openly, and sometimes very crudely, criticize the French national-sexual model because its most obvious features, for an outsider, are its stereotypical extremes. It seems that Anglo-Saxon queers living in France experience this cultural difference as an endless series of frustrations, disappointments, as disempowering invisibility, because they find it impossible to import a definition of (sexual) identity, the foundation of which they have long been taking for granted. The encounter between national cultural differences then gets perceived as a difference in the way in which a certain government, a certain society, treats queer people.[7] Such perceptions are skewed, however, by the fact that it is difficult to separate the way in which certain communities of people are treated by their native culture and the way in which they construct themselves with regard to the community in question. To a foreigner importing both his or her culture and the way in which his or her culture constructs queerness, there is no position from which such a distinction can be made except on an imaginary plane. A deep-seated mistrust of the other's model sets in due to the outsider's painful reaction to a radically new construction

7. Or black people, or women, as when someone remarks that there is "less racism" or "more racism" in France than in the United States, for example. As reassuring or alarming as such statements can be, they presuppose an internationally accepted definition of racism or sexism or homophobia, which I tend to find more and more problematic.

of identity—the other is primitive—and to the insider's resistance to the proposal of an imported theory—the other is imperialistic. Both sides feel it is their duty to accuse the other culture of preventing queer people from leading a politically and culturally rewarding existence.

Recently, Simon Watney was thus attacking a model that he obviously considers more than just undesirable. In a sense, his article functions as an echo to the French antighetto rhetoric. So far, no serious cultural dialogue has been initiated, and nothing is exchanged but mutual sarcasm and latent hostility. Watney states in his article that "there is little or no sense of 'homosexuals' as members of a distinct social constituency, which might have rights or entitlements. In other words, there is no real French equivalent to the Anglophone word 'gay'" (20). A little further on he notes: "lacking the type of gay identity we tend to take for granted, the very idea of 'community' is all but unimaginable to most French 'homosexuals'" (20). I doubt that his discourse of truth simply aims at satisfying his British public's anthropological curiosity for the way of life of the People-beyond-the-Tunnel. His is an undoubtedly violent indictment. Watney condemns "the limitations of French national identity" because he perceives the "little sense of collective identity" as "a terribly debilitating and inhibiting effect on 'homosexual' identities, preventing the very idea of what we think of as lesbian and gay culture." Watney's title, "Gai and Français," is an ironic reminder of Montesquieu's "comment peut-on être persan?" and his article is not meant as a philosophical treatise on the ways in which identities are constructed but as an anguished cry of revolt against the scandalous speed of HIV contamination in France.[8]

8. In spite of recent efforts (the "préservatif à un franc" [one-franc condom] campaign and the "3,000 scenarios contre un virus" [three thousand scripts against a virus], a series of short films broadcast between regular shows), France's reaction to the AIDS epidemic has proven particularly disorganized and ineffective. In 1994, Watney was comparing the 8,529 AIDS cases in England to the staggering number of about 30,000 in France. But, as philosopher André Glucksmann noticed a few days after the great "Sidathon" (a night-long TV show simultaneously broadcast on all of the French TV channels on April 7, 1994), France also failed its drug users and hemophiliac population, as in the scandalous episode of the so-called "l'affaire du sang contaminé" (contaminated blood scandal) which the Sidathon carefully ignored. According to Glucksmann, there is a certain degree of cynicism in preferring a grandiose public "redemption ceremony" (cérémonie de rachat) to institutional actions. See also his *La Fêlure du monde* (A crack in the world) for an example of how the national-sexual code is expressed in the philosopher's critique of certain stategic positions.

AIDS, it is true, makes it necessary and desirable to use every possible tactic, every effective argument. And in view of statistics confirming France's resounding failure to slow down the epidemic, I am tempted to say that if an argument is likely to be effective, I am willing to treat it as a catalyst regardless of its theoretical value. When I compare David Jones's aesthetic objection to queer ghettos and Watney's denunciation of France's pathetic failure in its fight against AIDS, the latter's arguments are rather more convincing.

And yet, I am not prepared to accept that the fight against AIDS neatly overlaps with queer culture. After all, by establishing a causal link between the spread of AIDS among queers and the French resistance to the idea of collective identities, Watney implicitly agrees with Jones's proposition ("queer culture equals AIDS"). I would like to believe that Watney is deliberately adopting shock tactics when he implicitly equates the anticommunity definition of queer sexualities in France with the spread of the virus. But such tactics have the major disadvantage of foreclosing the possibility of a transcultural dialogue between the two different definitions of the national-sexual.

Conversely, within each national discourse, differences and nuances will be encouraged as a sign of intellectual sophistication. In each country, theoreticians tend to question the premises of national-sexual constructions: to take the example of the United States, a certain dominant idea about the existence of queer culture and queer identity will be in competition with other theoretical constructions. When a North American writer provides her implied (North American) readers with a subtle and sophisticated critique of the hegemonic definitions of community and sexual identities, her positions may appear "obvious" and perhaps even "banal" to European readers who may choose to read her work as a confirmation of their own fear of ghettos. I am thinking about Judith Butler who writes, in *Bodies that Matter*:

> Although the political discourses that mobilize identity categories tend to cultivate identifications in the service of a political goal, it may be that the persistence of disidentification is equally crucial to the rearticulation of democratic contestation. Indeed, it may be precisely through practices which underscore disidentification with those regulatory norms by which sexual difference is materialized that both feminist and queer politics are mobilized. (4)

Here, Butler assumes that her readers will immediately understand the link between "identity politics" and some sort of political agenda. Her invitation to "disidentify" is therefore counterhegemonic and I suspect that she must show that her chosen tactic is a different way of reaching the same political goal for fear of being aligned with the enemy. And I suppose that Butler would feel misinterpreted and betrayed if French scholars were to appropriate or "recognize" her books as a confirmation that there can be no such thing as a queer community or a queer culture.

Tremblay's position is presumably just as ambivalent vis-à-vis his Québécois national-sexual code as Butler is vis-à-vis her own English-speaking North American circles. He opposes a certain discourse and simultaneously taps it as a source of supposedly common knowledge: when Tremblay introduces the notion of a double minoritization (the author is both gay and Québécois), he moves away from rejection of "ghettoization." He now seems closer to other forms of national discourses on identities—closer, for instance, to theories of "double consciousness" explored by African-American scholars (Gilroy). And I wonder how many of the readers of the *Magazine Littéraire* who had welcomed Tremblay's opposition to "ghettos" as a reasonable and intelligent stance suddenly felt alienated by what reads like an unpredictable contradiction.

At this point in my argument, I would like to insist that, perhaps contrary to appearances, I have no interest in deciding whether or not the existence of a separate queer culture is desirable in each and every culture. My hybrid reaction to Tremblay's hybrid discourse leads me in a slightly different direction: I would like to set up a theoretical space where a transnational-sexual dialogue is made possible. Such a comparatist practice would provide a hybrid and unstable ground from which I may be able to decide whether the aspects of Tremblay's theories that are bound to be read as original by a metropolitan French reader are not precisely those passages that would sound most familiar and banal to a Québécois reader. In other words, even if I am aware that some of the elements of Tremblay's thought seem to contradict each other, I feel no urge to launch into a close reading of the interview: I could only do so by agreeing to function within one logical and self-contained discursive universe, loosely identified as the North American paradigm. What I thus perceive as a self-contradiction is mainly my own inability to get out of one national-sexual mode, and what I would much rather do, in the rest of this article, is focus on the possible moments of Relation between different discourses. I would be happy if Tremblay's premises, in their transparent queerness, were revealed by their encounter with another self-referenced national-sexual discursive world.

Tremblay's interview is a site of invisible hybridity in the sense that there is immediate intercomprehension between the French and the Québécois. In fact, because I am so used to the idea that both the French and the Québécois speak "the same language" (French), even the word "intercomprehension" may sound like an exaggerated sensitivity to minute differences. Yet I claim that what we have here is a site of translation, a site of production of meaning that remains invisible to itself, a point of crossing that no one wants to police because it goes unnoticed, perceived as a banal conversation. This banal conversation could be imagined as a sort of inaudible noise, a noise whose frequency is so high or so low that human ears cannot detect it. And this parasitical noise, redoubling our conversations with a ghostly echo, would not function like an excess of information (like for example, static on the line), but rather like an excess of silence accumulating between two interlocutors without their being aware of it. It is as though two people talked to each other from within two different ideological closets without realizing how much difference lies between them.

Instead of consolidating and refining each of those imaginary positions, I would like to look for the hybrid points of crossing where both discourses become aware that the other's otherness is a product of one's transparent self-coherence. Consequently, I suggest that Tremblay's position is *both* self-evidently obvious and unacceptable for a reader who would not recognize that two languages, two national-sexual codes, are colliding inaudibly, not so much *within* the author's proposal (this is not a case of ambiguity) as between this interview and a certain French public. The margin of miscommunication is both immense and likely to be ignored, as though two subjects were quite happy to talk to each other in what they think is the same language when any third listener can tell that it is not the case at all.

Tremblay's position is all the more enlightening as its otherness remains relatively invisible. His version of nonfeminist Québécois "homosexual" forces two transparent ideologies to spell out their respective underpinnings. Naturally, Tremblay is not the only writer capable of generating revealing frictions within the abstract entity known as the Francophone world: surely, national-sexual silences develop in many other so-called Francophone novels. If I keep in mind the redoubling echoes of national-sexual layers of ideology, I will certainly gain a new perspective on Augustin Gomez-Arcos's *L'Agneau carnivore* or on Michel Tournier's *Les Météores.* Both books tell the stories of incestuous brothers, which would provide an interestingly similar basis to the study of differences produced by varying national contexts: Gomez-Arcos's text is saturated with the almost allegorical presence of the Spanish civil war while Tournier's twins' relationship to the Second World War appears secondary and insignificant in comparison.

Perhaps the hybrid moment of double silences and double minoritizations is best captured by the very last part of Tremblay's quotation, a strange and paradoxical allusion to the absence of "homosexualité" in his books: "I never spoke about homosexuality in my books; I spoke of homosexuals; that's not the same thing" (68). And once again, here is a distinction that I am, at the same time, ready to accept and incapable of understanding fully. The idea that there is a significant difference (it is not the same thing *at all*) between the subject of the novel and the identity of its characters is at the same time rather self-evident and difficult to grasp in Tremblay's case. Is this an implicit reference to a post-Foucaldian recognition of the difference between sexuality as a practice and sexuality as an identity? What exactly is this important difference between talking about "homosexuality" and talking about "homosexuals" in a novel? What is at stake and why has the memory of this unknown form of difference remained so powerfully alive that I could neither forget the opposition nor let it function freely within my own literary universe? When I try to conceptualize what could be the difference between a novel about queerness and a novel about queers, my mind hesitates a little painfully, torn between the temptation to give up on a meaningless distinction and the fleeting impression that I am on the verge of some sort of critical epiphany.

I am not suggesting that I accept Tremblay's remark as a definitive piece of critical wisdom concerning his own work. Not only has my academic training taught me to treat writers' explanations of their books as another layer of interpretable text, but I must admit that I simply do not see why *Le Coeur éclaté* can be used as an illustration of this principle of differentiation. Tremblay's latest novel is most certainly about queer characters and I don't know what argument could help me demonstrate that it is *not* about "homosexuality." The majority of its characters are queer, and overtly out. The hero and narrator is queer and his story is originally motivated by a painful separation from his young lover. Devastated by the end of a long relationship, Jean-Marc introduces us to all the (queer) friends who help him through his ordeal and especially a couple of lesbians, Jeanne and Marie-Hélène, who convince Jean-Marc to leave for Key West, setting the rest of the novel in a sort of stereotypical gay paradise. The narrator and the reader will meet a whole spectrum of queer characters among whom a few portraits stand out. It is true that no character is singled out as the representative of "homosexuality"; rather, some characters are more developed than others as the result of the hero's privileged interaction with them. Dan and Gerry, a rather pathetic Laurel and Hardy couple, own the bungalows and a restaurant, a favorite haunt of the whole queer community. They act as the center to which gravitates a whole array of arresting characters (the narrator hastens to dub them "la bande à Gerry"). Several couples fascinate the hero, including Jeanne and her lover, Catherine Burroughs, whose paintings are a powerful revelation to Jean-Marc: "In half an hour, Catherine S. Burroughs became my favorite painter of all times, of all schools" (216). Fascinating as well are Bill and Rob, an almost mythical pair of brothers, both separated and brought closer by AIDS; Rob is blind and can see only through Bill's narratives: "I immediately thought of an old Oedipus who would never have lost his eyesight and who was now guiding his young blind guide" (158). The whole novel could be read as a reflection on the effects of AIDS, a sort of symbolic master word that infiltrates the plot but also every metaphor, every dialogue, every image in the book. Across the miles, Jean-Marc keeps in touch with Luc, one of his ex-lovers, now a prisoner of hospital room 2731, and which the disease gradually transforms into a Kafkaesque "insect squashed on the windowsill" (273), into a "a poor little hairy caterpillar" (278). And when Jean-Marc finally agrees to spend a night with his new friend Michael, their sexual encounter is quite specifically inscribed within the "latex era" (253): "He came back and threw two little red squares of plastic on the bed between us. And the latex era blew up in my face" (253). In other words, *Le Coeur éclaté* does not seem to fulfill the preciously hybrid challenge proposed by Tremblay in his interview. Even the fact that the hero puts physical distance between himself and his culture of origin does not seem to constitute a very meaningful gesture: Montreal and the Keys appear like seamless environments for the gay character.

What would then be a novel about queers that does not talk about queerness? Could it be that, in order to imagine such an apparently asymmetrical universe, we need to visualize a world where queer practices are so completely dedramatized, banalized, as to make the concept of queerness irrelevant, uncomprehensible? *Le Coeur éclaté* certainly does not fit into that category, but perhaps Tremblay's interview is an invitation to look further than his own books.

Another Québécois novel may well provide a fruitful starting point: Daniel Sernine's *Chronoreg*. I would like to suggest that Sernine, who is best known for his science fiction novels, uses and twists the literary conventions of the genre, thus managing to achieve what *Le Coeur éclaté* could not really do: invent a "queer" hero that does not belong to any ghettoizable category of queerness. *Chronoreg*, a science fiction novel published in 1992, is a strange and disturbing text that will enable me to push to the extreme the logic of a possible "disidentification" between a queer character and any type of queer community.

This mysterious "chronoreg" represents danger, the unknown, and lawlessness: it is the name of a drug, of the very last drug that has not been legalized by the sovereign government of Quebec, for Quebec has become an independent national territory in this novel. The drug costs a fortune on the black market and even experts know practically nothing about its effects except that the subjects who swallow enough pills can "chronoregress," that is, project themselves into their own past. The year is 2005; this is obviously the universe of science fiction. Naturally, the advantage of science fiction as a literary genre is that it lets the author invent a symbolic universe that pays lip service to current ideological musts and must-nots. And if Sernine can indeed illustrate Tremblay's distinction, it is because he does not abide by any of the already accepted definitions of sexualities.

A change of mentalities, an alteration of the national-sexual code, is imagined here, and therefore enacted to a certain extent, thanks to the invention of the illegal, antisocial, antinarrative, and lethal drug called chronoreg. This powerful drug is capable of dissolving our definitions of sexuality and our storytelling. Sernine constructs his story by intertwining two inseparable and completely unrelated phenomena: on the one hand, a new conceptualizing of gender and sexual identities that I will describe as the "banalization" of queerness, and on the other hand, a science fiction narrative structure that we could call a chronoregressive construction, in the sense that it does to the narrative what the drug does to the hero who ingests it.

In *Chronoreg*, sex is not a theme, not even an important element of the plot. As in *Le Coeur éclaté*, most characters are attracted to people of their own sex, but their love affairs or sexual encounters are not what motivates the narrative nor what keeps it alive. In fact, the hero's (homo)sexuality is both so visible and of such little significance to the rest of the novel that it is a challenge even to talk about it: there is nothing left to say because there is nothing to discover, no secret, no suspense, no revelation, no surprise. Same-sex attraction is a completely banal element in this universe. In *Chronoreg*, the presence of queer sexualities is not meant as a celebration of oppressed identities. The goal is not to put an end to silence, and the alternative is not between telling or not telling, being out or being in the closet.

Even saying that queer characters are banalized is somewhat of an overstatement: the whole concept of queerness needs to be reinvented when talking about this book. I use it here as an economical key word although it is obvious that the banalization of so-called marginal sexualities is bound to have an impact on the definition of any sexuality and to make the word "queer" improper.

The hero's sexuality is not a form of social transgression; it is not even an identity, since there is no division of community along these lines. And yet, from the very first page of the novel, Denis Blackburn, like Jean-Marc in *Le Coeur éclaté*, is presented as a man attracted to men. In fact, his desire to go back into the past is motivated by the hope that he can save his friend Sébastien. When the novel opens, Denis's beloved friend Sébastien (whom he knew as a child and with whom he fell in love as a teenager) was killed in the war. Denis Blackburn's experiment with chronoreg is meant as an attempt to change the course of history. In the meantime, a series of one-night stands or short-lived affairs punctuates his search: he first meets Jodi, a teenager who soon becomes one of the main characters, then a young dancer in a bar, then a soldier who belongs to his own unit, and finally, he is reunited with his ex-lover and worst enemy, Jac Marin. Each encounter leads to sexual intercourse, which the text always describes in great detail, concentrating on visual details of the men's bodies. The narrator often focuses on one particular part of the partner's body, as if to reproduce the principle of cinematographic sex scenes. The novel zooms in on sexualized body parts, especially on the young men's ears, an apparently magic place where desiring and listening are confused.

There is no hint that the hero is ever trying to hide his sexual preference or that this preference is in any way remarkable. For example, the fact that Blackburn is a top-level officer in a military organization does not interfere with his sexuality. The old North American (U.S.) myth that gays are undesirable in the armed forces because of their specific vulnerability to blackmail could not function since all the officers in the story are attracted to men (Blackburn, Jac Marin, and a high-ranking officer dubbed "la Colonelle"). The novel, however, does not fall into the obvious trap of idealizing all queer characters: nobody pretends that blackmail would simply disappear if the military were composed of queer soldiers. Interestingly, the principle of blackmail sneaks back into the narrative when Blackburn threatens to use the information he has gathered on "La Colonelle" in order to protect Jodi, whom he fancies himself. Jodi is a male prostitute and he is guilty of spending a night of pleasure with Blackburn instead of a night of work with "La Colonelle," who had already paid for it. In other words, the blackmail issue is strangely turned inside out: the officer is not more vulnerable because he is queer, but the sexual being in him loses all power because of his role in the military when another (queer) officer blackmails him.

Knowing that an officer is queer does not constitute a piece of information. And yet, the textual indifference to homosexuality is not achieved through the invention of a narrative universe where every being is attracted to his or her own sex: nothing indicates that in Blackburn's society, queerness has become the dominant sexuality. *Chronoreg* is not an attempt at assimilation. In fact, banalization is almost the opposite of normalization, of mainstreaming: this novel has obviously no intention of portraying queer characters as "normal" and stable people whose social and private life is indistinguishable from the implicitly desirable model of the nuclear family. Symmetrically the novel shows no interest in suggesting that the straight male cruiser's practices are not so different from his gay counterpart's. Even within its own imaginary universe, the novel does not want to present Blackburn as a saint—far from it: his sexual preferences would be considered controversial in virtually any human group, including gay activists. Most of the spy's lovers are prostitutes, and to make things worse, Blackburn does have a rather inelegant tendency to claim that he cannot afford the bill and to get away with it. The text always insists on the significant age difference between Denis and the very young and powerless men to whom he is attracted. Frequent references to the adolescent bodies' "beauté aiguë [acute beauty]" leaves the reader poised uncomfortably between two ambiguous positions: no clear authorial or narrational signal indicates whether we are supposed to interpret Blackburn as a positive role model whose sexuality is now accepted by a more open-minded society, or if the officer's borderline incestuous desires are meant as a social critique. A series of vague allusions imply that Blackburn's practices are not an individual issue but rather a reflection of his age, which gives us no clear explanation as to how to theorize the distinction between same-sex attraction and the specific practices Blackburn engages in. Banalization remains poles apart from utopian normativization.

The interest of banalization is that it lets the text rearticulate minority sexualities rather than transgressing what is still perceived as a dominant rule in our world of "compulsory heterosexuality" (to use Rich's phrase). The whole conceptual opposition between heterosexuality and other sexualities becomes the excluded other in this novel. Since the beginning of my analysis, I have therefore been using the word "queer" inappropriately: in *Chronoreg*, there can hardly be any queer character, or culture, or sexuality, since all sexualities are queer in Blackburn's universe. I am practically sure that the word "homosexuel" never appears in the text, and even the idea of "same-sex" relationship is irrelevant due to the radical redefinition of each of the components of the phrase: the concepts of the "same" and of "sex" (also in the sense of biological gender) are not operative. And even if they were, they would be difficult to understand since the frontiers of the human body are completely reimagined in this typical science fiction world.

For example, Blackburn has a brief affair with a certain Lavilia, which could, in most national-sexual languages, encode him as a bisexual. But since the Lavilia in question is not a human, can we still talk about heterosexuality? Should our mental structures not rapidly invent a category for such cases: hetero- implies "other," but the word does not really give credit to Lavilia's different difference, to the fact that the kind of sex she has with Blackburn is "hetero-sexual" because they belong to different species rather than to different genders. The novel invents a universe where relationships between any member of the human race should be called "homo-erotic," the word "hetero-erotic" being reserved to those who fall in love with aliens. But even this extension of the similarity-difference paradigm is problematic because what we call "the same" is completely defamiliarized and denaturalized in *Chronoreg*: "the same" is nothing but an artificial construction. For example, when "la Colonelle" wants to ingratiate himself with Jodi, he presents him with five clones of a ferret, and the text explains, for the ignorant reader's benefit, that clones have become quite fashionable and quite valuable especially if the gift consists of many copies of a rare animal species. The same is an invention, a gadget.

As for the human body, its limits and its difference from mechanical contraptions have become so blurred that the vocabulary of sensations and desire often appears inadequate and obsolete. A series of rather incongruous and unexpected metaphors suggests that the difference between bodies and things has gradually disintegrated: when Blackburn swallows a drug that will let him read other people's thoughts or, rather, penetrate his enemy's brains, he feels that "his head resounded like a little squash court" (142). A little later, still under the effect of the drug, he feels like "a cushion among the cushions of the huge sofa" (149). His mind is invaded in turn by a woman who tries to steal his thoughts: "Stretched like a crumbling and pliable substance, his mind scatters in little bits of images, flickers in the emptiness where they float away" (113). Later, when Denis resists the woman's intrusion, his mind becomes a bizarre closet: "Painfully, he brings his mind together and shuts it up, slamming in the woman's face the door of a room that would be his life and that she would have started raiding" (113).

Feelings are expressed through similar metaphors: when Denis's acute jealousy is triggered by his chance encounter with Sebastien and his female lover (or friend?), he backs away from them "as if pulled by a rope attached to a hook plunged deep into his heart" (92). Each hero is a sort of undecidable monster, part human and part mechanical: even Blackburn does not know that he carries a transmitter implanted in his brain by alien powers. One of his lovers is a living bomb; the spy he intercepts can plug his artificial hand straight into the computer; this whole universe is saturated with drugs and video games. Minds are plundered like ordinary strongboxes and even the most intimate scenes can be watched on computer screens. As a result, each feeling is seen as a dangerous weakness, and when Denis craves intimacy, he blames himself for being "like those pitiful monsters born twenty years earlier in Ukraine with their hearts outside their rib cages, vulnerable to the slightest impact" (151). The novel hints that biology has become a direct consequence of political decisions: the pathetic monsters in question have been turned inside out as a result of irresponsible nuclear experiments. But whatever the cause of such dysfunctional reconstruction, the Ukrainian reinvented bodies metonymically raise the problem of how to define sexuality when our definition of the human collapses.

Because the private has disappeared from this universe, the novel offers a tacit critique of our currently accepted definition of the obscene, a rather difficult problem for gay activists or lawyers who need to play with the distinction between private and public when it comes to opposing sodomy laws, for example. In *Chronoreg*, the reader suddenly wonders what is "obscene": the graphic details of a love scene between Jodi and Blackburn in the shower, or this whole disciplined society where the police keeps the suspects "fantascopies" on file—apparently, a fantascopy is a video film of people's fantasms—and where war is waged by means of computer screens as if soldiers were playing video games, while video games themselves have become lethal, programmed to electrocute the loser.

From an ideological and political point of view, banalization is a complex and ambiguous stance. On the one hand, it authorizes a serene utopia, the legitimization of minority forms of sexual practices that our society either outlaws or reproves: different queer practices such as homosexuality, bisexuality, transvestism, and sex changes would not have to be in competition in their demand for recognition or equality. On the other hand, the utopia in question is not idealized and the novel reserves the right to criticize the ideological premises of this imagined future world. And this form of banalization is predicated on a radical reinvention of human bodies that goes hand in hand with a disturbing and original dissolution of narrative linearity. Because the body cannot be dissociated from the machine or from the object, the story of relationships between those cyborglike heroes cannot follow the rules of traditional narratives. In other words, the banalization of queer practices supposes a politics of style as well as a politics of values.

To put it briefly, Sernine's writing is comparable to the principle of those video games that have invaded every nook and cranny of Blackburn's universe. In a certain sense, this novel is a time(-killing) machine, but this killing of time must be understood literally: our conception of linearity is invalidated by the structure of *Chronoreg.* At first, it seems that the story is rather classically built. Denis Blackburn appears like the ideal hero of a traditional novel: he is a famous spy; he has a rather endearing personality; he has many friends and enemies and a relatively high number of lovers per chapter. And that is where all resemblance to a traditional nineteenth-century realist novel stops.

Critics have often said that Sernine's writing is reminiscent of film techniques, mimicking effects of discontinuous editing with its incessant flashbacks triggered by one character's memory. Yet the novel is not only inspired by cinematographic style. The drug chronoreg itself serves as an original metaphor for the specific unlinearity of narratives in a post-queer universe. The story simply does not believe that each subject experiences a linear conception of time: it moves forward or backward exactly like a hero under the influence of a dose of chronoreg, moving along what we can visualize as parallel universes. Chronoreg is no *nouveau roman,* it does tell a story, but the characteristic of this story is that it is immediately inscribed in self-repetition: the story, and each episode of the story, should always be told at least twice for the book to make any sense at all.

For example: a very young man is about to kiss Blackburn, who notices half-absentmindedly that his lover is wearing a different kind of earring. A bomb explodes, presumably killing both men. End of one chapter. At the beginning of the next chapter, with no indication that the narrative has moved backwards in time, Blackburn is alive, and like the reader, has a vague and puzzled recollection of what has just happened. I hesitate to call this a "memory" but it is as if both the reader and the hero had already seen the film: this time, Blackburn does research on this young man, and before letting him get any closer, he manages to remove the earring which he now recognizes for the fatal weapon it is. No narrative theory can really explain what happens in this scene and even the text must resort to images. As one of the characters suggests to Blackburn: "It is as if your time-line described very tight meanders and your consciousness could sometimes accidentally skip a few curves instead of following the whole line" (327). The interesting result of such spiraling constructions is that "le temps bégaie [time stutters]" (159). *Chronoreg* as a whole is a stuttering novel.

From a narratological point of view, stuttering is an interesting phenomenon: it is an involuntary form of speech and a very specific type of repetition. While a conscious act of repetition can be thought of as a pedagogical tool, a stutter is often perceived as a comic flaw, an error. The stutterer is both repeating and not repeating, because no repetition is complete, and because no statement is unique or ever completed. Stuttering may be theorized as a double form of impossibility, hovering uncomfortably between the always repeated original statement and always unachieved effect of real repetition. It questions the difference between the original and the copy by blurring the frontier between what is said the first time and what is repeated from the original. *Chronoreg* functions like a movie only if we imagine the viewer at home, sitting in front of a video, armed with the remote control that lets her or him move backward and forward at will. *Chronoreg* stutters, and our reading is contaminated by the stuttering structure.

Another example of stuttering structure appears toward the end of the novel: chapters 16, 17, and 18 all start with almost exactly the same sentence: "Twilight; the taiga is but a dark, ragged edge. Darkness is deep in the bluish grays of dawn" (223). The sentence itself is not particularly meaningful but its absence becomes important if we skip it or if we forget it: at the level of the narrative structure, it is crucial to be sensitive to its slightly modified return, since it is a marker of discontinuous time. Each chapter operates a backward move, providing us with a different version of a sequence of events. The stuttered sentence is a signal, a key. At first this frantic zapping-stuttering is not exactly easy to follow. I remember feeling a little like Blackburn himself, whose mind is imbued with chronoreg, and who is warned by a doctor that "your skull will burst like a ripe pomegranate" (50). At first, there is no way of understanding what is going on or when the sequence of events is taking place until we become aware that we have read the same sentence for the second or the third time. In my experience, it is quite possible to read on for a very long time without realizing that a stuttering narrative is unfolding slowly. My reaction at that point in the novel was that this process was rather painful, that it was difficult and taxing to follow. And somehow, the effort required of the reader seemed in contradiction to the principle of banalization, which evokes laissez-faire rather than a concerted effort to make a political or ethical statement, to intervene in the social realm.

On second thought, however, this stuttering technique could be imagined as a politics of queer editing: I suggest that it is through the attempt at banalizing but also through its nonlinear and quasi-repetitive structure that this novel comes close to illustrating Tremblay's formula of a novel about queer characters that does not make a point about queer identity. For a stuttering narrative no longer allows for a clear distinction between before and after, and, to me, this always-almost-already-said is a very apt metaphor of one of the founding elements of queer narratives: the coming-out moment. For "I am queer" is never enough. The formulation has to be redoubled and repeated and re-explained and requalified incessantly. Similarly, in *Chronoreg,* no real "truth" ever replaces an old "lie," everything is much more complicated. The stuttering narrative repeats without repeating, forces us to accept layers of slightly different and slightly similar pieces of some evolving truth. Each new version both includes the earlier ones and moves away from them, refusing to become the absolute reality of the narrative, building on the past while suggesting that it is always possible to go back, to have to start from scratch again. No coming-out is ever final. We keep adding or withdrawing new tiny pieces to a puzzle that remains ambiguously incomplete; no overarching version of what is going on can ever do complete justice to a narrative so complex that even the most flexible reader ends up feeling lost and frustrated. The stuttering technique of the novel enacts the mandatory yet impossible coming-out for which neither the hero nor the plot can be responsible in a context of banalization. The end of the novel performs the endlessly postponed reality of a final coming-out by refusing to privilege one unique conclusion, by refusing to choose between two possible endings. The last pages of the text are split in two separate and schizoid columns that follow two different directions without giving us any indication that one version is more plausible than the other: at the end of the novel, it is hard to say whether Blackburn has finally found Sebastien, his long-lost love, or if he is alone, trapped in timelessness, insane.

Naturally, the danger of endless stuttering, both for a reader and for a story-teller, is impending madness, the explosion of a multiple consciousness that is constantly ready to adapt to different contexts, differently hostile or welcoming environments. Blackburn is literally torn between two incompatible columns like any gay person oscillating daily between closetedness and overt outedness. For the split between both narratives is responsible for the multiplication of paradoxes and inner contradictions: the crazy intertwining of different coherent life stories is neatly captured by the almost surreal and mind-boggling effects of the chronoreg on our sense of chronology: after I decide to go back in time to change things, once a new present has replaced what the present should have been had I not gone back in time, I—but who am I anyway at this point?—cannot know what the present would have been without my intervention in the past: a classical science fiction problem. Another way of putting it is that Blackburn can never be sure that he was not hallucinating, that he did move backwards in time. In the same way as many friends and parents are capable of denying that any coming-out has ever occurred in their presence—nothing has changed after all—one of the experts consulted by Blackburn insists that he will never know whether he actually traveled in time because the only acceptable proof he could give would be "if your going backwards in time changed the course of events. But precisely, it would be changed and we would not know, would we?" (127).

And this painful paradox is also a very economical representation of the inextricable knot of discourses that obtains if the coming-out moment is complicated by the encounter between two or more national-sexual codes. Both determined by a national discourse and marginalized by dominant national values, both products of their cultures and intent on rejecting their homophobic components, queer subjects will never know what national-sexual code has shaped the definition of their desire and their demand for political, aesthetic, or social equality. Their own sexual words are sometimes an emanation of the national, they cannot tell for sure which one of their claims partakes in a hybrid transnational queer language, what formulation is sexually influenced by national stereotypes, what national criteria are deconstructed by sexual ideology. Similarly, because it is a painful and interminable form of listening, a stuttering reading resembles the strange dialogue between two subjects who are convinced that they speak the same language of desire when they are in fact separated by the illusion of being similarly queer, and by the added layer of cultural preconceived ideas about sexualities.

The originality of Sernine's novel is to denaturalize both the national and the sexual by inventing, on the one hand, a sovereign Quebec, which, for contemporary readers, can be but a leap of science fiction faith, and, on the other hand, a character whose sexual values are obviously determined by the imaginary creation of a nation. By redrawing national boundaries at the same time as it redefines the frontiers between bodies and their desires,

Chronoreg cannot address any specific political and social message to a queer reader anchored in any real contemporary culture. But if it offers no solution to the specific situation of "un homosexuel Québécois," it proposes a type of listening that we may consider adopting or at least experimenting with, whenever our national discourses get in the way of productive dialogues: when, for example, we encounter those queers of another nation who appear twice as foreign to us once they have shattered our illusions that our desire is the same.

Reference Matter

WORKS CITED

Abel, Sam. *Opera in the Flesh: Sexuality in Operatic Performance.* Boulder, Colo.: Westview Press, 1996.

[Abelard and Heloise]. *The Letters of Abelard and Heloise.* Trans., intro. Betty Radice. London: Penguin Books, 1974.

———. *Les Véritables Lettres D'Abeillard Et D'Héloïse.* Paris: Jean Musier, 1723.

Abelove, Henry, Michèle Aina Barale, and David M. Halperin, eds. *The Lesbian and Gay Studies Reader.* London and New York: Routledge, 1993.

Adam, Antoine. *Verlaine.* Paris: Hatier, 1965.

Albaret, Céleste. *Monsieur Proust.* Paris: Robert Laffont–Opera Mundi, 1973.

Allen, Louis, ed. "Letters of Huysmans and Zola to Raffalovich." *Forum for Modern Languages* 2.3 (1966): 214–21.

[Anon.] *Thousand Nights and a Night.* Trans. Richard F. Burton, 1885.

Anouilh, Jean. *Antigone.* Paris: La Table Ronde, 1946.

Anzieu, Didier. *The Skin Ego: A Psychoanalytic Approach to the Self.* Trans. Chris Turner. New Haven: Yale University Press, 1989.

Apter, Emily. *André Gide and the Codes of Homotextuality.* Stanford French and Italian Studies. Saratoga, Calif.: Anma Libri, 1987.

Aron, J.-P. and R. Kempf. *La Bourgeoisie, le sexe et l'honneur.* Brussels: Editions Complexes, 1984.

———. *Le Pénis et la démoralisation de l'occident.* Paris: Grasset, 1978.

Assouline, Pierre. "Du côté des femmes . . . " *Lire* 206 (November 1992): 26–30.

Augé, Marc. *Non-Lieux. Introduction à une anthropologie de la surmodernité.* Paris: Seuil, 1992.

Aumont, Jacques. *L'Oeil interminable, cinéma et peinture.* Paris: Librairie Séguier, 1989.

Bach, Gérard. *Homosexualités: Expression/Répression.* Paris: Le Sycomore, 1982.
de Balzac, Honoré. *La Comédie humaine.* Ed. Pierre-Georges Castex. Paris: Gallimard, 1976–81. 12 vols.
Bandy, W. T. and Claude Pichois, eds. *Baudelaire devant ses contemporains.* Paris: Editions du Rocher, 1957.
Barney, Natalie. *Album Secret.* Muizon: A l'Ecart, 1984.
Barthes, Roland. *Fragments d'un discours amoureux.* Paris: Seuil, 1977.
———. *Incidents.* Paris: Seuil, 1987.
———. *Michelet par lui-même.* Paris: Seuil, 1954.
———. *Le Plaisir du texte.* Paris: Seuil, 1973.
———. *Sade, Fourier, Loyola.* Paris: Seuil, 1971.
———. "Sur André Gide et son *Journal.*" *Magazine littéraire* 97 (February 1975): 23–28.
———. *S/Z.* Paris: Seuil, 1970.
Bartlett, Neil. *Who Was That Man? A Present for Mr Oscar Wilde.* London: Serpent's Tail, 1988.
Bataille, Georges. *L'Erotisme.* Paris: Minuit, 1957.
Baudelaire, Charles. *The Flowers of Evil.* Trans. James McGowan. Intro. Jonathan Culler. Oxford: Oxford University Press, 1993.
———. *Oeuvres complètes.* Paris: Gallimard (Pléiade), 1975. 2 vols.
———. *Correspondance.* Paris: Gallimard (Pléiade), 1973.
Baudrillard, Jean. *De la séduction.* Paris: Galilée, 1979.
———. *Oublier Foucault.* Paris: Galilée, 1977.
———. *Les Stratégie fatales.* Paris: Grasset, 1983.
———. *Le Système des objets.* Paris: Denoël-Gonthier, 1968.
———. *La Transparence du Mal. Essai sur les phénomènes extrêmes.* Paris: Galilée, 1990.
Beckett, Samuel. *Waiting for Godot.* New York: Grove Press, 1954.
Beizer, Janet L. *Ventriloquized Bodies: Narratives of Hysteria in Nineteenth-Century France.* Ithaca: Cornell University Press, 1994.
Bell, David F. *Circumstances: Chance in the Literary Text.* Lincoln: University of Nebraska Press, 1993.
———. "*Thérèse Raquin*: Scientific Realism in Zola's Laboratory." *Nineteenth-Century French Studies* 24.1–2 (Fall, Winter 1995–96): 122–32.
Benhabib, Seyla. *Situating the Self: Gender, Community and Postmodernism in Contemporary Ethics.* New York: Routledge, 1992.
Benjamin, Jessica. *The Bonds of Love: Psychoanalysis, Feminism, and the Problem of Domination.* New York: Pantheon, 1988.
———. "Master and Slave: The Fantasy of Erotic Domination." In *Powers of Desire: The Politics of Sexuality.* Ed. Ann Snitow, Christine Stansell, and Sharon Thompson. New York: Monthly Review Press, 1983. 280–99.
Benjamin, Walter. *Charles Baudelaire: A Lyric Poet in the Era of High Capitalism.* London: Verso, 1983.

Ben Jelloun, Tahar. "C'est dans un rêve . . . " *Le Monde* (May 14, 1993): 34.

———. *L'Enfant de sable.* Paris: Seuil [Points], 1985. Trans. as *The Sand Child* by Alan Sheridan. New York: Harcourt Brace Jovanovich, 1987.

———. *Harrouda.* Paris: Denoël, 1985.

———. *La Nuit sacrée.* Paris: Seuil, 1987. Trans. as *The Sacred Night* by Alan Sheridan. New York: Harcourt Brace Jovanovitch, 1989.

Bergmann, Emilie L., and Paul Julian Smith, eds. *¿Entiendes?: Queer Readings, Hispanic Writings.* Durham: Duke University Press, 1995.

Bernard, Leopold. *Les Odeurs dans les romans de Zola.* Conférence faite au Cercle Artistique. Montpellier: [n.p.], 1898.

Bersani, Leo. *Baudelaire and Freud.* Berkeley: University of California Press, 1977.

———. "Is the Rectum a Grave?" *October* 43 (Winter 1987): 197–222.

Bérubé, Allan. *Coming Out Under Fire: The History of Gay Men and Women in World War Two.* New York: Free Press, 1990.

Bhabha, Homi. *Nations and Narration.* London and New York: Routledge, 1990.

Binet, Alfred. "Le fétichisme dans l'amour." *Revue philosophique* 24 (1887): 143–67; 252–74.

Blackmer, Corinne E., and Patricia Juliana Smith, eds. *En Travesti: Women, Gender Subversion, Opera.* New York: Columbia University Press, 1995.

Boffin, Tessa, and Jean Fraser, eds. *Stolen Glances: Lesbians Take Photographs.* London: Pandora, 1991.

Bonnet, Marie-Jo. *Relations amoureuses entre les femmes du XVIè au XXè siècle.* Paris: Odile Jacob, 1995.

———. *Un choix sans équivoque: Recherches historiques sur les relations amoureuses entre les femmes XVIe–XXe siècle.* Paris: Denoël, 1981.

Borges, Jorge Luis. "The Zahir." In *Labyrinths: Selected Stories and Other Writings.* New York: New Directions, 1962.

Breton, André. *Manifestes du surréalisme.* Paris: Gallimard, 1985.

Brewer, E. Cobhan. *Dictionary of Phrase and Fable.* Philadelphia: Lippincott, 1896.

Brooks, Peter. *Body Work: Objects of Desire in Modern Narrative.* Cambridge, Mass.: Harvard University Press, 1993.

Buchen, Irving, ed. *The Perverse Imagination: Sexuality and Literary Culture.* New York: New York University Press, 1970.

Buci-Glucksmann, Christine. *La Raison Baroque.* Paris: Galilée, 1984.

Butler, Judith. *Bodies That Matter: On the Discursive Limits of "Sex."* New York: Routledge, 1993.

———. *Gender Trouble: Feminism and the Subversion of Identity.* New York: Routledge, 1990.

Butor, Michel. *Histoire Extraordinaire, Essay on a Dream of Baudelaire's.* Trans. Richard Howard. London: Jonathan Cape, 1969.

Brunel, Pierre. "Lesbos." In *Les Fleurs du mal. L'intériorité de la forme.* Paris: CEDES, 1989. 85–92.

Cahiers Gai-Kitsch-Camp: "Université 1: Histoire"; "Université 2: Histoire contemporaine"; "Université 3: Imaginaires et représentations." Lille, 1991.
Carlier, François. *La Prostitution antiphysique*. 1887. In Fernandez, *La Pédérastie*.
Case, Sue-Ellen. *Feminism and Theatre*. Basingstoke: Macmillan, 1988.
Castle, Terry. *The Apparitional Lesbian: Female Homosexuality and Modern Culture*. New York: Columbia University Press, 1993.
———. "Contagious Folly: *An Adventure* and Its Skeptics." In *Questions of Evidence: Proof, Practice, and Persuasion across the Disciplines*. Ed. James Chandler, Arnold I. Davidson, and Harry Harootunian. Chicago: The University of Chicago Press, 1994. 11–42.
Causse, Michèle, ed. *Berthe ou un demi-siècle auprès de l'amazone*. Paris: Tierce, 1980.
Certeau, Michel de. *L'Invention du quotidien 1: arts de faire*. Ed. Luce Girard. Paris: Gallimard, 1990.
Chalon, Jean. *Liane de Pougy: courtisane, princesse et sainte*. Paris: Flammarion, 1994.
———. *Portrait of a Seductress*. New York: Crown, 1979.
———. "Préface." In *Idylle saphique* by Liane de Pougy. Paris: Editions des Femmes, 1987.
Chambers, Ross, and Anne Herrmann, eds. *Reading the Signs. Lecture des signes*. Special Issue of *Canadian Review of Comparative Literature* 21.1–2 (1994).
Charcot, Jean-Martin, and Valentin Magnan. "Inversion du sens genital." *Archives de neurologie* 3 (1882): 53–60, 296–322.
Chauncey, George, Jr. "From Sexual Inversion to Homosexuality: Medicine and the Changing Conceptualization of Female Deviance." *Salmagundi* 58 (1982–83): 114–46.
Chevalier, Julien. *De l'inversion de l'instinct sexuel au point de vue médico-légale*. Paris: Octave Doin, 1885.
Churchill, Wainwright. *Homosexual Behavior among Males: A Cross-Cultural and Cross-Species Investigation*. New York: Hawthorn, 1967.
Courrousse, Claude. *Vocabulaire de l'homosexualité masculine*. Paris: Payot, 1985.
Crevel, René. *Mon corps et moi*. Paris: Pauvert, 1974.
———. "Trois Réponses à un Questionnaire sur la Sexualité Enfantine." *Le Roman cassé et derniers écrits*. Paris: Pauvert, 1989.
Darwin, Charles. *The Descent of Man and Selection in Relation to Sex*. Princeton: Princeton University Press, 1985 [1871].
———. *The Different Flowers of the Same Species*. Chicago: University of Chicago Press, 1986 [1877].
———. *The Various Contrivances by which Orchids are Fertilised by Insects*. 2nd ed., rev. 1877. Chicago: University of Chicago Press.
de Kuyper, Eric. "The Freudian Construction of Sexuality: The Gay Foundation of Heterosexuality and Straight Homophobia." *Journal of Homosexuality* 24.3–4 (1993): 137–44.
Deleuze, Gilles. *Cinéma I. L'Image-mouvement*. Paris: Minuit, 1983.

———, and Félix Guattari. *Anti-Oedipus*. Trans. Robert Hurley, Mark Seem, and Helen R. Lane. Minneapolis: University of Minnesota Press, 1992.

———. *Kafka: Toward a Minor Literature*. Trans. Dana Polan. Minneapolis: University of Minnesota Press, 1986.

———. *Mille plateaux (Capitalisme et schizophrénie, 2)*. Paris: Éditions de Minuit, 1972.

Derrida, Jacques. *La Dissémination*. Paris: Seuil, 1972.

———. *Glas*. Paris: Galilée e, 1974.

———. *Spectres de Marx*. Paris: Galilée, 1993.

Djebar, Assia. *Les Alouettes naïves*. Paris: Julliard, 1967.

———. *L'Amour, la fantasia*. Paris: Jean-Claude Lattès, 1985.

———. *Femmes d'Alger dans leur appartement*. Paris: Des Femmes, 1980.

Diagnostic and Statistic Manual of Mental Illness ("DSM"). New York: The American Psychiatric Association (rev. periodically).

Dollimore, Jonathan. *Sexual Dissidence: Augustine to Wilde, Freud to Foucault*. New York: Oxford University Press, 1991.

Dubarry, Armand. *Les Invertis (Le vice allemand)*. Paris: Chamuel, 1895.

Dumesnil, René. *Flaubert, son hérédité, son milieu, sa méthode*. 1905. Geneva: Slatkine Reprints, 1969.

Dumont, Jean-Paul, ed. *Les Ecoles présocratiques*. Paris: Gallimard, 1991.

Duras, Marguerite. *Blue Eyes, Black Hair*. Trans. Barbara Gray. New York: Pantheon Books, 1988.

———. *L'Amant*. Paris: Minuit, 1984.

d'Eaubonne, Françoise. *Eros minoritaire*. Paris: Balland, 1970.

Edelman, Lee. *Homographesis: Essays in Gay Literary and Cultural Theory*. New York: Routledge, 1994.

Ellis, Havelock, and John Addington Symonds. *Das konträre Geschlechstgefühl*. Trans. Hans Kurella. Leipzig: George H. Wiegand, 1896. Published in English as *Sexual Inversion*. London: University Press, 1897.

Ellman, Richard. *Oscar Wilde*. New York: Knopf, 1988.

Erickson, John. "Writing Double: Politics and the African Narrative of French Expression." *Studies in Twentieth-Century Literature* 15.1 (1991): 101–22.

Espé de Metz, G. (Georges Saint-Paul). *Plus fort que le mal. Essai sur le mal innomable*. Pièce en quatre actes. Paris: Maloine, 1907.

Ezine, Jean-Louis. "Le facteur sonne toujours trois fois." *Le Nouvel Observateur* (April 19–25, 1990): 69–71.

Fabre, Paul. "De l'hystérie chez l'homme." *Annales médico-psychologiques* 5th ser. 13 (1875): 354–73.

Fauvel, Maryse. "Jean-Philippe Toussaint et la photographie: *exposer* le roman." Unpublished presentation given at Twentieth-Century French Studies Colloquium (University of Colorado, 1993).

Fenichel, Otto. *The Psychoanalytic Theory of Neurosis*. New York: Norton, 1945.

Ferenczi, Sandor. "The Nosology of Male Homosexuality (Homoeroticism)." In Ferenczi, *First Contributions to Psycho-Analysis.* London: Hogarth, 1952 [1916]. 296–318.
Fernandez, Dominique, ed. *La Pédérastie.* 1857. By Ambroise Tardieu. *La Prostitution antiphysique.* By François Carlier. Paris: Le Sycomore, 1981.
Finkielkraut, Alain. *La Sagesse de l'amour.* Paris: Gallimard, 1984.
Fisher, Dominique. "Les non-lieux de Jean-Philippe Toussaint: brico(l)age textuel et rhétorique du neutre." *University of Toronto Quarterly* 66.2 (1996): 618–31.
———. "L'écrit, le jeu de la lecture et la mise en voix de l'écriture dans *La Vie matérielle* et dans *Les yeux bleus, cheveux noirs.*" *L'Esprit Créateur* 30.1 (1990): 76–85.
Flaubert, Gustave. *Correspondance.* 13 vols. Paris: Editions Louis Conard, 1926–54.
———. *Correspondance.* 3 vols. In *Oeuvres complètes.* Paris: Pléiade, 1980–91.
———. "La Légende de Saint Julien l'Hospitalier." In *Oeuvres.* Paris: Gallimard [Pléiade], 1952 [1877]. 2: 623–48.
Foucault, Michel. *The Birth of the Clinic: An Archaeology of Medical Perception.* Trans. A. M. Sheridan Smith. New York: Vintage Books, 1973.
———. *Histoire de la sexualité. Vol.* 1: La Volonté de savoir. Paris: Gallimard, 1976.
———. *The History of Sexuality: Volume* 1: An Introduction. Trans. Robert Hurley. New York: Vintage Books, 1980.
———. *Power/Knowledge. Selected Interviews and Other Writings,* 1972–1977. Ed. Colin Gordon. New York: Pantheon, 1980.
Fourier, Charles. *Vers la liberté en amour.* Ed. Daniel Guérin. Paris: Gallimard, 1975.
Fournier Pescay. "Sodomie." *Dictionnaire des sciences médicales* 51 (1821): 441–48.
Frappier-Mazur, Lucienne. "Marginal Canons: Rewriting the Erotic." *Yale French Studies* 75 (1988): 112–28.
Freud, Anna. *The Ego and the Mechanisms of Defense.* Rev. ed. New York: International Universities Press, 1966 [1936].
Fuss, Diana, ed. *Inside/Out: Lesbian Theories, Gay Theories.* New York: Routledge, 1991.
Gaillard, Sarra. "Oralité, écriture et intertextualité." In *Littérature et oralité au Maghreb: Hommage à Mouloud Mammeri.* Paris: L'Harmattan, 1992.
Gane, Mike. *Baudrillard: Critical and Fatal Theory.* London: Routledge, 1991.
Garat, Anne-Marie. *Aden.* Paris: Seuil, 1992.
Garber, Marjorie. *Vested Interests: Cross-Dressing and Cultural Anxiety.* New York: Routledge, 1992.
Gautier, Théophile. *Mademoiselle de Maupin.* Paris: Garnier-Flammarion, 1966.
Gellner, Douglas. *Jean Baudrillard: From Marxism to Postmodernism and Beyond.* Stanford: Stanford University Press, 1989.
Genet, Jean. *Fragments . . . et autres textes.* Preface by Edmund White. Paris: Gallimard, 1990.
———. *Funeral Rites.* Trans. Bernard Frechtman. New York: Grove Press, 1969.
———. *Journal du voleur.* Paris: Gallimard [Folio], 1949.
———. *Miracle of the Rose.* Trans. Bernard Frechtman. New York: Grove Press, 1966.
———. *Notre Dame des Fleurs.* Paris: Gallimard [Folio], 1948.

———. *Our Lady of the Flowers*. Trans. Bernard Frechtman. Intro. Jean-Paul Sartre. New York: Grove Press, 1976.

———. *Prisoner of Love*. Trans. Barbara Bray. Intro. Edmund White. Hanover, N.H., and London: Wesleyan University Press, 1992.

———. *Querelle*. Trans. Anselm Hollo. New York: Grove Press, 1974.

———. *The Thief's Journal*. Trans. Bernard Frechtman. Foreword Jean-Paul Sartre. New York: Grove Press, 1964.

Genette, Gérard. *Palimpsestes*. Paris: Seuil, 1982.

Gide, André. *L'Immoraliste*. Paris: Mercure de France, 1902.

———. *Journal* (1889-1939). Paris: Gallimard [Pléiade], 1959 [1951].

———. *Les Nourritures terrestres*. Paris: Gallimard, 1917.

———. *Oeuvres complètes*. 15 volumes. Paris: NRF, n.d.

———. *Romans; Récits et soties; Oeuvres lyriques*. Paris: Gallimard [Pléiade], 1958.

Gilroy, Paul. *The Black Atlantic: Modernity and Double Consciousness*. London and New York: Routledge, 1993.

Girard, René. *Deceit, Desire, and the Novel: Self and Other in Literary Structure*. Baltimore: The Johns Hopkins University Press, 1965.

———. *La Violence et le sacré*. Paris: Grasset, 1972.

Glissant, Edouard. *Poétique de la Relation*. Paris: Gallimard, 1990.

Glucksmann, André. *La Fêlure du monde*. Paris: Flammarion, 1994.

Goldberg, Jonathan. *Sodometries: Renaissance Texts, Modern Sexualities*. Stanford: Stanford University Press, 1992.

Goldstein, Jan. "The Uses of Male Hysteria: Medical and Literary Discourse in Nineteenth-Century France." *Representations* 34 (1991): 134–65.

Gontard, Marc. "Le Récit méta-narratif chez Tahar Ben Jelloun." In Mansour M'Henni, ed., *Tahar Ben Jelloun: Stratégies d'écriture*. Paris: L'Harmattan, 1993.

Gozlan, Martine, and Marion Lévy. "Homosexualité féminine: le monde du silence." *L'Evénement du jeudi*, October 3–9, 1991: 82–96.

Gracián, Baltasar. *L'Homme de cour*. Trans. Amelot de la Houssaie. Paris: Editions Champ Libre, 1980.

Grandville, J. J. *The Court of Flora. Les Fleurs animées*. Intro. Peter A. Wick. New York: Braziller, 1981.

———. *Scènes de la vie privée et publique des animaux*. Paris: Hetzel, 1842.

Greenberg, David F. *The Construction of Homosexuality*. Chicago: University of Chicago Press, 1988.

Griesinger, Wilhelm. "Über einen wenig bekannten psychopathischen Zustand." *Archiv für Psychiatrie und Nervenkrankheiten* 1 (1868–69): 626–35.

Guenette, Mark D. "Le Loup et le Narrateur: The Masking and Unmasking of Homosexuality in Proust's *A la recherche du temps perdu*." *Romanic Review* 80 (1989): 229–46.

Guibert, Hervé. *L'Homme au chapeau rouge*. Paris: Gallimard, 1992.

———. *L'Image fantôme*. Paris: Minuit, 1981.

Haggerty, George E., and Bonnie Zimmerman, eds. *Professions of Desire: Lesbian and Gay Studies in Literature.* Pref. Catherine Stimpson. New York: Modern Language Association, 1995.

Hahn, Pierre. *Nos ancêtres les pervers: La vie des homosexuels sous le Second Empire.* Paris: Olivier Orban, 1979.

Hatzfeld, Adolphe and Arsène Darmesteter. *Dictionnaire générale de la langue française du commencement du XVIIe siècle jusqu'à nos jours.* 2 vols. 1871–1888. Paris: Librairie Delagrave, 1924.

Hichens, Robert. *The Green Carnation.* Ed., intro. Stanley Weintraub. Lincoln: University of Nebraska Press, 1970.

Hocquenghem, Guy. *Le Désir homosexuel.* Paris: Editions Universitaires, 1972.

———. *Homosexual Desire.* New intro. Michael Moon, preface by Jeffrey Weeks, trans. Daniella Dangoor. Durham: Duke University Press, 1993 [Orig. ed.: London: Allison and Busby, 1978].

———. *La Dérive homosexuelle.* Paris: Jean-Pierre Delarge, 1977.

Holland, Eugene W. *Baudelaire and Schizoanalysis: The Sociopoetics of Modernism.* Cambridge: Cambridge University Press, 1993.

Horney, Karen. *Neurosis and Human Growth: The Struggle Toward Self-Realization.* New York: Norton, 1950.

———. *Our Inner Conflicts, a Constructive Theory of Neurosis.* New York: Norton, 1972 [1945].

[Invert]. [Letters to Emile Zola published anonymously as] "Le roman d'un inverti." Ed. Dr. Laupts (Georges Saint-Paul). *Archives d'anthropologie criminelle* 9 (1894): 212–15, 367–73, 729–37; 10 (1895): 131–38, 228–41, 320–25.

Irigaray, Luce. *Ce sexe qui n'en est pas un.* Paris: Minuit, 1977.

———. *Speculum de l'autre femme.* Paris: Minuit, 1974.

Irvine, Demar. *Massenet: A Chronicle of His Life and Times.* Portland, Ore.: Amadeus Press, 1994.

Jay, Karla. *The Amazon and the Page: Natalie Clifford Barney and Renée Vivien.* Bloomington: Indiana University Press, 1988.

Jefferson, Ann. "*De l'amour* et le roman polyphonique." *Poétique* 54 (1983): 149–62.

Joecker, Jean-Pierre. "De l'explosion gaie à la fin de l'homosexualité." *Masques* 25–26 (1985): 6–7.

Jones, David. "La Cul-ture homo" *Gay Défi* 12 (April–May 1994).

Kafka, Franz. "Penal Colony." In *Stories and Short Pieces.* Trans. Willa and Edwin Muir. New York: Schocken Books, 1948.

Kellogg, Stuart. "Introduction: The Uses of Homosexuality in Literature." *Journal of Homosexuality* 8.3–4 (1982–83): 1–12.

Kempf, Roger. *Sur le corps romanesque.* Paris: Seuil, 1968.

Khatibi, Abdelkébir. *Maghreb pluriel.* Paris: Denoël, 1983.

Kierkegaard, Sören. *Either/Or, Part* 1. Trans. and ed. Howard V. Hong and Edna H. Hong. Princeton: Princeton University Press, 1987.

Kinsey, A. C., W. B. Pomeroy, and C. E. Martin. *Sexual Behavior in the Human Male.* Philadelphia, Penn.: W. B. Saunders, 1948.

Knight, Philip. *Flower Poetics in Nineteenth-Century France.* Oxford: Clarendon, 1986.

Koestenbaum, Wayne. *The Queen's Throat: Opera, Homosexuality, and the Mystery of Desire.* New York: Poseidon, 1993.

Kopelson, Kevin. *Love's Litany: The Writing of Modern Homoerotics.* Stanford: Stanford University Press,

Krafft-Ebing, Richard von. "Über gewisse Anomalien des Geschlechtstriebs und die klinisch-forensische Verwerthung derselben als eines wahrscheinlich functionellen Degenerationszeichens des centralen Nerven-Systems." *Archiv für Psychiatrie und Nervenkrankheiten* 7 (1877): 291–312.

Kristeva, Julia. *Sèméiôtikè: recherches pour une sémanalyse.* Paris: Seuil, 1969.

———. *Soleil noir: Dépression et mélancolie.* Paris: Gallimard, 1987.

Kuzniar, Alice A., ed. *Outing Goethe and His Age.* Stanford: Stanford University Press, 1996.

Lacan, Jacques. *Ecrits: A Selection.* New York: Norton, 1977.

Laclos, P.-A.-F. Choderlos de. *Oeuvres complètes.* Paris: Gallimard [Pléiade], 1951.

———. *Les Liaisons Dangereuses.* Trans., intro. P. W. K. Stone. Harmondsworth: Penguin Books, 1972.

Lanteri-Laura, Georges. *Lecture des perversions. Histoire de leur appropriation médicale.* Paris: Masson, 1979.

Larousse, Pierre. "Femme." *Grand dictionnaire universel du XIXe siècle.* 1866–79. 17 vols. Geneva: Slatkine, 1982. 8: 202–24.

———. "Pédérastie." *Grand dictionnaire universel du XIXe siècle.* 1866–1879. 17 vols. Geneva: Slatkine, 1982. 12: 491–92.

Lasègue, Ernest. "Les hystériques, leur perversité, leurs mensonges." *Annales médico-psychologiques* 6th ser. 6 (1881): 111–18.

Laughlin, Henry P. *The Ego and Its Defenses.* New York: Appleton-Century-Crofts, 1970.

Dr. Laupts (Georges Saint-Paul). "Dégénérescence ou pléthore?" *Archives d'anthropologie criminelle* 23 (1908): 731–49.

———. "Enquête sur l'inversion sexuelle (Réponses)," [and editorial remarks to "Le roman d'un inverti."] *Archives d'anthropologie criminelle* 9 (1894): 105–8; 211–15; 367–73; 729–37; 10 (1895): 131–38; 228–41; 320–25.

———. "Lettre au Professeur Lacassagne en réponse au lettre de M. Raffalovich." *Archives d'anthropologie criminelle* 24 (1909): 693–96.

———. "A la mémoire d'Emile Zola." *Archives d'anthropologie criminelle* 22 (1907): 825–41.

———. *Tares et poisons. Perversions et perversités sexuelles. Une enquête sur l'inversion. Notes et documents. Le roman d'un inverti né. Le procès Wilde. La guérison et la prophylaxie de l'inversion.* Paris: George Carré, 1896.

Leakey, Felix William. "Baudelaire-Dufaÿs, Les lesbiennes: A Verse Novel? The Delacroix/Tasso Sonnet." *Forum for Modern Language Studies* 24.1 (1988): 1–26.

Le Garrec, Evelyne. *Des femmes qui s'aiment.* Paris: Seuil, 1984.

Lévinas, Emmanuel. *Noms propres.* Montpellier: Fata Morgana, 1976.

Littré, Emile. *Dictionnaire de la langue française.* Paris: Gallimard/Hachette, 1957 [1846–72].

Lucas, Prosper. *Traité philosophique et physiologique de l'hérédité naturelle.* Paris: Baillière, 1847–50.

Lucey, Michael. *Gide's Bent: Writing, Sexuality, Politics.* New York: Oxford, 1995.

Lyotard, Jean-François. *Economie libidinale.* Paris: Minuit, 1974.

———. *La Condition postmoderne: rapport sur le savoir.* Paris: Minuit, 1979.

———. "Prescription." In Robert Harvey and Mark S. Roberts, eds., *Toward the Postmodern.* Atlantic Highlands, N.J.: Humanities Press, 1993.

McCormack, Jerusha H. *John Gray: Poet, Dandy, and Priest.* Hanover, N.H.: Brandeis University Press, 1991.

Maeterlinck, Maurice. *Le Double Jardin.* Paris: Fasquelle, 1904.

———. *L'Intelligence des fleurs.* Paris: Fasquelle, 1907.

———. *La Vie des abeilles.* Paris: Fasquelle, 1901.

Maillou, Rioux de. *Souvenirs des autres.* Paris: Crès, 1917.

Mapplethorpe, Robert. *Flowers.* Foreword by Patti Smith. Boston, Toronto, and London: Bulfinch Press, Little Brown, 1990.

Marrouchi, Mustapha. "Breaking Up/Down/Out of the Boundaries: Tahar Ben Jelloun." *Research in African Literatures* 21.4 (1990): 71–83.

Martel, Frédéric. *Matériaux pour servir à l'histoire des homosexuels en France. Chronologie, bibliographie,* 1968–1996. Lille: Cahiers Gay-Kitsch-Camp, 1996.

———. *Le Rose et le noir. Les homosexuels en France depuis* 1968. Paris: Seuil, 1996.

Masques. Numéro spécial 25–26, Spring-Summer 1985.

"Medical Circular No. 1—Revised. Minimum psychiatric inspection." Reprinted in the *Journal of the American Medical Association* 116 (1941): 2059–61.

Meijer, Herman. "Can Seduction Make Straight Men Gay?" *Journal of Homosexuality* 24.3–4 (1993): 125–36.

Mendès-Leite, Rommel, and Pierre-Olivier de Busscher, eds. *Gay Studies from the French Cultures: Voices from France, Belgium. Brazil, Canada and the Netherlands.* Binghamton, N.Y.: Harrington Park Press, 1993.

Merleau-Ponty, Maurice. *L'Oeil et l'esprit.* Paris: Gallimard, 1964.

Merrick, Jeffrey, and Bryant Ragan, Jr. *Homosexuality in Modern France.* New York: Oxford University Press, 1995.

Micale, Mark S. *Approaching Hysteria: Disease and its Interpretations.* Princeton: Princeton University Press, 1995.

Milly, Jean. *Les Pastiches de Proust.* Paris: Armand Colin, 1970.

Mitzel. "Those Disgusting Flowers." "Common Sense." *Edge* (December 20, 1989): 38.

Monferrand, Hélène de. *Les Amies d'Héloïse.* Paris: Editions de Fallois, 1990.

———. *Les Enfants d'Héloïse.* Paris: Editions Double Interligne, 1997.

———. *Journal de Suzanne.* Paris: Editions de Fallois, 1991.

Morel, Bénédict. *Traité des dégénérescences physiques, intellectuelles et morales de l'es-*

pèce humaine et des causes qui produisent ces variétés maladives. Paris: Baillière, 1857.

Murail, Elvire. *Escalier C.* Paris: Sylvie Messinger, 1983. Trans. as *Stairway C.* New York: Avon, 1986.

Näcke, Paul Adolf. "Einteilung der Homosexuellen." *Allgemeine Zeitschrift für Psychiatrie* 65 (1908): 109–28.

———. "Le monde homosexuelle de Paris." *Archives d'anthropologie criminelle* 20 (1905): 182–85; 411–14.

N'Aït Attik, Mririda. *Les Chants de la Tassaout.* Trans. René Euloge. Casablanca: Belvisi, 1986.

Nordau, Max Simon. *Dégénérescence.* 2 vols. Trans. August Dietrich. Paris: Félix Alcan, 1894–95. Originally published as *Entartung.* Berlin: Carl Dunder, 1893.

Nye, Robert. *Masculinity and Male Codes of Honor in Modern France.* New York: Oxford University Press, 1993.

———. "Sex Difference and Male Homosexuality in French Medical Discourse, 1830–1930." *Studies in Homosexuality, vol.* 9: Homosexuality and Medicine, Health and Science. Ed. Wayne R. Dynes and Stephen Donaldson. New York and London: Garland Publishing, 1992. 168–87.

Painter, George. *Marcel Proust: A Biography.* 2 vols. London: Chatto and Windus, 1965.

Paris, Bernard J. *Karen Horney: A Psychoanalyst's Search for Self-Understanding.* New Haven, Conn.: Yale University Press, 1994.

Pasco, Allan H. *The Color-Keys to "A la recherche du temps perdu."* Paris: Editions Droz, 1976.

Pastre, Geneviève. *De l'amour lesbien.* Paris: Pierre Horay, 1980.

Perniola, Mario. "Logique de la séduction." *Traverses* 18 (1979): 2–9.

Perrin, Elula. *Les Femmes préfèrent les femmes.* Paris: Ramsay, 1977.

Pick, Daniel. *Faces of Degeneration, A European Disorder, c.*1848-c.1918. Cambridge: Cambridge University Press, 1989.

Pollard, Patrick. *André Gide: Homosexual Moralist.* New Haven, Conn.: Yale University Press, 1991.

Porter, Laurence M. *"The Interpretation of Dreams": Freud's Theories Revisited.* Boston: Twayne, 1987.

Pougy, Liane de. *L'Idylle saphique.* 1901. Paris: Editions des Femmes, 1987.

———. *Mes cahiers bleus.* Paris: Plon, 1977.

———. *My Blue Notebooks.* London: A. Deutsch, 1979.

Praetorius, Dr. Numa (Eugène Wilhelm). "A propos de l'article du Dr. Laupts sur l'homosexualité." *Archives d'anthropologie criminelle* 24 (1909): 198–207.

Proudhon. *De la justice dans la Révolution et dans l'Eglise.* 1860. Paris: Fayard, 1990. 4 vols.

Proust, Marcel. *A la recherche du temps perdu.* 4 vols. Paris: Gallimard (Pléiade), 1987–89.

———. *Contre Sainte-Beuve suivi de Nouveaux Mélanges.* Paris: Gallimard, 1954.

———. *Jean Santeuil.* Trans. Gerard Hopkins, pref. André Maurois. New York: Simon and Schuster, 1955.

Queneau, Raymond. *Zazie dans le métro.* Paris: Gallimard, 1959.

Rachilde. *Monsieur Vénus.* Paris: Flammarion, 1977.

Raffalovich, Marc-André. "L'affaire Oscar Wilde." *Archives d'anthropologie criminelle* 10 (1895): 445–77.

———. "Les groupes d'uranistes à Paris et à Berlin." *Archives d'anthropologie criminelle* 19 (1904): 926–36.

———. "A propos du roman d'un inverti et quelques travaux récents sur l'inversion sexuelle." *Archives d'anthropologie criminelle* 10 (1895): 333–36.

———. "Unisexualité anglaise." *Archives d'anthropologie criminelle* 11 (1896): 429–31.

———. "L'Uranisme. Inversion sexuelle congénitale." *Archives d'anthropologie criminelle* 10 (1895): 99–127.

———. *Uranisme et unisexualité. Étude sur différentes manifestations de l'instinct sexuel.* Paris: Masson, 1896.

Rivers, Christopher. *Face Value: Physiognomical Thought and the Legible Body in Marivaux, Lavater, Balzac, Gautier, and Zola.* Madison: University of Wisconsin Press, 1994.

Rivers, J. E. *Proust and the Art of Love: The Aesthetics of Sexuality in the Life, Times and Art of Marcel Proust.* New York: Columbia University Press, 1980.

Rivière, Joan. "Womanliness as a Masquerade." *International Journal of Psycho-Analysis* 10 (1929): 303–13. Repr. in Victor Burgin, James Donald, and Cora Kaplan, eds., *Formations of Fantasy.* London: Methuen, 1986. 35–44.

Rochester, Myrna Bell. *René Crevel: Le Pays des miroirs absolus.* Saratoga, Calif.: Anma Libri, 1978.

Romilly, Jacqueline de. *La Tragédie grecque.* Paris: PUF, 1973.

Rosario, Vernon, ed. *Science and Homosexualities.* New York: Routledge, 1996.

Rosset, Clément. *Joyful Cruelty: Toward a Philosophy of the Real.* Trans. David F. Bell. New York: Oxford University Press, 1993.

Rousseau, Jean-Jacques. *Oeuvres Complètes.* Paris: Gallimard (Pléiade), 1959–95. 5 vols.

Sade, D. A. F. (Marquis) de. *La Philosophie dans le Boudoir.* Paris: Gallimard, 1976.

Said, Edward. *The Word, the Text, and the Critic.* Cambridge, Mass.: Harvard University Press, 1983.

Saint-Paul, Georges. *Thèmes psychologiques. Invertis et homosexuels.* Paris: Vigot, 1930.

Sartiliot, Claudette. *Herbarium Verbarium: The Discourse of Flowers.* Lincoln: University of Nebraska Press, 1993.

Sartre, Jean-Paul. *Les Mots.* Paris: Gallimard, 1964. Trans. as *The Words* by Bernard Frechtman. New York: George Braziller, 1964.

———. *Saint Genet, comédien et martyr. Oeuvres complètes de Jean Genet, I.* Paris: Gallimard, 1952.

———. *Situations I.* Paris: Gallimard, 1947.

Schehr, Lawrence. *Alcibiades at the Door: Gay Discourses in French Literature.* Stanford: Stanford University Press, 1995.

———. *The Shock of Men: Homosexual Hermeneutics and French Writing.* Stanford: Stanford University Press, 1995.

———. *Rendering French Realism.* Stanford: Stanford University Press, 1996.

Schmidt, Joël. *Dictionnaire de la mythologie grecque et romaine.* Paris: Larousse, 1991.

Schor, Naomi. *George Sand and Idealism.* New York: Columbia University Press, 1993.

Sedgwick, Eve Kosofsky. *Epistemology of the Closet.* Berkeley: University of California Press, 1990.

———. *Between Men: English Literature and Male Homosocial Desire.* New York: Columbia University Press, 1985.

Sernine, Daniel. *Chronoreg.* Montréal: Editions Québec/Amérique, 1992.

Setz, Wolfram, ed. *Der Roman eines Konträrsexuellen.* Berlin: Verlag Rosa Winkel, 1991. German translation of Invert (1894–95).

Sewell, Brocard. *Two Friends: André Raffalovich and John Gray.* Aylesford, Kent: Saint Albert's, 1963.

Showalter, Elaine. *Sexual Anarchy: Gender and Culture at the Fin de Siècle.* New York: Viking, 1990.

Stambolian, George, and Elaine Marks, eds. *Homosexualities and French Literature: Contexts and Criticisms.* Ithaca: Cornell University Press, 1979.

Stein, Edward, ed. *Forms of Desire: Sexual Orientation and the Social Constructionist Controversy.* New York: Routledge, 1992.

Stendhal. *De l'amour.* Paris: Garnier-Flammarion, 1965.

———. *Lucien Leuwen.* Paris: Gallimard, 1952. In *Romans et nouvelles.* Ed. Henri Martineau. 1:733–1414.

Stoller, Robert J. *Observing the Erotic Imagination.* New Haven, Conn.: Yale University Press, 1985.

Tanner, Tony. *Adultery in the Novel: Contract and Transgression.* Baltimore: The Johns Hopkins University Press, 1979.

Tardieu, Ambroise. *Étude médico-légale sur les attentats aux moeurs.* 7th ed. Paris: J.-B. Baillière, 1878 [1857].

———. *La Pédérastie.* 1857. In Fernandez.

Thélot, Jérôme. *Baudelaire. Violence et poésie.* Paris: Gallimard, 1993.

Torgovnick, Marianna. *Gone Primitive: Savage Intellects, Modern Lives.* Chicago: The University of Chicago Press, 1990.

Toulouse, Edouard. *Emile Zola.* Paris: Société des Editions Scientifiques, 1896.

Tournier, Michel. *La Goutte d'or.* Paris: Minuit, 1986.

Toussaint, Jean-Philippe. *L'Appareil-photo.* Paris: Minuit, 1988.

Tremblay, Michel. *Le Coeur éclaté.* Montréal: Editions Lemeac, 1993.

———. "Une affaire de famille." Interview with Guy Cloutier. *Magazine Littéraire* 317 (January 1994): 68–70.

Troiden, Richard R. "The Formation of Homosexual Identities." *Journal of Homosexuality* 17.1–2 (1989): 43–73.

Ulrichs, Karl Heinrich. *Forschungen über das Räthsel der mannmännlichen Liebe.* 4 vols. Ed. Hubert Kennedy. Berlin: Verlag Rosa Winkel. 1994 [1864-79].

Veith, Ilza. *Hysteria: The History of a Disease.* Chicago: University of Chicago Press, 1965.

Verlaine, Paul. *Femmes. Hombres.* Ed. Jean-Paul Corsetti et Jean-Pierre Giusto. Paris: Le Livre à venir, 1985.

———. *Oeuvres poétiques.* Ed. Jacques Robichez. Paris: Garnier, 1969.

———. *Oeuvres poétiques complètes.* Ed. Y.-G. Le Dantec. Rev. ed. Jacques Borel. Paris: Gallimard (Pléiade), 1962.

———. *Women/Men (Femmes/Hombres).* Trans. William Packard and John D. Mitchell. New York: IASTA Press, 1977 (2nd ed.).

———. *Femmes Hombres, Women Men.* Trans. Alistair Elliot. London: Anvil Press, 1979.

———. *Royal Tastes: Erotic Writings, Paul Verlaine.* Trans. Alan Stone. New York: Harmony Books, 1984.

Vicinus, Martha. "The Adolescent Boy: Fin de Siècle Femme Fatale?" *Journal of the History of Sexuality* 5.1 (1994): 90–114.

Vivien, Renée. *Une Femme m'apparut.* Paris: Lemerre, 1904.

Waelti-Walters, Jennifer. *Feminist Novelists of the Belle Epoque: Love as a Lifestyle.* Bloomington: Indiana University Press, 1990.

Waller, Margaret. *The Male Malady: Fictions of Impotence in the French Romantic Novel.* Rutgers: Rutgers University Press, 1993.

Watney, Simon. "Gai et français." *Gay Times* (March 1994): 20.

———. *Practices of Freedom: Selected Writings on HIV/AIDS.* London: Rivers Oram Press, 1994.

Werner, Françoise. *Romaine Brooks.* Paris: Plon, 1990.

Westphal, Karl Freidrich. "Die conträre Sexualempfindung: Symptom eines neuropathischen (psychopathischen) Zustandes." *Archiv für Psychiatrie und Nervenkrankheiten* 2 (1869): 73–108.

Wheelwright, Julie. *Amazons and Military Maids: Women Who Dressed as Men in Pursuit of Life, Liberty and Happiness.* London: Pandora, 1990.

Wickes, George. *The Amazon of Letters: The Life and Loves of Natalie Barney.* New York: Putnam, 1976.

Wilhelm, Eugène. "Publications allemandes sur les questions sexuelles." *Archives d'anthropologie criminelle* 27 (1912): 301–9.

Wilkerson, Donna. "Hervé Guibert: Writing the Spectral Image." *Studies in Twentieth-Century Literature* 19.2 (1995): 269–85.

Wing, Nathaniel. *The Limits of Narrative: Essays on Baudelaire, Flaubert, Rimbaud and Mallarmé.* Cambridge: Cambridge University Press, 1986.

Winterson, Jeanette. *Art [Objects].* New York: Knopf, 1996.

Wittig, Monique. *Les Guérillères.* Paris: Minuit, 1969.

———. *The Straight Mind.* Boston: Beacon Press, 1992.

Wood, Elizabeth, "Sapphonics." *Queering the Pitch: The New Gay and Lesbian Musicology.* Ed. Philip Brett, Elizabeth Wood, and Gary C. Thomas. New York: Routledge, 1994. 27–66.

Woodhull, Winifred. *Transfigurations of the Maghreb: Feminism, Decolonization, and Literatures.* Minneapolis: University of Minnesota Press, 1993.

Žižek, Slavoj. *Enjoy Your Symptom!* New York: Routledge, 1992.

Zola, Émile. *La Curée.* In *Les Rougon-Macquart,* vol. I. Paris: Pléiade, 1963 [1871].

———. *Fécondité.* Paris: E. Fasquelle, 1899.

———. Preface. *Tares et poisons. Perversions et perversités sexuelles.* By Dr. Laupts (Georges Saint-Paul). Paris: George Carré, 1896. 1–4.

———. "Le Roman expérimental." *Oeuvres complètes.* Ed. Henri Mitterand. Lausanne: Cercle du Livre Précieux, 1968 [1880]. 1145–1203.

INDEX

In this index an "f" after a number indicates a separate reference on the next page, and an "ff" indicates separate references on the next two pages. A continuous discussion over two or more pages is indicated by a span of page numbers, e.g., "57–59." *Passim* is used for a cluster of references in close but not consecutive sequence. Entries are alphabetized letter by letter, ignoring word breaks, hyphens, and accents.

Library of Congress Cataloging-in-Publication Data

Articulations of difference: gender studies and writing in French / edited by Dominique D. Fisher and Lawrence R. Schehr.
p. cm.
Includes bibliographical references.
ISBN 0-8047-2974-3 (cloth: alk. paper)—ISBN 0-8047-2975-1 (pbk: alk. paper)
1. French literature—19th century—History and criticism. 2. French literature—20th century—History and criticism. 3. Homosexuality in literature. I. Fisher, Dominique D., 1954– . II. Schehr, Lawrence R.
PQ295.H65A77 1997
840.9'353—dc21 97-9683
CIP
Rev

This book is printed on acid-free, recycled paper.

Original printing 1997

Last number below indicates year of this printing:
06 05 04 03 02 01 00 99 98 97